# ROMANCE FOR SALE IN EARLY MODERN ENGLAND

*For Alinor*

# Romance for Sale in Early Modern England

## The Rise of Prose Fiction

STEVE MENTZ
*St. John's University, USA*

**ASHGATE**

rt of this publication may be reproduced, stored in a retrieval
ıy form or by any means, electronic, mechanical, photocopying,
ıout the prior permission of the publisher.

his moral right under the Copyright, Designs and Patents Act,
1988, to be identified as the author of this work.

Published by
Ashgate Publishing Limited
Gower House
Croft Road
Aldershot
Hants GU11 3HR
England

Ashgate Publishing Company
Suite 420
101 Cherry Street
Burlington, VT 05401-4405
USA

Ashgate website: http://www.ashgate.com

**British Library Cataloguing in Publication Data**
Mentz, Steve
 Romance for sale in early modern England : the rise of prose fiction
 1.Greene, Robert, 1558?—Criticism and interpretation 2.English fiction—Early
 modern, 1500-1700—History and criticism 3.Fiction—Appreciation—England—
 History—16th century 4.Fiction—Appreciation—England—History—17th century
 5.Books and reading—England—History—16th century 6.Books and reading—
 England—History—17th century 7.Romances—Adaptations—History and criticism
 I.Title
 823'.0850903

**Library of Congress Cataloging-in-Publication Data**
Mentz, Steve.
 Romance for sale in early modern England : the rise of prose fiction / Steve Mentz.
  p. cm.
 Includes bibliographical references and index.
 ISBN 0-7546-5469-9 (alk. paper)
 1. English fiction—Early modern, 1500-1700—History and criticism. 2. Fiction—
Appreciation—England—History—16th century. 3. Fiction—Appreciation—England—
History—17th century. 4. Books and reading—England—History—16th century. 5. Books
and reading—England—History—17th century. 6. Heliodorus, of Emesa—Appreciation—
England. 7. Romances—Adaptations—History and criticism. 8. Heliodorus, of Emesa.
Aethiopica. I. Title.

 PR836.M46 2006
 823'.0850903—dc22

2005012363

ISBN-10: 0 7546 5469 9

Printed and bound in Great Britain by MPG Books Ltd, Bodmin, Cornwall

Jacket illustration: Abraham Bloemaert, 1625, *Theagenes and Chariclea among the Slain Sailors*. By permission of the Stiftung Pressische Schlösser und Gärten Berlin-Brandenburg. Photograph: Roland Handrick, 1997.

# Contents

# Acknowledgments

Many of this book's readers will not need convincing that all books are collaborative efforts, and that the author's name on the title page hides a web of influences, personal and anonymous, institutional and private. But I am grateful that the genre of scholarly books provides this peritextual space for thanking the many people who have given this project critical attention and intellectual support, and the many institutions that have provided homes along its journey.

I'm grateful to all the scholars who have given my work their attention. All remaining faults are of course my own, but many helpful responses have come from (in alphabetical order) Derek Alwes, A. L. Beier, Craig Dionne, Margaret Doody, Elizabeth Eisenstein, John Fleming, Edward Gieskes, Heidi Brayman Hackel, Alexandra Halasz, W. Speed Hill, Victoria Kahn, Suzanne Keen, H. A. Kelly, Arthur Kinney, Jacques Lezra, Naomi Liebler, Kirk Melinkoff, Alice Miskimmin, Lori Humphrey Newcomb, Jonathan F. S. Post, Constance Relihan, Bryan Reynolds, Debora Shuger, Claire Sponsler, Goran Stanivukovic, Linda Woodbridge, Susanne Wofford, and Jessica Wolfe. I thank the English department at St. John's University, especially Stephen Sicari, Greg Maertz, John Lowney, Derek Owens, Robert Fanuzzi, Granville Ganter, Jennifer Travis, and Melissa Mowry. I also thank the English department at Iona College, especially Deborah Williams, Margo Collins, and Laura Shea. At Ashgate Publishing, I thank Ann Newell, Anne Keirby, Pete Coles, an anonymous reader, and especially Erika Gaffney for their exemplary professionalism.

This book began as a dissertation under the direction of Annabel Patterson and I am grateful for her early advocacy and scholarly example. I thank many early readers, including Lawrence Manly, David Quint, John Rogers, Elizabeth Dillon, Mary Floyd-Wilson, Laura King, Ramie Targoff, Roberto González Echevarría, Carlos Eire, Michael Anderson, Joseph Roach, Jenny Davidson, and Elizabeth Teare. I also thank the English department at UCLA for providing a congenial home away from home.

I'd like to thank my students at St. John's, Iona, and Yale for showing me how Heliodorus still appeals to modern readers. I am grateful to Harry Evans, Sharon DeLano, Sam Vaughan, and Random House, Inc., for introducing me to the modern book business some years ago. I thank the staffs of the University Libraries at St. John's and Yale, the Beinecke Library, the Folger Shakespeare Library, the New York Public Library, and the British Library.

For institutional support I thank St. John's University and the College and Arts and Sciences, especially Dean Jeffrey Fagen; Iona College, especially Deans Alex Eodice and Warren Rosenberg; the Folger Shakespeare Library; the Mellon

Foundation; the Beinecke Library; Yale University; the Yale Center for British Art; and Yale's Robert M. Leylan Fellowship in the Humanities, Chauncy Brewster Tinker Fellowship, and John F. Enders Grant.

Several sections of the book have appeared in print previously. A portion of Chapter 3 appeared as "The Thigh and the Sword: Genre, Gender, and Sexy Dressing in Sidney's *New Arcadia*," *Prose Fiction and Early Modern Sexualities*, Constance C. Relihan and Goran Stanivukovic, eds., (New York: Palgrave, 2003): 77-91, and another as "Reason, Faith, and Shipwreck in Sidney's *New Arcadia*," *Studies in English Literature* 44 (2004): 1-18. Part of Chapter 4 appeared as "Escaping Italy: From Novella to Romance in Gascoigne and Lyly," *Studies in Philology*, 101 (2004) 253-71, and part of Chapter 7 as "The Heroine as Courtesan: Dishonesty, Romance, and the Sense of an Ending in *The Unfortunate Traveler*," *Studies in Philology* 98 (2001): 339-58. I am grateful for permission to reproduce.

The painting on the cover, Abraham Bloemart's "Theagenes and Chariclea among the Slain Sailors" (1625), is reproduced courtesy of the Sansouci Museum in Potsdam, Germany, and the Stiftung Preußische Schlösser und Gärten Berlin-Brandenberg.

My most fundamental debts are to my ideal reader and most demanding editor, Alinor Sterling, and to Ian and Olivia, who were born while this project was in process.

# Introduction

# Why Early Modern Fiction?

> Thou mayst believe me, gentle reader, without swearing, that I could willingly desire this book (as a child of my understanding) to be the most beautiful, gallant, and discrete that might possibly be imagined; but I could not transgress the order of nature, wherein everything begets his like.
>
> Miguel de Cervantes, Author's Preface to *Don Quixote*[1]

In a prefatory letter to the second edition of *Pierce Pennilesse his Supplication to the Devil* (1592), Thomas Nashe insists that the first edition had been printed without his approval: "Faith, I am very sorry, sir, I am thus unawares betrayed to infamy."[2] What is notable about the letter is less its content – this disingenuous reluctance to appear in print is common – than its addressee. Nashe titles his letter, "A private Epistle of the Author to the Printer, wherein his full meaning and purpose in publishing this book is set forth" (49). Prefatory letters in Elizabethan books were usually addressed to patrons or potential patrons; Nashe's *The Unfortunate Traveler* (1594), like Shakespeare's narrative poems, was dedicated to the Earl of Southampton. These letters generally frame the books they introduce as gifts given freely to their noble addressees; Nashe calls *The Unfortunate Traveler*, "some little summer fruit" (252), and Shakespeare describes *The Rape of Lucrece* as the sole property of Southampton: "What I haue done is yours, what I haue to do is yours, being part in all I haue, deuoted yours."[3] By contrast, Nashe claims that the "meaning" and "purpose" of *Pierce Pennilesse* reside in the act of "publishing." Print publication, not noble patronage, conveys value. At the heart of the second edition of *Pierce Pennilesse*, Nashe places a professional exchange between himself, his printer Abell Jeffes, and his publisher John Busby.[4] The

---

[1]    Miguel de Cervantes, *Don Quixote*, Thomas Shelton, trans., (New York: P. F. Collier & Sons, 1937) 5. Translation originally published 1612.

[2]    Thomas Nashe, *The Unfortunate Traveler and Other Works*, J.B. Steane, ed., (Harmondworth: Penguin, 1972) 49. I cite *Pierce Pennilesse* and *The Unfortunate Traveler* from Steane's widely available edition.

[3]    William Shakespeare, *The Riverside Shakespeare*, 2nd ed., G. Blakemore Evans and J. J. M. Tobin, eds., (Boston: Houghton Mifflin, 1997) 1816. Further citations from Shakespeare to this edition in the text.

[4]    On this preface as Nashe's response to the first edition, printed by Richard Jones without any front matter by Nashe, see Lorna Hutson, *Thomas Nashe in Context*, (Oxford: Clarendon Press, 1989) 175-81. On the distinction between the printer (who produces the

assumption of commercial primacy displaces traditional claims that literary works were "trifles" (as Sidney termed his *Old Arcadia*). Literary meaning gets produced through the business of print publication.[5]

Two years later, writing a fictional peritext to *The Unfortunate Traveler*, Nashe radically expanded his sense of what printed books could do.[6] Following a letter in which he makes a patently insincere play for Southampton's patronage, Nashe added an "Introduction to the Dapper Monsieur Pages of the Court." Here the product of Nashe's transaction with his printer and publisher (Thomas Scarlet and Cuthbert Burby) becomes a talismanic object capable of many uses:

> A proper fellow page of yours, called Jack Wilton, by me commends him unto you, and hath bequeathed for waste paper here amongst you certain pages of his misfortune. In any case keep them preciously as a privy token of his good will towards you. If there be some better than other, he craves you would honour them in their death so much as to dry and kindle tobacco with them. For a need he permits you to wrap velvet pantofles in them also, so they be not woe-begone at the heels, or weather-beaten, like a black head with grey hairs, or mangy at the toes, like an ape about the mouth. But as you love good fellowship and ames-ace, rather turn them to stop mustard pots than the grocers should have one patch of them to wrap mace in: a strong, hot costly spice it is, which above all things he hates. To any use about meat or drink put them to and spare not, for they cannot do their country better service. Printers are mad whoresons; allow them some of them for napkins. (253)

Printed matter represents a series of social transactions redolent of Nashe's life in London's emerging print culture: his pages serve as "waste paper"; "privy tokens" of a special relationship among "pages" (the pun linking minor court figures to the leaves of a book is one of his central metaphors[7]); tobacco papers; wrappers for velvet pantofles; stoppers for mustard pots; or "any use about meat or drink." Even "mad whoreson" printers can use them "for napkins." Like his friend and sometime collaborator Ben Jonson, Nashe had a keen awareness of the physicality of his books. Even more than Jonson, Nashe seems aware of the destabilizing

---

book) and the publisher (who finances it), see Peter Blayney, "The Publication of Playbooks," *A New History of Early English Drama*, John C. Cox and David Kastan, eds., (New York: Columbia University Press, 1997) 383-422. Blayney notes that the terms "printer" or "bookseller" were used to describe both figures (389-92).

[5]    *Pierce Pennilesse* was Nashe's most successful work, re-published three times by John Busby (1592, 1592, and 1593) and once by Nicholas Ling (1595).

[6]    I take the term "peritexts," referring to prefatory letters, title-pages, etc., that are inside a literary text but not exactly part of it, from Gerard Genette's *Paratexts: Thresholds of Interpretation*, Jane E. Lewin, trans., (Cambridge: Cambridge University Press, 1997) 5.

[7]    On Nashe's pun on "page," see Jonathan Crewe, *Unredeemed Rhetoric: Thomas Nashe and the Scandal of Authorship*, (Baltimore: Johns Hopkins University Press, 1982) 69-70; and Margaret Ferguson, "Nashe's *Unfortunate Traveler*: The 'Newes of the Maker' Game" *ELH* 11 (1981): 166-7.

consequences of linking print publication to public self-presentation. Printed pages become social actors in Nashe's imagination; they pursue his readers and motivate their behavior. He continues:

> Memorandum: every one of you after the perusing of this pamphlet is to provide him a case of poniards, that if you come in company with any man which shall dispraise it or speak against it, you may straight cry, '*Sic respondeo*', and give him the stockado. It stands not with your honours, I assure ye, to have a gentleman and a page abused in his absence. Secondly, whereas you were wont to swear men on a pantofle to be true to your puissant order, you shall swear them on nothing but this chronicle of the King of Pages henceforward. Thirdly, it shall be lawful for any whatsoever to play with false dice in a corner on the cover of this foresaid Acts and Monuments. None of the fraternity of the minorites shall refuse it for a pawn in the times of famine and necessity. Every stationer's stall they pass by, whether by day or by night, they shall put off their hats to and make a low leg in regard their grand printed Capitano is there entombed. It shall be flat treason for any of this forementioned catalogue of the point-trussers once to name him within forty foot of an alehouse; marry, the tavern is honourable. Many special grave articles more had I to give you in charge, which your Wisdoms waiting together at the bottom of the Great Chamber stairs, or sitting in a porch (your parliament house), may better consider of than I can deliver. Only let this suffice for a taste to the text and a bit to pull on a good wit with, as a rasher on the coals is to pull on a cup of wine.
>
> Hey-pass, come aloft! Every man of you take your places, and hear Jack Wilton tell his own tale. (253-4)

This catalog of radical consequences associates reading fiction with a series of crimes, from playing false dice to dueling.[8] Reading also produces nascent class solidarity among "pages" dedicated to their "King." This passage has often been read as part of Nashe's idiosyncratic authorial manner, what Jonathan Crewe has termed Nashe's "scandal of authorship."[9] What seems particularly noteworthy, however, is how Nashe imagines the act of reading. He makes his imagined readers into Don Quixotes *avant la lettre* by asserting that reading about Jack Wilton will make them act in socially deviant ways. This sort of reading creates a subculture which bows to the "grand printed Capitano" in bookstalls and treats taverns as "honourable" places. I propose, and this book argues, that this flamboyant invocation of the consequences of reading owes less to Nashe's radical originality than to his insight into the changing conditions of print authorship in late Elizabethan England. Along with his sometime mentor Robert Greene and several other Elizabethan writers, Nashe defined himself as "a man in print" during an age that was discovering what that cultural construction would mean. This study proposes that Elizabethan fiction reveals the growing self-awareness of what

---

[8]   Ferguson suggests that this letter "presents the artist as a 'maker' who plays an inherently dangerous game when he creates fictions or 'counterfeits' that subvert established forms of authority" ("Newes of the Maker," 165).

[9]   See Crewe, *Unredeemed Rhetoric*.

would become the dominant mode of modern literary transmission: the speculative publication and sale of printed books to anonymous readers.

Reconsideration of Nashe, Greene, Philip Sidney, Thomas Lodge, and Elizabethan prose romance is urgent in early modern studies today because of a long tradition of marginalizing fiction that has only recently begun to be corrected.[10] The past quarter-century has seen vast expansions of the early modern canon, but despite this new breadth, early modern prose fiction, long ago mined as sources for Shakespearean drama, has often been overlooked. It is at once too familiar – all critical editions of Shakespeare's plays have notes to this material, and many contain selections – and too out of step with modern critical fashions. This combination of familiarity with lack of status means that even when *The Countess of Pembroke's Arcadia*, *The Unfortunate Traveler*, or more recently Mary Wroth's *The Countess of Montgomery's Urania* and Margaret Cavendish's *The Blazing World*, are discussed, they are generally presented as anomalous works, rather than products of the thriving, competitive, and influential culture of early modern English fiction.

Redressing this gap in our critical attention has begun through recent studies of "print culture" and the "history of the book." Driven by new strains of materialism and ongoing revolutions in scholarly editing (especially of Shakespeare's plays), the cultures of print have become a rising field in early modern studies.[11] Even though prose fiction is one of the substantial products of early modern print,

---

[10]   Several recent studies focus on popular fiction. See Lori Humphrey Newcomb, *Reading Popular Romance in Early Modern England*, (New York: Columbia University Press, 2002); Constance Relihan, *Fashioning Authority: The Development of Elizabethan Novelistic Discourse*, (Kent: Kent State University Press, 1994); Lorna Hutson, *The Usurer's Daughter: Male Friendship and Fictions of Women in Sixteenth-Century England*, (London: Routledge, 1994); Robert Maslen, *Elizabethan Fictions: Espionage, Counter-Espionage, and the Duplicity of Fiction in Early Elizabethan Prose Narrative*, (Oxford: Clarendon, 1997); David Margolies, *Novel and Society in Elizabethan England*, (London: Croom Helm, 1985); Derek B. Alwes, *Sons and Authors in Elizabethan England* (Newark: University of Delaware Press, 2004), Reid Barbour, *Deciphering Elizabethan Fiction*, (Newark: University of Delaware Press, 1993); Helen Hackett, *Women and Romance Fiction in the English Renaissance*, (Cambridge: Cambridge University Press, 2000); Caroline Lucas, *Writing for Women: The Example of Woman as Reader of Elizabethan Romance*, (Philadelphia: Open University Press, 1989); Suzanne Hull, *Chaste, Silent & Obedient: English Books for Women, 1475-1640*, (San Marino: Huntington Library, 1982); Tessa Watt, *Cheap Print and Popular Piety, 1550-1640*, (Cambridge: Cambridge University Press, 1991); and the growing field of work on Mary Wroth. Major earlier studies include Arthur Kinney, *Humanist Poetics: Thought, Rhetoric, and Fiction in Sixteenth-Century England*, (Amherst: University of Massachusetts Press, 1986), and Richard Helgerson, *The Elizabethan Prodigals*, (Berkeley: University of California Press, 1976).

[11]   On print culture, the "new materialism," and changes in editing as challenges to New Historicist orthodoxy, see Douglas Bruster, *Shakespeare and the Question of Culture: Early Modern Literature and the Cultural Turn*, (New York: Palgrave, 2003).

however, studies of early modern print culture by Douglas Brooks, Joseph Loewenstein, Alexandra Halasz, Wendy Wall, Joad Raymond, and David Scott Kastan, among others, tend to focus on some other aspect of print publication, often the specialized issues involved in printing dramatic texts.[12] Treating Ben Jonson at the key figure for the invention of what Joseph Loewenstein calls the "bibliographic ego, a specifically early modern form of authorial identification with printed writing," recognizes the striking place of Jonson's 1616 *Works* in the history of published poetry and drama, but it also slights the efforts of earlier fiction writers like Lyly and Greene to capitalize on their authorial personae.[13] Greene figures in Loewenstein's detailed unraveling of the competition between the "urban bookstall and the urban theater," in part because the "upstart Crow" attack reveals authorial jealousy, but his fictional output is largely overlooked.[14]

The historical record reveals a thriving marketplace for prose fiction in the late sixteenth century, including the works of Sidney, Greene, Nashe, Lodge, John Lyly, George Gascoigne, Barnebe Riche, and Thomas Deloney, among others.[15] Texts like Greene's *Menaphon*, Sidney's *New Arcadia*, Lodge's *Rosalynde*, or Nashe's *The Unfortunate Traveler* may seem "loose baggy monsters" to modern readers, but they thrived in the early modern literary economy. Understanding the historical roots of English narrative culture and complicating critical commonplaces like "the rise of the novel" require better ways of reading early modern fiction. Loewenstein's work on the "prehistory of copyright," Blayney's research into the practices of the Stationers' Company, and reconsiderations of early modern print like those of Chartier, Kastan, and Halasz have laid the groundwork for a more comprehensive model of the cultural status of early modern fiction. I propose seeking this model in the words of the practitioners themselves. Early modern prose fiction authors did not simply produce imaginative fictions; they also wrote combative, egotistical, contradictory prefatory letters and made

---

[12] See Douglas Brooks, *From Playhouse to Printing-House: Drama and Authorship in Early Modern England*, (Cambridge: Cambridge University Press, 2002), Joseph Loewenstein, *Ben Jonson and Possessive Authorship*, (Cambridge: Cambridge University Press, 2002), and *The Author's Due: Printing and the Prehistory of Copyright*, (Chicago: University of Chicago Press, 2002), Alexandra Halasz, *The Marketplace of Print: Pamphlets and the Public Sphere in Early Modern England*, (Cambridge: Cambridge University Press, 1997), Wendy Wall, *The Imprint of Gender: Authorship and Publication in the English Renaissance*, (Ithaca: Cornell University Press, 1993), David Scott Kastan, *Shakespeare and the Book*, (Cambridge: Cambridge University Press, 2001), and Joad Raymond, *Pamphlets and Pamphleteering in Early Modern Britain*, (Cambridge: Cambridge University Press, 2003).

[13] *Ben Jonson and Possessive Authorship*, 1. Loewenstein introduced the "bibliographic ego" in "The Script in the Marketplace," *Representations* 12 (Winter 1985): 101-14.

[14] See Loewenstein, *Ben Jonson and Possessive Authorship*, 53.

[15] See Paul Salzman, *English Prose Fiction, 1558-1700: A Critical History*, (Oxford: Clarendon, 1985).

thinly-veiled intertextual allusions. These moments reveal a generation of English authors coming to terms with print and the book market. The competitive, rapidly-changing market for Elizabethan fiction provides a wealth of keen observers and dissectors of their historical moment, and the intense self-consciousness of Elizabethan fiction opens a window onto this literary subculture.

By emphasizing the triumph of the public theater at the expense of printed fiction, early modern studies has long claimed for dramatists like Shakespeare a cultural independence that they did not have.[16] As we come to realize that our sense of Shakespeare's disinterest in print publication may have been overstated, we should also remember that the common practice of playwrights who were not also shareholders seems to have been to write prose pamphlets along with plays, as did Greene, Lodge, Nashe, Chettle, Munday, and others.[17] Sidney's supposed fear of the "stigma of print" has contributed to the assumption that print has minor relevance for many authors, but Sidney's early death and political ambitions make him a non-representative case. While it seems true that Shakespeare (like Heywood, among others) wrote plays first for performance, and Sidney wrote poems and fiction first for manuscript publication, these celebrated cases have distorted our understanding of how the printing press competed with and complemented the stage and the manuscript book as sites of literary circulation. (Spenser's relationship with William Ponsonby, Sidney's posthumous publisher, provides a better sense of how print culture helped shape authorial careers.)[18] The habit of separating the stage, the press, and the manuscript book has fed the relative lack of status of a literary genre that appears largely in print, early modern prose romance.[19]

When studies of Shakespearean drama accent the collective and performative aspects of the theatre, print culture is often explicitly dismissed. The image of early modern print as private and culturally marginal, however, relies on a simplified notion of print culture, as a revealing aside by Stephen Greenblatt makes clear. In the introductory essay to *Shakespearean Negotiations*, Greenblatt defines the

---

[16] Barbara Mowatt's salutary observation of the "permeability of the theater/literary-culture boundary and…the obvious dependence of the theater on nondramatic literary culture" ("The Theater and Literary Culture," *A New History of Early English Drama*, Cox and Kastan, eds., 218) is a notable counter-example.

[17] Recently Lukas Erne, among others, suggests that Shakespeare's antipathy toward print has been exaggerated. See *Shakespeare as Literary Dramatist*, (Cambridge: Cambridge University Press, 2003).

[18] See Jean Brink, "Materialist History of the Publication of Spenser's *Faerie Queene*," *Review of English Studies* 54:213 (Feb 2003): 1-26.

[19] The manuscript circulation of Sidney's *Arcadia* is an important exception, but after Sidney's death this work was published in several forms and was very influential in print circles. On Sidney's publication history, see Steve Mentz, "Selling Sidney: William Ponsonby, Thomas Nashe, and the Boundaries of Elizabethan Print and Manuscript Cultures," *TEXT* 13 (2000): 151-74.

Shakespearean stage through its radical contrast with prose fiction; the Elizabethan playgoer, he argues, "is not, as with the nineteenth-century novel, [an] individual reader who withdraws from the public world of affairs to the privacy of the hearth."[20] Using fiction as a straw man establishes the primacy of the theater, but at the cost of using a nineteenth-century image of print culture. Prose fiction in the Elizabethan era was anything but individual and private.[21] In fact, early modern printed fiction shares many of the transitory, changeable characteristics Greenblatt and others value in the theater. Print was not a retreat but a cultural sight in turmoil, as new markets for readers and writers threatened to destabilize, if not marginalize, the old protocols of court, church, and university.[22] As Alexandra Halasz has put it, "Print permanently altered the discursive field...by enabling the marketplace to develop as a means of producing, disseminating, and mediating discourse independent of the sites and practices associated with and sanctioned by university, Crown, and Church."[23] Elizabethan books were controversial objects, strange new media products whose meanings and uses were being negotiated by the culture at large. They were produced by multifaceted communities of interests and practices, including not just the author on the title page (if any), but also printers, booksellers, bookbinders, paper-makers, apprentices, compositors, and other figures involved in early modern print. These diverse communities establish the contexts for interactions between readers and books that were seldom private and solitary in Elizabethan England.

Printed books are complex artifacts, and their history is not just intellectual and textual, but also economic, social, and ideological.[24] What Roger Chartier calls the "order of books" produced at least two kinds of communities in early modern

---

[20] Stephen Greenblatt, *Shakespearean Negotiations: The Circulation of Social Energy in Renaissance England*, (Berkeley: University of California Press, 1988) 5.

[21] The case for privacy may be overstated even in regard to the nineteenth century, given communal practices like serialization and public readings.

[22] On the history of reading, see Robert Darnton, "First Steps Toward a History of Reading," *The Kiss of Lamourette: Reflections in Cultural History*, (New York: W.W. Norton, 1990) 154-187; Alberto Manguel, *A History of Reading*, (New York: Viking Penguin, 1996); and Roger Chartier and Guglielmo Cavallo, eds., *A History of Reading in the West*, (Amherst: University of Massachusetts Press, 1999). On early modern English readers, see Anthony Grafton and Lisa Jardine, "'Studied for Action': How Gabriel Harvey Read His Livy," *Past and Present* 129 (1990): 30-78; William H. Sherman, *John Dee: The Politics of Reading and Writing in the English Renaissance*, (Amherst: University of Massachusetts Press, 1995); Annabel Patterson, *Reading Holinshed's Chronicles*, (Chicago: University of Chicago Press, 1994); Sasha Roberts, *Reading Shakespeare's Poems in Early Modern England*, (New York: Palgrave, 2003), and Steven N. Zwicker, "The Reader Revealed," *The Reader Revealed*, Sabrina Alcorn Baron, ed., (Washington: Folger Library, 2001) 11-17.

[23] Halasz, *The Marketplace of Print*, 4

[24] See Adrian Johns, *The Nature of the Book: Print and Knowledge in the Making*, (Chicago: University of Chicago Press, 1998) 1-57.

England: book makers, which included artisans, craftsmen, and booksellers as well as writers and editors; and readers, which included more diverse if less clearly identifiable groups.[25] Traces of these two kinds of communities appear in the peritextual front matter of Elizabethan fiction as well as in the books' contents. Printed books provide different images of the author-audience relationship than those of the stage; they construct a series of imaginary relationships with their audiences, while dramatic scripts point towards literal encounters with filled playhouses. The most successful Elizabethan print author was not a player-shareholder like Shakespeare, but the self-mythologized, impoverished, proto-bohemian Robert Greene. Greene has long been famous for his apparent animosity toward the younger Shakespeare, but as the most prolific writer of printed fiction in the Elizabethan period, he may be a truer rival than our drama-centered criticism has allowed. Greene's career in print, like those of his contemporaries Lodge and Nashe, reveals a rival mode of authorship to the familiar model of the professional dramatist.[26]

Print, theater, and scribal publication represent three distinct strategies for aspiring authors and three intertwined literary sub-cultures. Comparing the relative inventories of playwrights and fiction writers clarifies the differences between these modes of authorial production. A playwright, if attached to a particular company, could draw on a patron (at least nominally), a troupe of adult and child actors, theatrical space, costumes, props, and other goods, as well as possibly hired co-authors. Authors of fiction, by contrast, had few resources, often just their names and professional contacts in the nascent publishing industry at St. Paul's, with which to build a marketable identity in print. The need to identify the author with the book gave rise to self-referential titles like *Greenes Never Too Late* and *Greenes Groatsworth of Wit*.[27] These print-specific titles demonstrate the author's

---

[25] See Roger Chartier, *The Order of Books: Readers, Authors, and Libraries in Europe between the Fourteenth and Eighteenth Centuries*, Lydia G. Cochrane, trans., (Stanford: Stanford University Press, 1992).

[26] Both models also contrast with the "self-crowned laureate" career patterns of some ambitious early modern English poets, including following the paths of Virgil (Spenser), Horace (Jonson), and Ovid (Marlowe). On these careers, see Patrick Cheney, *Spenser's Famous Flight: The Renaissance Idea of a Literary Career*, (Toronto: University of Toronto Press, 1993), and *Marlowe's Counterfeit Profession: Ovid, Spenser, Counter-Nationhood*, (Toronto: University of Toronto Press, 1997), and Richard Helgerson, *Self-Crowned Laureates: Spenser, Jonson, Milton, and the Literary System*, (Berkeley: University of California Press, 1983).

[27] Mentioning the author's name in the title was fairly common among fiction authors, as shown by Barnebe Riche (*Riche His Farewell to Military Profession*, 1581) and George Pettie (*A Petite Palace of Pettie His Pleasure*, 1576). While playtexts seldom followed this practice, it seems noteworthy that when clowns like Will Kemp and Robert Armin published collections of their jests, they made their names part of the books' titles. As David Wiles has noted, clowns were among the most individualist and anti-corporate of Elizabethan actors

(and publishers') manipulation of the culture of print authorship, just as the prologue of *Henry V* demonstrates the dramatist's self-conscious manipulation of theatrical form.

*Romance for Sale in Early Modern England* presents a comprehensive reconsideration of Elizabethan prose romance, especially the works of Greene, Sidney, Lodge, and Nashe. To make my intervention in literary history clear, I emphasize that my study also aims to undermine the still-current assumption that English fiction substantially began with the "rise of the novel" in the eighteenth century. Elizabethan prose romances are not, and should not be read as, "failed novels" or even embryonic novels.[28] Their prominence and sophistication, however, gives the lie to the nominal vacuum out of which the eighteenth-century novel rose. Before the eighteenth century, print had already become a major mode of literary transmission, and narrative prose fiction was becoming a major genre. The canonization of Defoe, Richardson, and Fielding represents the consolidation of a form that Elizabethan authors forced toward the mainstream.

The standard treatment of the rise of the novel is Michael McKeon's *The Origins of the English Novel, 1600-1740* (1987, re-issued 2002). McKeon's study presents a sophisticated dialectical model that places the novel on the boundaries of epistemological and sociological crises, but it largely maintains the canonical position that treats Defoe, Richardson, and Fielding as the first English novelists, previously established by Ian Watt's *The Rise of the Novel* (1957).[29] As responses to both Watt and McKeon have noted, this narrative of origins has a long history that dates to the eighteenth century and the efforts of Fielding, in particular, to contrast his "comic epic-poem in prose" to "those voluminous works commonly called Romances."[30] Two major strands of revisionism have challenged, but not

---

(*Shakespeare's Clown: Actor and Text in the Elizabethan Playhouse* [Cambridge: Cambridge University Press, 1987].)

[28] Lorna Hutson makes this point emphatically: "the project of excavating the 'origins' of the English novel from the mire of Elizabethan prose fiction has…obviously been a failure." See "Fortunate Travelers: Reading for the Plot in Sixteenth-Century England," *Representations* 41 (1993): 83-103. My project does not excavate origins so much as explore continuities. Another difference between my perspective and Hutson's is generic: she discusses novelle and I romances, the transmissions of which into modern fiction is more continuous.

[29] Michael McKeon, *The Origins of the English Novel 1600-1740*, (Baltimore: Johns Hopkins University Press, 1987); Ian Watt, *The Rise of the Novel: Studies in Defoe, Richardson, and Fielding*, (Berkeley: University of California Press, 1957).

[30] Henry Fielding, *Joseph Andrews*, Martin C. Battesin, ed., (Boston: Houghton Mifflin, 1961). On the history of the "rise of the novel" thesis, see William B. Warner, *Licensing Entertainment: The Elevation of Novel-Reading in Britain, 1684-1750*, (Berkeley: University of California Press, 1998) 1-44. As Warner details, critics narrate the rise of the eighteenth-century novel as a literary critical meta-romance, with many of the genre's

really dislodged, this canon. A series of influential studies have focused on the early eighteenth century and "amatory fictions" by women, especially Behn, Haywood, and Manley. Critics have suggested that what the canonical novelists dismissingly call "Romances" are actually examples of a rich, thriving subspecies of women's writing against which the male novelists were competing.[31] A second strand of revisionism, less visible in English studies, observes that the mid-eighteenth-century debate over romance has a French precursor in the seventeenth-century dialogue over French heroic romances, especially those of Scudéry.[32] Attempts to include these two categories in the discourse surrounding the eighteenth-century novel appear to be succeeding, but this revisionist shift, even when it attempts to define the novel broadly as, in William Warner's words, "a subset of the cultural history of print entertainments" shows little interest in printed fiction before Behn.[33] Warner's promising study sets out to define the novel in terms of "the onset of market-driven media culture" (xii), and he calls for a "fundamental resituating" (xiii) of the Watt/McKeon thesis, but even he stops short of acknowledging the rich media culture of Elizabethan fiction.

This omission suggests that Elizabethan fiction has something to teach rise of the novel criticism. McKeon notes that any genealogy of narrative fiction must consider the evolving history of prose narrative genres, some of which – especially romance – thrived before the novel. He writes that "genre theory cannot be divorced from the history of genres" (1), but rather than giving early modern romance a full share in this history, he re-affirms Watt's rise of the novel under the Marxist rubric of a "simple abstraction."[34] McKeon's category of "English novel" gives theoretical solidity to Watt, but cannot deal adequately with a problem McKeon identifies early in his introduction: "the persistence of romance...[and the] yet more fundamental problem [of] the inadequacy of our theoretical distinction between 'novel' and 'romance.'" (3). The historical continuity of romance bedevils McKeon's search for "origins"; even when he returns to Chrétien

---

recognizable features – the foundling (Defoe's early texts), the distinguished but obscure patrimony (Sidney and Cervantes), the episodic progress, and the eventual coronation.

[31]  See the introduction to John J. Richetti and Paula R. Backscheider, eds., *Popular Fiction by Women: 1660-1730: An Anthology*, (Oxford: Clarendon Press, 1996). See also Richetti, *Popular Fiction Before Richardson: Narrative Patterns, 1700-1739*, (Oxford: Clarendon, 1969); Ros Ballaster, *Seductive Forms: Women's Amatory Fiction from 1684 to 1740*, (Oxford, Clarendon, 1992); Linda S. Kaufmann, *Discourses of Desire: Gender, Genre, and Epistolary Fictions*, (Ithaca: Cornell University Press, 1986).

[32]  See Ioan Williams, *The Idea of the Novel in Europe, 1600-1800*, (New York: Macmillan, 1979); Joan E. DeJean, *Tender Geographies: Women and the Origins of the Novel in France*, (New York: Columbia University Press, 1991).

[33]  *Licensing Entertainment*, xi. There are no citations to early modern writers in the *Columbia History of the British Novel* (edited by Richetti) or in Warner's book.

[34]  McKeon, unlike Watt and other eighteenth-century critics, pays attention to premodern narrative forms, including *Don Quixote*.

de Troyes, the Spanish picaresque, or saints' lives, he remains bounded by his assumption that eighteenth-century novelists provide the key reformulations of the narrative models he discusses. This tactic relies on the distinction between romance and the novel that the opening pages of McKeon's study rightly question.[35]

It will be helpful at this point to kick away the crutch of the eighteenth-century canon, and replace Watt's defining feature of "formal realism" with a less sociological term.[36] The perspective of early modern romance clarifies this point: these writers do not rely on realistic sociological detail to tell their tales. What they do is tell fairly long, complex, coherent tales. I propose that the defining feature of Elizabethan fiction, the feature that distinguishes it from its medieval ancestors and connects it to the modern novel, is simply large-scale narrative coherence. This feature has been overlooked because our habits of reading have taught us to believe that length and coherence are marks of little distinction, but comparing Elizabethan fictions to their immediate predecessors supports my claim. Neither medieval romances of chivalry nor Renaissance novelle were organized this way. For Elizabethan romance writers plot became something to be shaped into a coherent and closed whole, and this innovation was key to the success and influence of their works. By narrative coherence I do not mean inventing new plots – Elizabethan fiction writers were as loose about borrowing storylines as dramatists – but rather articulating a lengthy story in a complex and closed form. Many kinds of fictional narratives existed in early modern England, from classical satire to medieval hagiography, but prose romance first explored formal continuity on a large scale.[37] Narrative coherence distinguishes Elizabethan prose romance from the seemingly endless episodes of chivalric cycles as well as the sudden plot-twists of novelle.

It may seem perverse to claim structural coherence as the defining feature of works that often prove so difficult for modern readers that one recent critic has pronounced them "in a basic sense, unreadable."[38] I suggest that this supposed unreadability is a function of historical distance, and that Elizabethan fictions assume coherence once we assimilate their generic codes and intertextual patterns. Even the less emphatic claim that early modern fictions cohere only according to patterns with which modern readers are unfamiliar – the argument for, in Alastair Fowler's terms, "a distinctly Renaissance mimesis" – seems to me too tentative a

---

[35] For a more dramatic approach to this conundrum, see Margaret Doody's full-scale assault on Watt's thesis, *The True Story of the Novel*, (New Brunswick: Rutgers University Press, 1996).

[36] McKeon notes problems with Watt's term (*Origins of the English Novel*, 1-3).

[37] By suggesting that previous fictions in English, including medieval romances, lack narrative coherence, I do not accuse them of formlessness or artistic failure; I rather claim that they lacked the formal continuity and closure that was a key feature of Elizabethan romances.

[38] Hutson, "Fortunate Travelers," 83.

way of integrating these works into English narrative culture.[39] When Elizabethan romance is placed among its generic and cultural peers, it stands out for its relative structural unity. The half-dozen elements that Fowler isolates as the distinct "narrative assumptions" of Renaissance fictions – allegorical content, discontinuity, multiple narratives, apparent inconsistency, apparent irrelevance, and schematic content – can help naturalize the structural peculiarities of these narratives.[40] Readers of early modern fiction should expect schematic and allegorical structures, be suspicious of apparent irrelevance and inconsistency, and discern behind discontinuity and multiple narratives formal patterns and intellectual consistency. Fowler's caveats describe a series of characteristic narrative strategies of early modern writers, but they need not separate these fictions from their modern descendents. Elizabethan fiction emerged during a period of cultural transition that included the expansion of literacy, rapid growth of the book market, revival of classical models, and competition between print, manuscript, and the theater. This ferment created the cultural conditions that made coherent narrative formulae marketable commodities. In this sense, romance was for sale in bookstalls in Elizabethan London.

A pattern of conflict and synthesis defines the interaction of chivalric romance, the novella, and Elizabethan romance in a way that parallels McKeon's "dialectical theory of genre" (20). The expansive but (to modern tastes) structurally incoherent episodism of medieval romance from Chrétien to Malory presents an initial position, widely popular in late medieval Europe. This form was challenged by the compact narrative resolutions of novelle, which came to rival chivalric romance by the fifteenth century. Faced with these two incompatible forms, Elizabethan prose romances devised a new configuration of narrative flexibility and coherence. Through its commitment to continuous closed narrative, Elizabethan prose romance represents a crucial development in the longer history of English fiction. Print made lengthy coherent narratives practical for transmitting in significant numbers to a broad readership.

I will clarify what narrative coherence meant to Elizabethan writers and readers through two apparently independent models. The first is the revival of Aristotelian critical theory through the circulation of the *Poetics* after the mid-sixteenth century. As is well-known, Aristotle valued plot as the most important aspect of a literary work. Not just any plot will do, either; he calls episodic plots "the worst" because "there is neither probability nor necessity in the sequence of its episodes."[41] In place of episodic plots, the popularity of which Aristotle connects

---

[39]   Alastair Fowler, *Renaissance Realism: Narrative Images in Literature and Art*, (Oxford: Oxford University Press, 2003).

[40]   Fowler no doubt intends his study to encourage the readability of Renaissance fictions. On the narrative assumptions listed above, see *Renaissance Realism*, 45-65.

[41]   Aristotle, *Poetics*, Ingram Bywater, trans., (New York: Modern Library, 1954) 235-6. Further citations in the text.

to the demands of "the players," Aristotle prefers a plot that is "complete in itself, as a whole of some magnitude" (233), and which is structured according to his famous three-part scheme:

> Now, a whole is that which has a beginning, middle, and end. A beginning is that which is not itself necessarily after anything else, and which has naturally something else after it; an end is that which is naturally after something itself, either as its necessary or usual consequent, and with nothing else after it; and a middle, that which is by nature after one thing and has also another after it. A well-constructed Plot, therefore, cannot either begin or end at any point one likes; beginning and end in it must be of the forms just described. (233)

Aristotle's emphasis on plot as a coherent whole requires literary narratives to be shaped in substantial and strongly closed forms. This formal imperative distinguished Elizabethan romance from the adventures of Arthur, Tristam, and Amadis, and from the brief plots of novelle.

The Aristotelian narrative template, which N. J. Lowe has recently labeled the "classical plot," can be usefully summarized as the tension between two features: economy and amplitude.[42] The first feature, economy, "maximise[s] the ratio of functionality to content in the narrative information presented to the reader" (62-3). In other words, as nearly as possible everything in the story should matter. The second feature, amplitude, appears in Aristotle's preference for a "whole of some magnitude." The art of classical plotting, Lowe suggests, lies in "reconciling the competing claims of amplitude and economy" (66), in creating a tale that feels both big enough to be impressive and coherent enough to be intelligible.[43] Plot-making is what Elizabethan prose romancers did well, and in making plots they not only supplied the public theater with a mine of usable material, but also established the long-lasting literary form of printed fiction in England.

Aristotle's theoretical abstractions are one important consideration in defining Elizabethan narrative coherence, but it is uncertain how well-known Aristotle was among English fiction writers in the 1580s and 1590s.[44] Elizabethan authors certainly did not consult Aristotle with the same fetishism that currently sells faux-

---

[42] N. J. Lowe, *The Classical Plot and the Invention of Western Narrative*, (Cambridge: Cambridge University Press, 2000). Citations in the text.

[43] The third feature of the Aristotelian plot, according to Lowe, is transparency: the author never steps out from behind the curtain in the classical plot. Even before modernism, this aspect of Aristotelian plotting was often violated, as the examples of Greene and Nashe show.

[44] On the obscurity of Aristotle, see Henry Turner, "Plotting Early Modernity," *The Culture of Capital: Property, Cities, and Knowledge in Early Modern England*, Henry S. Turner, ed., (London: Routledge, 2002) 86-7.

Aristotelian principles to aspiring Hollywood screenwriters.[45] I propose instead
that the most powerful vehicle for transmitting the classical plot to late sixteenth-
century English culture was not the *Poetics* but one of the supreme exemplars of
classical plotting, Heliodorus's *Aethiopica*. This late classical prose romance,
rediscovered in sixteenth-century Europe and widely published and translated, was
a – perhaps *the* – key structural model for Elizabethan prose fiction. As Lowe
notes, Heliodorus's sophisticated and complex plot was the best model of the
reconciliation of economy and amplitude: "The *Aethiopica* is the ancient world's
narrative *summa*, a self-consciously encyclopedic synthesis of a thousand years of
accumulated pagan plot techniques, of the game of story as a way of understanding
the world. For the next millennium and more, it remained the final word" (258). I
shall discuss the structure and influence of the *Aethiopica* in Chapters 1 and 2, but
I emphasize now that Heliodorus showed Elizabethan writers how to flesh out the
bare dicta of Aristotelian theory with a complex, suspenseful narrative structure
combining economy and amplitude. Borrowings from Heliodorus have been
documented in Shakespeare, Sidney, and Spenser, among others, but its larger
impact on literary structures and techniques of plotting has been underestimated.

My emphasis on Heliodorus over Aristotle contains a polemical subtext:
privileging practice over theory. More directly, I contend that practice implies
theory, that the efforts of professional writers like Greene, Lodge, Nashe, and
others to define their own works as worth a book-buyer's purse constitutes a
theoretical defense of prose fiction.[46] This study will draw its material for
articulating a theory of early modern narrative fiction from the practices of
professional authors and their self-constructions in the prefatory materials of their
books. These primary sources will supplement the sparse discussions of prose
narrative in early modern literary criticism. I argue that the practices of fiction
writers from Heliodorus to Greene reveal a practical approach to shaping narrative
that familiar sources like Sidney's *Defence of Poetry*, Puttenham's *Art of English
Poesie*, and the works of continental humanists seldom emphasize. The interaction
between Elizabethan fictions and the peritexts of print demonstrates the rise of a
new field of literary culture, driven neither by patronage nor the joint-stock
companies of the public stage, but by an implied contract between authors and
readers that expressed itself economically in the book market. The anonymous
transaction of buying a book first began to loom large in the imaginations of
professional English writers in the Elizabethan period, and this development drove

---

[45] Lowe suggests that cinema's "strongly classical form" underlies the persistent if often
uninformed homages to Aristotle in screenwriting manuals and courses.

[46] This method obviates Paul Salzman's objection that early modern England lacked "any
conception of a genre [i.e., the genre of prose fiction] constructed by the twentieth century
in response to the modern obsession with the novel" ("Theories of Prose Fiction in England:
1558-1700," *The Cambridge History of Literary Criticism*, Volume 3, Glyn P. Norton, ed.,
[Cambridge: Cambridge University Press, 1999] 295).

authors to seek out the Heliodoran plot as a flexible vehicle for displaying narrative artistry. Recovering this narrative form and its interactions with more well-known genres can place the Elizabethan age in contact with the longer sweep of English literary history, and also reorient our understanding of narrative itself as a constitutive aspect of that history.

The chapters that follow fall roughly into two parts: the first four explore the creation of Elizabethan-Heliodoran prose romance in the 1580s, and the next three investigate how Elizabethan writers departed from this model in the 1590s. The common figure in both parts is Robert Greene, whose career spans the many different contexts in which I read early modern English fiction. In the first four chapters, Greene is paired with Philip Sidney as co-initiators of the Heliodoran vogue; each articulates a different version of what I call Heliodorus's "anti-epic" model, with Sidney carving out a space for heroic agency and Greene delving into passivity and weakness. The following three chapters see Greene and his peers Lodge and Nashe become less classical and more devoted to urban popular readers. Greene's books stage combative relationships with the novella, his one-time protégés Lodge and Nashe, and even the circumstances of his own life. The conclusion treats the flurry of texts written about or under Greene's name after his death as English narrative culture's investigation of his legacy. The many "ghosts" of Robert Greene become, as I show, images of popular print authorship, a new phenomenon in early modern English culture.

# Chapter 1

# Early Modern Romance and the Middlebrow Reader

> Reading is thus situated at the point where *social* stratification (class relationships) and *poetic* operations (the practitioner's constructions of a text) intersect: a social hierarchization seeks to make the reader conform to the "information" distributed by an elite (or semi-elite); reading operations manipulate the reader by insinuating their inventiveness into the cracks in a cultural orthodoxy.
>
> Michel de Certeau, "Reading as Poaching[1]

Who read Elizabethan fiction, and why did they read it? Answering this question means moving beyond the claims Louis B. Wright made for "middle-class" readers with their "catholic curiosity and...uncritical judgment."[2] It also means reconsidering recent work on women readers by Lorna Hutson, Helen Hackett, Lori Humphrey Newcomb, and others.[3] Women did read Elizabethan fiction, and women readers were specifically addressed in the prefaces of many Elizabethan books, but educated men seem to have made up the bulk of the potential and actual readers in most cases.[4] The prominence of women readers may be taken as a symptom of changes in reading practices. Male aristocrats, who had once considered arms the only honorable career, were being reshaped by a world that valued textual more than military prowess.[5] Masculine social agency, once exclusively active and forceful, was becoming inward and passive, and both masculinity and reading were reevaluated as a result.[6] The new readers generated

---

[1]  Michel de Certeau, "Reading as Poaching," *The Practice of Everyday Life*, trans. Steven Rendall, (Berkeley: University of California Press, 1984) 172.

[2]  Louis B. Wright, *Middle-Class Culture in Elizabethan England*, (Ithaca: Cornell University Press, 1948) 83. Reprint of 1935 ed.

[3]  See Hutson, *The Usurer's Daughter*; Hackett, *Women and Romance Fiction in the English Renaissance*; Newcomb, *Reading Popular Romance in Early Modern England*.

[4]  For the notion that directing these texts to women readers was a strategy intended to resonate with male readers, see Hackett, *Women and Romance Fiction*, 10-11.

[5]  See Hutson, *The Usurer's Daughter*, and more generally Lawrence Stone, *Crisis of the Aristocracy, 1558-1641*, (Oxford: Clarendon Press, 1965).

[6]  On passive refigurations of heroism in seventeenth-century England, see Mary Beth Rose, *Gender and Heroism in Early Modern English Literature* (Chicago: University of Chicago Press, 2002).

by late sixteenth-century social conditions needed a model of heroic agency applicable to their own situations.[7]

Neither strict gender division nor the rise of a middle-class seems fully applicable to the social hierarchies of Elizabethan England, in which almost all educated readers may have qualified as elite.[8] The popularity and anti-courtliness of Elizabethan prose romance may be better read as initiating a distinct category of readers – the middlebrow –than exploiting the elite/popular divide.[9] Without re-examining the vexed category of the early modern middle class, I use middlebrow to signal the mediated positions of readers and writers of prose fiction on the margins of elite culture. Thus while, as Theodore Leinwand has observed, "it is not easy to describe the middling sort," it is possible to observe these writers defining their audience in terms that are neither purely elite nor popular.[10] Elizabethan prose romance thus initiates middlebrow narrative in a particular sense: while these works were not purely elite, they signaled their cultural affiliations more with elite culture (in this case, classical humanism) than with what later became known as "folk culture."[11] The position these books and their authors inhabit is neither courtly and exclusive nor broadly popular; the books teem with Latin tags and other references to exclusive university educations, but they define their readership

---

[7]    Newcomb notes that seventeenth century England developed a non-humanist model of reading influenced by the popularity of romance: extensive, relaxed, and empathetic ("Gendering Prose Romance in Renaissance England," *A Companion to Romance: From Classical to Contemporary,* Corinne Saunders, ed. [Oxford: Blackwell, 2004]: 121-39.)

[8]    For a critique of class as a category, see Pierre Bourdieu, "Social Space and Symbolic Space," *Practical Reason: On the Theory of Action,* Gisele Shapiro, trans., (Stanford: Stanford UP, 1998) 12 and *passim.* On early modern England as a "one-class society," see Peter Laslett, *The World We Have Lost: England Before the Industrial Age,* 2nd ed., (New York: Charles Scribner's Sons, 1971). On how misreading class distorts literary criticism, see A.L. Beier, "New Historicism, Historical Context, and the Literature of Roguery: The Case of Thomas Harman Re-opened," *Rogues and Early Modern English Culture,* Craig Dionne and Steve Mentz, eds., (Ann Arbor: University of Michigan Press, 2004): 98-119.

[9]    I adapt the term middlebrow from Janice Radway's *A Feeling for Books: The Book-of-the-Month Club, Literary Taste, and Middle-Class Desire* (Chapel Hill: University of North Carolina Press, 1997). While discussing contemporary American culture, she describes "middle-class longings for the prestige conferred by familiarity with high culture" (321) in resonant terms.

[10]    Theodore B. Leinwand, "Shakespeare and the Middling Sort," *Shakespeare Quarterly* 44 (1983): 289. Leinwand provides a valuable, if cautious, defense of the category of "middling" in this period.

[11]    Newcomb traces the shift in Greene's reputation to purely popular status (*Reading Popular Romance in Early Modern England*). By contrast, I emphasize that Greene's initial position was at least semi-elite.

in hybrid terms.[12] These writers appear to be some of the earliest in English literature to self-consciously imagine themselves in a middlebrow position: indebted to but slightly outside of elite culture.

Writers of Elizabethan prose romance distinguished themselves from their rivals within the field of narrative fiction and against other modes like drama and coterie verse.[13] Their collective acts of distinction and self-definition emphasize professional rivalries more than divisions of class or gender. Greene, Lodge, Nashe, and in a different sense Sidney, recognized that their careers in prose narrative represented something new in literary culture. As early modern studies reconsiders the "death of the author," Elizabethan prose fiction provides a detailed view of several self-generated authorial career paths.[14] These writers had, to begin with, an audience problem that operated differently than those of coterie poets or playwrights. Partly due to new technologies of transmission (the printing press and book market), and partly due to having a different literary history, Elizabethan prose romances defined themselves as a new subset of literary culture.

The audience problem of authors of Elizabethan prose fiction was fundamental: they did not know whom they were addressing, or even if anyone would read their works. The presumed heterogeneity of readers of printed fiction and of their reading practices distinguished them from more familiar kinds of audiences, like theater crowds, court and coterie circles, and groups that assembled in places like universities, churches, or the Inns of Court. Writers of printed books hoped to reach the unsounded but potentially broad readership made available by print technologies as well as the dwindling supply of literary patrons, but they had few explicit models for appealing to this diverse audience.[15] The inductions, prefaces,

---

[12]   On Latin in Elizabethan fiction, see Constance Relihan, "Humanist Learning, Eloquent Women, and the Use of Latin in Robert Greene's *Ciceronis Amor/Tullie's Love*," *Explorations in Renaissance Culture* 27 (2001): 1-19.

[13]   I do not consider verse miscellanies or sonnet sequences, which were also a popular (if non-narrative) form during this period. See, for example, Wall, *The Imprint of Gender*, 23-109.

[14]   The "death of the author" was announced by Barthes and Foucault in the 1970s, and has met increasing resistance since the mid-1990s. See Seán Burke, *The Death and Return of the Author: Criticism and Subjectivity in Barthes, Foucault, and Derrida*, 2nd ed., (Edinburgh: Edinburgh University Press, 1998), first ed. 1992; Jorge Gracia, *A Theory of Textuality: The Logic and Epistemology*, (Albany: State University of New York Press, 1995) and *Texts: Ontological Status, Identity, Author, Audience*, (Albany: State University of New York Press, 1996); and Adrian Wilson, "Foucault on the 'Question of the Author': A Critical Exegesis," *Modern Language Review* 99:2 (April 2004): 339-63.

[15]   This audience was constrained by, but not limited to, the number of literate readers. The practice of reading aloud allowed printed works to circulate among groups that were only partly literate. Roger Chartier has observed that the development of "popular" reading in the early modern period occurred on multiple levels, including the emergence of silent reading, the "sharing" of texts by elite and popular readers, and the book business's efforts to expand circulation of printed works. See "Reading Matter and 'Popular' Reading," *A History of*

and choruses of Elizabethan drama invoke the physical and social surroundings of the playhouse, and familiar lines like "this wooden O" or "the great globe itself" play upon limitations and opportunities particular to the stage.[16] Prose writers had few models to follow. Authorial figures from the classical and rhetorical traditions, like Homer's bard Demodocus and Cicero's Orator, did not speak to the circumstances facing writers of early modern prose fiction. These writers needed a new model for conceptualizing their relationship to a heterogeneous readership with varied reading practices.

Books of Elizabethan fiction addressed their readers directly through their front matter. These books (unlike most printed playscripts and privately circulated manuscripts) typically contained elaborate peritextual material: letters from the author to gentlemen or lady readers, dedications to wished-for patrons, and letters and poems from publishers, well-wishers, or even fictional characters.[17] In this prefatory matter, Elizabethan writers shaped diverse anonymous readers into an imagined community by suggesting how this group could (and should) read their books.[18] In *Mamillia* (1580), his first published book, Robert Greene's prefatory letter "To the Gentlemen Readers" describes the process by which potential customers might read his book: "For there is no chasser so charie, but some will cheape; no ware so bad, but some wil buy; no booke so yll but some will both reade it and praise it; & none again so curious, but some wil carpe at it. Wel, so many heades, so many wittes."[19] Greene shows himself at the start of his career to be the most strategic writer of Elizabethan prose fiction. He describes his book as a "ware" subject to many kinds of exchange; it will be "cheaped" (i.e., bargained for), "praised," "carped at," "bought," and (he hopes) "read." His readers resemble a hydra with "many heades" but no teeth. More heads are better, Greene implies;

---

*Reading in the West*, Cavallo and Chartier, eds., 269-83. On literacy rates, see David Cressy, *Literacy and the Social Order*, (Cambridge: Cambridge University Press, 1980) and Margaret Spufford, *Small Books and Pleasant Histories*, *Popular Fiction and Its Readership in Seventeenth-Century England*, (Athens: University of Georgia Press, 1982).

[16] On playing and writing in early modern drama, see Robert Weimann, *Author's Pen and Actor's Voice: Playing and Writing in Shakespeare's Theater*, (Cambridge: Cambridge University Press, 2000). On prologues and epilogues in relation to changing playscripts, see Tiffany Stern, "'A small-beer health to his second day': Playwrights, Prologues, and First Performances in the Early Modern Theater," *Studies in Philology* 101 (2004): 172-99.

[17] Front matter became more common in playtexts in the early seventeenth century, as authors like Jonson marketed their plays as literary works.

[18] On early modern paratextual material, see Kevin Dunn, *Pretexts of Authority: The Rhetoric of Authorship in the Renaissance Preface*, (Stanford: Stanford University Press, 1994), and Derek B. Alwes, "Robert Greene's Dueling Dedications," *English Literary Renaissance* 30 (2000): 373-97.

[19] Robert Greene, *Mamillia, The Complete Works in Prose and Verse of Robert Greene, M.A.*, Alexander Grosart, ed., 14 Volumes, (London: Huth Library, 1881-86) 2:10. Further citations given in the text by volume and page number.

the many-headed public ensures that someone will buy his book, although individual purchases seem governed purely by chance. The maxim about heads and wits was included in the 1520 edition of Erasmus's *Adagia*, and it became a common saying in early modern England.[20] For Greene, it presents an elegant solution to the dilemma of print authorship: plurality saves the day. He asks for many readers rather than an ideal reader. This description does not demonstrate a strategy for appealing to heterogeneous readers so much as it proclaims as an article of faith that his book will find such an audience.

This rhetoric strikes a different note than the metadramatic language of Elizabethan drama. The theatrical refrain of pleasing the crowd, of the applause that releases Prospero (or the actor playing Prospero) from his bonds, gets dispersed in Greene's celebration of divergent readings of his book. The hoped-for burst of applause nominally unifies a diverse playhouse crowd, but Greene accents the disparity of his readers ("so many heades") and also their interpretive practices ("so many wittes"). By contrast, Heming and Condell's letter "To the great Variety of Readers" in the First Folio (1623) suggest that the book should be used to repeat the unifying experience its readers presumably had in the theater: "Reade him, therefore; and againe, and againe" (95). The Folio appeals to its readers through the communal logic of the theater, even suggesting that if readers are confused by the plays, they should ask some "other of his Friends…[to] bee your guides" (95). *Mamillia*, by contrast, stakes its claim on a fragmentary and dispersed readership. Although Greene would become a successful playwright, he here initiates the distinction between printed fiction and dramatic playscripts that he would emphasize throughout his career.[21] Most (in)famously in his Upstart Crow attack, Greene consistently argued for the superiority of the page to the stage. In fact, the plea Greene makes in the Upstart Crow letter to his fellow dramatists (usually identified as Marlowe, Nashe, and Peele) is to give up playwriting for the nobler calling of the page: "O that I might intreat your rare wits to be imploied in more profitable courses."[22] There were a range of "more profitable courses" open to

---

[20] Erasmus's version reads, "Quot homines, tot sententiae." See Margaret Mann Philips, *The Adages of Erasmus: A Study with Translation*, (Cambridge: Cambridge University Press, 1964) 125. On the proverb in England, see Morris Palmer Tilley, *A Dictionary of the Proverbs in English in the Sixteenth and Seventeenth Centuries* (Ann Arbor: University of Michigan Press, 1950) 298, 438.

[21] For a survey of printed drama and fiction, see Charles Mish, "Comparative Popularity of Early Fiction and Drama," *Notes and Queries* (1952): 269-70. Mish notes that fiction surged in popularity around 1580, and that drama surpassed it around 1591.

[22] Robert Greene and Henry Chettle, *Greene's Groatsworth of Wit, Bought With a Million of Repentance (1592)*, D. Allen Carroll, ed., (Binghamton: Medieval & Renaissance Texts and Studies, 1994) 85. Carroll, among, others, doubts Greene's authorship of this book. Further citations in the text. See also Steve Mentz, "Forming Greene: Theorizing the Early Modern Author in the *Groatsworth of Wit*," *Robert Greene: Page and Stage*, Edward Gieskes and Kirk Melinkoff, eds., (Aldershot: Ashgate Publishing, forthcoming).

these gentlemen, but Greene's career amounts to a long argument in favor of the "profitability" (in several senses of the word) of prose fiction.[23]

The prominence of the description of the many-headed reader in Greene's career – it appears in the prefatory material to his first published book – demonstrates his preoccupation with the special audience problems of printed fiction. His letter asserts that readers will find his book, but his approach seems more brazen than strategic. In the same letter, he contrasts himself with more diffident authors who are "drenched in doubt of their abilities, & almost fortified for feare" (9) when offering their books to the marketplace. Greene's own position is hybrid; he attacks less erudite popular authors for producing "meete for the Pedler," but he also describes his own book as a "ware." He here defines the semi-elite position that I term middlebrow: more elite than other writers, but still accessible to heterogeneous audiences. Devising a more systematic way to appeal to the "many heades" of his readers would be one of the major tasks of Greene's career.

While his success in the print market is well known, it is not commonly recognized that Greene found a model for appealing to a diverse readership in one of his primary plot sources, Heliodorus's *Aethiopian History*. There were numerous classical models of prose fiction besides Heliodorus, but none offered as sophisticated a construction of its audience.[24] Heliodorus's tale, written a millennium before the age of print, explores the challenges of heterogeneous readers with diverse interpretive strategies. The construction of this readership begins in Heliodorus's celebrated opening scene. Readers of the *Aethiopian History* see a confusing tableau through the eyes of a gang of Egyptian bandits. A richly laden merchant ship sits at the mouth of the Nile next to a gruesome scene:

> But on the shore every place was ful of men, some quite dead, some halfe dead, some whose bodies yet panted, and plainly declared that there had ben a battell fought of late. But there coulde be seene no signes or tokens of any just quarrell, but there seemed to be an ill and unluckie banket, and those that remained, obtained such ende. For the tables were furnished with delicate dishes, some whereof laie in the handes of those that were

---

[23]   On humanist and other definitions of "profit," see Hutson, *Thomas Nashe in Context*.

[24]   Other ancient fictions include Xenophon's *Cyropaedia* (which Sidney praises alongside Heliodorus), Apuleius's *Golden Ass*, *Apollonius of Tyre*, Petronius's *Satyricon*, Lucian's *True History*, Longus's *Daphnis and Chloe*, and Achilles Tatius's *Clitophon and Leucippe*. These last two texts – usually grouped with the *Aethiopian History* as "sophistic" Greek romances – share some of Heliodorus's sophistication and were praised by some of the same authorities, but they transgress more than Heliodorus on the boundaries of humanist morality: their heroes do not remain chaste, and each work contains more than a whiff of parody. The *Satyricon* and the *True History* explicitly parody the *Odyssey*, which Lucian calls the founding text of a "school of literary horseplay" (*A True Story*, B. P. Reardon, trans., *Collected Ancient Greek Novels*, [Berkeley: University of California Press, 1989] 621). Heliodorus, by contrast, modifies Homer but does not mock him.

slaine, being in steede of weapons to some of them in the battaile, so souddenly begunne.[25]

Seemingly there is only one survivor: "A maid endued with excellent beautie, which also might be supposed a goddesse, sate uppon a rocke" (8-9). The bandits see her as Artemis (she carries a bow), Isis (a wounded man lies at her feet), or "some Priest of the Gods, that replenished with divine furie had made the great slaughter" (9-10). In this confusion they read the scene as a heterogeneous mass: "everie man gave his verdite, because they knew not the trueth" (11). The scene portrays reading as anarchy, a confused disorder of failed interpretations. What terrifies the bandits, however, attracts Heliodorus's readers, for whom not knowing the truth is a welcome introduction to a sophisticated entertainment. The opening scene contrasts the different results, terror on the one hand and interest on the other, of two strategies of reading.

The interrogation of divergent reading practices becomes more explicit when Heliodorus describes the opening scene as a spectacle: "To be briefe, God shewed a wonderfull sight in so shorte time, bruing bloude with wine, joyning battaile with banketting, mingling indifferently slaughters with drinking, and killing with quaffinges, providing such a sight for the theeves of Egypt to gaze at" (8). This image introduces another type of audience – watchers of a spectacle, or implicitly theatergoers – and raises questions about the reader's relationship to the text being read. Heliodorus's description contains three disjunctive ironies: the reader knows that the author, not the deity, has contrived the scene; that it is part of a prose romance, not a "wonderfull sight"; and that the intended audience is a literate reader, not an Egyptian bandit gang. This strategic inaccuracy of presentation is more sophisticated than Greene's willful construction of the desire of London's readers for his book; it articulates a recognizable strategy for entertaining a diverse readership.

Heliodorus's analogy portrays readers and bandits as different parts of a diverse audience and in this way draws together heterogeneous reading practices. The scene further imagines that a readership spread across space and time may be united by reconceiving individual acts of reading as mutual participation in a public performance. Placing bandits and readers in positions of ignorance, the text portrays different but coexisting strategies of reading.[26] There is no question that the bandits' way of reading is inferior – just as Greene presumably would prefer readers not to "carp at" his book – but their limited understanding, like some

---

[25] Heliodorus, *An Aethiopian History*, Thomas Underdowne, trans., George Saintsbury, ed., (London: Simpkin, Marshall, Hamilton, Kent, and Co., 1925) 7-8. This edition reprints the 1577 ed. Further citations in the text. This book's cover and frontispiece reproduce a painting of this scene by Abraham Bloemart from 1625.

[26] The more literal modern translation of J. R. Morgan describes the bandits as being "like the audience in a theater" (*Collected Ancient Greek Novels*, 354). Underdowne picks up the theatrical reference later.

carping, has its place. These authorial ploys – the counterfactual analogy to a public spectacle and the juxtaposition of the bandits with the readers – initiate the text's sophisticated articulation of the relationship between prose fiction and its heterogeneous readership.[27]

Heliodorus's text self-consciously embraces this readership. The work is a "wonderfull sight" for the Egyptian bandits" and a sophisticated romance for readers who understand the form.[28] It is an adventure story for readers eager to follow the plot, a travelogue for those who enjoy exotic places, a love story for sentimentalists, and a philosophical allegory for intellectual readers. Readers who crave military action receive the siege of Syene, and those who enjoy erotic intrigue get the Athenian traveler Cnemon's domestic imbroglio. While similar claims might be made for other ancient fictions, notably the *Odyssey*, the *Aethiopian History* constructs its appeal to a mixed readership as a conscious and systematic refinement on Homer.[29] The story's characters model different reading practices: the Egyptian sage Calasiris reads the tale as high-brow philosophical allegory, Cnemon treats it as middle-brow recreation, and the presumably illiterate bandits initially see it as tragic spectacle. In narratological terms, a single *text* allows readers access to multiple kinds of *story*, all superimposed on a substratum of unitary *fabula*.[30] Or, in Aristotelian terms, the dialectic between amplitude and economy strains as far as possible toward amplitude before unexpectedly resolving in an economic ending. Heliodorus's text displays and sanctions these multiple ways of reading. Calasiris's philosophy surpasses the other interpretive strategies, but even the low-brow bandits are welcome. Rather than being denigrated as Hamlet mocks the groundlings, the bandits gain respectability as the story continues; their chief, Thyamis, turns out to be Calasiris's son and eventually becomes high priest of Memphis. Early modern theatergoers encountered this

---

[27] John R. Morgan speaks for the consensus of recent criticism when he says that Heliodorus "was concerned in an almost theoretical way with problems of literary hermeneutics." See "Reader and Audiences in the *Aithiopika* of Heliodoros," *Groningen Colloquia on the Novel IV* (1991): 89.

[28] The dates of the extant Greek romances are uncertain, but the *Aethiopian History* is a late examples of the genre, perhaps as much as four hundred years after Chariton's *Chaereas and Callirhoe*. See Reardon, intro., *Collected Ancient Greek Novels*, 5.

[29] As I discuss in chapter 2, Heliodorus modifies Homer through explicit references to the *Odyssey*; the ghost of Odysseus appears and sets the stage for Heliodorus's careful rejection of the *Iliad* and his modification of the *Odyssey*. Tim Whitmarsh more generally argues that "The *Aithiopika*... undoes what might be taken to be the 'normative' or 'culturally consolidatory' aspects of the *Odyssey*." See "Heliodoros and the Genealogy of Hellinism," *Studies in Heliodorus*, Richard Hunter, ed., *Cambridge Philological Society Supplementary Volume 21* (1998): 93-124, 99.

[30] For an elaboration of this three-part schematic, see Mieke Bal, *Narratology: Introduction to the Theory of Narrative*, 2nd ed., (Toronto: University of Toronto Press, 1997).

priest-bandit more often than any other Heliodoran character; he is a primary model for Edgar in *King Lear*, and Duke Orsino mentions him in *Twelfth Night*.[31] Even "Egyptian theeves," it seems, can earn a place at the table.

The circumstances of Heliodorus's late classical era and Greene's early modern London appear radically different, and of course the innovations of print that meant so much to Greene have no clear parallel in the Second Sophistic. The exact nature of Heliodorus's dissemination and readership remains quite controversial – recent work has largely debunked earlier claims of an emerging middle class readership and, less definitively, of a growing class of women, young readers, or freed slaves as well – but the primacy of female characters, love stories, and human passivity suggests that new reading practices were being addressed.[32] Certainly the sophistication of these texts, with their wide allusions to classical literature and sophisticated interpretive games, suggests an educated audience, as Ewen Bowie has argued.[33] While further papyrus findings may advance our understanding of who read these works and when, the nature of the stories – idealized romances that revolve around human weakness and interpretive acumen – have suggestive parallels with the plights of the over-educated but unemployed courtiers of late sixteenth-century England. The fictions of both eras show a shift away from martial activity toward interpretive passivity.

The Heliodoran movement in English prose fiction began around 1580, with the publication of Greene's *Mamillia* and the (probable) manuscript composition of Sidney's *Old Arcadia*. (The Heliodoran turn in Europe began somewhat earlier, with the arrival of a Greek manuscript in Venice in 1526, as I discuss in the following chapter.) The trend's high-water mark came on the cusp of the 1590s, with Greene's *Menaphon* (1589), Sidney's *New Arcadia* (1590), and Lodge's *Rosalynde* (1590). Around this time the form became naturalized, and particularly associated with Greene, but its popularity outlasted his death in 1592 and continued in Nashe's *The Unfortunate Traveler* (1594) and Lodge's *A Margarite of America* (1596).[34] In these two decades, Heliodoran romance and Greene's elaboration of it renovated English prose fiction, producing a narrative form that would remain influential into the eighteenth century. While there can be no question that this genre lost its self-declared war with the Shakespearean stage, it

---

[31] Shakespeare drew the Edgar-Edmund-Gloucester subplot from Sidney's *New Arcadia* (Book 2). Duke Orsino, however, alludes to the *Aethiopian History* directly (5.1.117-9).

[32] See Susan A. Stephens, "Who Read Ancient Novels?", *The Search for the Ancient Novel*, 405-18.

[33] See Ewan Bowie, "The Readership of Greek Novels in the Ancient World," *The Search for the Ancient Novel*, 435-59.

[34] Heliodoran fiction changed dramatically in the seventeenth century, but authors like Mary Wroth, Margaret Cavendish, Aphra Behn, and William Congreve continued to adapt it. See Doody, *The True Story of the Novel*, and "Heliodorus Rewritten: Samuel Richardson's *Clarissa* and Frances Burney's *Wanderer*," *The Search for the Ancient Novel*, James Tatum, ed., (Baltimore: Johns Hopkins University Press, 1994) 117-31.

has a history of its own that can be recovered by breathing new life into the critical
term "genre."

## Genre and Literary Creation

> *The generic can be more intense than the concrete*...The generic (the repeated name, the
> type, the fatherland, the tantalizing destiny invested in it) takes priority over individual
> features, *which are tolerated only because of their prior genres.*
>
>                               Jorge Luis Borges, "A History of Eternity"

For much of the twentieth century, critics have treated both Greek romances and
Elizabethan prose romances as "genre fiction." Standard accounts denigrate
market-driven writers like Greene and Lodge, and even Nashe has served more as
oddity than exemplar. Courtier poets like Sidney pass muster, but marketplace
hacks do not. The similarities between Greene's and Sidney's prose works have
been explained away by common classical and Continental sources, or by the
convenient notion that Greene cribbed from a manuscript of the *Old Arcadia*.[35]
Major studies of Elizabethan fiction, like Arthur Kinney's *Humanist Poetics* and
Richard Helgerson's *Elizabethan Prodigals*, connect Sidney and Greene as
products of Elizabethan humanism but read them quite differently.[36] Accenting
their common use of Heliodoran form reminds critics that Greene and Sidney
worked with the same generic materials. Many critics refer to the "web" of sources
for Sidney's *Arcadia* first identified by John Hoskins around 1600: Heliodorus,
Sannazarro's *Arcadia*, and Montemayor's *Diana*.[37] When it is acknowledged that
Greene wove from the same web, and even that Greene's works, too, were named
"Arcadian," the comparison usually belittles Greene.[38]

Devaluing Greene has encouraged modern readers to disregard the Elizabethan
Heliodoranists other than Sidney. Without an approach that is both historicized and

---

[35] Recently Newcomb has revitalized this relationship by suggesting that Greene and
Sidney each dominated a particular medium: Greene popular printed romances, and Sidney
elite manuscript romances. See *Reading Popular Romance in Early Modern England*, 21-
76.

[36] Both treat Sidney as serious, learned, political, and philosophical, but Greene writes
"fictions of wonder" (Kinney) and is "less of a courtier" (Helgerson) than his peers. See
Kinney, *Humanist Poetics*, and Helgerson, *The Elizabethan Prodigals*.

[37] A. C. Hamilton has added *Amadis of Gaul*. See "Sidney's *Arcadia* as Prose Fiction: Its
Relation to Its Sources," *English Literary Renaissance* 2 (1972): 29-60.

[38] Calling Greene's fictions "Arcadian" was widespread: Nashe did it in the preface to
*Menaphon* (1589), Gabriel Harvey did it mockingly in *Foure Letters* (1592), and the
publisher John Smethewicke changed the title of *Menaphon* to *Greenes Arcadia* when he
republished it in 1610. By then, of course, the title alluded to Sidney.

generically informed, Elizabethan popular fiction has eluded modern criticism.[39] To recover the cultural impact of Elizabethan fiction requires a critical method sensitive to the ways generic form resonated with historical readers.[40] To accomplish this task, the often marginalized institution of genre criticism must be rigorously historicized.[41] Rather than renovating Frye's archetypalism, I shall localize Jameson's useful definition, "a genre is essentially a socio-symbolic message, or in other terms…form is immanently and intrinsically an ideology in its own right" (141). I suggest that a precise contextual definition of Elizabethan prose romance entails reconstructing the emerging ideology of middlebrow reading.[42]

Part of the problem is making sense of the repeated claims the Elizabethan Heliodoranists make for readerly pleasure, a suspect term both for sixteenth-century humanists and modernist critics. Sidney, as is well-known, dismissed his *Arcadia* as a "a trifle, and that triflingly handled," but Greene's self-conscious mixing of duty and pleasure strikes a more precarious balance.[43] Reading for pleasure, in the sixteenth century and today, involves the slow accumulation and

---

[39] See Hamilton, "Elizabethan Romance: The Example of Prose Fiction," *ELH* 49 (1982): 287-99; and "Elizabethan Prose Fiction and Some Trends in Recent Criticism," *Renaissance Quarterly* 37 (1984): 21-33. On "historical formalism," see Richard Helgerson, *Forms of Nationhood: The Elizabethan Writing of England*, (Chicago: University of Chicago Press, 1992) 7.

[40] Alastair Fowler has emphasized that genre, which he calls "the most important…of all the codes in our literary *langue*," plays an essential role in the interaction of readers with texts. See *Kinds of Literature: An Introduction to the Theory of Genres and Modes*, (Cambridge: Harvard University Press, 1982) 22. Similar claims come from both traditional and theoretical scholars; see E. D. Hirsh, *Validity in Interpretation*, (New Haven: Yale University Press, 1967), and Tzvetan Todorov, *The Fantastic: A Structural Approach to a Literary Genre*, Richard Howard, trans., (Ithaca: Cornell University Press, 1975).

[41] Critics often relate generic systems to other systems. The most prominent metaphors views genres in one of four ways: as products of quasi-Darwinian evolution; as a system of Wittgensteinian "family resemblances"; as sets of purely literary conventions; or as part of a system of Austinian speech-acts. On these four analogies, see David Fishelov, *Metaphors of Genre: The Role of Analogies in Genre Theory*, (State College: Penn State University Press, 1993). Fishelov valuably identifies the blind spots of each metaphor: for evolution, see 22-5; family resemblances, 54n; literary conventions, 89-90; and speech-act theory, 120-1 and 121n.

[42] For recent work in historicist genre theory, see Alastair Fowler, "The Formation of Genres in the Renaissance and After," *New Literary History* 34:2 (Spring 2003): 185-200; Thomas Pavel, "Literary Genres as Norms and Good Habits," *New Literary History* 34:2 (Spring 2003): 201-210 (207-8 on French Heliodoranism); Farrell, "Classical Genre in Theory and Practice." Farrell's notion that the practices of ancient poets constitutes an "implied theory" (402) parallels my analysis of early modern fiction.

[43] Sir Philip Sidney, *The Countess of Pembroke's Arcadia*, Maurice Evans, ed., (Harmondsworth: Penguin, 1977) 57. Further citations in the text.

testing of generic certainty.[44] We read less for novelty than for the pleasure of recognizing variations on familiar patterns. As Umberto Eco has noted about mass market narrative, "the hunger for entertaining narrative based on these mechanisms is a *hunger for redundance*."[45] What Greene and Sidney repeat in their narratives, however, has seldom been specified: they repeat, with variations, the narrative structure of classical romance, especially the *Aethiopian History*.

Choosing Heliodorus as their model, rather than Malory or Bandello, gave classical status to these romances. To be sure, as Helgerson has emphasized, all literary efforts were examples of prodigal excess in Elizabethan humanist culture.[46] The relative prestige of Heliodorus, however, distinguished fiction based on this model from chivalric romance and the novella, as well as the public stage. The Elizabethan Heliodoranists declared their literary ambition with their choice of generic model; they "dar[ed] to compete with Heliodorus," as Cervantes phrased it.[47] Since Heliodorus was an approved text, imitating his genre allowed Greene and others to locate their narrative gifts inside humanist establishment. Modern readings of these fictions have forgotten or ignored this ambition and its roots in inter-generic competition.[48]

Recognizable shifts in generic positioning place the fictions of Greene, Sidney, Lodge, and Nashe in a doubly mediated position: between public drama and the humanist university on the one hand, and between novelle and chivalric tales on the other. These distinctions in generic form were quite clear to early modern readers, and the rhetoric of Elizabethan front matter depends on the intelligibility of generic rivalries to prospective book buyers. (In this sensitivity to small generic shifts, early modern readers parallel modern media consumers, who readily distinguish between different genres.) As Roger Chartier has observed, early modern popular narratives operated through "the recurrence of extremely coded

---

[44]   See Heather Dubrow, *Genre*, (London: Methuen, 1982) 1-44. More technically, Iser describes the act of reading as "a dialectic of protension and retention" (*The Act of Reading: A Theory of Aesthetic Response*, [Baltimore: Johns Hopkins University Press, 1978] 111-12), with "protension" or expectation being a term adapted from Husserl.

[45]   Umberto Eco, "The Myth of Superman," *The Role of the Reader: Explorations in the Semiotics of Texts*, (Bloomington: Indiana University Press, 1979) 120.

[46]   See *The Elizabethan Prodigals*, esp. 1-43.

[47]   Cervantes makes this claim about his final work, *Persiles and Sigismunda* (1617), in the prefatory letter to *Exemplary Novels* (1613). See *Novelas ejemplares I*, Harry Sieber, ed., (Madrid: Ediciones Cátedra, S. A., 1995) 53.

[48]   The decline of "reader-response" criticism after the 1980s may have hindered attention to this aspect of early modern fiction. For a witty reading that fingers Stanley Fish's 1981 review of Iser's *The Act of Reading*, see Michael Bérubé, "There is Nothing Inside the Text, or, Why No One's Heard of Wolfgang Iser," *Postmodern Sophistry: Stanley Fish and the Critical Enterprise*, Gary A. Olsen and Lynn Worsham, eds., (Albany: State University of New York Press, 2004) 11-26.

forms."[49] These codes created the "field" (in Bourdieu's sense) of early modern fiction, stimulating rather than inhibiting creativity.[50] The language of this field is predominantly the language of genre.

Genres, as scholars have long recognized, provided creative models for early modern writers. In Rosalie Colie's influential formulation, "[L]iterary invention – both 'finding' and 'making'– in the Renaissance was largely generic, and that transfer of ancient values was largely in generic terms, accomplished by generic instruments and helps."[51] This creative understanding of genre distinguishes early modern genre theory from its Romantic and post-Romantic descendents. Inter-generic competition underwrites the ongoing struggle between the norms of classical humanism and new literary experiments like tragicomedy, Ariostan verse romanzi, or prose romance. Renaissance critics defended Aristotelian and Horatian categories while they hotly debated hybrid works like Dante's *Commedia*, Guarini's *Il Pastor Fido*, and Ariosto's *Orlando Furioso*.[52] Generic mixing was controversial, but also so common that it invited parody, as in Polonius's list of theatrical genres, "tragedy, comedy, history, pastoral, pastoral-comical, historical-pastoral, tragical-historical, tragical-comical-historical-pastoral" (*Hamlet*, 2.2.396-9).[53] This absurd list parallels his fatherly advice to Laertes; it spoofs a meaningful set of choices facing the early modern writer.

The interpenetration of generic conventions through "imitatio" and "contaminatio" situates the climate in which Elizabethan prose romance emerged.[54] Prose romance's lack of a classical exemplar before Heliodorus's rediscovery was both a lack of authority and also a paradoxical freedom; unlike Tasso, prose fiction

---

[49]  *The Order of Books*, 14.

[50]  See Pierre Bourdieu, *Distinction: A Social Critique of the Judgment of Taste*, Richard Nice, trans., (Cambridge: Harvard University Press, 1984). For application of Bourdieu to early modern fiction and Greene in particular, see Newcomb, *Reading Popular Romance in Early Modern England*.

[51]  Rosalie Colie, *The Resources of Kind: Genre-Theory in the Renaissance*, Barbara K. Lewalski, ed., (Berkeley: University of California Press, 1973) 17.

[52]  As Colie has noted, defenses of these forms – "Mazzoni's defense of Dante, Guarini's of pastoral drama, Pigna's of romance" – never questioned "the rightness of genre-theory." See *Shakespeare's Living Art*, (Princeton: Princeton University Press, 1974) 17. For Italian critical debates on these issues, see Bernard Weinberg, *A History of Literary Criticism in the Italian Renaissance*, (Chicago: University of Chicago Press, 1960). See also Daniel Javitch ("Italian epic theory"), Paul Salzman ("Theories of Prose Fiction in England: 1558-1700"), and Glyn P. Norton with Marga Cottino-Jones ("Theories of prose fiction and poetics in Italy: *novella* and *romanzi* [1525-1596])" in *The Cambridge History of Literary Criticism, Volume 3: The Renaissance*, Glyn P. Norton, ed., (Cambridge: Cambridge University Press, 1989).

[53]  See also Nicholas Holmes Pearson, "Literary Forms and Types; or, A Defence of Polonius," *English Institute Annual 1940*, (New York: AMS Press, 1965).

[54]  On "contaminatio" and "imitatio," see Louise G. Clubb, *Italian Drama in Shakespeare's Time*, (New Haven: Yale University Press, 1989) 33.

writers did not need to devise elaborate Virgilian-Christian allegories of their works. The sudden return of Heliodorus set the stage for a new ambition in prose fiction, which now could claim high humanist sanction. The genre Heliodorus provided was not a stale template but "a structural model, [and] an invitation to the actual construction of the work of art."[55] Writers accepted the "invitation" of generic form, and proceeded (to misapply Pound's phrase) to "make it new." The model of the *Aethiopian History* solved the cultural problems posed by the previous lack of an exemplary classical prose text and the immorality (and Catholicism) of Continental forms.[56]

As a generic category, romance has always been a problem. The term's problems mirror those of genre theory as a whole, in that both romance and genre theory promise more than they usually deliver. For scholars of prose fiction, also, romance has served mainly as whipping boy for the novel. Genre theory and the category of romance are bedeviled by competing claims of precision and practicality: the more precise they become, the less useful, and vise versa. Some mixture of similarity and difference inheres in the term itself; it derives from Aristotle's *genos*, which means an essential attribute common to a plurality of things which are different from each other in their specifics.[57] This etymology suggests that genre definitions necessarily poise themselves between specificity and generality. If the term romance designates any pre-modern work that is of a certain length and (mostly) in prose, than it ends up not being very useful for literary analysis.[58] Part of the problem is romance's long history and incessant variation; it is difficult to determine the common ground between texts as formally and historically distinct as the *Odyssey*, *Erec and Enide*, *Wuthering Heights*, and a contemporary mass-market paperback. In modern criticism, romance's meaning has varied widely: it is one of four archetypal literary modes for Northrop Frye, an outdated critical term for Margaret Doody, an ideological construct for Frederic Jameson, and for many less systemic thinkers a nearly empty gesture, which describes either a literary work's idealistic core or its naiveté. Attempts to do

---

[55]   Claudio Guillén, *Literature as System: Essays Toward the Theory of Literary History*, (Princeton: Princeton University Press, 1971) 119.

[56]   As Guillén has observed, "A genre endures...insofar as it continues to be a problem-solving model," (*Literature as System*, 386).

[57]   See *Topica* 1.5.102a. Quoted in Guillén, *Literature as System*, 117.

[58]   Doody's assault on Watt's rise of the novel thesis takes exactly this transhistorical approach. As she puts it, "Romance and the Novel are one. The separation between them has been part of a problem, not part of a solution" (*True Story of the Novel*, 15). Drawing on Greek romance and updating Bahktin and Frye, Doody finds common tropes and *topoi* in over two millennia of narrative prose. The problem with collapsing these generic terms is that it produces a vague definition of the remaining category, "novel": "A work is a novel if it is fictional, if it is in prose, and if it is of a certain length" (16). I sympathize with Doody's polemic against Watt's excessive influence on English studies and the concomitant focus on "realism" in modern fiction.

without the term, however, either by expanding the "novel" into classical antiquity or by treating purported romances as hybrid "tragicomedies" that draw on two established Aristotelian genres, risk being unable to account for the puzzling consistencies of a narrative form that has remained in many ways recognizable over more than two millennia. For critics who work in early modern fiction, the term has two problems: it is indispensable, in that it describes the common ground of a series of narratives in a way that no other term does, and it is also imprecise and overused.[59]

Romance as a category links together an otherwise unassimilated group of works of early modern English fiction, those that derive neither from medieval sagas of chivalry nor from Continental novelle. In this case, romance can be defined as not only one of the major strains of Western narrative from Homer forward, but also as a new category applied to something left out of an established set of options. The term romance has historically often functioned in this way. Designating works that did not fit current generic paradigms as "romances" was exactly what Edward Dowden did in 1877 when he initiated a fourth generic category for Shakespearean drama.[60] Similarly, Frye used romance to complete his set of four narrative mythoi.[61] As a *tertium quid*, romance takes on a more precise meaning when it is historically localized: while I do not claim that all romances mediate between chivalry and the novella, this locally intense sixteenth-century rivalry facilitates a reasonably precise definition of Elizabethan prose romances: this genre comprises any narrative fictions that take recognizable steps to distinguish themselves from both chivalric romance and the novella.[62] While this definition remains subjective – some readers might argue that Sidney's *New*

[59]  Critics of Shakespeare's late plays have been particularly vocal in doubting the practicality of the term. See, for example, Stanley Wells, "Shakespeare and Romance," *Later Shakespeare*, John Russell Brown and Bernard Harris, eds., (London: Edward Arnold, 1966); Simon Palfrey, *Late Shakespeare: A New World of Words*, (Oxford: Clarendon, 1997) 14; Howard Felperin, "Romance and Romanticism: Some Reflections on *The Tempest* and *Heart of Darkness*, Or When is Romance No Longer Romance?", *Shakespeare's Romances Reconsidered*, Carol McGinis Hay and Henry Jacobs, eds., (Lincoln: University of Nebraska Press, 1979). On using "comedy" and "tragedy" but not "romance" in describing Shakespearean theater, see Lawrence Danson, *Shakespeare's Dramatic Genres* (Oxford: Oxford University Press, 2000) 11-13.

[60]  See Edward Dowden, *Shakspere*, (London: Macmillan, 1877) 55-6. On Dowden's category, see Barbara A. Mowat, "'What's in a Name?': Tragicomedy, Romance, or Late Comedy," *A Companion to Shakespeare's Works, Volume 4: The Poems, Problem Comedies, Late Plays*, Richard Dutton and Jean E. Howard, eds., (Oxford: Blackwell, 2003): 129-49.

[61]  Northrop Frye, *The Anatomy of Criticism: Four Essays*, (Princeton: Princeton University Press, 1957), esp. 107-8, 186-206.

[62]  Barbara Fuchs' recent elaboration of romance as a "strategy" more than a genre reached me too late to influence my argument, but it resonates with my sense of romance as a strategic choice by early modern authors. See *Romance*, (London: Routledge, 2004).

*Arcadia*, for example, intends to reform rather than rebut chivalric fictions – it is much more exact than many uses of romance. It allows us to identify *Menaphon*, the *New Arcadia*, and *Rosalynde* as Elizabethan romances, while designating *The Palace of Pleasure* and *The Seven Champions of Christendom* as respectively a novella collection and a chivalric romance.[63]

Elizabethan prose romances derive from loss-wandering-recovery narratives from Homer's *Odyssey* through the prose fiction of Byzantium, saint's lives, medieval biography, jestbook tales, chivalric legends, and Italian verse *romanzi*, among other forms. The transhistorical continuity of the genre invokes an archetypal mythos (in Frye's term) and a dense literary genealogy.[64] Romance arrived in Elizabethan England with roots in myth and ritual and literary exemplars in classical poetry, Celtic legends, and medieval chivalric cycles.[65] My claims for prose romance in Elizabethan England exploit the distinction between the anti-epic tradition of Heliodorus and the interlaced adventures of medieval romance.[66] While the vernacular romances that emerged in the "twelfth-century Renaissance" remained popular, chivalric fictions became problematic for Elizabethan writers in early modern England.[67] They lacked Aristotelian-Heliodoran narrative coherence, and they were mostly Catholic, especially those that came from Spain. For Elizabethan writers, the Heliodoran model provided a valuable alternative to the chivalric tradition that stretched from Chrétien de Troyes and the "Vulgate" cycle to Malory and *Amadis*. Elizabethan romance becomes legible to modern readers when we distinguish with some degree of precision between competitive elements within the history of distinct romance forms.

---

[63] By focusing on prose fiction, I exclude verse romances like Spenser's *Faerie Queene* or the poems of Daniel, Drayton, and Marston, although Spenser especially drew on Heliodoran form.

[64] Mowat perceptively notes that both terms persist because they invoke this complex genealogy: "Within the context of inherited codes, of genre as a set of works connected by family resemblances, *romance* and *tragicomedy* become truly useful names for Shakespeare's late plays" ("'What's in a Name?'" 134).

[65] On the transmission of Celtic myth into early modern fiction, see Edward Dudley, *The Endless Text: Don Quixote and the Hermeneutics of Romance* (Binghamton: State University of New York Press, 1997).

[66] Mowat observes that when the term romance was (rarely) used in early modern England, it usually referred to medieval verse romances of chivalry ("'What's in a Name?'" 133).

[67] On twelfth-century romances, see Eugène Vinaver, *The Rise of Romance*, (Oxford: Clarendon, 1971), and W. P. Ker, *Epic and Romance: Essays on Medieval Literature*, (New York: Dover, 1957) repr. of 1905 ed. On romance "interlace" and narrative endlessness, see Vinaver, 76. On Malory's partial transformation of the form, see Vinaver, 123-39. On this period as a precursor to early modern and modern prose fiction, see McKeon, *The Origins of the English Novel*, 33-9.

## The Competitive Genre System of Elizabethan Prose Fiction

> The accuracy of all further study depends upon the accuracy of classification.
>
> V. Propp, *Morphology of the Folktale*[68]

By providing the most substantial model for connecting with a heterogeneous audience, the *Aethiopian History* made an important intervention in the genre system of early modern fiction.[69] For writers working in the suspect form of prose fiction, the Heliodoran model was valuable because it shared the cultural prestige of the classical revival and avoided the problems English humanists saw in continental fiction.[70] Heliodorus's plot of love and adventure replaced the amoral trickery of the novella with moral constancy, albeit a constancy that operated through indirection. It also replaced the bloody combat of chivalric adventure with a battle of wills won by feminine constancy.[71] The Heliodoran model positioned Elizabethan writers to distinguish themselves from the amoral cynicism of the novella and the moral anarchy of chivalric romance.

Both chivalric romance and the Italian novella were attacked by early modern humanist culture. The attack on chivalry began, as Robert P. Adams has noted, with the generation of More and Erasmus and was part of the anti-medievalist attitude of the New Humanism, which has its roots in Petrarch.[72] Montaigne explains with unconcealed pride that he read only Ovid in his "tender age": "For as regards the Lancelots of the Lake, the Amadises, the Huons of Bordeaux, and such books of rubbish on which children waste their time, I did not even know their names, and I still do not know their substance."[73] In Roger Ascham's *The Scholemaster* (1570), books of chivalry define a licentious and Catholic reading:

---

[68]   V. Propp, *Morphology of the Folktale*, Laurence Scott, trans., Louis A. Weagner, ed., Svatava Pirkova-Jacobson and Alan Dunde, intro., (Austin: University of Texas Press) 5.

[69]   My discussion of the Elizabethan genre system has affinities with Helgerson's "system of authorial roles" (*Self-Crowned Laureates*, 2-7).

[70]   Helgerson emphasizes the lack of a classical model. See *Elizabethan Prodigals*, 1-15. Carmine di Biase applies this point specifically to the career of Robert Greene in his edition of *Gwydonius, or The Card of Fancy*, (Ottawa: Dovehouse Editions, 2001) 14-15.

[71]   In the Elizabethan period, other kinds of prose fiction, like pastoral, satire, and picaresque, usually appeared in the context of another major genre. Thus Sidney's *Arcadia* and Greene's *Menaphon* can be accurately called "pastoral romances," but the emphasis should fall on romance. In Fowler's terms, "pastoral" was a mode or sub-genre, not a full genre (*Kinds of Literature*, 106-11).

[72]   See Robert P. Adams, "Bold Bawdry and Open Manslaughter: The English New Humanist Attack on Medieval Romance," *Huntington Library Quarterly* 23 (1959-60): 33-48. See also Lewis, *English Literature*, 28-30.

[73]   "Of the Education of Children," (1.26), *The Complete Essays of Montaigne*, Donald Frame, ed. and trans., (Stanford: Stanford University Press, 1958): 130.

In our forefathers tyme, whan Papistrie, as a standying poole, couered and ouerflowed all England, fewe bookes were read in our tong, sauying certaine bookes of Cheualrie, as they sayd, for pastime and pleasure, which, as some say, were made in Monasteries, by idle Monkes or wanton Chanons: as one for example, *Mort Arthure*; the whole pleasure of which booke standeth in two special poyntes, in open mans slaughter and bold bawdrye.[74]

But newer forms of fiction like the novella were equally problematic:

These be the inchantementes of *Circes,* brought out of *Italie,* to marre mens maners in England...Mo Papistes be made by your mery bookes of *Italie* than by your earnest bookes of Louain... ten *Morte Arthures* do not the tenth part so much harme as one of these bookes made in *Italie* and translated into England. They open, not fond and common wayes to vice, but such subtle, cunnyng, new, and diuerse shiftes, to cary yong willes to vanitie, and yong wittes to mischief, to teach old bawdes new schole poyntes, as the simple head of an English man is not hable to inuent, no neuer was hard of in England before (2-4).

Ascham's attack situate the cultural climate in which Elizabethan-Heliodoran romance constructed itself. The challenge was to defuse the criticism without losing the appeal of these forms.

The Elizabethan Heliodoranists entered a crowded market. Works of fiction published in this period included books by Anthony Munday, Henry Robarts, Mary Wroth, Margaret Cavendish, Henry Chettle, Emmanuel Forde, Barnebe Riche, John Lyly, William Baldwin, George Pettie, William Painter, Geoffrey Fenton, Richard Johnson, Thomas Deloney, John Grange, Brian Melbancke, William Warner, George Whetstone, and George Gascoigne. These authors mostly did not write Heliodoran romances, although several clearly knew the form. Home-grown chivalric romances like Munday's *Zelauto* (1580), Johnson's *Seven Champions of Christendom* (1596) and *Tom a Lincoln* (1599), and Forde's *Ornatus and Artesia* (1595) catered to a common taste long since denounced by the humanist

---

[74] Roger Ascham, *The Scholemaster, Elizabethan Critical Essays*, G. Gregory Smith, ed., Two volumes (Oxford: Oxford University Press, 1904) 1: 3-4. Further citations in the text. Neo-Aristotelian theorists like Jacques Amyot also attacked chivalric fiction; in the preface to his translation of Heliodorus Amyot writes, "They are usually so dissonant and so removed from any resemblance to truth that they are more similar to the dreams of a sick man who raves in his fits of fever than to the inventions of a man of acumen and judgement....[There is] no erudition, no knowledge of antiquity, nor a single thing, in truth, from which one may profit" (Quoted in Forcione, *Cervantes, Aristotle, and the 'Persiles,'* 59). Amyot's metaphor – "the dreams of a sick man" – emphasizes that these works fail on the level of structure: they do not have, as Aristotle requires, a beginning, middle, and end. As I emphasize in Chapter 2, it was on neo-Aristotelian grounds that Amyot produced his (qualified) endorsement of Heliodorus.

establishment.[75] A racier trend included cycles of novelle based on Italian or French originals, including Pettie's *Petite Pallace of Pettie his Pleasure* (1576), Painter's *Palace of Pleasure* (1565), Riche's *Farewell to Military Profession* (1581), Whetstone's *Heptameron of Civill Discourses* (1582), and Warner's *Pan his Syrinx* (1584).[76] The courtly fictions of Gascoigne, Lyly, and their imitators were closely related to these novelle.[77] Deloney's and Dekker's tales of shoemakers and apprentices constitute another subgenre, and idiosyncratic works like Baldwin's *Beware the Cat* (1570) sit uneasily between categories.

These books' prefatory material reveals that Elizabethan authors and publishers defined their products by positioning them against their generic rivals. To a large extent these efforts were marketing gambits, but in marketing their books authors defined their literary ambitions. The front matter of most books of Elizabethan fiction reveals broad similarities – all claim they want to please the reader, and most apologize to anyone who is not pleased – as well as aggressive efforts to distinguish themselves from their rivals. Several strategies were well-established by 1580. Novelle sold themselves by being courtly, clever, and wanton; chivalric romances offered a slightly chastened version of traditional violence and erotic play; classical texts peddled their erudition; and sermons or moral pamphlets appealed to the desire for ethical improvement. The Elizabethan Heliodoranists intervened in this competition by offering a hybrid package: humanist morality and classical status in a pleasurable narrative package. Reading the front matter of the three main fictional forms of the latter Elizabethan era – the novella, chivalric romance, and Heliodoran romance – provides snapshots of three competing genres of Elizabethan fiction.

Exploring how front matter anticipates and shapes reading practices gives historical specificity to what Hans Robert Jauss has termed the "aesthetics of reception."[78] Jauss's work, alongside his colleague Wolfgang Iser's phenomenology of reading, emphasizes that the consumption of works of art is an

---

[75] On chivalric romance in England, see John Joseph O'Connor, *'Amadis de Gaule' and Its Influence on Elizabethan Literature*, (New Brunswick: Rutgers University Press, 1970), and Alex Davis, *Chivalry and Romance in the English Renaissance*, (Cambridge: D. S. Brown, 2003).

[76] On the novella, see Jean Kirkpatrick, *English and Italian Literature from Dante to Shakespeare: A Study of Source, Analogue, and Divergence*, (London: Longman, 1995), and Robert J. Clements and Joseph Gibaldi, *Anatomy of the Novella: The European Tale Collection from Boccaccio and Chaucer to Cervantes*, (New York: New York University Press, 1977). There was considerable variation among these collections: Pettie's novelle are more classical than most, Fenton's more moral than Painter's, and Warner's take a Biblical rather than pagan setting.

[77] For a recent study of 1570s fiction, especially Lyly and Gascoigne, see Maslen, *Elizabethan Fictions*.

[78] See Hans Robert Jauss, *Toward an Aesthetic of Reception*, Timothy Bahti, trans., Paul de Man, intr., (Minneapolis: University of Minnesota Press, 1982).

essential part of their cultural impact: "literature and art only obtain a history that
has the character of a process when the succession of works is mediated not only
through the producing subject but also through the consuming subject – through
the interaction of author and public."[79] What Jauss calls the "horizon of
expectations" (25) of a literary work finds concrete representation in the imagined
readers addressed in peritextual letters.[80] Jauss's summary of this way of reading
explores the historical interaction between genres: "Such kinds of structural
analysis…could gradually lead to a synchronic cross-section in which the
organization of the traditional and the noncanonized genres appears not as a logical
classification, but rather as the literary system of a definite historical situation"
(87). Like Jauss, I believe that literary scholarship should produce this richly
"historical" reading of genre to supplement and correct any purely "logical"
classification or analysis.

The front matter of George Pettie's *A Petite Pallace of Pettie His Pleasure*
(1576) exemplifies the subterfuge and rhetorical gamesmanship of the Elizabethan
novella. With its self-referential title and tag from Horace – *Omne tulit punctum,
qui miscuit utile dulci* ("He who mixes the useful and the pleasing wins every
prize"), the motto Greene would take after 1584 – Pettie's book offers
sophisticated narrative pleasure. In the first of three peritextual letters, he addresses
his text exclusively to "Gentlewomen Readers." Pettie's avowed preference for
women readers conceals his ironic masculine humor: "For to speake my fancy
without feigninge, I care not to displease twentie men, to please one woman: for
the friendship amongst men, is to be counted but cold kindesse, in respect of the
fervent affection beetweene men and women: and our nature, is rather to doate of
women, then to love men."[81] In the word "our" Pettie tips his hand: his primary
intended audience is male courtiers, whom he titillates by claiming to write only to
women.[82] His novelle, this letter implies, will model the erotic discourse with
which men lure women into "fervent affection."

The remaining peritextual letters include one from "G.P." to "R.B." desiring
that he "not impart [these tales] to others" (5), and one from the Printer apologizing

---

[79]　Jauss, "Literary History as a Challenge to Literary Theory," *Toward an Aesthetic of
Reception*, 15.

[80]　In "Theory of Genres and Medieval Literature," Jauss charts the distinctions between
epic, verse romance, and the novelle in a way that parallels my notion of inter-generic
competition in Elizabethan fiction (*Toward an Aesthetic of Reception*, 83-7).

[81]　George Pettie, *A Petite Pallace of Pettie His Pleasure*, Herbert Hartman, ed., (New
York: Barnes and Noble, 1970, repr. of Oxford University Press, 1938) 3. Further citations
in the text.

[82]　Caroline Lucas has developed feminist strategies for the "resisting reader" of this and
other sixteenth-century texts (*Writing for Women*). Most other recent critics, however,
including Hackett, Maslen, and Hutson, agree that Pettie addresses male courtiers who
would have relished the joke. I engage Juliet Fleming's designation of Pettie's works as
"ladies' texts" in Chapter 5.

for publishing tales that may be "to[o] wanton" (8). Inverting Greene's "many heades," these letters emphasize the pseudo-private nature of the book: Pettie's letter is ostensibly meant only for his intimate friend "R.B," and the printer implies that the book has reached a public readership without the author's consent. The front matter's atmosphere of lewd intrigue derives from the pseudo-anonymity of the initials (perhaps aping Gascoigne's *Adventures of Master F.J.*), the claim to be part of a courtier's "private pleasure" rather than a public "commoditie" (5), and the Printer's statement that he has used "discretion in omitting such matters as...might seeme offencive" (9).[83] This collection of novelle appeals to an audience of educated male courtiers who enjoy rhetorical games.

If Pettie's prefatory material promises eroticized play behind a rhetorical veil, the front matter of chivalric romances was more straightforward. This genre was familiar to readers of early printed books like *Le Morte D'Arthur* (1485), but in the late sixteenth century Malory's heroes were supplanted by Amadis of Gaul and Palmerin of England.[84] One of the original Elizabethan romances of this type was Anthony Munday's *Zelauto: The Fountaine of Fame* (1580), which followed the newer Iberian tradition of eschewing adulterous love affairs.[85] *Zelauto*'s front matter peddles a chaste and modest version of chivalric romance. Unlike Pettie's book, which contains an apology only from the printer, *Zelauto* presents Munday's profuse apologies for the book's hedonistic qualities. Munday's letter "To the well disposed Reader" claims that he has tempered Arthurian excess: "[S]ome will suppose heere are rare exploytes of martial mindes to be seen: which when they haue prooued, they finde it to[o] faint. Othersome will desire for *Venus* daintie dalliances: but *Iuno* dealeth so iustly in this cause, that their also they misse their mark."[86] He appears to have taken Ascham's attack on chivalric bawdry and manslaughter to heart.

---

[83] The Printer's description of his editing of the tales – "if I have not gelded to[o] much, I think I have deserved the lesse blame" (9) – echoes Gascoigne's presentation of himself as *poemata castrada* in his 1575 revision of *Master F.J.* See Richard McCoy, "Gascoigne's 'Poemata castrada': The Wages of Courtly Success," *Criticism* 27 (1985): 29-55, and Felicity Hughes, "Gascoigne's Poses," *Studies in English Literature* 37 (1997): 1-19.

[84] See Mary Patchell, *The* Palmerin *Romances in Elizabethan England*, (New York: Columbia University Press, 1937). For a chronology, see Paul Scanlon, "A Checklist of Prose Romances in English, 1474-1603," *The Library*, n.s. 33 (1978): 143-52. *Le Morte D'Arthur* was repeatedly published between 1485 and 1578, but not again in the Elizabethan period after the *Amadis* and *Palmerin* cycles began to appear around 1580.

[85] At nearly the same time Munday began his lifelong labor as translator of chivalric romance; see Gerald R. Hayes, "Anthony Munday's Romances of Chivalry," *The Library*, 4th ser. 6 (1925-6): 57-81. Patchell notes that "English readers of these fictions had a decided preference for fidelity and chastity." See *The* Palmerin *Romances*, 57-9, 113. See also Hackett, *Women and Romance Fiction*, 55-7.

[86] Anthony Munday, *Zelauto: The Fountaine of Fame (1580)*, Jack Stillinger, ed., (Carbondale: Southern Illinois University Press, 1963) 7. Further citations in the text.

Munday's letter seems quite modest compared to those of other Elizabethan writers.[87] His front matter praises "that *Lilly* whose sent is so sweet" (8) and hopes that his work can ride on the fame of Lyly's Euphues volumes.[88] Munday offers wanton pleasure, but diffidently: "I may be deemed (courteous Reader)," he writes, "more wanton than wise, and more curious than circumspect" (7). When he concludes by writing, "I wishe my woorkes may prooue as profitable to you in the reading: as they were delightfull to me in the writing" (8), the emphasis is on the self-evident unity of profit and delight. Like Pettie, Munday offers more *dulce* than *utile*, but he lacks Pettie's rhetorical edge.

Greene's *Menaphon* (1589), by contrast, is not content to seem simple like *Zelauto* or coy like Pettie's *Pallace*. Its front matter instead claims to be the sophisticated public face of a new kind of prose fiction. *Menaphon* was published at the height of Greene's success, and its presentation demonstrates Greene's (and his publisher, Sampson Clarke's) conception of him as man of the hour. The book's front matter transforms the brazen hopes of *Mamillia* into a full elaboration of Greene's appeal for heterogeneous readers. It borrows strategically from other Elizabethan writers, combining a Lylyian subtitle ("Camilla's Alarm to slumbering Euphues in his melancholy cell at Silexedra"), a Sidneian half-title, ("Arcadia / The reports of the shepherds") and the Horatian tag Greene had taken over from Pettie ("Omne tulit punctum").[89] These signs market Greene as rightful heir of courtly writers and humanist classicism as well as reigning master of narrative entertainment.

*Menaphon*'s front matter – a dedication to Lady Hales, celebratory poems from Henry Upchear and Thomas Brabine, a letter from Greene to "the Gentlemen Readers," and a lengthy preface by the as-yet unknown Thomas Nashe – captures the ambition of Greene's Heliodoranist program.[90] Nashe's preface and the poems

---

[87]   Munday was enough of a marketplace tactician to publish his books in multiple volumes, because "a man grutched not so much at a little money payd at severall times, as hee doth all at once." This tactic failed for *Zelauto*, as the promised continuation never appeared, but worked for his multivolume translations of the *Amadis* and *Palmerin* cycles. See Patchell, *The* Palmerin *Romances*, 19-20.

[88]   *Zelauto* was published near-simultaneously with Lyly's *Euphues and his England*, when both Lyly and Munday were servants of Oxford.

[89]   It is possible that in 1589 the title "Arcadia" was not yet associated with Sidney. (The *New Arcadia* was first printed in 1590, though manuscript editions of the *Old* version had been in circulation for several years.) See H. R. Woodhuyson, *Sir Philip Sidney and the Circulation of Manuscripts, 1558-1640*, (Oxford: Clarendon Press, 1996), and Mentz, "Selling Sidney."

[90]   Brenda Cantar suggests the dedication should be considered "scandalous," since Lady Hales's husband had been imprisoned for fraud and then drowned himself in 1554 after his release (DNB). As Cantar emphasizes, "there is no evidence that Greene was successful in his suit for patronage." See Robert Greene, *Menaphon*, Brenda Cantar, ed., (Ottawa: Dovehouse Editions, 1996) 176. Further citations in the text.

of Upchear and Brabine declare Greene the best prose writer in England. Both poems notably denigrates Greene's competition. Upchear takes aim at rivals in narrative fiction, rejecting the "Lily once I lov'd" for the "Greener objects [that] are my eyes' abode" (78). Brabine attacks the rival medium of theater by claiming that playwrights will "View [in] *Menaphon* a note beyond your reach"(79).[91] Nashe finally claims elite status for Greene, lauding his "*Arcadian Menaphon* whose attire...doth entitle thee above all other to that *temperatum dicendi genus* which Tully in his *Orator* termeth true eloquence" (82). Nashe's Ciceronian language praise Greene's style and learning, as well as promoting, with the nod toward "Tully," Greene's other 1589 romance, *Tullie's Love*.[92] These statements distinguish *Menaphon* from Lyly's novella-based fiction and from public drama while linking him to Ciceronian humanism. (Chivalric romances do not draw any fire, though Nashe parodies them elsewhere.) Nashe goes on to emphasize that Greene's fame does not rest exclusively on courtly or high humanist criteria: "give me the man whose extemporal vein in any humor will excel our greatest art-master's deliberate thoughts." (82). Greene's fiction is announced as a superior kind of writing, combining Tully's eloquence and the pleasures of extemporaneity.

Greene's contributions to the front matter distinguish his way of appealing to the reader from his rivals' techniques. In the Dedication, he nominates his text as a "recreation" (75) for the recently widowed Lady Hales, thus carving out a virtuous female readership in contrast to Pettie's sly voyeurism. His letter, "To the Gentlemen Readers, health," carefully mentions his most recent previous book (*Euphues his Censure to Philautus*, 1587) to make sure everyone knows that he has taken over Lyly's position as the leader of Elizabethan fiction. He also signals a literary ambition that distinguishes him from Munday:

> If, Gentlemen, you find my style either *magnis humile* in some place, or more sublime in another, if you find dark enigmas or strange conceits as if Sphinx on one side and Roscius on the other were playing the wags, think the metaphors are well meant, and that I did it for your pleasures, whereunto I ever aimed my thoughts. (80)

---

[91]  Alwes plausibly identifies Brabine as Greene's sometime patron Thomas Burnaby, to whom he dedicated *Franciscos Fortunes* (1590) and *A Quip for an Upstart Courtier* (1592), and who wrote commendatory poems for *Menaphon* and *Ciceronis Amor* (1589). See *Sons and Authors in Elizabethan England*, 23, 159-60n.

[92]  *Tullies Love*, also called *Ciceronis Amor*, seems to have been written either just before or just after *Menaphon*. See A.F. Allison, *Robert Greene 1558-1592: A Bibliographical Catalogue of the Early Editions in English (to 1640)*, (Old Woking: Unwin Brothers, 1975) 21. René Pruvost believes *Tullies Love* was the prior text (*Robert Greene et ses romans: Contributions à l'histoire de la Renaissance en Angleterre*, [Paris: Société d'Editions 'Les Belles Lettres,' 1938] 333ff). This text circulated among the semi-collaborative publishers Nicholas Ling, John Busby, and John Smethwicke (whose relationship I discuss below); it was reprinted in 1597 (Busby); 1601, 1605 (Ling); 1609, 1611, 1616, 1628, and 1639 (Smethwicke).

This letter asserts that Greene's writing has become hard to decipher. From "a toy to passe away the time" (*Mamillia*; 2:10), the tale has become a Sphinx, requiring Oedipal ingenuity to pry out its dark meaning. *Menaphon* also remains a pleasing entertainment, in the manner of the Roman comic actor Roscius Quintus. As Greene's letter describes it, these two projects – the literary riddles of the Sphinx, and the comic display of Roscius – are not opposites but complements.[93] Literature and comic play, high art and the marketplace, Greece and Rome: all become compatible through the structure for appealing to heterogeneous reading practices that Greene adapted from Heliodorus. His book will appeal to bandit-readers who want entertainment and philosophical readers like Calasiris. Greene describes alternative ways of reading of his book "playing the wags," implying that diverse reading practices can enjoy the book.

This ambitious claim of literary preeminence contains no direct references to the *Aethiopian History*, although *Menaphon*'s oracle and shipwreck wear their Heliodoran colors openly. The first English translation of Heliodorus, however, suggested in its front matter how the model could serve writers seeking respectability for prose fiction. Thomas Underdowne, Heliodorus's Elizabethan translator, claimed that the *Aethiopian History* embodied a superior form of adventure story and an antidote to chivalric romance. In a prefatory letter added to the second (1577) edition, Underdowne writes, "If I shall compare it to other of like argument, I think none commeth neere it. Mort Darthure, Arthur of little Britaine, yea, and Amadis of Gaul, accompt violent murder, or murder for no cause, manhoode: and fornication and all unlawful luste, friendly loue. This book punisheth the faultes of euil doers, and rewardeth the well liuers."[94] Underdowne's letter groups Heliodorus with chivalric romances as texts of "like argument," but asserts the *Aethiopian History*'s superiority in moral terms. Underdowne asserts that Heliodorus will appeal to readers of chivalric romance, because it solves the moral problems of that genre.

Underdowne's efforts to distinguish Heliodorus were not exclusively ethical. He further suggests that high humanist morality was partly a marketing strategy: "I am not ignorant that the stationers shops are to[o] full fraughted with bookes of smal price, whither you consider that quantitie or the contents of them, and that the losenesse of these days rather requireth graue exhortations to vertue, than wanton allurements to leudnesse, that it were meeter to publish notable examples of godly

---

[93]  Helgerson notes that Greene's fiction, while devoted to literary pleasure, rejected the stance of pure entertainment that dominated the novelle of Painter, Pettie, and Barnebe Riche. See *Elizabethan Prodigals*, 92-3.

[94]  Heliodorus, *An Aethiopian Historie*, Thomas Underdowne, trans., (London: Francis Coldocke, 1577), sig. ¶3. Further citations in the text.

christian life, than the most honest (as I take this to be) historie of love" (sig. ¶3).[95] Underdowne's letter assures prospective readers that his book is a moral tale, but it is a "historie of love," not an example of "godly christian life." Some readers wanted morality, others pleasure, and this text provided both. This heterogeneous readership was exactly the composite audience to which Greene, Sidney, and the other Elizabethan Heliodoranists imagined their works addressing.

## Strategies for Reading Early Modern Prose Romance

> Romances, properly so call'd, are Fictions of Love-Adventures, artfully form'd and deliver'd in Prose, for the Delight and Instruction of the Readers.
> Pierre-Daniel Huet, "The History of Romances" (1670)[96]

The front matter of early modern English fictions reveals the competition between fictional genres. Applying this insight to the fictions themselves leads to a series of guiding strategies for reading Elizabethan prose romance. When the force of intergeneric competition is kept in mind, the narrative habits of these writers assume coherent shape. I shall therefore read these texts "for the plot," and argue that their various plots constitute an ongoing public debate about printed narrative in English culture.[97] Greene and his Heliodoran peers staked their claim on a particular classical narrative form, and their works articulate this claim both in front matter and narrative structure. Four narrative principles distinguish Elizabethan-Heliodoran romances: 1) the priority of the heroine over the hero, 2) the power of passivity, 3) the beneficence of supernatural (but not human) threats, and 4) the value of moral deception. These four strategies define an Elizabethan-Heliodoran text's distance from its main competition. The first two, the heroine's priority and the power of passivity, reveal a text's rejection of chivalric romance and its masculine agency. (The emphasis on passivity also recalls the shifting of masculine agency from active to passive qualities that I mentioned at the start of this chapter.) The second pair, supernatural power and moral deception, describes

---

[95] On the vexed question of price, it is difficult to know how expensive Coldocke's editions of Heliodorus were. The 1569 edition was a quarto, but the 1577 and 1587 editions were small octavos, and presumably less expensive. For comparison, most of Greene's works were published in small black-letter quartos, but Sidney's *Arcadia* (1590) was a large quarto in new italic type.

[96] Huet's *Traite sur l'origine des Romans* was published 1670; the above passage is from Samuel Croxall's *Select Collection of Novels and Romances* (London: John Watts, 1720) i. For a partial modern reprint see Ioan Williams, *Novel and Romance 1700-1800: A Documentary Record*, (London: Routledge and Kegan Paul, 1970) 43-55.

[97] This phrase comes from Peter Brooks's study of the European novel, *Reading for the Plot: Design and Intention in Narrative*, (Cambridge, MA: Harvard University Press, 1984). Hutson adapts Brooks's terminology in "Fortunate Travelers."

its distance from the novella and its trickster plots. Taken together, these strategies define the Elizabethan Heliodoranists' alternatives to novelle and tales of chivalry. Observing the application of these narrative principles in different texts allows the reader-text interaction – which Iser has described as an ongoing process of "consistency-building" – to become historically specific and theoretically meaningful.[98] Through this plot – the first fully classical plot in English prose fiction – the Elizabethan Heliodoranists defined a new form of mainstream prose narrative.

Variations in these tactics reveal the relative generic affinities of different texts. Greene's focus on female characters, which led Nashe to dub him the "Homer of women," accents his resistance to the masculine force idolized by chivalric romance (and, as Nashe well knew, by Homeric epic).[99] As Greene's collections of short fiction show, he was less clearly opposed to the tricksters of the novella. Sidney's princes, on the other hand, while feminized through disguise, never become wholly passive. Sidney's attachment to martial valor indicates that he, like Lodge, retains elements of chivalric romance in his fiction.[100] Taking the *Aethiopian History* as a model gave these writers a way to include narrative material of dubious provenance – the novella for Greene, chivalric romance for Sidney and Lodge, picaresque for Nashe – while aligning themselves with humanist condemnations of these genres.

Reading Elizabethan prose romances through inter-generic competition and audience construction corrects a still-prevalent error, the belief that these texts are crude and sentimental. Sophisticated misdirection is fundamental to these works. This sophisticated deceptive core, as I shall show in Chapter 2, is the heart of the Heliodoran legacy. Failing to recognize the place of misdirection has led generations of scholars to oversimplify both Greek and Elizabethan romances.[101] In fairness, this misreading is partly due to the surface content of these fictions, which emphasizes the virtue and fidelity of the heroine and (to a lesser extent) the hero. The temptations of the superficial, however, are part of the machinery of narrative romance. Readers who take the characters' protestations of virtue and fidelity as

---

[98] See *The Act of Reading*, 118-25.

[99] Nashe, *The Anatomy of Absurdity, The Works of Thomas Nashe*, R.B. McKerrow, ed., F.P. Wilson, rev., 5 volumes (Oxford: Basil Blackwell, 1958) 1:12. I discuss this epithet in chapter 4 below. Further citations from Nashe in the text.

[100] Sidney's apology for Amadis in the *Defence* is well known: "Truly, I have known men that even with reading *Amadis de Gaule* (which God knoweth wanteth much of a perfect poesy) have found their hearts moved to the exercise of courtesy, liberality, and especially courage" (*Sir Philip Sidney*, Katharine Duncan-Jones, ed., [Oxford: Oxford University Press, 1989] 227). Further citations in the text.

[101] Even Mikhail Bahktin makes this error in his analysis of Greek romance. See "Forms of Time and the Chronotope in the Novel," *The Dialogic Imagination: Four Essays*, Michael Holquist, ed., Michael Holquist and Caryl Emerson, trans., (Austin: University of Texas Press, 1981) 86-95.

indicative of the work's moral simplicity read no more perceptively than the Egyptian bandits who see Heliodorus's fiction as a "tragic show."

The Elizabethan-Heliodoran plot develops through a double structure: what you see for most of the tale is not what you get in the end.[102] Reading with Aristotle's dialectic of economy and amplitude in mind unlocks the full play of narrative possibilities. Simply put, we know how the story ends, but read to discover how it gets there. In Elizabethan prose romance, the redemptive ending emerges neither from the heroes' swordarms (as it would in chivalric romance) nor from their cleverness (as in a novella), but from Providential (and authorial) control. Thus informed readers must pay special attention to extrahuman events. I do not mean to encourage an algorithmic approach in which each text is run through the mill of genre and the expected results come out. Rather, highlighting varied narrative strategies in generically similar texts exposes the ways Elizabethan romances rearticulate the wandering-recovery masterplot. Readers of any period's romances recognize the basic pattern: chaos and danger dominate the story, but these events eventually lead to redemption and triumph. In these tales, all errant wanderers, including the disoriented reader, eventually return home. In an important sense these romances are, in Frank Kermode's phrase, "end-determined fictions."[103] Given the certainty that Sidney's princes will not be executed at the end of the *Old Arcadia*, for example, the eventual solution of their plight – the faux-resurrection of Basilius, which reprises Chariclea's return from supposed death in the *Aethiopian History* – clarifies Sidney's connection to Heliodorus. At the climax of his tale, Sidney rewards the passivity of the imprisoned princes, thus fixing his text generically as a Heliodoran rather than a chivalric romance.[104]

For passivity and moral deception to triumph, the heroes and heroines of Elizabethan-Heliodoran romances must suffer. Many common narrative elements of these texts create suffering. Among these elements is the prototypical plot motif of shipwreck, which Northrop Frye has called Greek romance's "standard means of transportation."[105] Shipwreck is caused by the inscrutable powers that drive the heroine and hero forward through the story. This same hidden "deity" – on one narratological level a figure for divine power, on another the author – stages the opening "spectacle" of the *Aethiopian History*. A list of other typical narrative elements suggests that readers enjoy seeing heroines threatened: these tales feature orphanings, ambiguous oracles, love at first sight, assault by pirates or bandits,

---

[102] Frank Kermode suggestively describes Aristotle's ideal plot as "a double take." See *The Sense of an Ending: Studies in the Theory of Fiction*, (London: Oxford University Press, 1966) 52-3.

[103] *The Sense of an Ending*, 6.

[104] The fractured nature of the three *Arcadia*s – the *Old*, *New*, and hybrid (1593) editions – makes any conclusion about the ending speculative. On the revision as a defense of fiction, see Alwes, *Sons and Authors in Elizabethan England*, 89-111.

[105] See Northrop Frye, *The Secular Scripture: A Study in the Structure of Romance*, (Cambridge: Harvard University Press, 1976) 4.

rape (usually not carried out), cannibalism, fear of incest, atheism, witchcraft, a magical chastity test (often by fire), the sudden death of a protector, the heroine's seduction of a villain (usually unconsummated), the conversion of a villain, resurrection, and a concluding trial. These narrative features can be culled from the plots of Elizabethan prose romances, but they also comprise a virtual plot summary of the *Aethiopian History*.[106] Heliodorus treats his readers to the full course of exile, love, shipwreck, sorcery, false deaths, and real deaths before Chariclea's recovers her position at the Aethiopian court. Many Elizabethan-Heliodoran romances deviate from this model, but all use these elements. In the 1590s, however, major revisions appear; the rape in *The Unfortunate Traveler* is quite real, and the conversions of Greene's hero-villains are never trustworthy. The accumulation of these tropes produces chaos on the narrative surface of these works. This chaos entertains the reader, especially if he or she is well-schooled enough in generic expectations not to be misled.[107]

These narrative elements fall into three categories: human threats, supernatural threats, and supernatural rescues. The logical fourth category, human rescues, tends not to appear; key plot developments are kept out of human hands. (This omission contrasts with the novella and chivalric romance; in those genres, human agency – cunning or martial valor – usually carries the day.) These categories roughly correspond to the four narrative strategies I enumerated earlier: divine threats must be accepted by the heroine's passivity, divine rescues encouraged by the priority of the supernatural over human agency, and human threats defended through moral deception. Human rescues, the primary tasks of chivalric heroes or clever tricksters, have little place in texts that typically give priority to heroines over heroes.[108]

The largest of these categories, human threats, includes pirates, bandits, rapists, and other villains. The heroine and hero must resist, defeat, or passively withstand these threats. More dangerous to their lives and peace of mind, however, are supernatural threats like shipwreck, witchcraft, and love at first sight. To the well-schooled reader these are not really threats, because while the forces that control the genre may be opaque, they are beneficent. The plot motifs that guarantee deliverance, including resurrection, sudden repentance, and a *deus ex machina*

---

[106] In Propp's terms, this list comprises the "chain of variants" out of which Elizabethan prose romances are built. See *Morphology of the Folktale*, 114. On Propp's legacy, see Bal, *Narratology*.

[107] This disordered surface has led one critic, Walter Davis, to a completely different reading of the genre. Davis claims that in these texts, "life in the world is almost pure chaos" (*Idea and Act in Elizabethan Fiction*, [Princeton: Princeton University Press, 1969]). I believe this reading overemphasizes the first of the two stages of the narrative: chaos always gives way to order.

[108] Among the Elizabethan Heliodoranists, the major exception appears to be Sidney's *New Arcadia*, which focuses on two male princes in addition to two princesses. As I discuss in Chapter 3, Pyrocles especially is significantly feminized in Arcadia.

conclusion, emerge from the same beneficent supernatural dispensation as storms and blind love. Jameson's understanding of romance as providing an "imaginary 'solution' to...[a] real contradiction" emphasizes the importance of the supernatural in these texts.[109]

Examining the development of the Elizabethan-Heliodoran romances reveals an increasingly varied recombination of the building blocks of the genre.[110] Heliodoran romance led not only to *Menaphon* and the *New Arcadia*, but also to Greene's repentance tracts, *A Margarite of America*, and *The Unfortunate Traveler*. Part of the challenge seems to have been seeing how far the genre could be stretched: thus Greene exports the conventions of romance to his cony-catching exposés and deathbed autobiographies, and Nashe strains these conventions to (or past) their limits in *The Unfortunate Traveler*.[111] These texts expand the notion of genre as a creative force: the conventions of Elizabethan romance produced many similar texts and many disparate works as these writers strained and distorted the match between matter and form.

The twenty-year run of Elizabethan-Heliodoran romances reveals how a widespread taste for a form both new and ancient enabled a generation of writers to renovate English fiction. The rise of a new kind of narrative, often claiming to be "novel," is an oft-repeated event in literary history. These rises embody something basic in the human appetite for narrative. Readers' tastes are historically determined, and they want narratives that are both up-to-date and culturally sanctioned. In the Elizabethan period, this combination led to a generation of Heliodoran fictions. The genre these texts created remains paradoxical: a combination of naiveté and shrewdness, of sentimental faith and conscious gamesmanship. From its fertile soil grew the strains of prose fiction that lead to, and beyond, the rise of the modern novel as the dominant purveyor of narrative formulae in the language.

---

[109] See *The Political Unconscious*, 118.

[110] In Greene's case, this variety has confused critics, who have produced baroque listings of his career: Pruvost lists eleven phases in *Robert Greene et ses romans*. A clearer understanding of romance streamlines our understanding of his career; see Chapter 4.

[111] On Greene's cony-catching pamphlets as romances, see Mentz, "Magic Books: Cony-Catching and the Romance of Early Modern London," *Rogues and Early Modern English Culture*, 240-58.

# Chapter 2

# Heliodorus and Early Modern Literary Culture

Who is not earnestly affected with a passionate speech, well penned, an elegant Poem, or some pleasant bewitching discourse, like that of Heliodorus, *ubi oblectatio quaedam placide fluit, cum hilaritate conjuncta* [where quiet pleasure joins with merriment]?

Robert Burton, *The Anatomy of Melancholy* (2.2.4)[1]

In 1526, following the sack of Buda by the Turks, a German mercenary carried a Greek manuscript of the *Aethiopica* from the library of King Matthias Corvinus of Hungary to Venice.[2] Little is known of this man, but the consequences of his action would ripple across early modern Europe. Heliodorus's story was written in North Africa in the third or fourth century C.E. and then lost in the Middle Ages.[3] Once in Venice, it found its way into the hands of the international community of humanists who printed Greek texts, and soon was edited by Vincentus Obsopoeus and printed by the office of Hervagiana in 1534 in Basel. Many editions and translations soon followed, beginning with a French translation (Paris, 1547) by the noted humanist Jacques Amyot, and followed by a Latin version (Basel, 1552) by the Polish knight Stanislaus Warschewiczki. In 1569, the first English version appeared in London,

---

[1]  Robert Burton, *The Anatomy of Melancholy*, Holbrook Jackson, ed., (London: J.M. Dent & Sons, 1932) 88, my translation.

[2]  See Alban K. Forcione, *Cervantes, Aristotle, and the 'Persiles,'* (Princeton: Princeton University Press, 1970) 49. Forcione's chapter, "Heliodorus and Literary Theory" (48-87), remains the best introduction to the *Aethiopica* in sixteenth-century Europe.

[3]  The date remains controversial. Reardon cites a range between the third and the late fourth century (*Collected Ancient Greek Novels*, [Berkeley: University of California Press, 1989] 5). Gerald Sandy cites the standard bibliography in "Characterization and Philosophical Decor in the *Aethiopica*," *Transactions of the American Philological Association* 113 (1984): 154n. See also Gerald Sandy, *Heliodorus*, (Boston: Twayne Publishers, 1982).

translated by Thomas Underdowne and published by Frances Coldocke, who would later become Master of the Stationers' Company.[4]

The clearest testimony to the *Aethiopian History*'s popularity was its speedy translation across the continent. Versions appeared in every major language.[5] In England, the tale's influence on Sidney, Spenser, Shakespeare, and others has become a standard theme in scholarly commentary.[6] Across the continent, writers from Montaigne to Cervantes to Rabelais to Racine to Scudéry mentioned him prominently.[7] Missing from standard accounts of this text's appeal, however, is detailed consideration of what about Heliodorus attracted early modern readers and writers. My claim that Heliodorus was the decisive example of the classical plot suggests that the *Aethiopian History* gave Elizabethan writers two important things: an alternative to chivalric romance and the Italian novella, and a sophisticated way of exploiting the varied interpretive practices of readers of narrative fiction.[8] I have already suggested how the *Aethiopica*'s opening scene models the diverse relations between the text and the diverse practices of its readers. Underneath this technical innovation, however, lay Heliodorus's philosophical core, which resonated powerfully in the sixteenth century. The *Aethiopica*'s narrative strategies present an

---

[4]    Francis Coldocke's rise in the Company began after he published Heliodorus. He became Junior Warden in 1580-2, Senior Warden in 1587-9, and then was twice Master of the Company, in 1591-2 and again in 1595-6. See Michael Brennan, "William Ponsonby: Elizabethan Stationer," *Analytical and Enumerative Bibliography* 7:3 (1983): 91; and R.B. McKerrow, *Dictionary of Printers and Booksellers in England, Scotland, and Ireland, and of Foreign Printers of English Books, 1557-1640*, (London: Bibliographical Society, 1910) 72.

[5]    The Greek *editio princeps* appeared in Basel in 1534, and translations rapidly followed: French (Amyot, 1547), Latin (Stanislaus Warschewiczki, 1552), Italian (Leonardo Ghini, 1556), Spanish (anonymous translator, 1554), German, (Johannes Zschorn, 1559), and finally English (Thomas Underdowne, 1569).

[6]    See Samuel Wolff, *The Greek Romances in Elizabethan Prose Fiction*, (New York: Columbia University Press, 1902).

[7]    Montaigne mentions Heliodorus in passing; see "Of the affection of fathers for their children," *The Complete Essays of Montaigne*, Donald M. Frame, trans. (Stanford: Stanford University Press, 1957) 291. I quote Burton and Rabelais as epigrams in this chapter, and discuss Racine's fascination with Heliodorus below. Cervantes's final work, *Persiles and Sigusmunda*, as noted above, is announced as an attempt to "compete with Heliodorus" in the preface to his *Exemplary Stories*. Mlle. de Scudéry declares in her preface to *Artamène ou Le Grand Cyrus* (1649-53) that her "only models" are "l'immortal Héliodore et le Grand Urfe" (quoted by Wolfgang Stechow, "Heliodorus' *Aethiopica* in Art," *Journal of the Warburg and Courtauld Institutes* 16 [1953]: 144-52, 145). On French Heliodoranism, see Pavel, "Literary Genres as Norms and Good Habits," 207.

[8]    Forcione notes that in Spain Heliodorus was considered as superior to chivalric romances as Virgil was to the verse romances of Ariosto and Boiardo (*Cervantes, Aristotle, and the 'Persiles*, 50, 87).

intricate model of the place of human agency in a mysteriously-ordered universe. Heroism in Heliodorus mixes strategic passivity with active dissembling, and outwardly rejects epic martialism.

In Heliodoran romance, weakness and dependency define the human condition. (This emphasis on human weakness resonates with the basic tenets of early modern Protestantism, as I discuss below.) Faced with their own impotence, Heliodoran characters devise sophisticated practices to align themselves with a providentially-ordered plan. This stance, which is one of patience and careful interpretation more than direct action, I call "conspiring with fate." Its portrait of human agency remains largely passive (thus conforming to the narrative model outlined in Chapter 1), and this passivity highlights Heliodorus's anti-epic status. The encouraged stances are faith and delay, not wrath or polytropic trickery. (Though, as I shall show, Odysseus's trickery is closer to Heliodoran virtue than Achilles's rage or even Aeneas's piety.) Heliodorus's characters, through strategic deception and a sometimes maddening refusal to draw conclusions too soon, allow the Providential plot to guide them toward a happy ending. The Aethiopian holy man Sisimithres, perhaps the wisest and most mysterious of Heliodorus's characters, explains how this process works during the final recognition scene: "Sisimithres, who had withelde himself a good while, for al that he knew the whole matter that was in handling, till it were bolted out, which little by little came to light" (280). Sisimithres's strategic delay and accommodation with Providence contrasts sharply with the neo-Stoic resignation proposed by Latin moralists like Seneca and Cicero (and Elizabethan fiction writers like Lyly).[9] The Heliodoran combination of passivity and activity created a model that was attractive for frustrated courtiers like Sidney and market-driven writers like Greene, Lodge, and Nashe.

The plot of Heliodorus's now-forgotten story was so well known in Elizabethan England that Duke Orsino in *Twelfth Night* (1601-2) could allude to the minor character Thyamis and expect the audience to recognize him.[10] "Why should not I," the Duke asks, "(had I the heart to do it), / Like th' Egyptian thief at point of

---

[9] Heliodorus's ideas about Fate and Providence have various sources in classical literature, including Homer, Herodotus, and Greek tragedy. While Herodotus, in particular, presents comparable narrative elements (oracles, shipwrecks, etc.), Heliodorus's notion of an abstract controlling Tyche differs from Herodotus's (and Homer's) jealous and wrathful gods. On the "jealousy of the gods" in Herodotus, see Susan O. Shapiro, "Herodotus and Solon," *Classical Antiquity* 15 (1996): 348-64.

[10] The plot begins with the birth of Chariclea, the white-skinned daughter of the Aethiopian King Hydaspes and Queen Persinna. Persinna, afraid that her daughter's white skin, caused by her contemplation of a painting of Andromeda during conception, will make Hydaspes think her unfaithful, entrusts the infant to her priest Sisimithres and tells the King she died in infancy. Sisimithres passes her to the Greek Charicles, who raises her until she is stolen from him by the Egyptian sage Calasiris and Theagenes, a Greek who falls in love with her. Escaping from Greece to Egypt, these three make their way to Aethiopia where Chariclea's heritage is finally revealed. Heliodorus's presentation is much more complicated than this summary, as I discuss below.

death, / Kill what I love?" (5.1.117-9). By the time of Shakespeare's play, Heliodorus's story appears to have become a typical literary recreation for self-indulgent lovers like the Duke.[11] Orsino exemplifies a reading of Heliodorus as sentimental and soft-headed, a characterization that dominated reception of the *Aethiopian History* (and classical romance) as recently as the mid-twentieth century. The Duke is as far off the mark as the bandits who read the opening tableau as a tragedy – and, in fact, by imagining more bloodshed than the story contains, he makes nearly the same interpretive error they do.

Orsino refers to a moment of misreading in Heliodorus: the bandit-chief Thyamis (whose men capture Theagenes and Chariclea in the opening scene) has fallen in love with Chariclea, and when he believes she will be stolen by rival bandits, he kills her, or so he thinks. In fact, he has slain another Greek woman, Thisbe, instead. His mistakes do not end with his failure to distinguish the heroine from a minor character. If he had simply waited, he would have found that he was not "at point of death"; he survives the attack and eventually recovers his patrimony, although he never marries Chariclea. Thyamis's error, at its most basic level, is generic; like Malvolio, he appears stranded in the wrong genre. Greek romance asks more faith, patience, and indirection from its heroes than Thyamis possesses.

This pattern of generic misdirection continues throughout the opening books of the *Aethiopian History*. Chariclea's particular skill is her ability to manipulate generic patterns to mislead potential antagonists. After Thyamis and his men capture her, instead of revealing the details of her arrival, she laments her fate in general terms: "Apollo (said she) how much more grievous punishment doest thou take of us then we have deserved? Hast thou not beene sufficientlie revenged on us for that that is past? For as much as wee were taken by Pyrates, and subject to six hundred daungers more by Sea, but that nowe againe wee must on the Lande fall into the handes of theeves and robbers: beside, who knoweth whether any thing worse is like to light upon us? When wilt thou make an ende?" (14). The events behind this description remain obscure, but the narrative elements – separation, pirates, shipwreck, and thieves – identify the genre of her story: she is in a Greek romance. Starting from this scene, the *Aethiopian History* confronts its characters with all the trials the genre has to offer. At times Chariclea and Theagenes begin to lose hope, as

---

[11]   In seventeenth-century France, Racine's youthful obsession with Heliodorus testifies to the continuing link between this romance and excessive emotionalism. As Reardon relates the story, "From the seventeenth century there is the story of how the young Racine, having twice had his copy of Heliodorus (probably in Amyot's translation) confiscated at Port-Royal as un-suitable reading, acquired yet another copy, which he took the precaution of learning by heart" (*Collected Ancient Greek Novels*, 13). Winkler considers this anecdote the "a perfect emblem of the genre we now call the ancient novel, or romance." See "The Invention of Romance," *The Search for the Ancient Novel*, 38.

Chariclea does here, but maintaining faith is their basic job as co-conspirators with fate.[12]

Chariclea mixes activity and passivity, waiting for the right moment and using indirect means – verbal skill, manipulation, and even mendacity – to help Providence along. When Thyamis wants to marry her immediately, she delays him with a story.[13] She claims that she and Theagenes are brother and sister, Ionians and priests by birth, who have been shipwrecked in Egypt and who defeated their first attackers in combat, thus producing the bloody scene which opens the narrative. The shipwreck she describes is the stereotypical wreck of romance: "After we had ended the greatest parte of our voiage, a tempest soudainely arose, and a vehement winde, with fearefull blastes, moving great waves of the sea, caused us to leave our determined journey, and the governour overcome with the greatnes of the daunger, gave over the governement, and within a while after, coming out of the hulke committed the rule thereof to Fortune" (30-1). Perhaps because of her surrender to "Fortune," or because Thyamis was persuaded, "partly willing, partly agaynst his will" (31), he delays the marriage until Chariclea can perform certain rites at a temple of Apollo.

Chariclea's story, however, is pure fiction. She is not a priestess of Apollo, nor an Ionian, and especially not Theagenes's sister. While she and Theagenes have been victims of shipwreck in their journey from Greece to Egypt, the most recent landfall was not a wreck, as the fully-laden, intact ship bears witness. Chariclea's words arise from tactical necessity: she delays her marriage so that the gods can rescue her. As she tells Theagenes, who is confused by her apparent assent to Thyamis and by the lie that he is her brother, her tale pretends to yield to Thyamis while actually giving herself and Theagenes over to Providence: "All which thinges I foreseeing, by my present talke, committed my selfe to him, commending that, which shall followe to the Goddes, and the Angell, that at firste hath obtayned the tuition of our love" (34). Chariclea's fiction mirrors Heliodorus's, in that both invoke and rely on a preordained (generic) plan. Thus Chariclea's defense of her lie – "For that manner of a lie is tollerable, whiche profiteth the inventor, and hurteth not the hearer" (34) – stands for Heliodorus's defense of his fiction.

An especially valuable element of the Heliodoran fictional structure, for his Elizabethan heirs, was his nonspecific and omnipresent Providence, which Elizabethan writers assimilated into their Christian worldview.[14] Not embodied in Homeric or Virgilian gods, Heliodorus's supernatural infrastructure is invisible and

---

[12] Theagenes, as I discuss below, does not roll with Fate's punches as well as Chariclea, but his relative inflexibility only underlines that the romance is her story primarily.

[13] The reader does not yet know it, but Thyamis is Calasiris's lost son, driven into banditry because his younger brother has displaced him as priest in Memphis. In pretending to accept Thyamis, Chariclea nearly makes Calasiris, her adopted "father," her actual father-in-law.

[14] On the Renaissance transformation of classical *Fortuna* into Christianized Providence, see Frederick Kiefer, "Fortune and Providence in the *Mirror for Magistrates*," *Studies in Philology* 74 (1977): 146-64.

all-encompassing. Providence is on one level the plot principle in the story, the *fabula* in narratological terms; it is the ordering substructure that presides over the tale's unfolding. Heliodorus, more than any other writer of Greek romance, singled out this mechanism for self-conscious reflection.[15] His wisest characters – Calasiris, Chariclea, and Sisimithres – recognize the outlines of Providential control, and negotiate the crises they encounter accordingly.

Some modern critics have dismissed Heliodoran Providence as a simplistic fictional order in which good things happen to good people.[16] While Heliodoran romance (unlike that of Achilles Tatius and Longus) lacks the skepticism about human perfection that many modern readers value, its commitment to virtue was eagerly consumed by early modern readers. Philip Sidney typifies a certain kind of early modern reader when he calls the "sugared invention of that picture of love in Theagenes and Chariclea" an "absolute heroical poem."[17] Heliodorus's Providence may be, as J. R. Morgan says, "Plot in disguise,"[18] but plot has become a tool for ethical teaching. In a world where divine control is never doubted, humankind has two central tasks: to recognize supernatural control and to collaborate with it.

The key term Heliodorus uses to describe Providence is *Tyche* (Τνχη) which means "Good Fortune" or "Chance."[19] This multivalent Greek word is one of many

---

[15]    It is because of this interest in Providence and interpretation that I believe Heliodorus to have been more influential on Elizabethan writers than Longus (whose was part of the pastoral tradition) or Achilles Tatius (who satirizes mainstream Greek romance). Tim Whitmarsh has recently emphasized that Achilles Tatius was also interested in manipulating readers' responses; see "Reading for Pleasure: Narrative, Irony, and Erotics in Achilles Tatius," *The Ancient Novel and Beyond*, Stelios Panayotakis, Maaike Zimmerman, and Wytse Keulen, eds., (Leiden: Konnninklijke Brill, 2003) 191-205.

[16]    This view contributed to Heliodorus's critical neglect in the early twentieth century. See Reardon, introduction to *Collected Ancient Greek Novels*, and Sandy, *Heliodorus*.

[17]    Sidney, *Defence of Poesy*, 218.

[18]    Morgan, introduction to *An Ethiopian Story, Collected Ancient Greek Novels*, 350. Morgan doubts Heliodorus's moral seriousness: "I cannot find any consistency in the attribution of events to nonhuman agencies and am inclined to think the whole divine apparatus a literary device to give the plot a sense of direction, purpose, and eventual closure, rather than a statement of belief intended to instruct its readers in the ways of god" (350-1). As will become clear, I believe Morgan's statement to be misleading, especially for early modern readings of Heliodorus. Early modern readers would have rejected Morgan's position, since they were trained to seek utility and pleasure together.

[19]    See *The Oxford Classical Dictionary*, Hammond, N. G. L., and Scullar, H. H., eds., [Oxford: Clarendon Press, 1970] 1100-1, on this word, which can mean success either through luck or through skill "in such matters as navigation, warfare, and government" (1100). Oedipus, as the *OCD* notes, calls himself "child of Tyche" because he comes to the throne through his own hand not by birth. Sophocles's plot reveals him to be Tyche's child in a more sinister sense (1101).

that Heliodorus uses for Fate, Chance, or Fortune in the *Aethiopian History*.[20] Tyche lies at the heart of the Heliodoran project because it can mean either blind Chance, as Cnemon uses it in Book 1 (82),[21] or Providence, as Calasiris uses it when he first speaks (152). Faced with these divergent meanings, Chariclea's basic interpretive task is to distinguish Calasiris's Providence from Cnemon's Chance.

Chariclea's connection to Tyche becomes increasingly close as the romance progresses. In fact, she proves so powerful toward the end of the tale that even the bandits' original misreading – that she is a goddess who caused the massacre – proves true in a sense. Once the nested narratives that take up nearly half of the *Aethiopian History* reveal the origin of the massacre, we learn that Chariclea, with her hidden ally Calasiris, incited the massacre by setting the two chief pirates against each other. At the tale's end, also, she recovers her patrimony in Aethiopia and becomes priestess of the Moon, which links her to Artemis or Isis. The problem with the bandits' initial interpretation is not the results they reach but the reasoning they use. Dazzled by Chariclea's beauty, they assume she is superhuman and capricious. Heliodorus requires a more discerning standard.

## The Heliodoran Tradition

> [T]he world of Greek romance is an *alien world*: everything in it is indefinite, unknown, foreign.
>
> Mikhail Bahktin, "Forms of Time and of the Chronotope in the Novel"[22]

Although Heliodorus's text was lost to western Europe before the sixteenth century, a tradition of neoplatonic allegorization grew up around the tale in late antiquity. This tradition, while presumably unknown in the early modern period, has suggestive parallels with the uses early modern Heliodorists made of his plot. The clearest surviving example of the tradition is by "Philip the Philosopher," a pseudonymous author whose commentary appears in a twelfth-century manuscript of the *Aethiopian History*. (As Robert Lamberton notes, the fragment is undateable; if the name "Philip" is meant to refer to Philip of Opus, Plato's student, this intentional anachronism does not help.)[23] Philip's commentary

---

[20] Nancy Lindheim notes Tyche's importance in the *Aethiopian History*, although she accents the meaning of the word as "Chance" rather than "Good Fortune." See *The Structures of Sidney's Arcadia*, (Toronto: University of Toronto Press, 1982) 120.

[21] References to the Greek text are to Aristide Colonna, ed., *Le Ethiopiche di Eliodoro*, (Torino: Unione Tipografico-Editrice Torinese, 1987), cited in the text.

[22] Mikhail Bahktin, *The Dialogic Imagination: Four Essays*, Michael Holquist, ed., Michael Holquist and Caryl Emerson, trans., (Austin: University of Texas Press, 1981) 101.

[23] See Robert Lamberton, *Homer the Theologian: Neoplatonist Allegorical Reading and the Growth of the Epic Tradition*, (Berkeley: University of California Press, 1989) 148-9n, for various attempts to dating the fragment. Lamberton notes that Colonna found Theophanes the Keramite using the pseudonym in the tenth-eleventh centuries, but it could also be as early

represents a mode of reading Heliodorus popular sometime between late antiquity and the early medieval era. Philip the Philosopher, like Philip Sidney and Robert Greene, reads Heliodorus as an ethical pedagogue who advocates indirect rather than direct action.

Philip frames his commentary as a defense of Chariclea. When a crowd ridicules Heliodorus's book, Philip's friend Nikolaos calls on him to defend it: "Lover of Chariclea that I am, I am hurt by this [attack] and, by your wisdom, I entreat you not to let the modest girl be insulted, but rather call to her defense 'your wit and your gentleness' [*Od.* 11.202-3] and show these babbling quacks that the story of Chariclea is beyond all reproach!" (306).[24] That the book should need defense from charges of frivolity reveals that its romantic character was suspect even in Philip the Philosopher's day. The cultural prejudice against romances as "trifles" that remained potent in Sidney's self-criticism of the *Old Arcadia* and Greene's deathbed repentances haunted the *Aethiopian History* as well.

Philip defends Chariclea by arguing that she requires a special kind of reading. What may seem idle or licentious reveals its ethical value to a superior reader.[25] "This book," argues Philip, "is very much like Circe's brew: those who take it in a profane manner, it transforms into licentious pigs, but those who approach it in a philosophical way, in the manner of Odysseus, it initiates into higher things" (307). Philip equates Heliodorus's meaning with a neoplatonist allegory of the *Odyssey*. He argues that Heliodorus's romance presents moral instruction, and he describes Calasiris and Chariclea as ideal teacher and perfect student in ethical matters.

But the ethics Calasiris teaches, Philip argues, are not boilerplate neo-platonism. The Egyptian sage instructs not just "reverence for the divine" but also right use of problematic techniques: "how to use falsehood as you would a drug, when you are determined to come to the aid either of friends or of yourselves, neither harming your neighbor nor pledging a falsehood in violation of an oath, but rather how to manage your words with wisdom and to be careful and pleasing in your speech" (308). Even for a moralist like Philip, romance is the genre of misdirection. The recommended moral stance relies on two things: personal judgment to determine how the strong medicine of "falsehood" should be applied, and rhetorical "care" to make one's speech "pleasing." Tactical falsehood

---

as the fifth century. Doody suggests a date in the earlier half of this range (*True Story of the Novel*, 100).

[24] Philip the Philosopher, "An Interpretation of the Modest Chariclea from the Lips of Philip the Philosopher," Robert Lamberton, trans., *Homer the Theologian*, 306-11. Further citations in the text. The bracketed notes are Lamberton's.

[25] In its outlines, Philip's "philosophical" method of reading appears analogous to the typological method of assimilating Old Testament and pagan material to a Christian world-view, as described by Augustine and others.

does not taint Heliodorus's characters because, as Philip notes, they use falsehood in a "philosophical way" and with "reverence for the divine" (308).[26]

According to Philip, Chariclea's tactical falsehood relies on two qualities: self-restraint and acceptance of human weakness. Her willingness to place her fate in divine hands is clear from the opening scene of the *Aethiopian History*. For Philip, this self-restraint is Chariclea's defining quality. She and Theagenes are "models of self-restraint...Chariclea was so clothed in self-restraint that she avoided intercourse with her lover even in dreams and fantasies" (308). Chariclea combines Calasiris's mendacity with her own self-restraint, of which personal chastity is the outward symbol. Philip goes on to provide an elaborate neoplatonic reading of the heroine, in which "Chariclea is a symbol for the soul and of the mind that sets the soul in order" (309), but late antiquity's taste for elaborate allegory should not obscure the ethical content of Philip's reading.

Rejecting the "profane manner" of reading only for the plot, Philip finds in the *Aethiopian History* a powerful moral subtext. "For the story itself cries out!," he says, "The very letters all but speak!" (308). Philip sees Heliodorus's subtext as a recipe for moral living: "[E]ven when you are treated unjustly, be content with the anomalies of chance and bear them nobly, suffering with Theagenes and Chariclea, so that your end may be rich and prosperous" (309). The insights of a late-antique reader are remarkably compatible with, and premonitionary of, those of the early modern readers who themselves became authors of Elizabethan romance.

Modernist critics, whose standards underwrite our own reading practices, rejected the allegorical and moralistic readings that appealed to Philip the Philosopher.[27] Recently, however, a surge of work on Heliodorus and Greek romance has begun revising critical opinion by returning to the hermeneutic questions that Philip finds so engaging. It is not just that, as Margaret Doody has noted, "The Zeitgest whispers now of a revival of interest in the classical novel."[28] Rather, Heliodorus's self-conscious exploration of narrative methods fascinates a variety of modern critics, especially now that narratological methods have encouraged a return to well-worn plotlines.[29] The first one-volume English translation of all extant Greek romances, *Collected Ancient Greek Novels* (1989) marks the re-entry of these works into critical awareness.[30] The readership of these

---

[26] Philip's notion that Calasiris embodies virtuous deceit has recently reappeared in the work of modern classicists. See Winkler, "The Mendacity of Kalasiris," and Sandy, "Characterization and Philosophical Décor."

[27] On post-Enlightenment skepticism of the allegorical tradition, see Lamberton, *Homer the Theologian*, 298-305.

[28] Doody, *True Story of the Novel*, xvii.

[29] See Lowe, *The Classical Plot*, for a recent use of narratological and cognitive theories to reconsider classical narrative from Homer to Heliodorus.

[30] For recent work, see, among others, B. E. Perry, *The Ancient Romances: A Literary-Historical Account of Their Origins* (Berkeley: University of California Press, 1967), Arthur Heisermann, *The Novel Before the Novel* (Chicago: University of Chicago Press, 1977), To-

texts in the classical period is hotly debated, as is the readership of Elizabethan fiction. Without solving these perhaps unanswerable questions, it seems clear that both the late classical and early modern worlds saw a flourishing of narrative fiction and, not coincidentally, a shift from epic, martial models to passive interpretive ones. By the time of the rediscovery of Heliodorus in the sixteenth century, this model became a real alternative to epic martialism.

Heliodorus's anti-epic structure emerges in recent reconsiderations of the Greek text. Perhaps the most influential study is Winkler's, "The Mendacity of Kalasiris and the Narrative Strategy of Heliodoros' *Aithiopika*."[31] Like Philip the Philosopher, Winkler believes that Heliodorus models crafty deception: "Kalasiris [is] the crafty narrator, who fools various audiences, and yet seems in some sense to maintain his integrity and lofty morality in the service of divine providence" (93-4).[32] Calasiris's most blatant falsehood, noted by Winkler and others,[33] is a refusal to reveal his true history and motives; he conceals that he came to Delphi at the behest of Queen Persinna to look for Chariclea. Instead, Calasiris insists that he came solely to learn from the oracle (105-6). This lie is essential to Calasiris's larger plan; his two goals, seeking Delphic wisdom and returning Chariclea to Aethiopia, are compatible only if he does not reveal the latter to anyone.

Laboring under the handicap of mixed knowledge and ignorance, the reader (like Calasiris and Chariclea) navigates between two alternatives: fear of misinterpretation, and faith in God's (or the gods') beneficent plan. Like Iser's

---

mas Hägg, *The Novel in Antiquity* (Berkeley: University of California Press, 1983), B. P. Reardon, *The Form of Greek Romance* (Princeton: Princeton University Press, 1991), James Tatum, ed., *The Search for the Ancient Novel* (Baltimore: Johns Hopkins University Press, 1994); Gerald Sandy, *Heliodorus*, (Boston: Twayne Publishers, 1982); Shadi Bartsche, *Decoding the Ancient Novel*, (Princeton: Princeton University Press, 1989); David Konstan, *Sexual Symmetry: Love in the Ancient Novel and Related Genres*, (Princeton: Princeton University Press, 1994); Simon Goldhill, *Foucault's Virginity: Ancient Erotic Fiction and the History of Sexuality*, (Cambridge: Cambridge University Press, 1995); Suzanne MacAlister, *Dreams and Suicides: The Greek Novel from Antiquity to the Byzantine Empire*, (London: Routledge, 1996); J. R. Morgan, "A sense of the ending: the conclusion of Heliodorus' *Aethiopika*," *Transactions of the American Philological Society* 99 (1989): 299-320; Maria Futre Pinhiero, "Calasiris' Story and its Narrative Significance in Heliodorus' *Aethiopica*," *Groningen Colloquia on the Novel* IV (1991): 69-83. This list is partial, and does not include numerous attempts to relate the Greek romances to areas outside of classics, some of which I discuss below.

[31]   References in the text.

[32]   I follow Winkler, Morgan, Sandy, Pinhiero and others in seeing Calasiris as a serious figure, but this opinion is largely a product of recent scholarship. Even as recently as 1977, Arthur Heiserman could call Calasiris a "charlatan" (*Novel before the Novel*, 191) and compare his moral character unfavorably with Philostratos's Apollonius of Tyna, and the Acts of Paul (203-10).

[33]   For other studies of Calasiris's lie, see Sandy, "Characterization and Philosophical Décor," and Pinhiero, "Calasiris' Story."

dialectic of protesion and retention, or Aristotle's tension between economy and amplitude, this dialogue frames the reader's engagement with Heliodorus's narrative. The first of these, fear of misinterpretation, motivates Calasiris's duplicity toward Cnemon and Heliodorus's toward the reader: neither tells the whole story because neither is sure it will be properly understood. In fact, Persinna's initial decision to exile her infant daughter, also hinges on fear of misinterpretation: Persinna fears King Hydaspes would wrongly interpret Chariclea's white skin as evidence of adultery.[34] As Winkler phrases it, Chariclea's plight parallels that of the text: "Fear of misinterpretation is Persinna's motive for withholding her daughter/knowledge from Hydaspes and for launching her child/text rather into the uncertain world of coincidence and happenstance where ignorance and ambiguity are the rule" (120). The task for Chariclea, and the reader of the *Aethiopian History*, is to resist misinterpretation until Providence and the author bring the right meaning forward.

The deceptions in which Persinna, Calasiris, and Chariclea engage are not simply cases where ends justify means, because for Heliodorus narrative facility and interpretative duplicity are higher moral values than simple truth. Winkler's comment on Calasiris's lie holds true generally: "It is as an actor in the gods' complicated plot at Delphi that Kalasiris appears duplicitous, but the justification of his behavior is not that he acts basely in the service of a higher cause, rather *duplicity itself* is the proper moral attitude, duplicity in the sense of carefully weighing alternatives and respecting the volition of all the characters" (136). This tactic of "passivity and reluctance to intervene" (136) is Calasiris's anti-epic heroism. As an alternative to epic force and the novella's trickery, it would become the heart of Elizabethan prose romance.

### Heliodorus in the Renaissance

> Pantagruel, stretched out on a cross-sail at the end of the hatchway, slumbered, holding a Greek Heliodorus in his hand.
>
> Rabelais, *Pantagruel* (Book 4)

Heliodorus's prestige with Renaissance scholars like Julius Caesar Scaliger, El Pinciano, and Jacques Amyot contributed to his high status among early modern humanists. Continental commentators praised his innovative handling of plot. The most substantial discussion comes from Scaligar, who calls Heliodorus a "splendid" model of narrative technique in *Poetices libri septem* (Lyon, 1561):

---

[34]   For a reading of Persinna's shrewdness in avoiding this accusation, see Michael J. Anderson, "The ΣΟΦΡΟΣΥΝΗ of Persinna and the Romantic Strategy of Heliodorus' *Aethiopica*," *Classical Philology* 92 (1997): 314-18.

> Hoc ipsum igitur quod pro principio sumes, ne statuas in principio, ita enim auditoris animus est suspensus: querit enim quod nondum extat. Ea sane vel unica vel praecipua virtus, auditorem quasi captiuum detinere...Hanc disponendi rationem splendidissimam habes in Aethiopica historia Heliodori. Quem librum epico Poetae censeo accuratissime legendum, ac quasi pro optimo exemplari sibi proponendum.

> [Accordingly you should not set forth at the beginning what you select for the beginning, so that the mind of the listener is held in suspense, for he seeks something that does not yet exist. This, to be sure, is the unique or outstanding virtue, to hold the listener as if he were a captive....This most splendid manner of constructing a work is observed in Heliodorus's *Aethiopian History*, a book which, I think, should be read with great attention by the epic poet, and which should be proposed to him as the best model possible.][35]

Heliodorus is "the best model" because his narrative structure draws the reader into his work. In this way, he ensures that the author's "delightful teaching" (to use Sidney's phrase from the *Defence*), will have a fit audience, held in place like captives ("quasi captiuum detinere").[36]

While Scaliger stops short of granting Heliodorus's genre co-equal status with Virgilian epic, his was one of many influential voices celebrating the Greek romance model. Tasso, despite his contempt for Ariostan romance, cites Heliodorus in *Dell Arte poetica* as an example of the proper use of a love-plot in an heroic poem.[37] Amyot celebrated Heliodorus in terms similar to Scaliger's, although he also censured Theagenes because he does not perform "any memorable feat of arms."[38] (Amyot considered his translations of Plutarch superior because they were histories, but he valued the fictions of Heliodorus, Homer, and Virgil as "disguised histories.")[39] In Spain, El Pinciano's praise in *Philosophía antigua poética* (1596) was more effusive: "Gift of the sun is Heliodorus, and in this matter of tying and untying knots, he is unsurpassed, and in the other

---

[35]    Julius Caesar Scaliger, *Poetices Libri Septum*, (Stuttgardt: fromman-holzbog, 1987) 144. I use Forcione's translation; see *Cervantes, Aristotle, and the 'Persiles,'* 65-6.

[36]    On Heliodorus's use of suspense, see Terence Cave, *Recognitions: A Study in Poetics*, (Oxford: Clarendon Press, 1988) esp. 16-21, and "'Suspendere animos': Pour une histoire de la notion de suspens," *Les commentaires et la naissance de la critique littéraire, France/Italie (XIVe-XVIe siècles)*, Gisèle Mathieu-Castellani and Michel Plaisance, eds., (Paris: Aux Amateurs de Livres, 1990) 211-18.

[37]    See Lawrence F. Rhu, *The Genesis of Tasso's Narrative Theory*, (Detroit: Wayne State University Press, 1993) 109. Forcione notes that the praise was expanded in Tasso's later *Del poema eroica* (*Cervantes, Aristotle, and the 'Persiles,'* 67).

[38]    Jacques Amyot, trans., *L'Histoire Aethiopique de Heliodorus*, (Paris: Estienne Groulleau, 1547). See also Forcione's comments on Amyot (*Cervantes, Aristotle, and the 'Persiles,'* 63) and Victor Skretkowicz, Jr., "Sidney and Amyot: Heliodorus in the Structure and Ethos of the *New Arcadia*," *Review of English Studies* n.s. 27 (1976): 171-4.

[39]    See Forcione, *Cervantes, Aristotle, and the 'Persiles,'* 63.

techniques of composition, he is excelled by but a few."[40] Ultimately these European critics influenced Pierre-Daniel Huet's *Traité de l'origine des romans* (1670), which singles out Heliodorus as an originary text for seventeenth-century prose romance: "Until then nothing more artfully contrived had been seen, nothing more finished in the art of writing *romans*, than the adventures of Theagenes and Charikleia....[I]t served as a model to all writers of *romans* who followed it, and it may be said just as truthfully that they have all drawn upon it, as it is said that all poets have drawn upon the model of Homer."[41] This French and Spanish tradition, however, operated somewhat differently in England.[42]

Although writers like Greene and Sidney may have read several editions of Heliodorus's work, the Latin version would have been especially striking. About two-thirds of the way down the title-page of the 1552 Latin edition of Heliodorus appears the name of Philip Melanchthon, the *Praeceptor Germiniae* ("teacher of Germany").[43] (Philip Sidney may have especially noticed: he was named after Philip of Spain but likely considered Melanchthon a more admirable namesake.) The name appears in type nearly as large as that of the author, Heliodorus, or the translator, Stanislaus Warschewiczki. For most early modern English readers, Melanchthon's name was the most famous of the three. The Latin text, published by Johannes Oporinus in Basel in 1552 and re-issued in Antwerp in 1556, bore the identifying marks of low country Protestantism. Melanchthon's contribution to the text is not clear from the title page, and it was, in fact, limited to a bare paragraph, but the name was a powerful draw, especially for ambitious Protestants like Sidney and University men like Greene.

With Melanchthon's name and introduction, the Latin Heliodorus recalled for Sidney the world from which his Queen's disfavor barred him. To modern readers, however, Melanchthon's prominence on the title page, out of proportion to his brief contribution to the volume, suggests a commercial motive. The publisher, Oporinus, apparently wanted to sell the romance to a readership that could be

---

[40] See Forcione, *Cervantes, Aristotle, and the 'Persiles,'* 72. El Pinciano even considers Heliodorus to be superior to Homer and Virgil (75) – perhaps, as Forcione notes, because the literary dilemma in Spain was how to beat back the prose tradition of *Amadis*, for which Heliodorus was better suited than any verse model.

[41] Pierre-Daniel Huet, *Lettre-trait sur l'origine des romans*, Jean Chapelain, ed., (Paris: Edition A.-G. Nizet, 1971) 77-80. I use Forcione's translation (*Cervantes, Aristotle, and the 'Persiles,'* 53-4). On Huet, see also Doody, *True Story of the Novel, passim.*

[42] On Greek romances in early modern England, see Darlene C. Greenhalagh, "Love, Chastity, and Women's Erotic Power: Greek Romance in Elizabethan and Jacobean Contexts," *Prose Fiction and Early Modern Sexualities in England, 1570-1640*, Constance C. Relihan and Goran V. Stanivukovic, eds., (New York: Palgrave Macmillan, 2003) 15-42.

[43] Cited in Sachiko Kusakawa, *The Transformation of Natural Philosophy: The Case of Philip Melanchthon*, (Cambridge: Cambridge University Press, 1995) 1.

attracted to Melanchthon's imprimatur.[44] For the browsing bookbuyer in northern Europe in the mid-sixteenth century, Heliodorus and Warschewiczki were obscure names, but Melanchthon placed the book in a specific cultural milieu.

In Sidney's case, Melanchthon's influence was just one step removed from being personal, since Hubert Languet, Sidney's confidant and mentor, had been a student of Melanchthon's at Wittenberg.[45] Sidney cannot have failed to notice the reverent terms in which Languet spoke of his former teacher. In a letter to Sidney in 1574, Languet explained his tendency to be generous by citing his "master" Melanchthon. Languet claimed that Melanchthon taught him to sympathize with human foibles: "I have never yet repented of my master, nor of my education, nor will I be seduced to give them up by the animadversions of men who are more strict, or more bitter than myself."[46] When Sidney opened the Latin edition, the prominent display of Melanchthon's name would have produced a frisson not just of authority, but of recognition.

The title page displays Melanchthon's judgment as advertising. Just below the title, it quotes his opinion of the author: "Adiectum est etiam Philippi Melanthonis de ipso autore, & hac eiusdem conuersione, iudicium."[47] ("Philip Melanchthon has read this author thoroughly, and judged his style of writing.") The key term here is "iudicium," judgment. Melanchthon has read Heliodorus and judges him to be appropriate. The authority of the sober Lutheran refutes the charges of frivolity that had attached to Heliodorus since the medieval period, and which the dedication to the earl of Oxford would revive in England. Melanchthon's approval of the *Aethiopian History* would at least have confirmed Sidney's decision to use Heliodorus as a narrative model; it may even have inspired it.

When delving into the large 1552 Quarto, Sidney would have found that Melanchthon's presence was limited to a scant 150-word introductory paragraph, addressed to his "dearest friend" Johannes Oporinus. Publicity blurbs, often in the form of laudatory poems, were a well-established means of advertising in early modern publishing. After skimming Melanchthon's effusive thanks to Oporinus

---

[44]   For the career of Oporinus, a prominent publisher and intellectual in Basel, see Martin Steinmann, *Johannes Oporinus: Ein Basler Buchdrucker um die Mitte des 16. Jahrhunderts*, (Basel, 1967).

[45]   Sidney met Languet in Paris in 1572, after witnessing the massacre of the Huguenots on St. Bartholomew's Day. Sidney's commitment to the international Protestant cause solidified on this trip to France, and Languet's teaching became central to his political ideas and ambitions. See Duncan-Jones, *Sir Philip Sidney, Courtier-Poet*, 60-62, and A. G. D. Wiles, "Sir Philip Sidney: The English Huguenot," *Transactions of the Huguenot Society of South Carolina* 45 (1940): 24-37.

[46]   Hubert Languet and Sir Philip Sidney, *The Correspondence of Sir Philip Sidney and Hubert Languet*, Steuart A. Pears, ed., (London: William Pickering, 1845) 88.

[47]   Heliodorus, *Aethiopicae Historiae*, (Basel: Johannes Oporinus, 1552), unsigned leaf. Further citations from this edition are given in the text. Translations are my own unless otherwise indicated.

and the closing comments in praise of the translation, readers would have been left with a three-sentence core in which Melanchthon describes why he judges Heliodorus to deserve a wide audience:

> Scio te ipsum prudenter & recte iudicare de scriptis: & tibi notum esse autorem existimo. Oratio est nitida, & non tumida. Et mira est uarietas consiliorum, occasionum, euentuum, & adfectuum: & uitae imagines multas continet. (1552 ed., unsigned leaf)

> [I know you judge writing prudently and correctly, and I judge this author is known to you. The style is polished, and never pompous. The diversity of counsels, occasions, events, and states of mind is wonderful. It also contains many images of life.]

Melanchthon's focus on the story's diversity must be read within the sixteenth-century interest in the utility of fiction. The many images of life that Heliodorus contains are useful, according to the Horatian model, because they show good behavior rewarded and evil acts punished. Melanchthon singles out Heliodorus as exemplary in Horatian terms, noting not just the external "events" in his story, but also the associated "states of mind." This attention to internal moral decisions may have been one reason humanist readers and critics preferred Heliodorus to Arthurian legends and the numerous progeny of Amadis of Gaul.

A common legend about Heliodorus (now discounted) saw him as the bishop of Tricca who rejected the church for fiction. The story, repeated by Montaigne and Burton, relates that the *Aethiopica* was written in Heliodorus's youth, and when he later became bishop it caused a scandal among young readers. Confronted by church elders with the choice of renouncing his book or his office, Heliodorus chose the book.[48] In part by valuing his romance, Heliodorus became for English writers a model for combining romance narrative with cultural ambition. As the student of Languet, who was the student of Melanchthon, Sidney in particular would have welcomed Heliodorus, the author his master's master recommended. He and his peers found there not simply a felicitous plot but also a model of the interaction between predeterminate Fate and human free will, and a way of making romance a serious intellectual enterprise. They also may have linked Heliodorus's Tyche to Protestant understandings of Providence, which Melanchthon discussed in his 1532 *Commentarii ad Epistolam Pauli ad Romanos*.[49] Commentaries on this epistle, which contains the Protestant rallying cry of justification by faith alone

---

[48] This rejection of the clerical hierarchy would have recommended Heliodorus to Protestants like Melanchthon and Sidney.

[49] See Kusakawa, *Transformation of Natural Philosophy*, 164, for the place of this commentary in Melanchthon's career.

(*iustificati igitur ex fide* in the Vulgate [5:1]),[50] were rhetorical battlefields in the religious pamphlet wars of sixteenth-century Europe. Melanchthon's commentary presents a version of Providence compatible with the generic structure of Greek romance. His believer, like Heliodorus's heroine, clings to faith and virtue to preserve herself for God's mysterious ends.

The starting point for Melanchthon's discussion of Providence is human impotence. Human beings can do nothing to relieve sin: "Non enim possunt homines per solam rationem naturalem statuere, quod Deus velit remittere peccata."[51] ("It is certainly not possible for human beings to stand by their natural reason alone, but only if God wills to remit their sins.") Melanchthon asserts that the believer cannot succeed by any human means; models like Achilles's force of arms, Odysseus's tricks, and even Aeneas's piety are all futile. Rather, like a romance-heroine, the Protestant believer triumphs by submitting to and cooperating with Divine will.[52] Since Heliodorus's heroine relies on Tyche for rescue, his plot requires a belief in human weakness comparable to Melanchthon's. Whatever Heliodorus's own religious beliefs were,[53] the English Heliodoranists' conversion of Tyche into Christian Providence was facilitated by substantial analogies between Heliodoran romance and Protestant theology.

In Greek romance, the happy ending emerges out of two parallel movements: the heroine's defense of her chastity and the dispensation of the gods. For Melanchthon, two things combine to produce redemption: "duas esse praecipuas partes universae scripturae, legem et promissionem reconciliationis" (34). ("The important parts of the universal scripture are twofold: the law, and the promise of salvation.") The law corresponds to romance's behavioral imperatives of self-defense and chastity. For both Melanchthon and Heliodorus, however, the key

---

[50]   *Biblia Sacra: Iuxta Vulgatam Versionem*, (Stuttgart: Württembergische Bibelanstalt, 1975) 1754.

[51]   Philip Melanchthon, *Commentarii ad Epistolam Pauli ad Romanos, Melanchthons Werke*, (Gütersloh: Gütersloher Verlaghshaus Gerd Mohn, 1965) 70. Further citations in the text. Following translations are my own unless otherwise noted.

[52]   In the language of sixteenth-century theology, sin is not imputed or external to humans, but is the result of a corrupt nature: "Peccatum originis non est tantum imputatio, qua posteri Adae propter ipsius delictum rei sunt sine naturae corruptione, sed est etiam corruptio naturae secuta lapsum Adae" (171). ("Original sin is not anything to be reckoned as a merit or a fault, since subsequent to Adam's sin things are corrupt by nature, and corrupted nature declines because of Adam's sin.")

[53]   As Doody notes, the Greek romances have often been associated with the mystery cults of late antiquity, especially by Karl Kerenyi, *Eleusis: Archetypal Image of Mother and Daughter*, Ralph Mannheim, trans., (Princeton: Princeton University Press, 1991), and Reinhold Merkelbach, *Roman und Mysterium in der Antike*, (Munich: Beck, 1962). Despite some doubts, Doody endorses the view that the Greek romances have a fundamentally religious point of view (*True Story of the Novel*, 160-72). Other recent readers have been skeptical.

events emerge from divine action, according to the *promissionem reconciliationis,* rather than being caused by human virtue. What Melanchthon calls the promise of salvation, Heliodorus calls Tyche.

The necessary human component of salvation, obeying the law, does not mean placing one's hopes in any human institution. Rather, as Melanchthon explains, the law's observation requires inward discipline: "Lex requirit notitiam Dei, timorem Dei, oboedientiam erga Deum in omnibus operibus divinis, in morte et aliis afflictionibus" (224). ("The law requires knowing God, fearing God, and therefore obeying God in all divine things, even in death and other afflictions.") The key terms here, *notitiam, timorem, oboedientiam,* indicate not outward actions but emotional states. Knowing, fearing, and obeying God take place in the heart of the believer. Likewise a romance heroine's greatest powers are internal and psychological; she resists outward temptations and thereby collaborates with her fate.

For Melanchthon, the task of the faithful is to believe that God's mercy will remit human sin in the end. The believer, according to Melanchthon, must never doubt the Divine plan. In *Loci communes* (1521), Melanchthon defines faith as the certainty that God will have the last word:

> ...to have faith is to believe the promises, that is, to trust the mercy and goodness of God against the wickedness of the world, sin, death, and even the gates of hell... "the assurance of things hoped for" [Hebrews 11:1] is called "faith." Therefore, those who do not hope for the promised salvation do not believe.[54]

Faith for Melanchthon centers on the "promised salvation" and calls up an image of God devising a master-plot to rescue creation. God's plot makes human history a massive romance with salvation at the end; faith thus underwrites Heliodoran narrative strategies that emphasize the rewards of passivity. Faith in God's "promised salvation" mirrors the reader's (or, in Heliodorus, the heroine's) faith that the conventions of romance will produce a happy ending. Melanchthon's approval thus encouraged English writers to imagine Heliodorus's narrative to be compatible with Protestant Providence.

In addition to the Latin translation, the other crucial sixteenth-century version of Heliodorus was Thomas Underdowne's English translation. Translated from the Latin, not the original Greek (with some apparent cribbing from Amyot's French), this edition was first published in London by Francis Coldocke in 1569, and then re-issued with slight changes twice during Elizabeth's reign (1577, 1587).[55] These

---

[54]   Quoted in Kusakawa, *Transformation of Natural Philosophy*, 160, his translation.

[55]   Heliodorus was published in England six more times before 1640: three more editions of Underdowne (1605, 1606, 1622), and three of William L'Isle's verse couplets (1631, 1631, 1638).

editions attest to the work's popularity in Elizabethan England: even Sidney's *Arcadia*, arguably the most influential prose text of the era, was only published three times under Elizabeth (1590, 1593, and 1598).

Unlike the Latin edition, Underdowne's front matter does not bear the marks of international Protestantism. This book is dedicated to "the Right Honorable Edward Deuire, Lord Boulbecke, Earle of Oxenford."[56] The de Vere family rivaled the Sidney/Dudley/Leicester faction at court, and Edward de Vere would quarrel publicly with Sidney on the tennis court in 1579.[57] Oxford was the patron of Greene's rival Lyly, and critics often cite him as an example of the Italianate decadence that Protestants like Sidney wanted to purge from English culture. While Melanchthon's approval of Heliodorus commanded respect, Oxford's association with the English translation may have seemed disturbing. Oxford was frivolous where Melanchthon was serious, papistical where Melanchthon was Protestant,[58] and part of a faction that would ally England with the Roman church while Melanchthon, and Languet, stood for Sidney's dream of an international Protestant alliance. To Greene, Oxford would have been unreliable as both Lyly's patron and a crypto-Catholic.

Even the subtitles in the Underdowne editions might have given Elizabethan writers pause, as they expose the text's lighter side. The title page of the 1569 edition describes the work as "very wittie and pleasaunt," and the 1577 and 1587 editions read "no lesse wittie than pleasaunt." While all readers of Heliodorus concur on his wit, humanist readings accented the romance's capacity to teach. "Et mira est uarietas," writes Melanchthon, but this miraculous variety is not just "wittie and pleasaunt" but of serious ethical importance. The divergence between Underdowne's "wittie and pleasaunt" Heliodorus and Melanchthon's "moral" Heliodorus duplicates a rift common in Renaissance responses to literature, the gap between Horace's *utile* and *dulce*. These two editions of Heliodorus literalize that gap: Melanchthon's book is *utile*, Underdowne's *dulce*. Since to be witty without utility is to fail poetically, the Underdowne edition's emphasis on pleasure over teaching trivializes the text. This version truly is what Sidney half-seriously calls his *Old Arcadia*: "a trifle, and that triflingly handled."[59]

---

[56]   Heliodorus, *An Aethiopian History*, Thomas Underdowne, trans., (London: Francis Cold-ocke, 1569) sig. ¶2. Further citations in the text.

[57]   See Duncan-Jones, *Sir Philip Sidney: Courtier Poet*, (New Haven: Yale University Press, 1991) 163-7. This quarrel came at the height of Sidney's unpopularity at court due to his outspoken disapproval of Elizabeth's proposed marriage to the Duc d'Alençon.

[58]   When Oxford returned from the Continent in 1580, he pronounced himself a Catholic. When he recanted his conversion, perhaps to retain favor at court, he subsequently informed on his comrades for the same crime. Duncan-Jones suggests that he "seems to have been a crypto-Catholic" (*Courtier-Poet*, 166).

[59]   This phrase appears in the prefatory letter to his sister Mary, the Countess of Pembroke. The current Oxford editors have concluded that, despite being reprinted in virtually every edition of the *Arcadia* since 1590, this letter should properly be applied to the *Old Arcadia* only. See Jean Robertson, ed., *The Countess of Pembroke's Arcadia (The Old Arcadia)*,

As I discussed earlier, Underdowne, if not Oxford, offered Heliodorus as a corrective to unchaste chivalric romance. The romance's lovers were not Christian, like those in Cervantes's *Persiles y Sigismunda*, but the Heliodoran world produced examples of virtue compatible both with Sidney's muscular Protestantism and Greene's appeal to multiple reading practices. Underdowne's preface provides succinct phrasing of the problems facing the Elizabethan Heliodoranists; they needed to avoid the "wittie and pleasaunt" decadence of the Oxford circle, and also the violent, lustful play of Arthur, Amadis, and their kin. Steering a middle course between Oxfordian sophistication and medieval excess, they took from Heliodorus an example of female chastity and constancy, combined with strategic activity, triumphant in the end. The example of Melanchthon's Heliodorus, moreover, would have helped them claim that Heliodorus's providentialism was not simply a matter of narrative convenience. Heliodorus's pleasure was serious business.

The influence of these editions of Heliodorus cannot be rigorously proved; it is possible (but unlikely) that Sidney, Greene, Lodge, or Nashe relied on the Greek text only, or on Amyot's French translation. Examining these editions, however, provides evidence of these writers' motives in turning to the *Aethiopian History* as a structural model. Both Heliodoranism and English Protestantism wanted counterbalance Oxfordian "pleasure." In this way, Melanchthon's "judgment" becomes an essential component of Elizabethan-Heliodoran romance; it was this judgment that told young writers that their narrative experiments were worth carrying out. Hidden in the pagan setting of the *Aethiopian History*, they found a narrative practice and image of Providence compatible with Protestant ideas of destiny and divine control.

### Conspiring with Fate

> Heaven didn't forget to aid them, and by an occurance so unusual they took it for a miracle.
>
> Cervantes, *The Trials of Persiles and Sigusmunda*[60]

The complex relation between human virtue and Fortune/Providence in Heliodorus depends largely on a technical aspect of the Heliodoran model that I have already discussed: his exaggerated self-consciousness about narrative technique. Heliodorus's classical plot was more than just a strategy for appealing to diverse

---

(Oxford: Oxford University Press, 1973) 3, 418; and Victor Skretkowicz, Jr., *The Countess of Pembroke's Arcadia (The New Arcadia)*, (Oxford: Oxford University Press, 1987) 504.

[60]   Miguel de Cervantes, *The Trials of Persiles and Sigusmunda*, Celia Richmon Weller and Clark A. Colahan, trans., (Berkeley: University of California Press, 1989) 31.

reading practices; it was also a way of depicting complex truths in a heterogeneous world. As such, it was as valuable to Sidney, whose *Old* and *New Arcadia*s circulated in private manuscripts, as to Greene, who sold his books at St. Paul's. The act of narrating often takes center stage in Heliodorus, and the narrative model that Heliodorus espouses is a form of open-ended authorial conspiracy, in which his characters facilitate Providence's completion of their story.

The initial model of this practice is Calasiris. As primary teacher and narrator, Calasiris dominates the first half of the text. When Calasiris enters the tale, his first words to Cnemon echo Odysseus's retrospective narrative to King Alkinoos: "Ἰλιοθεν με ΦερωνθΦ" (*Odyssey* 58; 9.38). (Literally, as Morgan explains in his note, the phrase means, "You are carrying me from Troy.")[61] The phrase introduces Calasiris as quasi-Homeric hero, in narrative skill if not feats of arms. He may not equal Odysseus on the battlefield, but he thrives as a storyteller.

The importance of Calasiris's narrative practice has led recent critics to consider him the most important character in the *Aethiopian History*.[62] As Calasiris tells the story of Chariclea and Theagenes to the Athenian Cnemon,[63] Heliodorus educates his readers in the art of narrative. Cnemon's fascination with the lovers represents a naive response to the romance genre.[64] Cnemon wants all the luxuries associated with Greek romance: pageants, voyages, danger, beautiful young people falling in love at first sight, etc. When Calasiris wants to omit a description of a ceremony at Delphi, Cnemon protests that the story would not be complete without it: "Nay Father (quoth Cnemon, interrupting him) it is not done yet, seeing your talke hath not made mee also a looker thereon. But you slippe from me, who desire wonderfully to beholde the whole order thereof, no lesse than one (who as the proverb is) came after a feast, in as much as you have but opened the Theatre, and straight shut it up againe" (75). Cnemon's way of reading is to give himself over

---

[61] See Reardon, ed., *Collected Ancient Greek Novels*, 394n. Both Thomas Underdowne, in the sixteenth century, and J. R. Morgan, in the twentieth, avoid translating this phrase literally. Underdowne renders it, "You cause me...to remember many troubles" (58), and Morgan, "It is an Odyssey of woe" (394).

[62] As Winkler puts it, "the analysis of Kalasiris's religiosity and craftiness is simply a test case for our understanding of Heliodoros' religious and narratives strategies in general" ("The Mendacity of Kalasiris," 94).

[63] Heliodorus's characters reveal a geographic chauvinism regarding wisdom. The least wise characters, Cnemon and Theagenes, are Greek; the next wisest, Calasiris and Thyamis, are Egyptian; and the wisest of all, Chariclea and Sisimithres, are Aethiopian. For Heliodorus's elaboration of this ascending scale of wisdom, see 106, which reveals that Calasiris's time in Aethiopia has made him wiser than the typical Egyptian. Morgan's note suggests Philostratos's *Life of Apollonios* (6.6) as a possible source (*Collected Ancient Greek Novels*, 436n), which also appears in Herodotus. The sense of wisdom increasing as one travels east and south substantiates Doody's thesis that the "ancient novel" came to Europe from Africa and Asia (*True Story of the Novel*, 15-32).

[64] See Morgan, "Reader and Audience in the *Aithiopika* of Heliodoros," 99-100.

"wonderfully" to the dazzling theatricality of romance narrative.[65] For him the "wittie and pleasaunt" aspects of Heliodorus predominate; it is easier to imagine him reading the English rather than the Latin translation. Heliodorus's tale gives his reader both Cnemon's spectacle and Calasiris's philosophy, and it allows readers to choose either or both.

The spirited narrative style that Calasiris, ex-high priest of Memphis,[66] calls (in Morgan's translation) "showmanship" (422) defines his position. Rhetorical flourishes were *au courant* in the Second Sophistic as in Elizabethan England, and Calasiris's self-conscious oratorical technique would have appealed to early modern rhetoricians. When Calasiris explains that he knows about Theagenes's love for Chariclea, he plays his prophetic role to the hilt:

> I thought I then a fitte time to glose with him, and to guesse at that, which I knewe well inough. Therefore looking uppon him cherefully, I sayd, Although you bee ashamed to tell me, yet nothing canne be hidde from my wisedome, and the knowledge of the Goddes. And after I had lifted up my selfe a little, and made as though I woulde have caste some accounte with my fingers, and spreade my haire aboute mine eares, like one that would have prophesied, I saide, My Sonne thou art in love: hee started at that worde, and when I had added, with Caridlia [sic], then hee supposing I had knowen it of God, missed but a litle, that he had not fallen downe and worshipped me. (89-90)

Calasiris pokes fun at Theagenes, but he sympathizes with the young lover he advises. He never questions the oracle, nor does he doubt that the gods will clear up the feud between his own sons as a consequence of the larger story. Calasiris's "primary quest," as Winkler observes, is for "divine wisdom" and insight into the gods' plan for human affairs.[67] This sympathy with the machinations of Tyche, despite its habit of bruising individual humans,[68] marks Calasiris as model narrator for Heliodoran romance.

After Calasiris's death, Chariclea takes over his combination of active duplicity and passive faith. Her verbal prowess has marked her as Calasiris's heir and best

---

[65]  On Cnemon, see J. R. Morgan, "The Story of Knemon in Heliodoros' *Aithiopika*," *Journal of Hellenic Studies* 109 (1989): 99-113. He provides an acute response to Winkler's "Mendacity of Kalasiris" (104-6) that emphasizes Heliodorus's appeal for both Calasiris-readers and Cnemon-readers.

[66]  In a subplot, Calasiris left Memphis to avoid the temptations of the courtesan Rhodope and to avoid seeing his two sons fight over his legacy. This plot would eventually become the subplot of *King Lear*, via Sidney's episode of the Paphlagonian King (see Wolff, *The Greek Romances in Elizabethan Prose Fiction,* 312-13, 366n).

[67]  Winkler, "The mendacity of Kalasiris," 102, 138.

[68]  When Calasiris first enters, he complains that Fate prevents him from having a good day: "I cannot, quoth he, for that fortune will not so" (58). This comment appears to be one of the sage's careful truths, since he would not want a good day unless it were good because fate had chosen it. Significantly, he uses the word Tyche for fate.

pupil since the opening scene. By the tale's climax, she even sounds like Calasiris, especially when she corrects Theagenes's interpretation of his dream: "My deere harte Theagenes, our continuall calamitie maketh you take all at the woorste. For commonly men applie their minde to that which accustomable happeneth. But I thinke that thy answere seemeth to foreshewe better lucke than you suppose" (216-7).[69] From the duplicitous lover who manipulates Thyamis in the opening scene, Chariclea has become a wise interpreter of dreams, teaching Theagenes what Calasiris has taught her.

Chariclea's intelligence drives the first two narrative strategies I outlined in Chapter 1, the primacy of heroine over hero and the value of indirection. Theagenes, as Amyot and other early modern readers complained, never achieves heroic status. A descendent of Achilles, and thus a holdover from the martial world that Heliodorus abandons, he falls into the same interpretive error as the opening scene's bandits: he imagines his situation is tragic. At one point, fearing Chariclea is dead, he cries, "Farewell...this day my life, let here all feare, daungers, cares, hope, and love, have end, and be dissolved, Cariclea is dead, Theagenes is destroyed, in vaine was I unhappie man afraide, and content to betake my self to flight...O marveilous crueltie, and unspeakable wrath of the Gods" (41-2). This attribution of divine rage appears foolish when Cnemon reminds him that Chariclea is still alive. Theagenes makes the same error Thyamis had; he mistakes the slain Thisbe for Chariclea and misinterprets his own genre. He is not in a tragedy, where Fate is against him, but a romance, where Providence will be on his side once he endures its tribulations. In a world where narrative sophistication and interpretive acumen are the highest values, Theagenes's devotion to Chariclea barely counteracts his muscle-bound simplicity.

Chariclea's central task consists of learning to interpret her world correctly; she is the heroine as ideal reader. The Heliodoran world teems with violent brigands, pirates, mutinies, wicked women, and lustful men who assault the heroine. Supernatural phenomena, oracles, and prophetic dreams mislead or confuse her. These trials, however, are waystations on the providential path. After Calasiris's death, Chariclea produces the clearest expression of the way Tyche operates. After her chastity (and a magic jewel) has preserved her from being burnt at the stake, Chariclea realizes how her world works:

> For (quoth she) this strange kinde of deliverie may be though in deede to proceede of God. But still to be afflicted with such miseries, and torments without all measure, is rather a token of those who are plagued by God, and are like to fall into

---

[69] Theagenes's prophecy does seem happy: "To morrow shalt thou with the maide escape Arsaces band: / And soone be brougth with her into the Aethiopian land" (216). Theagenes interprets the maiden, "kore," as the Queen of Hades, "Aethiopian land" as the netherworld, and his freedom as death, which is not as absurd a misreading as it sounds, since the Greek "kore" could refer to Persephone, and the question of Aethiopia's dark lands being Hades had perplexed Calasiris when was interpreting an earlier prophecy (Book 4).

greater inconveniences, except there bee some more hidden mysterie which casteth into extreame perill, and when all hope is past, findeth a remedy. (215-16)

Chariclea solves her own riddle. Even though she still must reclaim her family and nationality, this speech is an interpretive triumph: she realizes that Providence is her ally, and she discovers how it operates. Here she adduces the remaining two of my four narrative strategies: the beneficence of supernatural powers and the power of passivity. At this point she recalls the dead Calasiris's words in her dream: "An easy thing to Parcae tis / though els right strange to see" (216).[70] Like Calasiris, she gives herself over to benevolent Tyche. With Providential insight and interpretive acumen, she replaces her teacher and foster-father.

The final scene of the *Aethiopian History* returns to the experiment with audience control with which the opening scene began. While the first scene divided itself to embrace diverse reading practices, the closing scene – an elaborate mixture of anagnorisis, trial by combat, and interrupted sacrifice at the Aethiopian court – initially restages this separation only to orchestrate its reunification. The models to which the text appeals include the dramatic spectacle alluded to in the opening scene as well as the equity court of King Hydaspes of Aethiopia, thus suggesting both the communal experience of the theater and the more serious and political space of a courtroom. The scene influences numerous forensic conclusions in early modern fiction – notably the trial in Sidney's *Old Arcadia* – but more broadly, Heliodorus's elaborate game of audience construction provides a conclusive model for the practice of prose fiction authorship.

This scene replaces the Egyptian beach with the Aethiopian throne room. The people of Aethiopia, the final image of a popular audience in Heliodorus, greet Hydaspes "as if he had bene a god" (262) and then settle into a space that seems half theater, half church: "[Hydaspes] sate in a tabernacle made ready before for that purpose.... In an other tabernacle hard by this upon places above were set the images of that countrey Gods, and the pictures of noble men, especially of Memmon, Perseus, and Andromeda, whom the kings of Aethiopia supposed to be the authors of their stocke. In other seates beneath sate the Gymnosophistes, and had in maner their Gods over their heades" (262-3). The stage divides into three – a space for Hydaspes and his family, one for Gods and mythological figures, and one for philosophers – and is surrounded by soldiers, thus indicating the heterogeneous structural basis of the kingdom and the show that will follow.

The basic narrative tactic of the recognition scene is delay: Chariclea, who knows very well that Hydaspes is her father and that she can prove it, puts off revealing her identity until she deems the time ripe. Theagenes's frustration calls attention to her delay: "But Cariclia why do you not nowe manifest your selfe? What other time do you looke for hereafter? Wil you tarrie till one come to cutte

---

[70] Here Underdowne uses the Latin *Parcae* for the Fates. Morgan's translation is clearer: "Miracles may come to pass: for Fate 'tis easy game" (528).

our throtes?" (265). The emphasis on Chariclea's reluctance suggests that delay lies at the heart of her strategy of self-presentation; in this context, the emphasis on the virginity of both heroine (265) and hero (264) can be read as a symbol of an interpretive gambit, in which something valuable must be concealed in order to reveal it later under more propitious terms. The Aethiopian sage Sisimithres also begins this scene by refusing to communicate with the masses: when he and his Gymnosophists reject the blood sacrifice demanded by Aethiopian custom, Sisimithres speaks "in Greeke, that the people might not heare it" (266). This reminder of the linguistic heterogeneity of the scene – a mass who speak only Aethiopian watching an elite who also speak Greek – marks the self-conscious division of the audience that precedes the reunification of family and nation.

This reunion progresses through a combination of public spectacles, especially the virginity tests and Theagenes's wrestling against a bull and an Aethiopian champion and private communications, especially Chariclea's private conference with her mother which finally makes her identity clear (284). Chariclea's claim to be Hydaspes's daughter gets greeted with skepticism, and the king rejects it precisely because it seems too much like fiction: "Is not the maide starke mad? Who of singular boldnes with lies seeketh to avoyde death, and saith she is my daughter, as if it were a Comedie?" (268). The analogy to drama, and implicitly to the opening scene, gets raised as a challenge – Chariclea's ploy seems too theatrical to be credible – but the people are not as discerning as the king: "The whole multitude of the Aethiopians… would not suffer him to lead Cariclea one foote further, but cried out suddenly alowde Save the maide, save the bloud royall, save her whom the Goddes will have saved" (279). The three explanations they offer – Chariclea's singular status, her royal blood, the Gods' manifest will – suggest that the crowd reads according to narrative conventions also but they are less hostile to melodramatic flourishes.

The distinction Heliodorus draws between the spectacle as Hydaspes wishes to present it, in which a king holds firm to the customs of his land even at the cost of a long-lost daughter, and that which the crowd prefers, in which the maid's return allows the abnegation of ancient custom, makes the narrative's final turn against sacrifice an endorsement of middlebrow reading practices. The preferences of the crowd, however, while not shared by their king, match those of the super-elite Gymnosophistes, who return to preside over the refusal of human sacrifice. Even the crowd's ability to express an opinion is something of a miracle, since much of the conversion has taken place either in Greek, in private, or both. When the crowd bestows its approval, Hydaspes's sneering reference to drama gets recast: "The people in another place rejoyced, and almost daunced for joy, and with one consent were all gladde of that which was donne, marry all they understoode not, but gathered the most part of Cariclea. Perhappes also they were styrred to understand the truth by inspiration of the Gods, whose wil it was that this should fal out woonderfully, as in a Comedie" (288). At this moment Sisimithres changes his linguistic relation to the masses: "Thereunto Sisimithres answered not in Greeke, but in the Aethiopian tongue, that all might understand him" (288). The final revelation of heroine and hero's identity leads not only to the expected marriage and installation of Chariclea and Theagenes as priest-kings of Aethiopia, but also to the religious improvement of the nation. Sisimithres provides a national moral for the spectacle: "Lette us therefore suffer divine miracles to sinke in our mindes, and be healpers of their will, and doo more acceptable sacrifices to them, and leave murthering, of men, and women for ever hereafter" (288). This finale, which Sisimithres himself calls "the ende and conclusion of this comedie" (288), combines the diverse reading practices invited into the text by the opening tableau: the philosophical reader gets moral edification, the sentimental reader a long-deferred marriage, the political reader a revitalized nation, and the purely hedonic reader an elaborate game of artfully delayed narrative wonder. Heliodorus's romance shows that mass appeal and narrative sophistication need not be mutually exclusive, and for a generation of English writers learning to build careers through the marketplace of print, this insight proved invaluable.

# Chapter 3

# Anti-Epic Traditions: Sidney's *New Arcadia*

Atrides' ghost gave answer: "O bless'd son
Of old Laertes, thou at length hast won
With mighty virtue thy unmatched wife.
How good a knowledge, how untouch'd a life,
Hath wise Penelope! How well she laid
Her husband's rights up, whom she loved a maid!
For which her virtues shall extend applause
Beyond the circles frail mortality draws;
They deathless in this vale comprising
Her praise in numbers into infinites rising."

*The Odyssey* (24)[1]

One reason romance has been poorly defined, in the early modern era and the present day, is the lack of any classical exemplar. A Heliodorus revival cannot fully redress this problem, since his name will never rival Homer's or Virgil's. The problem, however, is less the lack of a model than the co-opting of an ideal text into a rival genre. Romance, it should be clear, has an early forerunner in Homer's *Odyssey*. As Hubert McDermott notes, "the term romance seems to express perfectly the essential dissimilarity which exists between the *Odyssey* and the *Iliad*."[2] The *Odyssey* contains the building blocks of all subsequent romances: a formal pattern of loss, wandering, and recovery, a disguised or unknown hero, a prominent heroine, a belated recognition scene, and greater emphasis than epic on the domestic and feminine. Plot motifs like shipwreck, prophecy, capture, and disguise exemplify the plot, and while combat and masculine force are not absent, they do not dominate. Odysseus is as much conniver as warrior; even the slaughter of the suitors, his most martial exploit, is facilitated by foresight and indirection rather than overpowering rage.

---

[1]  George Chapman, trans., *The Odysseys of Homer*, Richard Hooper, intro., 2 vols. (London: John Russell Smith, 1857) 2:257. Orig. published 1614-15.

[2]  See Hubert McDermott, *Novel and Romance: The* Odyssey *to* Tom Jones, (London: Macmillan, 1989) 12. See also Robert J. Ellrich, "Prolegomenon: or, Preliminary Musings to make the gentle reader think, or fume, or snort. In which we modestly propose to deal with the origin, history, and meaning of the Romance," *Para-doxa* 3 (1997): 273-4.

The importance of Penelope provides strong evidence that the *Odyssey* should be re-classified as romance. She does not travel in the wandering-phase of the story, as Chariclea and her Elizabethan descendents will, but her cunning and rhetorical skill complement her husband's heroism. As John Winkler observes, "Penelope, constrained as she is by the competing and irreconcilable demands of social propriety, exerts some degree of real control over events and makes possible the homecoming of her husband, outwitting many deadly enemies and a few friends in the process."[3] Her deceptions, including unweaving of Laertes's shroud, announcing of the archery contest, and the trick she plays on Odysseus about the great bed, establish a pattern for the romance-heroines who follow her.[4]

The problem for early modern and modern literary criticism is that the *Odyssey* has been since Aristotle misleadingly categorized as epic. As neo-Aristotelian categories became prominent in sixteenth-century Italy, claims for the its epic status hardened. That Virgil's *Aeneid* drew on both the *Odyssey* and the *Iliad* helped solidify all three poems as epics. Italian epic theory engaged early modern verse *romanzi*, attacking or defending the poems of Ariosto and Boiardo in relation to epic norms. Even for defenders of romance, entering this debate often meant accepting Aristotle's mono-generic format; Pigna's defense of Ariosto refuses to distinguish between romance and epic.[5] As the debate continued, romance became a battleground for the struggle between ancients and moderns. Neo-Aristotelians like Minturno and Tasso claimed that romance was "a defective and transgressive kind of heroic composition," while Cinthio countered that romance was a "new kind of poetry [that] could not be judged by ancient epic norms."[6] Thus when Scaliger, Amyot, Underdowne, and others defended Heliodorus as an epic poet, they side-stepped this Italian polemic. If Heliodorus was a viable model, prose writers could avoid choosing between Aristotle and Ariosto. These scholars stopped short of theorizing Heliodoran romance as distinct from the epic, but that should not prevent modern critics from seeing its anti-epic qualities.

Once we reconsider the generic sameness of the *Odyssey* and the *Iliad*, the esteem of sixteenth-century humanists for Heliodorus seems particularly telling. The *Odyssey*, and Ulysses himself, were undergoing reevaluation in early modern Europe, with medieval distaste for the lying hero being replaced by early modern admiration for the politician. The anti-Greek polemics of redactors from Pindar to Dictys and Dares were giving way to a new appreciation of the wily hero. For humanists like Ascham and Elyot, Ulysses was a hero of "policy," a virtuous

---

[3] *The Constraints of Desire: The Anthropology of Sex and Gender in Ancient Greece*, (London: Routledge, 1990) 133.

[4] Winkler notes that in tricking Odysseus, Penelope reveals how Homer has been tricking the reader into underestimating female power (*Constraints of Desire*, 158).

[5] See Javitch, "Italian epic theory," *The Cambridge History of Literary Criticism*, Volume 3, 211.

[6] See Javitch, "Italian epic theory," 213, 211.

Machiavel, and this picture colors depictions of his exploits in Sidney, Spenser, Peele, and Greene.[7] Heliodorus's return also highlighted the anti-epic elements of the *Odyssey*. The *Aethiopica*, indebted to the *Odyssey* and polemically engaged with modifying its form, became known as a "splendid" model for literary construction, but the works that followed this model bore little resemblance to Iliadic epic.

Heliodorus self-consciously modeled himself on the *Odyssey* in a combative way. Given the *Aethiopian History*'s interest in virtuous deception and mendacious narration it seems inevitable that Odysseus would be important. In fact, Heliodorus moves beyond allusion to give the Ithacan hero a role in his story. Odysseus's presence clarifies how Heliodorus distinguishes himself from Homer. Heliodorus welcomes romance indirection but dismisses epic violence. He also privileges the chaste heroine over the martial hero.

In Book 5, halfway through the narrative, Chariclea and Theagenes are stranded on an island with Calasiris. The night before they leave, Calasiris has a prophetic dream:

> After wee had eaten a slender supper, and were gone to bedde, an olde man appeared to me in my sleepe, whose bodie was dried up, yet he had a dish tied to his girdle, who seemed in his youth to have beene a tall man: he had a hatte on his head, and seemed by his countenaunce , that he had bene a wise, and subtile man: marry he halted a little, as if he had gotten some wound in his thigh: who after hee came neare me, smiled a little with an angrie countenaunce, and said: You good man, alone of all that have sailed by Caphalene, and looked upon my house, and accoumpted it a great matter to know my renoune, have had no respect to mee, but have set to light by mee, that you would not speake to mee, which everie man dooth, for all I dwelt so neere you, but you shall ere long bee punished for this, and shall have like perilles as I had, and fall into your enemies hand, as well by land as seas. As for the maide that thou carriest with thee, speake to her, and greete her, in my wives name, because she esteemeth more of her virginitie, then any thing in the world, wherefore she shall have a lucky end. (136)

That the shade of Odysseus berates Calasiris suggests that Heliodorus does not simply place his story under Homer's wing. The exchange underlines the contrast between Homer's solitary warrior-hero and Heliodorus's ancient Calasiris and virginal Chariclea. The allusions in Heliodorus's description of Odysseus present a complex picture.[8] The strong thigh (which Underdowne renders as being a "tall man") and leather helmet (called a "hatte") accent martial prowess, but the

---

[7] See W. B. Stanford, *The Ulysses Theme: A Study in the Adaptability of a Traditional Hero*, 2nd ed. (Ann Arbor: University of Michigan Press, 1968), 296-303.

[8] Morgan catalogs the allusions in his footnote: "The withering of age refers to the disguise given by Athene at *Odyssey* 13.398ff; the strong thigh comes from *Odyssey* 18.66ff.; the leather helmet from *Iliad* 10.261ff.; the Homeric words for "cunning" and "of many wiles" from *Odyssey* 13.332 and 1.2, respectively; the wound in the leg is the boar-inflicted scar from *Odyssey* 19.392ff" (*Collected Ancient Greek Novels*, 462n).

reference to his dried-up body echoes his disguise as a beggar upon returning to Ithaca, and Odysseus wore the leather helmet, the property of his maternal grandfather, the thief Autolycus, during a night raid in the *Iliad*.[9] Even these martial accoutrements thus accent his trickster qualities. Explicit references to Odyssean indirection follow in the words "wise" and "subtile." (The Greek is *polytropos*.) The description mutes the military hero of the *Iliad* to accent the romance mode of the *Odyssey*. Heliodorus's narrative sever the two halves of the Homeric model, and present in polytropic tricksters who have no martial, Iliadic aspect. Odysseus's attack on Calasiris reinforces the notion that he and Chariclea reject the warlike half of the Homeric model.[10]

Penelope's message to Chariclea further highlights the *Aethiopian History*'s reworking of the *Odyssey*. Each story chronicles a lengthy quest to return home, but Chariclea's benediction comes from Penelope, not Odysseus, because her chastity, not her strength, proves essential for her "lucky end." She takes chastity from Penelope and wiles from both her and Odysseus, but never needs the hero's strong sword.[11] She does slay a number of bandits, notably with bow and arrows, weapons that Odysseus uses to slay the suitors at Penelope's request.

Even before this rejection of Odysseus, Calasiris has provided a radically untraditional reading of Homer. While telling Cnemon how he brought Chariclea and Theagenes to Egypt, Calasiris states that Homer was Egyptian, not Greek. This bizarre claim about the poet's birth enables Calasiris to draw two explicit connections between Homer and himself. First, he argues that Homer's poetry, like his own search for Chariclea's homeland, is motivated by the quest for divine presence in mortal affairs: "the skillful Homer, like an Egyptian, and one well instructed in the holy doctrine, secretly and closly signified in his verses, leaving it to the understanding of such as could attaine thereto" (87). By making Homer an exiled Egyptian wandering from city to city, Calasiris imagines him to be in the same situation as himself and Chariclea:

> he was our Countryman, an Egyptian, borne at Thebes, which hath an hundred gates, as of him self a man may know, and his father a Priest, as some thinke, and not Mercurie, as is falsely fained. His father was supposed to be a prieste, because that the God lay with his wife doing certain sacrifices after the manner of the countrie, and fell on sleepe in the temple, and there ingendred Homer, who had about him token of unlawfull generation, for on both his thighs there grewe from his birth a great deal of hair (87-88).

---

[9]   On Odysseus's "Autolycan" side, see Stanford, *The Ulysses Theme*, 8-24.

[10]  Calasiris recognizes the shade and sends an ally to sacrifice to him at Ithaca. Calasiris's sudden death in Book 7 may recall Odysseus's curse, but by that time the Egyptian sage has passed his knowledge to Chariclea.

[11]  The one martial episode in the *Aethiopian History* comes in Book 9, and it relates the triumph of the managerial tactics of Xenophon's Cyrus more than the heroics of the *Iliad*. The siege of Syene refers obliquely to Homer's siege of Troy, but Hydaspes's methodical strategy and self-control are far from the rage of Achilles.

Like Chariclea's white skin, the hair on Homer's thighs brands him an exile. Chariclea's triumph over her exile, her return to the court of Aethiopia, indicates Heliodorus's rapprochement with half of Homer's legacy. This combative relationship with epic frames the Heliodoran fictions of Sidney, Greene, and the other Elizabethan Heliodoranists.

## Reason, Faith, and Shipwreck

> Woe unto him who seeks to pour oil upon the waters when God has brewed them into a gale!
>
> *Moby-Dick*

The *New Arcadia* begins with shipwreck. Sidney's narrator portrays "a sight full of piteous strangeness: a ship, or rather the carcase of the ship, or rather some few bones of the carcase hulling there, part broken, part burned, part drowned – death having used more than one dart to that destruction" (66). Amid the wreckage float mutilated corpses and a "great store of rich things" (66). This scene, when juxtaposed with the text's other shipwrecks, reveals a fictional structure through which Sidney explores the relative merits of reason and faith in understanding human experience. As one might expect from an incomplete text, the *New Arcadia* does not yield any simple conclusions, but its elaboration of the shipwreck *topos* shows Sidney using Heliodoran romance to debate views of reason and faith that are neither as neoplatonic nor as Calvinist as some critics have assumed. In three scenes of shipwreck, Sidney treats faith as superior to reason but sees the two as interactive, a position which allows him to qualify the Reformation's attack on this-worldly values with his hopes for human intellect. The standard means of transportation in Greek romance becomes for Sidney a vehicle for humanist and theological debate. His fiction focuses on the Heliodoran strategies of passivity and acceptance of supernatural control as it rewrites the epic as theological speculation.

Investigating this topic brings one face to face with the unsettled status of reason and faith in Sidney studies. Where critics once held that Sidney – "that rare thing, the aristocrat in whom the aristocratic ideal is truly embodied," as C. S. Lewis called him – embodied Renaissance humanism, recent work has emphasized his eclectic nature.[12] The question has become not whether Sidney was a humanist, but which strain – civic, neoplatonic, Erasmian, Stoic, Ciceronian, hybrid – best fits him. Critical opinion has shifted from John Danby's confident description of

---

[12] See C. S. Lewis, *English Literature in the Sixteenth Century Excluding Drama*, (Oxford: Clarendon, 1954) 324. On Sidney's humanism, see also, John Danby, *Poets on Fortune's Hill: Studies in Sidney, Shakespeare, Beaumont and Fletcher*, (London: Faber & Faber, 1952), and Walter Davis, *A Map of Arcadia: Sidney's Romance in Its Tradition*, (New Haven: Yale University Press, 1965).

Sidney's "conjunction of the Christian and the Nichomachean ethics" to studies that emphasize "contradiction and irresolution."[13] Recent studies have made it clear that the tradition of describing Sidney as a "Platonist Protestant" does not do justice to his intellectual range and critical rigor.[14] Arthur Kinney calls him "a man of contradictions" who not only embraced humanism but also produced "a considered reexamination of the precepts and practices advocated by Tudor humanists."[15] Richard Helgerson further claims that the *Arcadia* represents a retreat from humanist principles, even though Sidney's first readers denied this.[16] Wesley Trimpi has pointed out that Sidney's *Defence*, often called neoplatonic, rejects neoplatonic analysis for a Ciceronian/Aristotelian approach.[17] At every turn, Sidney's attacks on intellectual folly counterbalance his hopes for human reason; every "erected wit" has its "infected will."

Protestantism provides an alternate focus for Sidney's career, but his religion appears no less contradictory than his humanism.[18] Sidney was part of the political faction of Leicester and Walsingham, who advocated an alliance with Dutch Protestants and sympathized with Calvinism.[19] The notion that Elizabethan theology contained a "Calvinist consensus" regarding grace and election, however,

---

[13] Danby, *Poets on Fortune's Hill*, 47; Richard McCoy, *Sir Philip Sidney: Rebellion in Arcadia*, New Brunswick: Rutgers Univ. Press, 1979), x. Other recent scholars have accented Sidney's intellectual range: Nancy Lindheim emphasizes his "this-worldly" rejection of neoplatonism (*Structures of Sidney's Arcadia*, 10); Joan Rees his "exploratory mode" and evolving opinions (*Sir Philip Sidney and Arcadia*, [Cranbury, NJ: Associated Univ. Presses, 1991], 8); O. B. Hardison, Jr., the "two distinct and discordant voices" of the *Defence* ("The Two Voices of Sidney's *Apology for Poetry*," *English Literary Renaissance* 2 [1972]: 97); and Stephen Greenblatt the *Arcadia*'s "mixed mode" (Sidney's *Arcadia* and the Mixed Mode," *Studies in Philology* 70 [1973]: 269.)

[14] For an uncritical use of the old categories, see Blair Worden, *The Sound of Virtue: Philip Sidney's* Arcadia *and Elizabethan Politics*, (New Haven: Yale Univ. Press, 1996), 32.

[15] *Humanist Poetics*, 235-36.

[16] *Elizabethan Prodigals*, 127-8 and *passim*.

[17] Wesley Trimpi, "Sir Philip Sidney's *An apology for poetry*," *The Cambridge History of Literary Criticism, Volume 3: The Renaissance*, Glyn Norton, ed., (Cambridge: Cambridge Univ. Press, 1989), 187.

[18] The seminal study is Andrew Weiner, *Sir Philip Sidney and the Poetics of Protestantism*, (Minneapolis: Univ. of Minnesota Press, 1978). See also Duncan-Jones, *Sir Philip Sidney: Courtier-Poet*; Alan Sinfield, *Literature in Protestant England, 1560-1660*, (London: Croom Helm), 20-48; Michael McCanles, *The Text of Sidney's Arcadian World*, (Durham: Duke Univ. Press, 1989) 125-34; Rees, *Sir Philip Sidney and Arcadia*, 135; Lindheim, *Structures of Sidney's Arcadia*, 25; and Kinney, *Humanist Poetics*, 236-7.

[19] Worden claims that neither Sidney nor his Huguenot mentor Languet was strictly a Calvinist (*Sound of Virtue*, 32, 52). Penry Williams also notes that the Elizabethan church contained "doctrines that were closer to those of Calvin than to any other Continental reformer, but could only misleadingly be called 'Calvinist'" (*The Later Tudors, 1547-1603*, [Oxford: Clarendon Press, 1995] 458).

has been challenged since the 1980s.[20] Although the Book of Common Prayer took a semi-Calvinist position on the Eucharist, and godly preachers like William Perkins and Arthur Dent were popular on the pulpit and in print, the English Reformation was ideologically very mixed.[21] When considering the four strains of English Protestantism that Penry Williams sees as influential during the late Tudor period – reformers like Grindal, anti-Presbyterians like Whitgift, proto-Arminians like Andrewes, and advocates of reason and natural law like Hooker – it has been standard to link Sidney to the reformers.[22] (The tribute to Grindal in Spenser's *Shepheardes Calendar*, a text dedicated to Sidney, emphasizes the point.) In the *New Arcadia*, however, Sidney appears less hostile to human reason than many reformers. Sidney's defense of reason never becomes as explicit (or anti-Puritan) as Hooker's, but he strains against the orthodox reformed position.[23] Sidney had no doubts about the superiority of faith to reason, but he did not reject reason entirely.

Shipwreck in the *New Arcadia* provides Sidney's most striking image of absolute Providential control. The wrecks complement the project of his friend, the Huguenot theologian Philip de Mornay, in the treatise *De La Vérité de la religion chrestienne* (1581): making divine Providence appear reasonable to human minds.[24] For Mornay,

> Prouidece [sic] is nothing els but a wise guyding of things to their end, and that euery reasonable mynd that woorketh, beginneth his worke for some end, and that God (as I haue said afore) the workmaister of all things, hath (or to say more truely) is the soureine mynd, equall to his owne power: doth it not follow that God in creating the worlde, did purpose an end?(Sig. L7v)[25]

The crucial term, for Mornay and Sidney as Protestants, and for Sidney as a writer of romance, is "end." A purposed end imagines God as a Supreme Author,

---

[20] See Christopher Haigh, ed., *The English Reformation Revisited*, (Cambridge: Cambridge University Press, 1987).

[21] See, for example, Christopher Haigh, *The English Reformations: Religion, Politics, and Society under the Tudors*, (Oxford: Oxford Univ. Press, 1993); Williams, *The Later Tudors*; Peter Lake, *Anglicans and Puritans?: Presbyterianism in English Conformist Thought from Whitgift to Hooker*, (London: Unwin Hyman, 1988).

[22] See *The Later Tudors*, 489.

[23] Williams claims that Hooker's embrace of the "Gradual Improvement of Human Reason" was "perhaps his most important contribution to the ideological base of the Church of England" (*The Later Tudors*, 488-9).

[24] Sidney would begin translating this work soon after he left off revising the *New Arcadia*. Modern critics believe that Sidney's contribution to the translation was small, probably no more than a draft of eight chapters (out of thirty-four), all of which Golding subsequently revised. See Duncan-Jones, *Sir Philip Sidney*, 251-74.

[25] Philip du Plessis Mornay, *A Woorke Concerning the Trewnesse of the Christian Religion*, (Delmar, NY: Scholars' Facsimiles and Reprints, 1976), 174. First ed. 1587. I first encountered this passage in Kinney, *Humanist Poetics*, 287.

maneuvering the history of humankind according to His elaborate plotline. The end of the story redeems its beginnings. For Sidney's fictional characters, this problem becomes literal, as shipwrecks make their "ends" seem likely to be death by drowning.

The tautology at the heart of Mornay's definition of Providence opens the door for Sidney's literary experiment. Mornay's God, "the workmaister of all things," controls events in the world, but His "end" is irrevocably aloof from human experience. God is "the souereine mynd, equall to his owne power," but He is only "reasonable" in His own terms. Human reason cannot grasp the divine mentality. In a pre-Christian fiction, however, Sidney is released from religious orthodoxy into an arena of intellectual freedom. His pagan surrogates rely on human mental ingenuity without the saving crutch of faith. The *New Arcadia*, by combining a pagan setting with disembodied determinist control, creates a haven for speculation into theological truisms.

Sidney's concern with the status of reason in a fallen world, as Åke Bergvall has noted, has made him "a focal point for a broader investigation of the interaction between humanism and reformation."[26] Observing that a hard line between human reason and divine power was defended by Erasmus as well as Luther and Calvin, Bergvall suggests that Sidney demonstrates the compatibility of humanism and Protestantism.[27] By exploring the shipwrecks in the *New Arcadia*, I hope to complicate Bergvall's observations. I believe that "compatibility" goes too far; the relationship Sidney explores is fraught and combative. In fact, Bergvall's reading of the *Arcadia* – that it "warn[s] against the dangers accompanying the trespass over" the boundary between the "two Kingdoms"[28] – fails to recognize how shipwreck problematizes that very boundary.

Even the most emphatic reformed spokesmen, as Bergvall observes, did not dismiss reason outright. Rather, Luther, Calvin, and their followers valued reason so long as it kept "within its boundaries."[29] According to Calvin, reason by itself is "suffycyente for ryghte gouernaunce," but should not presume to judge questions of "personal ethics" or "moral laws."[30] Luther, in his debate with Erasmus, emphasizes the complementary point: "Human Reason . . . is blind, deaf, stupid, impious, and sacrilegious with regard to all the words and works of God."[31] Despite the appeal (for modern as well as Renaissance humanists) of Erasmus's working-together ("*synergos*") between human will and divine power, early modern Protestantism strictly limited reason's value. Sidney, while rejecting

---

[26]   Åke Bergvall, "Reason in Luther, Calvin, and Sidney," *Sixteenth-Century Journal* 23 (1992): 115.

[27]   See Bergvall, "Reason," 115, 117-21.

[28]   Bergvall, "Reason," 122.

[29]   Bergvall, "Reason," 117.

[30]   Calvin, *Institutes*, II.ii.3; quoted in Bergvall, "Reason," 119. Bergvall, "Reason," 121.

[31]   Luther and Erasmus, *Luther and Erasmus: Free Will and Salvation*, E. Gordon Rupp and Philip S. Watson, eds., (Philadelphia: Westminster Press, 1969) 230.

Erasmian compromise, was not content to let the barrier between human and divine
remain impenetrable. The *New Arcadia* uses shipwreck to interrogate this barrier
from a mortal perspective.

Examining the heroes' attitudes toward shipwreck reveals that, for Sidney,
unlike Luther, reason is only partially blocked from the divine. Reason is valuable
because it rejects false explanations, intuits Providential control, and then
recognizes its limits. This modest hermeneutic accomplishment does little to
alleviate terror on a sinking ship. It does, however, clarify the relation between
reason and faith in Sidney's fiction. The two Kingdoms are not absolutely separate,
and reason can recognize the point at which it must not claim more knowledge
than it possesses. As in Heliodorus, human virtue is passive and interpretive,
waiting for truth to emerge.

Sidney's narrator offers no explanation for the opening wreck. His only
conclusion is negative; he warns against false interpretations. Like Calasiris and
Chariclea, he defers untenable conclusions. All he claims is that the sea is not
entirely to blame: "And amidst the precious things there were a number of dead
bodies, which likewise did not only testify both elements' [the sea's and the
storm's] violence, but that the chief violence was grown of human inhumanity . . .
which [blood] it seemed the sea would not wash away that it might witness it is not
always his fault when we condemn his cruelty" (66). Sidney's narrator rejects the
assumption that the wreck was caused by divine wrath or caprice. "[H]uman
inhumanity" is a contributing cause, and human causes should be sought before
divine ones. This modest but rational approach forestalls misinterpretation without
advancing a coherent explanation. Neither weather nor poor sailing are to blame; it
is "a shipwreck without storm or ill-footing" (66). The cause remains a mystery of
the deep, which is not cleared up for some three hundred pages.[32]

Like Heliodorus's bandits, the fishermen who accompany Musidorus offer a
rival interpretation. The fishermen are pagans, but like rigid reformed believers
they believe the wreck's cause is purely supernatural: "assuredly it was some God
begotten between Neptune and Venus that had made all this terrible slaughter"
(66). They see no role for human malice. Full of "superstition" (66), the fishermen
"ma[ke] their prayers" (67) instead of throwing Pyrocles a line. Their pagan
naiveté, however, should not obscure their possible insight into the wreck. The
fishermen are not wrong to seek a supernatural explanation; they simply invoke the
wrong supernatural vocabulary. Their interpretation presents an extreme version,
or pagan parody, of Calvinist predestination.[33]

---

[32] The evil Plexirtus paid the ship's crew to kill the princes, as Pyrocles reveals much later
(370-6).

[33] As William Elton notes, the *Arcadia* explores Christian ideas from a pagan perspective
(King Lear *and the Gods*, [San Marino: Huntington Library Press, 1969] 34-62).

In contrast to these alternatives is Sidney's ideal understanding of shipwreck, the Biblical wreck of Saint Paul (Acts 27-8).[34] When Paul and his companions fear for their lives during "a tempestuous wind," Paul is granted a saving vision: an "angel of the Lord" comes to him and says "Fear not, Paul . . . and, lo, God hath given thee [safety for] all that sail with thee" (Acts 27:23-4).[35] Paul and his companions take heart in divine revelation and conquer their fears.[36] Sidney's heroes, unfortunately, do not ship with Saint Paul. The assurance Paul receives from the angel they can only struggle toward with unaided reason. Like Pamela refuting Cecropia, they must derive the core of Christianity without angels or sacred texts. The challenge of shipwreck in the *New Arcadia* is duplicating the results of Paul's faith without receiving his vision.

Sidney's romance begins by juxtaposing the fishermen's faux-Calvinist submission to divine power against the narrator's claims for "human inhumanity." Reconciling these points of view becomes one of the text's central interpretive challenges. Shipwrecks recur at two other crucial junctures in the plot. These moments are scattered within the expanse of the *New Arcadia*, but their prominence as romance *topoi* suggest they should be read against each other. All three wrecks initiate important narrative transitions. Wrecks drive the two young princes to Asia Minor (initiating the adventures of Book 2) and later to Arcadia (for Book 1), and a final wreck brings Euarchus to them for the dénouement (Book 5). These episodes are structurally identical: shipwreck wrenches control from the heroes' hands, and Sidney's plot shifts direction.

Shipwrecks subject Sidney's heroes to trials in which the virtues of dry land – especially humanist reason – becomes weaknesses rather than strengths. Looking at Pyrocles, Musidorus, and Euarchus as shipwrecked sailors inverts the standard hierarchy in which Euarchus is a model king, Musidorus a prince-in-training, and Pyrocles a youth who cannot contain his desires. (This reading has been challenged recently, but still claims impressive advocates.) Pyrocles, whose reason falls most abjectly to his passion, gains the most insight from shipwreck; Musidorus remains largely baffled; and Euarchus learns nothing at all. This new hierarchy among these heroes implies a critique of reason and ethical rectitude; these virtues are valuable in crises like shipwreck only to the extent that they recognize and accept human dependence on extra-human forces.

Since the details of Sidney's revision will never be known, it is uncertain which shipwreck he wrote first. I shall examine the wrecks in order of increasing comprehension by the primary hero involved, starting with Euarchus's failure to

---

[34]   On Paul's adventure in relation to classical depictions of shipwreck, see Susan Marie Praeder, "Acts 27:1-28:16: Sea Voyages in Ancient Literature and the Theology of Luke-Acts, " *The Catholic Biblical Quarterly* 46 (1984): 683-706.

[35]   Authorized Version.

[36]   Praeder argues that Paul and his companions become an image of Christian community and thereby depart from classical depictions of shipwreck ("Theology," 699-700).

understand his wreck, then Musidorus's politicized oversimplification of the wreck off Asia Minor, and last Pyrocles's partial explanation of the opening mystery, the wreck that brings the princes to Arcadia. This three-part reading may appear schematic, but it has the virtue of exposing a basic structural feature of Sidney's romance. In these episodes Sidney develops a positive interplay between the resources of reason and the demands of faith. The princes do not understand Providence any more than Chariclea does Tyche, but by refusing false explanations Pyrocles perceives more than his father or cousin. Acknowledging powers that he cannot explain leads him to a middle position between the rationality of the narrator and the superstition of the fishermen. He uses reason to move toward partial recognition of divinity, which is as far as reason can take him.

### *"An extreme tempest": Euarchus and the Failure of Reason Alone*

Euarchus's shipwreck, one of the few revisions Sidney made to Book 5, presents the simplest handling of the *topos* in the *New Arcadia*.[37] It portrays the limits of unaided reason. This wreck replaces Euarchus's sudden decision in the *Old Arcadia* to make "a long and tedious journey to visit his old friend and confederate the duke Basilius."[38] A meeting that once arose from Euarchus's fellow-feeling for a neighboring head of state is now caused by God's storm. Book 5 needs Euarchus to step into the power vacuum Basilius's false death has left in Arcadia, but it is not his political acumen that gets him to the troubled kingdom.

The tempest that re-directs Euarchus's ship is simple and inexplicable: "[Euarchus] had in a short time run a long course when on a night, encountered with an extreme tempest, his ships were so scattered that scarcely any two were left together" (790). In the phrase, "encountered with an extreme tempest," not very different from the *Old Arcadia*'s "terrible tempest," Euarchus's navy and his earthly kingdom disappear, leaving the king a solitary adventurer on the "unhappy coast of Laconia" (790) – exactly where the young princes were cast away in Book 1. Once again, shipwreck shifts a Greek prince from political adventures (the princes' exploits in Asia Minor, Euarchus's defeat of Byzantium) to interpersonal ones (the princes' love affairs, Euarchus's judging of the Arcadian crisis).

---

[37] For post-1590 revisions to the *New Arcadia*, see William Leigh Godshalk, "Sidney's Revision of the *Arcadia*, Books III-V," *Philological Quarterly* 43 (1964): 171-84. These revisions may have been made by Mary Sidney or Fulke Greville in accordance with Philip Sidney's wishes, or for reasons of their own.

[38] Sir Philip Sidney, *The Old Arcadia*, Katharine Duncan-Jones, ed., (Oxford: Oxford Univ. Press, 1985) 305. Only the initial wreck appears in the *Old Arcadia*: "But so it pleased God, who reserved [Pyrocles and Musidorus] to greater traverses, both of good and evil fortune, that the sea to which they committed themselves, stirred with terrible tempest, forced them to fall far from their course upon the coast of Lydia" (10). In addition, Pyrocles as Cleophila invents a tale of shipwreck to explain his arrival in Arcadia (33).

Euarchus, however, fails to realize that the game has changed. His attempt to apply rigorous justice and reason to the Arcadian crisis nearly causes disaster.

Euarchus is an ideal king, but events in Arcadia expose him as overly dogmatic. His errors stem from his inability to make the cognitive leap shipwreck requires. He trusts human reason and forgets superhuman control. The first four Books of the *New Arcadia* idealize him, but always in a political context, on dry land. Musidorus describes him as the perfect king: "For how could they choose but love him, whom they found so truly to love them? ... In sum ... I might as easily set down the whole art of government as to lay before your eyes the picture of his proceedings" (255-6). Like Xenophon's Cyrus, Euarchus represents the political duty that Sidney's generation felt it owed the Elizabethan state.[39]

Scattering Euarchus's navy and casting him ashore in Arcadia turn the ideal king into an untutored romance hero. Viewing his character this way can clarify one of the critical controversies surrounding Book 5, in which the ideal legislator appears willing to execute his own son. Numerous recent critics have pointed out flaws in Euarchus's justice.[40] While Pyrocles and Musidorus use their shipwrecks to start new phases of education, Euarchus enters Arcadia believing his rational code is all he needs to know. I concur with critics who see Book 5 as criticizing Euarchus, but even Stephen Greenblatt's conclusion that the trial shows that "wisdom can be hopelessly inadequate"[41] fails to account for Sidney's interweaving of human reason and divine power. Wisdom alone is inadequate, but the text does not abandon its reader to the impotence Greenblatt suggests. The *New Arcadia* suggests that human reason can be trusted only so far, but it replaces "wisdom" with a combination of reason and a partial perception of extra-human Providence. The lesson Euarchus misses is the lesson of Paul's tempest: do not judge what you cannot know. Recognition of divine control, which is (barely) comprehensible to human reason, can supplement the rational humanism that Greenblatt and others rightly see Book 5 criticizing.[42]

---

[39] Helgerson sees the conflict between prodigal literary forms like romance and practical careers as statesmen as "the dilemma of Sidney's generation" (*Elizabethan Prodigals*, 16-43, 139).

[40] See, e.g., Elizabeth Dipple, "'Unjust Justice' in the *Old Arcadia*," *Studies in English Literature* 10 (1970): 83-101, 93-4; Greenblatt, "Mixed Mode," 277-8; Hamilton, "Sidney's Arcadia," 135; Arthur Kinney, "Intimations of Mortality: Sidney's Journal from Flushing to Zutphen," *Sir Philip Sidney: 1586 and the Creation of a Legend*, Jan van Dorston, Dominic Baker-Smith, and Arthur Kinney, eds., (Leiden: Leiden Univ. Press, 1986), 125-48; Lindheim, *Structures*, 158-60; McCoy, *Rebellion in Arcadia*, 213-4; and Karen Saupe, "Trial, Error, and Revision in Sidney's *Arcadias*," *Sidney Newsletter and Journal* 12 (1993): 22-29, 24-6.

[41] Greenblatt, "Mixed Mode," 278.

[42] Myron Turner suggests that the revised text combines "the pride and self-sufficiency of the hero with Christian humility and dependence upon God" ("The Heroic Ideal in Sidney's Revised *Arcadia*," *Studies in English Literature* 10 [1970]: 63-82, 63). I argue that

Euarchus's problem is his limited point of view. He cannot understand shipwreck because it is not subject to rational interpretation; he is an excellent prince, but a poor theologian. A political triumph added to the *New Arcadia* further highlights this disjunction. Before leaving Macedonia, Euarchus provides an example of statecraft at its best, discouraging a rebellion by the Latines. He pre-empts their violence with a show of force and maintains his kingdom equitably for all. His tactics impersonate the tempest that will later cast him ashore: "[Euarchus] by many reasons making them see that though in respect of place some of them might seem further removed from the first violence of the storm, yet being embarked in the same ship, the final wreck must needs be common to them all" (788). This attempt to make a tempest part of a political program inverts the status of storms in Heliodoran romance. Euarchus's ship of state cannot accommodate the *topos* that makes a shipwreck an occasion for supplementing human reason with the direct manifestation of divine will. Understanding this aspect of shipwreck falls to younger heroes than Euarchus.

### "Cruel winds": Musidorus's Political Errors

Learning from shipwreck is not easy for any of Sidney's heroes. Musidorus, like Euarchus, fails because he cannot escape politics. Unlike Euarchus, however, Musidorus recognizes the mystery of shipwreck. When he narrates his adventures to Pamela, he interprets the shipwreck off Asia Minor as a cruel act of fate:

> [W]hen the conspired heavens had gotten this subject of their wrath upon so fit a place as the sea was, they straight began to breathe out in boisterous winds some part of their malice against him, so that with the loss of all his navy, he only with the prince his cousin were cast a-land far off from the place where their desires would have guided them. O cruel winds, in your unconsiderate rages why either began you this fury, or why did you not end it in his end? (229)

Musidorus fails to see that the "cruel winds" make possible his adventures with Pyrocles in Asia Minor, which not only advance his education but also comprise the narrative of his courtship of Pamela.[43] Musidorus sees only the "boisterous winds" and their "malice," rather than the Providential plot they advance. He does ask "why" the storm strikes him, and this acknowledgment exceeds his uncle's self-sufficiency. He recognizes the role of supernatural forces. He is no more open to reevaluating shipwreck, however, than Euarchus.

---

shipwreck helps produce this humility in Pyrocles. While Turner sees Pamela as the ideal Christian heroine, I believe that Pyrocles models a more practical Heliodoran virtue.

[43]  Lindheim argues that Musidorus's seriousness "reassert[s] the proper 'ethical' alignment between public and privates actions" (*Structures*, 120). Shipwreck asserts a different hierarchy, in which political reason must recognize its subordination to faith.

Tailoring his speech to appeal to Pamela, heir to the Arcadian throne, Musidorus makes politics his governing metaphor. For Musidorus, the sea can be only loyal subject or traitor. When he and Pyrocles set sail, "The wind was like a servant, waiting behind them so just, that they might fill the sails as they listed; and the best sailors, showing themselves less covetous of his liberality, so tempered it that they all kept together like a beautiful flock which could so well obey their master's pipe" (260). The pastoral relation between shepherd and flock subtends this fantasy of perfect transparency between power and service, of a "beautiful flock" that loves to "obey their master's pipe." Musidorus describes a world he can control. Playing on a metaphor common in Tudor poetry, Musidorus and the fleet "consider the art of catching the wind prisoner to no other end but to run away with it" (260). Conventionally "catching the wind" is an image of futility, but for this crossing of the Mediterranean, it works just fine.

As readers no doubt expect, Musidorus's idyll falls apart. The storm that arises shatters the fleet:

> For then the traitorous sea began to swell in pride against the afflicted navy under which, while the heaven favoured them, it had laid so calmly, making mountains of itself over which the tossed and tottering ship should climb, to be straight carried down again to a pit of hellish darkness; with such cruel blows against the side of the ship (that, which way soever it went, was still in his malice) that shortly there was left neither power to stay nor way to escape. And shortly had it so dessevered the loving company which the day before had tarried together, that most of them never met again but were swallowed up in his never satisfied mouth. (261)

Musidorus shows some awareness that the ideal service of wind and sea has been the result of heavenly favor, but his vocabulary mingles the language of traitors and faithful servants with the "pit of hellish darkness." The pit is a more nearly Christian image than the fishermen's Neptune and Venus, but Musidorus interprets divine hostility in the same simplistic way they had. He omits any role for "human inhumanity," or mortal error. The "traitorous sea" is his ultimate villain.

As so often in Sidney, paired images, in this case the calm and the storm, comprise an interpretive test. Musidorus reads the shift from calm to storm in political terms, and this method precludes seeing the storm as part of a divine plan. The storm, as even Musidorus knows, is not a traitorous servant, but an unknowable power: "[T]he ship wherein the princes were (now left as much alone as proud lords when fortune fails them) though they employed all industry to save themselves, yet what they did was rather for duty than hope to escape" (261). That he feels himself left alone "when fortune fails" exposes Musidorus's failure to accept predeterminism, in which fortune (or Providence) never fails. Musidorus and his cousin remain trapped, waging a continual struggle "rather for duty than hope to escape." The alternative Musidorus never considers is that shipwrecks may be beneficial, not malicious, as he thinks, or even capricious, as the fishermen believe.

Musidorus rails against "the tyranny of the wind and the treason of the sea" (262) as he fetches up on Asian shores. In these terms, the cost of the storm is immense. The fleet is destroyed, and Leucippe and Nelsus, brothers who have loyally served the princes, must sacrifice themselves for their masters (263). (Leucippe's name, from Achilles Tatius's *Leucippe and Clitophon*, places this episode in the context of Greek romance.) The ship's rib on which the four float provides a keen metaphor for hard political decisions in a world of scarce resources. The rib will only float two, so the servants must give way to the masters or become traitors. The servants do not present their sacrifice in zero-sum terms, but their deaths suggest that the politics of Musidorus's wreck are strikingly cold-blooded: either servants or masters must die. Musidorus accepts their sacrifice as a matter of course, explaining that he and Pyrocles had ransomed them from captivity. The servants' ultimate fidelity, however, further undercuts Musidorus's insistence on "treason" as a governing metaphor.

The shipwreck divides the two princes, and Pyrocles washes up in hostile Phrygia, while Musidorus arrives in friendly Pontus. Pyrocles's fate in Phrygia, as Musidorus narrates it, takes him from oceangoing storms to a land-locked one: "And in this plight, full of watchful fearfulness, did the storm deliver sweet Pyrocles to the stormy mind of that [Phrygian] tyrant" (266). The tyrant's "stormy mind" reprises Musidorus's flawed interpretation: he reads storms as political acts, tyrannies of wind and sea. The princes' political education – the new task to which this shipwreck brings them – begins with Pyrocles being held captive in Phrygia and Musidorus maneuvering for his release outside. Musidorus remains bound by political reason. Pyrocles, by contrast, refuses Musidorus's explanations when he describes the subsequent wreck off Arcadia. His refusal to pronounce decisively is as close as any Arcadian prince gets to understanding how shipwreck operates in their world.

### *"That little all we were": Pyrocles and the Challenge of Human Weakness*

Sidney matches each prince's weak point with the subject of his narrative. Thus Musidorus, whose strengths are active and political, narrates a shipwreck, which, if interpreted better, might reveal the need to accept supernatural control. Pyrocles, by contrast, narrates a shipwreck which is not a direct product of supernatural power. At the end of Book 2, Pyrocles finally explains the mysterious opening disaster. Unlike Musidorus, he condemns not disloyal service but the entire bloody episode:

> But while even in that little remnant, like the children of Cadmus, we continued still to slay one another, a fire which (whether by the desperate malice of some, or intention to separate, or accidentally, while all things were cast up and down) it should seem had

taken a good while before, but never heeded of us (who only thought to preserve or revenge) now violently burst out in many places and began to master the principal parts of the ship. Then necessity made us see that a common enemy sets at one a civil war; for that little all we were (as if we had been waged by one man to quench a fire) straight went to resist that furious enemy by all art and labour: but it was too late, for already it did embrace and devour from the stern to the waist of the ship; so as labouring in vain, we were driven to get up to the prow of the ship, by the work of nature seeking to preserve life as long as we could: while truly it was a strange and ugly sight to see so huge a fire, as it quickly grew to be, in the sea, and in the night, as if it had come to light us to death. (374)

With the simile of Cadmus's children, Pyrocles laments "human inhumanity" more than Plexirtus's treachery. Calling the battling mariners "that little all we were" emphasizes the crisis's role as a microcosm of human experience. Pyrocles refuses Musidorus's political metaphor. The fire still "master[s]" and "devour[s]" the ship, but Pyrocles does not name it or the sea a traitorous servant. He remains unwilling to pass judgment on the fighting men or even on the fire itself, which paradoxically appears "as if it had come to light us to death."

Plexirtus's captain exposes the nihilistic end-point of his master's treachery when "with a loud voice [he] sware that if Plexirtus bade him, he would not stick to kill God himself" (374). The captain transforms "human inhumanity" into a fantasy of superhuman power. He wants to invert the mechanism of shipwreck and strike a human blow against divinity. Pyrocles replies to the captain in the only words he speaks aloud during the episode: "Villain . . . dost thou think to over-live so many honest men whom thy falsehood hath brought to destruction?" (375). He recognizes that the captain's violence is based on "falsehood," even if he has no straightforward truth with which to replace it.

Amid this chaos, Pyrocles and Musidorus distinguish themselves by abstaining from violence. Pyrocles describes their refusal as a moral victory: "For my cousin and me, truly I think we never performed less in any place, doing no other hurt than the defense of ourselves and succoring them who came for it drave us to, for not discerning perfectly who were for us and who against us, we thought it less evil to spare a foe than spoil a friend" (373). Compared to the zero-sum game that forces Leucippe and Nelsus off the ship's rib, Pyrocles's reticence is striking.[44] As the melee progresses to the point where "no man almost could conceive hope of living but by being the last alive" (373), Pyrocles refuses the role of judge and executioner. Pyrocles's careful distinctions cede judgment to extrahuman dispensation: he will not decide who is to live or die, but resigns the choice to fortune and fire. He knows by his reason to abandon reason.

---

[44]  Bergvall reads this storm as the "sea of passion" into which Pyrocles falls, but he does not consider Pyrocles's combination of reason, acceptance, and resigned effort. See "The 'Enabling of Judgement': An Old Reading of the New *Arcadia*," *Studies in Philology* 85 (1988): 477.

Accepting his fate does not force Pyrocles into passivity. From the text's first image of him clinging to the ship's mast, he always struggles to preserve himself. The initial description of this moment, however, seems misleading: "For holding his head up full of unmoved majesty, he held a sword aloft with his fair arm, which often he waved about his crown as though he would threaten the world in that extremity" (66). While "unmoved majesty" captures Pyrocles's combination of semi-passive resignation with unabated effort, the gesture need not be a threat against the world. The narrator's narrow focus on "human inhumanity" interprets everything as a struggle between antithetical forces. Pyrocles, when he re-narrates the scene, makes it clear that the fewer violent actions he performs, the better. He recognizes that his best victory will be avoidance of error. The interpretive problem – why does Pyrocles wave his sword? – embodies the larger mystery of the wreck. Rather than striking out blindly, Pyrocles calls attention to himself and his plight while waiting for rescue.

When Pyrocles narrates the scene (374-5), he reveals that he was not, in fact, threatening the world. He slays the evil captain, but he never bewails his fate, nor does he rail against the treachery of wind and water. Rather, after killing the captain, he sits patiently on the mast: "there myself remained, until by pirates I was taken up" (375). Pyrocles balances on the cusp of active struggle and passive resignation. He sends the captain who has proven himself evil "to feed the fishes" (375), but then gives himself over to the pirates. Throughout the episode, he never loses hope. He cannot know if his shipwreck is Providential plan, but he refuses to act on any motivation he knows to be erroneous.

Pyrocles's refusal to draw conclusions about the shipwreck is a partial victory. His hope approximates the imperfect knowledge of shipwreck that the reader has at the text's opening: these disasters are mysteries and opportunities, occasions for the divine Author to surprise with His story. Pyrocles will not judge individual sailors in the shipboard melee, nor will he judge the way he arrives in Arcadia. He cannot reach the Christian solution available to Sidney, but he refuses error. The image of Pyrocles atop the mast epitomizes his interpretive high-point: he maintains hope in a plan of which he knows nothing. The conclusion of the romance, had Sidney lived to write it, would presumably have requited this patient endurance.[45]

## Ends Human and Divine

The endings of literary romance parallel but do not precisely mirror the Providential "end" that Mornay describes. Theologically, the end of salvation

---

[45] It seems logical, as Michael McCanles has argued, that Sidney's plans for the end of the *New Arcadia* were not all that far from the *Old* version, given the approximate sameness of the Oracle in both versions (*Text*, 142). Moreover, since Sidney was writing a romance, a "happy ending" was a generic imperative.

comes to the elect in the next world, while a romance presents this ending in a (fictional) human world. Romance condenses the Christian overplot into a human drama. In absolute terms, fiction miniaturizes the Christian *telos*, giving Sidney a scale model for his experiment. Sidney may have feared that a conventional ending would trivialize his theology. Much of the revision of the *Arcadia* appears a sustained attempt to reinforce his text's seriousness. Even an updated version of the ending of the *Old Arcadia* might have slighted the revised version's more somber tone. Sidney's literary dilemma, which he never solved, was how to write a human triumph for his heroes that would not minimize the unreachable insights toward which they have been striving.

In bringing together reason and faith, the shipwreck scenes in the *New Arcadia* explore how difficult it is to cling to Providence in the face of catastrophe. The princes' struggle to comprehend shipwreck's causes of divine fiat and "human inhumanity" echoes Sidney's intellectual struggle with reason and faith. Accepting Mornay's notion of Providence as God's "end," Sidney found in Greek romance a world that operates under an analogous dispensation. He used Heliodoran fiction as a human model to approximate God's design. In both schemes, danger (shipwreck/the Fall) opens the door for the complex workings of Providence to create an unlooked-for triumph (the happy marriage/Christian revelation). Learning to accept shipwrecks, and even thrive in a world suffused with them, becomes Sidney's literary analogy for imagining the interrelation of human reason and divine Providence. The unfinished text gestures toward a mutual accommodation between reason and faith.

The final irony is that the *New Arcadia*, unlike most Heliodoran romances, has no end. The fragmentary revision leaves the Providential ending incomplete. Speculation about Sidney's reasons for breaking off the revision, or his plans had he lived to continue it, are ultimately fruitless, but in religious terms the rupture makes perfect sense. The *Aethiopian History* imagines the happy ending of romance as a theological triumph on mortal soil: the hero and heroine become high priest and priestess, and the nation of Aethiopia eschews human sacrifice forever. For a Protestant like Sidney, however, placing divine grace inside a literary fiction exceeds the province of mortal artistry. The final end rests in divine hands. Sidney's abandonment of the revision and subsequent early death ceded the *New Arcadia*'s "end" to God and posterity alone.[46]

---

[46] Other authors rushed to plug the hole in Sidney's text. Gervase Markham and Anne Weamys, among others, wrote continuations of the *Arcadia* in the seventeenth century, and several writers, beginning with William Alexander in 1621, wrote bridge-passages filling the gap between the revised Book 3 and the concluding Books of the *Old Arcadia*.

## Cross-Dressing in Captivity

> When you meet a human being, the first distinction you make is "male or female?"
> and you are accustomed to make this distinction with unhesitating certainty.
>
> Sigmund Freud, "Femininity"[47]

Shipwrecks and oracles were the main plot devices Sidney took from Heliodorus, but the non-Heliodoran topos of cross-dressing shows even more clearly Sidney's struggle to preserve epic qualities in his revised text. The *New Arcadia* fuses epic martialism with romance indirection rather than discarding the former. In the Captivity Episode of Book 3, the conflict between romance passivity and epic activity becomes explicit. Outside the besieged castle, two knights, Amphialus and Musidorus, fight in the traditional manner of knights errant. Inside, the princesses and Pyrocles as Zelmane struggle against weakness and immobility. This juxtaposition clarifies Sidney's tense relationship with the Heliodoran model. Unlike the Greek romancer, he maintains a place for the worldly values of epic. Pyrocles carves out a space for activity within his role as victimized heroine. His active-passive strategy oscillates between fighting and accepting divine control. As Stephen Greenblatt says about Sidney himself, Pyrocles must learn to be a "connoisseur of doubt"[48] who puts off final judgment until God's plan shows itself.

By focusing on the captivity episode, I shall show how the *New Arcadia* recasts the dominance of the heroine in Heliodoran fiction. The key trope is one that Sidney found in Continental fiction (including Book 11 of the French *Amadis*) but not Heliodorus: cross-dressing. Pyrocles's hybrid gender constructs a heroism that is active and passive, male and female, epic and romance. This hybridity has its clearest emblem in the clothes Pyrocles wears when he disguises himself as Zelmane. The cross-dressing episode, and its description of Zelmane, have long been controversial, with critical debate oscillating between historicist readings of Sidney as a spokesman for the masculinist pieties of his humanist teachers, and sympathetic portraits of him as a feminist *avant la lettre*.[49] To bypass this stalemate, I shall juxtapose two scenes of Zelmane's cross-dressing, the initial moment when she first appears to Musidorus, and her battle with Anaxius and his brothers at the end of the revised section of Book 3. In this scene, which breaks off mid-sentence, Sidney stages the conflict between epic and romance and their mutual critique and interaction.

---

[47] Freud, Sigmund, *New Introductory Lectures on Psychoanalysis (1933), The Standard Edition of the Complete Psychological Works of Sigmund Freud*, James Strachey, ed., (London: Hogarth Press, 1964) 22:113.

[48] "Mixed Mode," 274.

[49] Duncan-Jones opens her biography of Sidney by placing herself firmly in the latter cam "In Sidney's work," she writes, "misogyny is never allowed to stand uncorrected" (*Sir Philip Sidney: Courtier-Poet*, 2).

Cross-dressing enters the *New Arcadia* as an act of provocation. The shock of seeing Pyrocles abandon armor for a dress provokes a debate with Musidorus and within Sidney criticism. Mark Rose epitomizes the once-standard reading that supports Musidorus against Pyrocles: "Sidney, I believe, intended his audience to find Pyrocles' disguise offensive."[50] Rose relies on a normative understanding of sexuality in which the two genders are easily distinguished and completely separate. Feminist criticism, especially since the 1970s, has significantly increased attention to moments of tension within the orders of gender. Rose's position, however, finds some support in the humanist ideals that Sidney was taught. His education, as Richard Helgerson has noted, valued the public over the private, the male over the female, and reason over passion.[51] The *New Arcadia* demonstrates, however, that Sidney – writing in the "prodigal" form of romance – critiques these humanist ideals.

The opposite camp's position is stated most directly by John Danby: "[Sidney] would seem to be insisting that man is capable of a synthesis of qualities that includes the womanly yet avoids the hermaphroditic."[52] Here Pyrocles/Zelmane embodies bi-gendered perfection. Some version of this point of view typifies many recent reconsiderations of this scene, especially those influenced by feminist scholarship. Mary Ellen Lamb, for example, sees the cross-dressing as signifying "an inner change" in Pyrocles; David Cressy shifts the emphasis slightly by arguing that cross-dressing per se was not "so transgressive"; and Casey Charles sees the costume as part of the creation of "a new masculine social identity" within "the male lover who accepts himself as a sexual subject."[53] For all these critics, as for Rose, Pyrocles's costume epitomizes his unstable social status. Changing clothes has changed the man.

The debate between the Rose and Danby camps centers on the emotional or psychological function of the Zelmane disguise. In Sidney's text, the debate between Pyrocles and Musidorus prefigures this critical controversy. Musidorus argues for reason, male clothing, and Rose; Pyrocles counters in favor of love, cross-dressing, and Danby. Most recent critics, especially feminists, hew to the Pyrocles/Danby side, although attention to Sidney's understanding of sexuality and the relationship between the princes has nuanced Danby's celebration.[54] Sidney's

---

50   Mark Rose, "Sidney's Womanish Man," *Review of English Studies* n.s. 15 (1964): 354.

51   See Helgerson, *The Elizabethan Prodigals.*

52   Danby, *Poets on Fortune's Hill* 57.

53   See Mary Ellen Lamb, "Exhibiting Class and Displaying the Body in Sidney's *Countess of Pembroke's Arcadia,*" *Studies in English Literature* 37 (1997): 63; David Cressy, "Gender Trouble and Cross-Dressing in Early Modern England," *Journal of British Studies* 35 (1996): 439; and Casey Charles, "Heroes as Lovers: Erotic Attraction between Men in Sidney's *New Arcadia,*" *Criticism* 34 (1992): 479-80.

54   Winfried Schleiner and John O'Connor place cross-dressing in the context of its source in *Amadis of Gaul.* See Winfried Schleiner, "Male Cross-Dressing and Transvestitism in

text does not conclude this debate so much as break it off, and criticism must grapple with his apparent sympathy with both Pyrocles and Musidorus.

The impact of Zelmane's cross-dressing may be psychologically undecidable, but in terms of narrative coherence its function seems straightforward. Much of Sidney plot relies on the hero's female clothing. The costume sets the main plot in motion. Basilius's retreat to the countryside may be initiated by his misreading the Delphic oracle, but Zelmane's disguise keeps him waiting and hoping in pastoral Arcadia.

Above all, Zelmane's clothes provoke. They provoke incontinent desire in Basilius, and later Zoilus, a tortured surrender to passion in Gynecia, and a slightly more controlled passion in Philoclea. They further provoke Musidorus (and readers like Rose) to despair of the prince's reason. Zelmane's costume contributes to the disruption of generic expectations: characters who should be warriors, governors, queens, or princesses instead become lovers. Zelmane, in the final scenes of the revision, repositions martial valor in Sidney's heroic ideal. Her hybrid male-female heroism is neither the humanist ideal of Danby, for whom the decision to dress as an Amazon seems straightforwardly positive, nor the hopeful egalitarianism of feminist critics like Lamb or Duncan-Jones, but rather a heroism on the far side of provocation and despair.[55] The image of the original Zelmane, who died for love of Pyrocles, recalls the potential cost of erotic attachment. Zelmane unsettles herself and the kingdom, creating chaos in Arcadia. As I shall show, the broken sentence of the revision's end can serve as a metaphor for the price, for author and character, of this experiment in gender and genre.

Zelmane's appearance begins Sidney's use of the pronoun "she" to describe this character. The pronoun repeats the provocation of the costume: each time Sidney uses the word "she" for a character we know is a "he," the frisson of blurred genders increases.[56] The two princes have been separated by shipwreck, and Musidorus finally discovers Zelmane in a "little wood" (130) after scouring Arcadia for his lost cousin. Zelmane is thus the object of a semi-erotic quest before she is known to be feminine. Chance and a tired horse[57] lead Musidorus to a lady who banishes all thought of sleep: "It was...a lady who, because she walked with her side toward him, he could not perfectly see her face, but so much he might see of her that was a surety for the rest that all was excellent" (130). This sentence previews the description that follows: Zelmane is partly hidden and not easy to see, but her visible parts incite desire for what is covered.

---

Renaissance Romance," *Sixteenth-Century Journal* 19 (1988): 605-19; and O'Connor, *Amadis de Gaule and Its Influence on Elizabethan Literature*.

[55] While Pyrocles does cross-dress in the *Old Arcadia* (under the name Cleophila) the *New* version's emphasis on recovering heroic values within a pastoral space places greater tension on the trope, especially on the connection between erotic desire and martial rage.

[56] I follow Sidney by calling the cross-dressed hero "she" and "Zelmane" throughout.

[57] The tired horse might allegorically indicate a weakness of the flesh, the very weakness Musidorus will deny in his debate with Zelmane.

The motif of partial covering, of a costume that reveals and conceals, dominates the description of Zelmane. A creature of paradox, she shows and hides, exposes and covers, and finding her in a wooded glen is itself an act of discovering:

> Well might [Musidorus] perceive the hanging of her hair in fairest quantity in locks, some curled and some as it were forgotten, with such a careless care and an art so hiding art that she seemed she would lay them for a pattern whether nature simply or nature helped by cunning be the more excellent: the rest whereof was drawn into a coronet of gold richly set with pearl, and so joined all over with gold wires and covered with feathers of divers colours that it was not unlike to an helmet, such a glittering show it bare, and so bravely it was held up from the head. Upon her body she ware a doublet of sky-colour satin, covered with plates of gold and, as it were, nailed with precious stones that in it she might seem armed. The nether part of her garment was so full of stuff and cut after such a fashion, that though the length of it reached to the ankles, yet in her going one might sometimes discern the small of her leg, which with the foot was dressed in a short pair of crimson velvet buskins, in some places open, as the ancient manner was, to show the fairness of the skin. (130-1)

The play between what is revealed, by carelessness or subtle art, and what covered, by hair or helmet, coronet or armor, announces the arrival of Zelmane as provocative object. She mixes martial gear and soft, feminine garments, as the description shifts from curls to helmets, from doublets to armor, and finally to the small of her leg. The narrator's eye travels the length of Zelmane's body from head to toe and concludes by lingering on the "fairness of...skin" of her exposed foot. Even the Arcadian princesses, who have so far appeared only in paintings, would be hard pressed to beat this entrance.[58]

Musidorus sees Zelmane first, but the first attempt to interpret her is not his rational masculinist disgust, but rather Pyrocles's choice of emblem. The device expresses ambivalence and hope: "a Hercules...with a distaff in his hand, as he once was by Omphale's commandment, with a word in Greek but thus to be interpreted, 'Never more valiant'" (131). This motto splits critical response into its predictable camps; Rose insists that the Renaissance despised the distaff-spinning Hercules, while the Danby camp praises Pyrocles for showing himself never more valiant than when serving love.[59] Sidney had already written about the emblem in the *Defence*, where he noted that that the image "breedeth both delight and laughter: for the representing of so strange a power in love procureth delight, and

---

[58]   When Zelmane describes Philoclea, she revives this style: "[Philoclea's] body (O sweet body!) covered with a light taffeta garment, so cut as the wrought smock came through it in many places, enough to have made your restrained imagination have thought what was under it" (146). To the extent that Philoclea reminds the reader (and Musidorus) of Zelmane, it may be that feminine beauty is always cross-gendered in this text.

[59]   Rose, "Sidney's Womanish Man," 361. Rose cites the opposing viewpoint from Wolff, *The Greek Romances in Elizabethan Prose Fiction*, 338.

the scornfulness of the action stirreth laughter" (245). This scornful laughter and delight, however, are not as simple as the "offensive[ness]" Rose imagines the disguise produces.

Sidney designs the emblem to be ambiguous and provocative. Delight and scorn work together ironically, and the emblem reveals both vulnerability and instability. Zelmane, like Sidney, acknowledges the dangers of her provocative disguise. Sidney's text suggests that Pyrocles can be admired for assuming the distaff, but that is not to say (with Danby) that he must be admired unconditionally. Scorn remains the risk of cross-dressing, and the laughter that the disguise creates resists interpretation. Motto and costume remain mixed.

Sidney concludes Zelmane's description by turning to the sword on her thigh. This last glimpse of her body brings to a climax the intermingling of erotic and martial subtexts. The image unsettles Sidney's narrator, who cannot decide whether sword or thigh is more dangerous: "[O]n her thigh she ware a sword which, as it witnessed her to be an Amazon...so it seemed but a needless weapon, since her other forces were without withstanding" (131). Zelmane unsettles the common homology in which love becomes a battlefield; she is literally at home in love and war. She wields sword and thigh, battlefield and bedroom, and this radical juxtaposition unsettles as it attracts.

As this character strides through Basilius's kingdom, nearly all who see her are provoked to uncontrollable desire. Even Musidorus succumbs to her charms. Her transgressive costume inflames him before he recognizes his old friend. When he finally recognizes her as Pyrocles, Musidorus appears "as Apollo is painted when he saw Daphne suddenly turn into a laurel" (132). The analogy seems clear; like Apollo, Musidorus is frozen exactly as he loses what he desires. This scene produces not so much delight as eroticized pathos. Musidorus loses both a convenient shield for homosocial/sexual eros, and also a potential female object of desire. Casey Charles notes that Sidney's delicate touch allows "the unmentionable monstrosity of homosexual behavior...into discourse,"[60] but Sidney's blurring of genders puts both hetero- and homosexual feelings on display.

After Musidorus, the list of Zelmane's conquests comprises nearly everyone in the Arcadian royal family. With the constant provocation of her clothes and her body, she seduces Basilius, Gynecia, and Philoclea. Each of the three reads the relationship of clothing to body differently, and thus each succumbs to different charms. Basilius reads the clothing naively, accepts her as a woman, and offers his "doting love" (149). Gynecia pierces the disguise and desires the Hercules beneath the dress. Philoclea, less worldly than her mother but shrewder than her father, does not attempt to resolve Zelmane's gender ambiguity, but accepts the costume and the feelings it provokes: "Away then all vain examinations of why and how. Thou lovest me, excellent Zelmane, and I love thee" (244). These passions testify

---

[60] Charles, "Heroes as Lovers," 478.

to Zelmane's provocative range, inciting desire in foolish old men, shrewd middle-aged women, and innocent young girls.

Zelmane's provocation contrasts sharply with the text's portraits of the wholly feminine Arcadian princesses. Zelmane models a heroic femininity that makes her both more powerful and more Heliodoran than Pamela or Philoclea. Pamela, especially, is a rock of certainty and constancy, but this constancy makes her a flawed heroine. Her refutation of Cecropia's atheism, among the most commented-upon passages in Book 3,[61] marks her as a fixed point within the Captivity Episode. This refutation provides Sidney's closest fictional approximation of the justification of Christian faith he found in Mornay. For Pamela, the key to faith is "constancy," a trait that isolates the most morally straightforward aspect of Heliodoran passivity. Pamela builds her argument against Cecropia on her certainty that the Divine will must be constant. Cecropia's skepticism, which combines antitheological ideas from Lucretius, Lucian, and perhaps Montaigne,[62] cannot shake Pamela's faith. Despite her nominal paganism, Pamela adopts semi-Calvinist attitudes typical of Sidney and his Huguenot mentors.[63]

Pamela's proof of God's existence relies on her certainty of a Providential "end" to Creation. Instead of the chance-ruled universe of Cecropia (and Machiavelli), Pamela describes a world in which what looks like chaos reveals itself to be part of a Providential plan. For Pamela, as for Melanchthon, Mornay, and (in a literary context) Heliodorus, "eternity and chance are things unsufferable together" (489). Faced with the choice between Chance and Providence, she chooses the divine plan, but unlike Calasiris she does not think it requires any action on her part to help it along. Her absolute passivity puts her at odds with the hybrid heroism of Zelmane.

Sidney's text gives Pamela his highest possible approbation: "So foully was the filthiness of impiety discovered by the shining of her unstained goodness...that there was a light more than human which gave a lustre to her perfections" (492). Contrasting her with Zelmane and Chariclea, however, suggests that she is too passive. Her triumph comes only after Cecropia assaults her. Her passivity during the rest of the captivity episode does not evoke such glowing praise. In converting chance to Providence, she ignores the other resonance of Tyche, which refers to something gained through merit. Pamela's famous prayer, which the imprisoned Charles I supposedly read before his execution, relishes the annihilation of her own will:

---

[61]   See Elton, King Lear *and the Gods*, 34-64, and D. Walker, *The Ancient Theology: Studies in Christian Platonism from the Fifteenth to the Eighteenth Century*, (London: Duckworth, 1972), 132-63.

[62]   See Elton, King Lear *and the Gods*, 46-8.

[63]   Elton, King Lear *and the Gods*, 38, 40.

But yet, my God, if in Thy wisdom, this be the aptest chastisement for my unexcusable folly; if this low bondage be fittest for my over-high desires; if the pride of my not-enough humble heart be thus to be broken, O Lord, I yield unto Thy will, and joyfully embrace what sorrow Thou wilt have me suffer. (464)

Her strength flows from her embrace of "whatever Thou wilt have me suffer" and her refusal to place her own wisdom in competition with God's. Later, when Artesia reveals a plot to poison Amphialus, Pamela rejects any action against her captors: "As for me, let the gods dispose of me as shall please them; but sure it shall be no such way nor way-leader by which I will come to liberty" (520). Unlike Chariclea, Pamela refuses to conspire with Fate.[64]

Philoclea, by contrast, supplements passivity with an indirection that first emerges when Pyrocles finishes the story of his arrival in Arcadia. He then asks Philoclea to tell him about Erona and Plangus,[65] but he will not let her talk for kissing. This dilemma comically anticipates her problem with Amphialus, whose passion overcomes him more drastically. Pyrocles, too, cannot control himself; he "could not choose but rebel so far as to kiss her" (376). The word "rebel" uncomfortably anticipates the central action of Book 3. Rather than chastising Pyrocles for his love, however, Philoclea deflects him, saying, "How will you have your discourse...without you let my lips alone?" (376). Her playful refusal guides Pyrocles back to reasoned "discourse" and away from physical passion.[66] Philoclea's stratagem is only a delaying action, because Pyrocles turns to her hands with new fervor after being denied her lips. It falls to Miso's interruption to change the scene, but witty evasion has become part of Philoclea's repertoire.

This indirect agency emerges after her surrender to love. The extended description of Philoclea choosing to trust her feelings displays Sidney's painstaking emotional description (238-44).[67] Philoclea does not strive for knowledge outside her grasp, but rather, like a good Protestant or shrewd reader of Heliodorus, trusts unseen powers. She acknowledges her love and gives herself to

---

[64] Pamela's rigid passivity bends only when forced by her love for Musidorus. The conclusion of her prayer contains a *sotto voce* appeal that King Charles, presumably, did not repeat: "And, O most gracious Lord...whatever become of me, preserve the virtuous Musidorus" (464). This aside remains cloaked in the theological language of "grace" and "virtue," but it is also simply a young woman's plea for special treatment for her love. This slip from the ideal to the personal reveals that Pamela's arguments do not complete her portrait.

[65] On the Erona/Plangus subplot, see Winfried Schleiner, "Differences of Theme and Structure of the Erona Episode in the *Old* and *New Arcadia*," *Studies in Philology* 70 (1973): 377-91.

[66] Philoclea uses rhetoric to protect herself from unwanted sexual attention at earlier moments in the text (331, 357). These moments recall Chariclea's pacifying Thyamis in the *Aethiopian History*.

[67] See Danby, *Poets on Fortune's Hill*, 58.

it. In the refrain of her lovesick poem, she implicitly critiques her sister's constancy: "And [I] witness am, how ill agree in one / A woman's hand with constant marble stone" (242). Philoclea does not reject Pamela's constancy, but softens it with a "woman's hand." Philoclea's attempt to understand her feelings provides a microcosm of the larger questions of reason and passion in the *New Arcadia*. Philoclea's solution, to pledge silent faith to love and tell no one (except, soon, Zelmane herself), recalls Calasiris's patient deferral and Chariclea's reluctance to speak publicly. These examples suggest a compromise between strict rules and the freeplay of passion.

A median path between duty and passion proves difficult to find in the *New Arcadia*. Philoclea' balances these imperatives through Heliodoran deception. In the crucible of Book 3, she lies to preserve herself. Early in her captivity, Philoclea delays Cecropia's attempts to marry her to Amphialus by claiming not to care for marriage. "I know not...what contentment you speak of," Philoclea tells her aunt, "but I am sure the best you can make of it (which is marriage) is a burdenous yoke" (460). A far cry from Pamela's forceful debating style, Philoclea's ruse deflects Cecropia into a wickedly comic speech extolling the virtues of marriage and bewailing the loss of her husband (460-1). Philoclea's manipulation of Cecropia becomes stronger, however, when she invokes Amphialus, the one person Cecropia might love: "'If,' said [Philoclea], 'the common course of humanity cannot move you...yet let the love you have often told me your son bears me so much procure, that for his sake one death may be thought enough for me'" (552). Despite the unsettling pun on "procure," which is exactly what Cecropia wants to do for her son, Philoclea uses Amphialus's unwelcome love as a tool to blunt Cecropia's rage.[68]

Philoclea's deceptions add an active component to Pamela's stoicism. One moment in particular emphasizes Philoclea's closeness to the Heliodoran model. Echoing Chariclea's return after her supposed death, she stages a false-resurrection as a test of Pyrocles's love. This test echoes Parthenia's testing of Argalus after he believes her dead (105-6), Penelope's testing of Odysseus, and other false deaths in the romance tradition. Philoclea pretends to be a "poor gentlewoman" (566) so that she can see how Pyrocles has reacted to her apparent death. Satisfied with his grief, she returns to him with new openness, saying, "'Dear Pyrocles...I am thy Philoclea, and as yet living: not murdered as you supposed; and therefore be comforted,' and with that she gave him her hand" (568). As resurrected lover, Philoclea gives Pyrocles her hand in a gesture both human and sacramental. The willing gift of Philoclea's hand reprises and defeats Pyrocles's impulsive seizing of it earlier. Philoclea's deceptive tactics show her that "death was not strong enough to divide thy love from me" (570). Philoclea's deceptive triumph, which might seem beside

---

[68] Her tactics are less direct than Chariclea's manipulation of Thyamis, because Philoclea must manipulate her lover's mother rather than him directly.

the point with all three characters still imprisoned, underscores the success of Chariclean mendacity in emotional as well as practical terms.

The culmination of Sidney's revision of Heliodoran virtue appears in the struggle of Zelmane against Anaxius and his brothers. At this point, the transsexual disguise, which fools everyone except Gynecia, provides an emblem of his combined virtues. As Amazon, both woman and warrior, Pyrocles/Zelmane embodies both the active virtues of chivalric combat and the passive virtues of the princesses. Pyrocles is not perfect, and his inability to keep from kissing Philoclea typifies the lack of self-control that makes him the least Cyrus-like of Sidney's major heroes.[69] When he fights Anaxius and his brothers, Pyrocles uses both active and passive modes. These hypermasculine antagonists lust after their prisoners, so Zelmane opposes them not as a rival knight but as an assailed woman. Her costume now provokes violence as well as desire, creating in the brothers an "evil consort of love and force" (588). Implicitly defending her own consort of love and force, Zelmane seduces them with her now-swordless costume and fights them with stolen weapons. The revision breaks off during the struggle with Anaxius, but her complex tactics suggest that Zelmane embodies Sidney's most sophisticated version of heroism.

When she first encounters Anaxius, Zelmane's provocative dress forces him to listen to her, because "the excellency of her beauty and grace made him a little content to hear" (582). She speaks, and he stares: "sometimes with bent brows looking upon the one side of her, sometimes of the other" (582). Like Musidorus in the wood, Anaxius is transfixed by Zelmane's mixture of eroticism and force. Simply being stared at, however, does not give Zelmane any advantage.

Trapped within her generic and gendered confines, she cannot engage the brothers as a knight. Thus when she challenges Anaxius to "choose thee what arms thou likest" (582), he merely smiles. Searching for a way back to anger and combat, Zelmane conjures by her male name, Pyrocles, whom Anaxius hates.[70] Like the disguised heroines of comic drama, Zelmane plays on her hidden identity: "I tell thee, no creature can be nearer of kin to [Pyrocles] than myself: and so well we love, that he would not be sorrier for his own death than for mine" (583). This witticism, however, fails to bring Anaxius to combat.

Zelmane then turns to a familiar feminine ruse, pretending to agree to an unwanted marriage proposal in order to buy time. Pamela refuses to go along, arguing that even this minor deception is "flatter[ing] adversity" (584). Zelmane cannot argue against her resolve, so she reminds her that blind faith is impractical. She convinces Pamela to play along by hoping for a last-minute reversal. "While that [time] may bring forth any good," Zelmane argues, "do not bar yourself

---

[69] Argalus is an exemplary, controlled lover, Musidorus combines chastity with strong leadership, and even Amphialus, although a poor lover, is a great general. Pyrocles's only military leadership role, notably, is at the head of the Helot rebellion in Book 1.

[70] Pyrocles killed Anaxius's uncle Euardes in Book 2.

thereof" (585). Philoclea agrees with this plan easily, but convincing Pamela marks a clear victory for Zelmane.

The ruse gains a trip to the Delphic oracle, which for the moment postpones the crisis. Unlike the tale's first oracle, however, the new oracle is not mysterious. It refuses to endorse the marriages, and this refusal drives Anaxius back to violence (586-8).[71] Even the journey to Delphi does not buy much time, as it occupies only two pages of text. Feminine tactics of delay, apparently, can do no more than a masculine direct challenge.

Having exhausted male and female tactics separately, Zelmane combines them in the revision's final pages. Pursued by Zoilus, she plays the part of the coy Amazon who must engage her spouse in ritual combat before marriage. She emphasizes that this combat will be a formality, saying, "Therefore, before I make mine own desire serviceable to yours, you must vouchsafe to lend me armour and weapons, that at least with a blow or two of the sword I may not find myself perjured to myself" (589). The word "perjured" highlights a complex game of identities: a man dressed as a woman asks for male gear in order to pretend to effect a womanly submission to male desire. Zelmane's request, notably, is for the rest of her disguise. She wants to complete her Amazon garb by re-arming herself, and she emphasizes the sword's place in an eroticized costume. Inflamed by her sexuality, Zoilus loses control and assaults her, so that "she should quickly know what a man of arms he was" (588). This phrase demonizes Zoilus as one who believes rape to be the ultimate expression of masculinity, but it also uncomfortably echoes Zelmane's earlier defense of female clothing: "there is nothing I desire more than fully to prove myself a man in this enterprise" (136). Proof of masculinity appears in the loss of control created by feminine clothes.

In embracing Zelmane, Zoilus plays into her hands. Their physical contact crosses the boundaries of the disguise, and he ends up wrestling a better warrior than himself. Having seduced him into her embrace, Zelmane emerges from it with Zoilus's sword in her hands. Now fully dressed as an Amazon, she can play a martial part again. From this point on, Zelmane returns to her double role as hero and heroine.

Zelmane's warrior's role is significantly altered by her status as pursued woman. Her martial exploits are undercut by the unchivalric slaughter of the two younger brothers. She exerts power in and through female clothes, but when she takes up the sword she nearly debases her masculine identity. Sidney's narrator mirrors her slip back into masculinity by calling her "Pyrocles" four times (593-4) before returning to "Zelmane" on the final pages. In her first re-masculinized action, she attacks Zoilus, who flees back to his brothers. Zelmane kills him "even as he came to throw himself into their arms for succour" (590). Even more than

---

[71]   For the second Oracle's un-Delphic tone, see Michael McCandles, "Oracular Prediction and the Fore-conceit of Sidney's *Arcadia*," *ELH* 50 (1983): 240-43.

Amphialus's slaughter of Argalus and Parthenia, this killing does not seem chivalric.

Lycurgus, Zelmane's next opponent, falls before her in unequal combat. She steals his sword in addition to Zoilus's, and thus doubly masculinized – "two swords against one shield" (591) – she drives him to his knees. His plea for mercy starts to work on her "repressed" (591) emotions, but Lycurgus gets betrayed by an article of clothing. Eroticized clothes here activate male violence. Zelmane notices on Lycurgus's arm "a garter with a jewel which...[Zelmane] had [previously] presented to Philoclea" (592). This garter, ripped off Philoclea's arm, acts as a "cypher" (592) for Zelmane's jealousy and rage. It incites her to deny mercy and butcher the kneeling Lycurgus. Once again, the juxtaposition of a male body and female clothing – Lycurgus's arm and Philoclea's garter – provokes a loss of self-control.

The final combat – in a sense the "end" of the revised text – matches the heroic Anaxius against Pyrocles/Zelmane, who now wears both sexual identities at once. In an explicit moment of generic self-consciousness, Sidney links Anaxius to Achilles. Anaxius wields "a huge shield, such, perchance, as Achilles showed to the pale walls of Troy" (594). Anaxius, previously described as a knight without courtesy, is the last opponent for Zelmane as cross-dressing tactician. At first the pair's martial prowess links them via the chivalric trope of brothers in arms: "So that they both, prepared in hearts and able in hands, did honour solitariness there with such a combat as might have demanded, as a right of fortune, whole armies of beholders" (593). The word "fortune" intrudes on this image to remind the reader that the *New Arcadia* is not epic but romance, dedicated less to martial combat than the indirect ways of fortune.

The status of fortune in the final combat recalls the generic hybridity of the *New Arcadia*. Anaxius appears to be a character out of Homer's *Iliad* – Ajax if not Achilles – but Sidney's primary model is not Homer but Heliodorus. Unlike his classical exemplar, however, Sidney stages his critique of martial valor through a bloody swordfight. The link between the two combatants continues in an extended simile that brings the battle under the sign of romance:

> But like two contrary tides, either of which are able to carry worlds of ships and men upon them with such swiftness as nothing seems able to withstand them, yet meeting one another, with mingling their watery forces and struggling together, it is long to say whether stream gets the victory; so between these, if Pallas had been there, she could scarcely have told whether she had nursed better in the feats of arms. The Irish greyhound against the English mastiff; the sword-fish against the whale; the rhinoceros against the elephant, might be models, and but models, of this combat. (593)

This simile moves Sidney's text from the epic *Iliad* to the romance of the *New Arcadia*. Pallas, goddess of war and patron of Odysseus, cannot interpret the scene. The "contrary tides" move the warriors from the battlefield to the sea, where what looks like chaos recedes to reveal a Providential plan. The models suggested for the two combatants, greyhounds and mastiffs, sword-fish and whales, rhinoceros and elephants, remain "but models" because the sea itself is the dominant metaphor. In generic terms, the tides represent epic (Anaxius) and romance (Zelmane), and in the presumed triumph of Zelmane romance defeats epic. The combat, moreover, parodies the heroic ideal since Zelmane has neither armor nor shield. The tides snatch final agency away from the two heroes and place it where it belongs, above them, in divine hands.

The final exchange reveals that force of arms cannot win the day. For the epic hero Anaxius, this realization comes as a shock. Raging against his fate, Anaxius despises the gods who will not let him overcome a woman: "'I think,' said he, 'what a spiteful god it should be who, envying my glory, hath brought me to such a wayward case'" (594). This reference to supernatural control allows Zelmane to demonstrate her superior knowledge of gender and genre. She replies that the gods are just: "'Thou dost well indeed,' said Zelmane, 'to impute thy case to the heavenly providence, which will have thy pride find itself, even in that whereof thou art most proud, punished by the weak sex which thou most contemnest'" (594). The distinction between Anaxius's "spiteful god" and Zelmane's "heavenly providence" could not be clearer. Zelmane revels in her identity as "this weak sex." Her speech, the last in the revision, shows Zelmane in the midst of an heroic battle recalling her feminine nature. She has inverted her own emblem, so that Hercules now fights as well as spins. Although Pyrocles presumably would have shed his Amazonian mask had Sidney lived to complete the revision, at this juncture he wields both identities together.

A few lines later, the revision breaks off mid-sentence. We cannot know how Sidney intended to conclude Book 3, but the combat in progress when the rupture occurs merits special scrutiny. I suggest that Sidney broke the text here so as not to upstage a moment that is both Zelmane's triumph and her fall, her acceptance of a mutually intertwined male and female nature. Her combination of seduction and warfare, of being both an object of lust (from Zoilus) and herself incited to excessive desire (by Philoclea's garter), personalizes the provocation of her cross-dressing. Given the new complexity of her character, any purely martial triumph cannot but be anti-climactic. At this moment she is violent and unsettling, neither the passive woman of classical romance nor the chivalric man of medieval romance but an unstable mixture, like Sidney's narrative. She has become her costume, and Sidney has written himself into a corner. He has combined martial and erotic values, but his plot still needs each separately: Zelmane's sword to end the Captivity Episode, and her seductive dress to entice the Arcadian royal family back to Arcadia. Sidney may have been reluctant to return exclusively to either arms or eroticism. In the teeth of this dilemma, I speculate, Sidney laid down his pen, and the war in Holland prevented him from taking it up again. Zelmane's cross-dressing had become so central to the author's multigeneric narrative practice that he could not bring himself to write the scenes where she would lay her clothes aside.

# Chapter 4

# Anti-Epic Traditions: Greene's Romances

I write to your iudgements, hoping as my intent is to please all, if it might bee
without offence, so I shal be pardoned of al, though not presuming to[o] farre.

Robert Greene, "To the Gentlemen Readers," *Penelopes Web* (5:144)

Only the poet, disdaining to be tied to any such subjection, lifted up with the vigour
of his own invention, doth grow in effect another nature.

Philip Sidney, *Defence of Poesy* (216)

Greene and Sidney flank Heliodoran romance's entrance into Elizabethan prose
fiction. The aristocrat and the hack make an odd pair. Sidney was the presumptive,
if ultimately disappointed, heir of Robert Dudley, Earl of Leicester, and for a time
the focus of Protestant hopes at court.[1] Greene was a self-made man whose family
origins remain in doubt.[2] They both attended university, but Sidney left Christ
Church, Oxford, without a degree, while Greene graduated from St. John's,
Cambridge, and went on to receive Master of Arts degrees from both universities.[3]
Greene was an urban figure, and Sidney, while living in both court and country,
wrote primarily in the country.[4] In literary terms, they shared a taste for

---

[1]   See Duncan-Jones, *Sir Philip Sidney: Courtier-Poet*.

[2]   On Greene's life, see Charles W. Crupi, *Robert Greene*, (Boston: Twayne Publishers,
1986), John Clark Jordan, *Robert Greene*, (New York: Oxford University Press, 1915), and
Nicholas Storojenko, "The Life of Robert Greene," *Works*, vol. 1, and René Pruvost, *Robert
Greene et ses romans*. W. W. Barker considers Greene's life as a model for his fiction in
"Rhetorical Romance: The 'Frivolous Toyes' of Robert Greene," *Unfolded Tales: Essays on
Renaissance Romance*, George M. Logan and Gordon Tesky, eds., (Ithaca: Cornell
University Press, 1989) 74-97.

[3]   Greene received his MA in 1583, and a second from Oxford in 1588. The second
apparently was a courtesy extended from one university to the other, but it enabled Greene
to style himself "Utriusque Academia in Artibus Magister" in *Greenes Mourning Garment*
(1590) and later works.

[4]   Greene's project owes much to his urban environment. London provides a backdrop for
the "providential destiny" advanced in pamphlet literature, as Lawrence Manley has argued
(*Literature and Culture in Early Modern London*, [Cambridge: Cambridge University Press,
1995] 297).

Heliodorus, but had different ideas about how his genre should operate. Their different understandings of passivity and heroism define the field within which Elizabethan prose romance developed. Greene embraced the romance passivity Sidney doggedly resisted.

At stake in the rivalry between Sidney and Greene as writers of romance is a clearer sense of the social positioning of their texts. My claims for Greene as a middlebrow figure who aligns himself with but broadens the appeal of elite conventions become sharper when his work is juxtaposed against Sidney's. Sidney, while in many ways a failed courtier, was an elite figure with elite literary, political, and philosophical aspirations. The intricately plotted *New Arcadia* dwarfs any of Greene's numerous books; Sidney's greater ambition motivates the greater amplification (in Aristotle's sense) of his fiction. But each writer also defined his aspirations in detail, and comparing their authorial self-images reveals more than the old picture of superlative poet and marketplace hack. Greene's self-conscious celebration of his books makes a compelling, and on some level convincing, riposte to Sidney's cultural elitism.[5]

Sidney's *Defence of Poesy* has long been viewed as Elizabethan England's most important work of literary criticism.[6] Greene produced no comparable free-standing treatise, but the peritextual material of his books implicit rebukes to Sidney. By juxtaposing Greene's peritexts with Sidney's *Defence*, I extend my claim that the authorial self-justifications found in Elizabethan front matter are best read as practical works of literary theory. Where Sidney "defends" poetry on moral and philosophical grounds, Greene celebrates the circulation of books as literary commodities. For generations, Greene's use of Sidney's romance motifs has seemed a trivialization of high art. Gabriel Harvey makes precisely this point when he notes, "The Countesse of Pe[m]brookes Arcadia is not greene inough for queasie stomakes, but they must have *Greenes* Arcadia."[7] If we see Sidney and Greene as co-experimenters in a new literary kind, then these two authors expose a

---

[5]    Comparisons between Greene and Sidney are common, including recently Newcomb's: "In Bourdieu's terms, Sidney aspired to the dominant fraction of the dominant class, the elite group whose cultural dabbling was supposed merely to ornament substantial socioeconomic responsibility, while Greene, educated beyond his economic position, at best occupied the dominated fraction of the dominant class, the Bohemian group whose economic vulnerability Greene confirmed by his allegedly willful poverty" (*Reading Popular Romance in Early Modern England*, 32). Newcomb's treatment has been very valuable for me, though I focus on Greene's middlebrow status more than his later transformations into a popular figure.

[6]    Posthumously published like all of Sidney's work, the *Defence* (also published as the *Apologie for Poetry*) was most likely written around 1580, after the *Old Arcadia* but before the revision. It apparently began as a response to Stephen Gosson's *School of Abuse* (1579), an anti-theatrical tract dedicated to Sidney.

[7]    Gabriel Harvey, *Foure Letters and certain sonnets*, G.B. Harrison, ed., (London: Bodley Head, 1922) 41.

debate about what prose fiction would be in Elizabethan culture: high humanist poesy or marketable commodity?

Sidney's *Arcadia*, in both its *Old* and *New* versions, is a fictional experiment designed for an audience which shares an intellectual (and political) point of view. The romance, at least in its early version, was written for and read to Sidney's sister, the Countess of Pembroke, at her home in Wilton, and it approaches "poesy" as a rhetorical sport, in which verbal dexterity and stylistic display are ends in themselves and ways to debate human agency and control in political, philosophical, and theological arenas.[8] Sidney's *Defence* fights a rear-guard battle for high humanistic "poesy" as separate from, and superior to, the products of a debased market. The poesy Sidney calls the "first light-giver to ignorance" was not for sale. Sidney celebrates coterie literature as a form of rhetoric that resists political compromise, ethical collapse, and theological truancy. The courtly, humanist Sidney circle exemplifies the "golden" world of poesy; it is a world under siege from "brazen" power politics at Court and crass mercantilism in the City. This culture needed Sidney's defense.[9]

Greene shared Sidney's Protestant humanism, though without his politicized evangelism, but he spoke for (and from) a very different culture. His front matter celebrates the material and brazen elements of literary creation that Sidney excludes. For Greene, who repeatedly calls his writings "toyes" or "follies," his books' imperfections create value for different kinds of readers. Greene's works are "toyes" in more literal sense than Sidney's assertion that the *Old Arcadia* is a "trifle, and that trifilingly handled" (57). Greene celebrates his folly, while Sidney sees his literary errors as images of human insufficiency. Greene's playful self-castigation, his repeated dismissals of his works as "sundry wanton Pamphlets" (9:119) provides a radical alternative to Sidney's poetics. Greene values the "imperfect" in his work, the contingent, spontaneous quality that Nashe in the preface to *Menaphon* describes as his "extemporal vein" (82). For Greene, the rewards of literary discourse accrue through the circulation of his "toyes," which leads to the pleasure (and, perhaps, the edification) of his readers.

Greene's and Sidney's understandings of literary creation seem incompatible. Sidney's *Defence* argues that poetry arises from inspired glimpses of a divine plan. The concepts of the "fore-conceit" and the poet as *vates* suggest that, for Sidney, the poet serves as a conduit for things beyond mortal ken: "for any understanding knoweth the skill of each artificer standeth in that *idea* or fore-conceit of the work, and not in the work itself" (216). The language is neoplatonic, but the spirit, as several recent critics have noted, is Calvinist. Through the "fore-conceit," Sidney marries the foibles of individual poets to a transcendental conception of Poesy. He also joins humanist idealism with Calvinist focus on mortal weakness, making

---

[8]   On the politics of the *Old Arcadia*, see Worden, *The Sound of Virtue*. The allegory is much less central to the *New* version.

[9]   On the *Arcadia* as "great house" literature, see Danby, *Poets on Fortune's Hill*.

poetry a vehicle for Providential insight without deifying individual poets. Poetry allows inspired men and women to glimpse the divine plan as it manifests itself in history. Poetry thus contributes to Providential history by "bestow[ing] a Cyrus upon the world to make many Cryuses" (217).

Greene, on the other hand, locates his work's origins and social power in the London marketplace. Starting in *Mamillia*, he abjures any sense of himself as a vatic poet, instead hoping that his "unperfect...follie" will please a diverse crowd. The "many heades" define Greene's hoped-for audience; he asks only to appeal to as many of them as possible. Sidney, of course, was aware that the "many heades" of his audience might disagree with each other, but he emphasizes that reason should struggle to make accurate judgments, no matter how difficult it might be. Thus, after the "Ister Bank" eclogue in the *Old Arcadia*, when the narrator relates that "diverse judgements straight followed," the reader is not led to think that this heterogeneous pleasure is itself a triumph; rather, it speaks to the allegorical density of the passage, and the difficulty of speaking truths in a repressive political environment.[10] In relating the fable that "old Languet had me taught" (222) as an allegory of the crisis of his Protestant faction in Elizabeth's court, Sidney appeals to the most educated and discerning "wittes" he can find. In Heliodoran terms, he writes for Calasiris, not Cnemon – though Sidney's ideal reader is more politically involved than Heliodorus's hermit.

The refrain of Greene's epistles is the hope to please all readers. His ambition is antithetical to Sidney's: the latter aims high, constrained by mortal imperfections; the former low, aided by the pleasures of the dashed-off and incomplete. In *Perimedes the Blacksmith* (1588), Greene emphasizes that the book represents nothing more than "my old course, to palter up some thing in Prose" (7:7).[11] Books that are "palter[ed] up" cannot sustain high philosophical claims for Poesy, but they can appeal to the many-headed hydra of the marketplace. Greene's obsessive desire to change with the taste of his readers underlies the repeated voltes-face of his career.

In place of inspiration, Greene values commodification. Greene repeatedly called his books "toyes," "small trifles," or "pamphlets."[12] His description of *Arbasto* typifies his ambivalent assertion of commodification: "So Gentlemen, if

---

[10] On the *Arcadia* and censorship, see Annabel Patterson, *Censorship and Interpretation: The Conditions of Writing and Reading in Early Modern England*, (Madison: University of Wisconsin Press, 1984) 32-51.

[11] Greene calls his books "imperfect" five times, in *Mamillia* Part 1, *Morando* Part 1, *Arbasto*, *Gwyndonius*, and *Pandosto*.

[12] He calls his books "toyes" four times, in *Mamillia* Part 1, *Mamillia*, Part 2, *Morando* Part 1, and *Greenes Never too Late*. He calls *Pandosto*, a "small trifle" and an "imperfect Pamphlet" in the dedication to George Clifford (4:230-1). He calls his books "pamphlets" five times, in *Pandosto*, *Perimedes the Blacksmith*, *Alcida*, *Greenes Mourning Garment*, and *The Defence of Cony-Catching* (the last published under the pseudonym, "Cuthbert Cony-Catcher").

some to[o] curious carpe at your courtesye, that vouchsafe to take a view of this unperfect pamphlet, I hope you will answere, though it be not excellent, yet it is a booke" (3:177). Greene concedes his work's lack of excellence, but emphasizes its substance: it is a thing that will be bought, sold, and read. He writes in the letter preceding *Tullies Love* (1589) that his book is, "if not *Bucephalus*, yet a horse" (7:101).[13] An easy-riding nag rather than an emperor's steed, a pleasure-producing "toy" rather than a high-minded "fore-conceit," Greene's books celebrate themselves as commodities whose places is in bookstalls begging to be bought.

Sidney, by contrast, never intends that his *Defence* (or any of his works) be sold to the public. Anxiety about his "unelected vocation" (212) reinforces his sensitivity to the so-called "stigma of print."[14] He treats the appeal of literary rhetoric as more problem than solution. The *Defence* opens with a cautionary example of the persuasive force of language. Learning horsemanship from John Pietro Pugliano at Vienna, Sidney falls under his spell. Pugliano tells him that horses are "masters of war and ornaments of peace, speedy goers and strong abiders, triumphers both in camps and courts" (212), and Sidney believes virtue inheres in the bodies of horses.[15] His deliverance from this ludicrous horse-loving position – itself a pun on his name, "phil-(h)ippus" – comes from reason. Sidney writes, "if I had not been a piece of a logician before I came to him, I think [Pugliano] would have persuaded me to have wished myself a horse" (212). The wish to become the thing desired, to succumb to Pugliano's "strong affections and weak arguments" (212), recalls Greene's market-centered ambitions. Greene's self-description embraces "strong affections and weak arguments," and Sidney rejects this course for the same reason he rejects Pugliano, because obsessions with material form (horses or books) misplace human reason and hierarchical control. The horse cannot lead the rider, nor the book market the writer. Sidney would resist the market until his death, but his books then became as marketable as Greene's.[16] The *Arcadia*, among the most popular stories in English literature

---

[13] As numerous critics have observed, Greene did not shy away from plagiarizing himself; he had previously made the Bucephalus analogy in the epistle preceding *Arbasto* (1584).

[14] See J. W. Saunders, "The Stigma of Print: A Note on the Social Bases of Tudor Poetry," *Essays in Criticism* 1 (1951): 139-59. On work influenced by Saunders, see Daniel Traister, "Reluctant Virgins: The Stigma of Print Revisited," *Colby Quarterly* 26 (1980): 75-86. For a potent rejoinder, see Stephen W. May, "Tudor Aristocrats and the Mythical 'Stigma of Print,'" *Renaissance Papers* 10 (1980): 11-18. May focuses on aristocrats, including King James VI and I, who sought printed publication during their lifetimes. His findings do not fully quite his conclusion that "no 'stigma of print' is discernible during the Tudor age" (17). Rather, print carries both stigma and practical value for aristocrats in this period. On the mutual implication of print and manuscript cultures, see Mentz, "Selling Sidney."

[15] Horsemanship was a traditional emblem of the will's control over the body.

[16] Sidney's calls his *Defence* "this ink-wasting toy of mine" (249), accenting its status as a product of pen and ink, i.e., a manuscript.

through the eighteenth century, played out Sidney's fears by becoming, in essence, a horse that generations of publishers would ride.[17]

Both Greene and Sidney, as Helgerson has observed, turned to religious subjects late in their careers, but even here the split between them remains clear.[18] For Greene, fiction with a religious focus, what he calls in the *Spanish Masquerado* the attempt "to discouer my conscience in Religion" (5:241), was a tactical move in his mercantile maneuvering. His long dance of repentance, which he calls "the reformation of a second Ovid" (*Greenes Mourning Garment*; 9:121) and announces numerous times after 1590, appears designed to maintain commercial viability. His conversions strain the reader's credulity, especially since his books never stray from the masterplot of romance. Repentance for Greene is never a moral absolute, but a clever tactic, a trick to convert failure into triumph.

For Sidney, religion meant a Reformed understanding of human frailty. The gap between "wit" and "will" sets stark limits for the success of literary efforts. Given the contrast between their initial understandings of literary art, it seems surprising that both writers found the Heliodoran classical plot to be so useful. In using the Heliodoran template, however, Greene and Sidney diverge. Both emphasize the four Heliodoran narrative strategies I outlined in chapter 1: the primacy of heroines, passivity, indirection, and absolute supernatural control. But Greene embraces Heliodoran passivity and its idolization of femininity uncritically, while Sidney struggles to revise heroic force and epic masculinity.

Greene's celebration of mendacity underlies another of his favorite descriptive terms, "counterfeite."[19] For Greene, counterfeits became "books" through sales. The notion that counterfeits could be redeemed by sales balances whatever seems essentially deceptive about a writer's appeal to the marketplace.[20] The act of conversion – transforming something worthless into something valuable – was a dominant theme of Greene's career. Especially near the end of his life, Greene made conversion the preferred grist for his mill, as he changed himself from wanton pamphleteer to patriotic exposer to pious moralist. That each shift exported his narrative style to a slightly different readership cannot have been far from his mind, although one suspects that some readers may have simply followed Greene from genre to genre.

---

[17] On reception of the *Arcadia* into the eighteenth-century, see Peter Lindenbaum, "Sidney's *Arcadia* as Cultural Monument and Proto-Novel," *Texts and Cultural Change in Early Modern England*, Cedric C. Brown and Arthur F. Marrotti, eds., (New York: St. Martin's, 1989).

[18] See Helgerson, *Elizabethan Prodigals*.

[19] He calls his work a "counterfeite" three times, in the front matter to *Mamillia* Part 1, *Morando* Part 1, and *Arbasto*.

[20] "Counterfeit" in the early modern period could be used to mean to imitate with intent to deceive (*OED* 1-4) or without that intent (*OED* 7-9).

Both Sidney and Greene died young, each in exemplary fashion. After dying of wounds suffered fighting for the cause of international Protestantism in Zutphen against the Spanish in 1586, Sidney received an elaborate state funeral and became a national hero.[21] Six years later, Greene expired after a "surfett of pickle herring and rennish wine" in a London tavern.[22] The contrast between Sidney's martyrdom, celebrated in numerous elegies and Fulke Greville's hagiographic *Life*, and Greene's "fatall banquet" could not be more stark. Sidney died a hero, Greene a disgrace. In literary terms, however, Greene's model for how turning an author's name into a popular brand may have had as much impact on the English literary marketplace as Sidney's aristocratic example.

## Greene and Heliodorus at the Marketplace

> [W]hatsoeuer the lawes of Philosophy perswade me, I will at this time giue the raynes of libertie to my amorous passions.
>
> Robert Greene, *Mamillia* (2:34)

Where Sidney struggled to reconcile romance with his political ambitions and religious rigor, Greene reveled in the loose but predictable structure of the genre. For him, the formulaic quality of Heliodoran romance created a sheltered space for rhetorical play. While Sidney's heroes struggle against passivity, Greene's heroines accept it as a matter of course. The distinction between Sidney and Greene establishes two clear models for romancers who would follow them: either strain against the genre's limits, or accept the form and play within it.

Greene's earliest work of fiction, *Mamillia* (1583) simply presents a love story to the book market.[23] Notably, it contains one of two places in which Greene refers to Theagenes and Chariclea by name.[24] This early reference may suggest that the Heliodoran model helped initiate Greene's career, and it certainly demonstrates Greene's knowledge of the *Aethiopica* by 1580. Greene exaggerates Heliodoran romance by emphasizing human helplessness. In the early texts especially, the passive heroine – abandoned, pursued, and defenseless – takes center stage.

---

[21] See Duncan-Jones, *Courtier-Poet*, 275-303.

[22] Harvey, *Foure Letters*, 13.

[23] A presumed first edition of 1580 is lost; the earliest surviving copy is from 1583. In 1583, Ponsonby published the second part of under the subtitle, "The Triumph of Pallas."

[24] See Wolff, *Greek Romances in Elizabethan Prose Fiction*, 367-458, 381; and Greene, *Works*, 2:67, 91. The other reference is in *Alcida Greenes Metamorphoses* (1588) 9:80. Wolff stresses Greene's affinity with Greek romance by claiming that when Greene borrowed from Boccaccio, he took only elements which Boccaccio drew from Greek romance. See *Greek Romances in Elizabethan Prose Fiction*, 374-5.

*Mamillia* rejects heroic masculinity in its sub-title: "A Mirrour or looking-glasse for the Ladies of England."[25] Greene, whom Nashe called "the Homer of women," sells himself directly to women readers.[26] He may have learned this tactic from Lyly, but Greene's decision to make his central character female was not Lyly's: Euphues is not a warrior, but he is a man.[27] Sidney's *Arcadia* feminized itself by addressing to Sidney's sister in its title, but Greene's efforts seem much less vexed than Sidney's heady combination of female and male virtues: in Greene's romance the heroine unabashedly outshines the hero. Greene's full sub-title denigrates male heroism: "Wherein is deciphered, howe Gentlemen under the perfect substance of pure loue, are oft inueigled with the shadow of lewde luste: and their firme faith, brought asleepe by fading fancie: vntil wit ioyned with wisdome, doth awake it by the help of reason" (2:3). The syntax outlines the basic structure of Greene's romance: his gentlemen heroes (and readers) fall passively before the power of "lewde lust" and "fading fancie." Only after they lapse into sin do the forces of "wit ioyned with wisdome" and "reason" awake an unclear "it" that presumably is the "firme faith" previously lost.

In the 1583 edition, the earliest copy of *Mamillia* that survives, Greene manipulated the front matter with a shrewdness no other Elizabethan romancer would equal. Dedicating the text to "his very good Lorde and Maister, Lorde Darcie of the North," Greene emphasizes the book's marketability. He offers the text to Darcie as a form of currency, "the first payment" of the social debt he owes the Lord.[28] Marketability was again the issue in his epistle "To the Gentlemen Readers," which reads like a riposte to Sidney's as-yet unpublished letter to the Countess of Pembroke introducing the 1590 *Arcadia*. As noted earlier, Greene made frivolity a selling point: "If Gentlemen will take my booke as a toy to passe away the time...if I say, they shall shew me this curtesie, it shal be both a spurre to prick me forward to attempt further, and a sufficient recompence for my trauell" (2:10). Here is a trifle that makes no apologies for its trifling nature.

---

[25]   This sub-title appears in Thomas Woodcocke's 1583 edition, entered into the Stationers' Register on October 3, 1580.

[26]   Quoted by Lucas, *Writing for Women*, 74, as part of her diagnosis of misogyny in Greene's suffering women. Lucas fails to recognize the value, moral and psychological, that Greene places on passivity and other prototypically female virtues. Kinney notes that Greene likes "having it both ways" and plays to misogynist stereotypes as well as celebrating heroically resistant women. See "Marketing Fiction," *Critical Approaches to English Prose Fiction 1520-1640*, Donald Beecher, ed., (Ottawa: Dovehouse Editions, 1998) 45-61. I discuss Nashe's epithet in chapter 5.

[27]   Greene's early works are highly indebted to Lyly; see Pruvost, *Robert Greene*; Jordan, *Robert Greene*; and Jaroslav Hornat, "*Mamillia:* Robert Greene's Controversy with *Euphues*," *Philologica Pragensia* 5 (1963): 210-18.

[28]   Brenda Richardson suggests that Greene, possibly raised in Yorkshire, may have known Darcie in his pre-Cambridge years. See "Robert Greene's Yorkshire Connections: A New Hypothesis," *Yearbook of English Studies* 10 (1980): 160-80.

*Mamillia* presents Greene's romance-masterplot in its simplest form: virtuous Mamillia loves inconstant Pharicles, she hides her love, and he leaves her for the younger Publia, only to return in the second part, *Mamillia: The Triumph of Pallas.*[29] Mamillia claims a Heliodoran model for her key virtue, constancy in love. Twice Mamillia mentions Heliodorus's characters by name, citing them as models of constancy: "be thou but *Theagines,* and I will try my selfe to be more constant than *Caniclila*" (2:67), and later, "What perilles suffered *Theagines* to keepe his credit with *Caricha*?" (2:91). Despite Greene's, or his compositor's, variable spellings of Chariclea's name, Mamillia defines herself in Heliodoran terms. In fact, she suggests that while Theagenes would be a good model for Pharicles, she herself will be "more constant" than Chariclea. Constancy is the virtue *par excellence* of Greene's heroines, and Mamillia explicitly names its Heliodoran source.

After Pharicles declares his love, Mamillia turns to Chariclea's tactics of indirection. At this point, she combines the stance that Helgerson calls "passive resignation"[30] with an indirection reminiscent of both Heliodorus and of Greene's efforts to fashion himself as a marketable author. She wants to appeal to diverse ways of reading her. Mamillia never becomes as active as Zelmane, but instead imitates Chariclea:

> Although these wordes of *Pharicles,* Gentlemen, did not greatly displease *Mamillia,* because it is very harde to anger a woman with praising her, and especially if she think as much of her selfe as others speake, yet she would have hid fire in the straw, and haue danced in a net, striuing as much as shee could, with a discontented countenaunce to couer a contented mind, and to seeme as cruel as a Tygre, though as meeke as a Lambe, least either by outward shewe or words hee might coniecture some hope of good happe, she gaue him this cold confect for his hotte stomacke. (2:62)

The sly "Gentlemen" reminds readers that Greene's address to women readers (like those of Lyly, Pettie, and Riche) are to be read voyeuristically by male courtiers. Mamillia's acknowledgment of Pharicles's love and manipulation of its postponement recalls Chariclea playing off Thyamis or Zelmane manipulating Zoilus. This task is complicated for Greene's heroine because she cannot trust Pharicles. Her lover's inconstancy weakens her position. Caught in the "net" of eros, Mamillia goes on to describe constancy as her only defense: "A womans heart is like the stone in *Aegypt,* that will quickly receiue a forme, but neuer chaunge without cracking" (2:64). With a nod toward Heliodorus's eastern Mediterranean milieu, Mamillia posits constancy as her ideal virtue, but also cites

---

[29] This two-part structure copies Lyly's two volumes of Euphues. On the legacy of Lyly in Greene and Lodge, see Nancy R. Lindheim, "Lyly's Golden Legacy: *Rosalynde* and *Pandosto,*" *Studies in English Literature* 15 (1973): 3-20.

[30] *Elizabethan Prodigals,* 82

constancy as a reason to conceal her own love. Her dilemma would not find a
solution until later in Greene's career.


### "A Note Beyond Your Reach": *Menaphon* and Elizabethan Heliodoranism

> Come forth, you wits that vaunt the pomp of speech,
> And strive to thunder from a stage-man's throat,
> View *Menaphon* a note beyond your reach,
> Whose sight will make your drumming descant dote.
>> Thomas Brabine, introductory verses to *Menaphon* (79)


*Menaphon*, Greene's most ambitious fiction, was a media sensation in Elizabethan
publishing.[31] Along with Lodge's *Rosalynde*, which appeared one year later,
*Menaphon* represents the high-water mark of Elizabethan Heliodoranism. I have
already explored how its front matter parades the cultural ambition of Elizabethan
fiction. In specifically contrasting itself with the stage – Thomas Brabine's poem
presumably fingers Marlowe as the "thundering" playwright – *Menaphon* claims to
be a new form of literary excellence. Its lengthy publication history, which
parallels that of *Rosalynde*, suggest that these boasts were not mere bravado.
*Menaphon* was published by Sampson Clarke in 1589, re-issued in 1599 and 1605
by Nicholas Ling, and then passed to John Smethwicke, who re-published it under
the title *Greenes Arcadia* in 1610 and 1616, for a total of 5 editions in just over 25
years.[32] This does not quite make it Greene's best-selling fiction – that honor goes
to *Pandosto* – but it seems worth recalling that no Shakespearean play is reprinted
so often during this time.[33]

*Rosalynde*, even more strikingly, was published in nine editions between 1590
and 1634.[34] Perhaps unsurprisingly, given the close contact between Greene and
Lodge at this time, in which Greene served as Lodge's agent when he was at sea,
these two publishing ventures show considerable overlap. *Rosalynde* was
published, separately and together, by four members of the Stationers' Company:
Nicholas Ling, John Busby, Thomas Gubbins, and John Smethwicke. Ling and
Smethwicke also produced four of the five editions of *Menaphon*. The way this
group reprinted Elizabethan-Heliodoran fiction makes a powerful argument for this

---

[31] For recent praise of *Menaphon*, see Davis, who calls it "Greene's masterpiece" (*Idea and Act*, 171); Barker, "Rhetorical Romance," 84; Salzman, *English Prose Fiction*, 65-8; Margolies, *Novel and Society*, 127-8; and Cantar's introduction, 11-74.

[32] The copyright was assigned from Ling to Smethwicke on November 19, 1607. See *STC*, 1:537.

[33] On *Pandosto* see Newcomb, *Reading Romance in Early Modern England*.

[34] Of contemporary romances, only Greene's *Pandosto* went through more editions. *Pandosto* was published twelve times between 1588 and 1640, with the later editions going by the title, *The Pleasant Historie of Dorastus and Fawnia*.

fiction's status as marketable object. While the relationships among these four appear informal, in publishing *Menaphon* and especially *Rosalynde* they operated as a *de facto* consortium. The first edition of *Rosalynde*, in 1590, was published jointly by Gubbins and Busby, and the group subsequently passed the book amongst themselves: Gubbins and Busby again in 1592, Ling and Busby in 1596, Ling and Gubbins in 1598, Ling alone in 1604, and the last four editions (1609, 1612, 1623, and 1634) by Smethwicke, who became Ling's literary heir in 1609. It seems noteworthy that Ling, who appears to have owned the rights when he bequeathed them to Smethwicke, was not the publisher of the first edition in 1590. He was, however, one of the two men (along with Busby) to whom the book was entered in the Stationers' Register on October 6, 1590.

These two texts make a valuable comparison with the publication of two more prestigious Elizabethan romances, Sidney's *Arcadia* (1590, 1593, 1598) and Spencer's *Faerie Queene* (1590, 1594). These canonical texts were published by the up and coming Stationer William Ponsonby.[35] The Ling-Busby consortium (if they deserve such a name) did not manage such long-term success, but as a group they capitalized on the popular taste for romance fiction. Along with Thomas Newman, to whom John Smethwicke was apprenticed in 1598-7, these men published *Greenes Mourning Garment* (Newman, 1590); *Greenes Never too Late* (Ling and Busby, 1590, Ling, 1600, 1602, 1607, Smethwicke, 1611); *Greenes Vision* (Newman, 1592); and Lodge's *Robin the Devil* (Ling and Busby, 1591), *Euphues' Shadow* (Busby, 1592), and *A Margarite of America* (Busby, 1596). Thus over little more than a quarter-century these five publishers produced 22 separate editions, or nearly one per year, of Elizabethan prose romances. In selecting *Rosalynde, Robin the Devil*, and *A Margarite of America* out of Lodge's writings, they focused on Lodge's fiction, rather than his social satire, verse, or moral criticism. These works represent a significant fraction of the total fiction publications of Greene and Lodge, and also a noteworthy part of the output of these publishers. For John Smethwicke, Ling's professional heir, publishing these fictions was part of a distinguished career; he became Master of the Company in 1639.[36]

In *Menaphon*, Greene's professional ambition gets combined with a conventional plot that shifts its focus down the social scale. The work highlights Greene's middlebrow paradox: he makes high claims for the book, but pitches his tale to less-than-elite readers. There is a royal wedding in *Menaphon*, but it is off stage and downplayed. By emptying out heroic agency, *Menaphon* contrasts with romances like *New Arcadia* (presumably unread by Greene at this time) or *Amadis of Gaul*. Greene's heroine Sephastia cannot take up a sword like Zelmane, and she has no knight-errant battling for her. Instead, she relies on her wits, rhetorical

---

[35] Ponsonby also published two books by Greene, *Mamillia* part 2 (1583) and *Gwyndonius* (1584).

[36] He also, as a partner of John Jaggard, had a share in the first two Shakespeare folios.

acumen, and above all Fortune. Her extreme passivity suggests that Greene's version of the anti-epic tradition cuts all ties to martial values: there are few warriors anywhere in Greene.

According to Smethwicke's 1610 title, *Menaphon* is both a fictional *Arcadia* –a re-presentation of Sidney's material – and also the work of *Greene* – a publication tailored to popular taste. More than any other Elizabethan prose writer, Greene internalized the tastes of his readers. John Clark Jordan speaks for a generation's assumptions about Greene when he asserts that to say that Greene "wrote for his living explains Greene as fully...as any single statement can."[37] This backhanded praise was once a reason to dismiss Greene, but it also suggest that his career reveals prose fiction's emergence in England. Greene's prefatory letters suggest that he conceived of the book market itself as a species of romance, in which the wandering reader-heroine seeks the perfect hero-author. The pun Greene often made on his name as meaning "young" or "untried" suggests that he is the key ingredient needed to bring brash new energy to "Arcadia."

The two most prominent plot devices *Menaphon* takes from Greek romance are the two Sidney also borrowed from Heliodorus: oracles and shipwreck. The oracle, which presents itself as an insolvable mystery, is *Menaphon*'s hermeneutic key. It defines Greene's distinction from Sidney, because it is less a puzzle than an enigma. It cannot be solved, but must be accepted. Greene's oracle is longer and less plot-driven than Sidney's, and it requires a supernatural solution.[38] Instead of paradoxes about Basilius's adultery with his own wife, this oracle describes a universe at odds with itself:

> When Neptune riding on southern seas
> > Shall from the bosom of his leman yield
> Th'Arcadian wonder, men and gods to please,
> Plenty in pride shall march amidst the field,
> > Dead men shall war, and unborn babes shall frown,
> > And with their falchions hew their foemen down.
>
> When lambs have lions for their surest guide,
> > And planets rest upon th'Arcadian hills,
> When swelling seas have neither ebb not tide,
> When equal banks the ocean margin fills,

---

[37] *Robert Greene*, 201.

[38] As Cantar notes, Greene could have gotten this device from Heliodorus or Achilles Tatius. Combined with the Arcadian setting of the tale, and the pastoral disguise of the noble couple Sephastia and Maximus, the evidence for some knowledge of Sidney seems powerful, even though Sidney's romance was not yet in print. See Cantar, ed., *Menaphon*, 186-7. Paul Scanlon suggests that *Menaphon* draws from both the *Old Arcadia* and the *New*, but does not sustain the *New*'s narrative complexity. See "Greene's Later Prose Romances," *Cahiers Elisabethains* 24 (1983): 11.

> Then look Arcadians for a happy time,
> And sweet content within your troubled clime. (95-6)

Three uses of the word "Arcadia" highlight the Sidneian/Sannazarran parallel, but this oracle is much darker than Sidney's. "Th'Arcadian wonder" is the heroine Sephastia, but the world around her is grim indeed: dead men war, unborn babes frown, and mysterious "foemen" fall. Unlike in the *Old Arcadia*, misinterpreting the prophecy does not initiate the main plot. Instead, the original error that starts Greene's tale – Sephastia's being exiled for marrying against her father's wishes – is independent of the oracle. This world is less errant than indecipherable.

Struggling to interpret prophecy is less important in Greene's romance than Sidney's. The oracle is more a statement of events – a coded summary of the plot – than a challenge to human ingenuity. It describes a climax that arrives without any human intervention: the concluding duel between Sephastia's husband and son. The "dead" Maximus fights his "unborn" son while King Democles, Sephastia's father, looks on. At this point, Providence (and the oracle) intervene. An old woman "attired like a prophetess" (173) appears to interpret the oracle, pronouncing Democles the "lion [which] were guide unto the lambs" and claiming that "the seas that had neither ebb nor tide was the combat 'twixt the father and the son that gave the waves of the seas in their shields, not able to vanquish one another but parting with equal victory" (173). This metaphorical interpretation explains the oracle and reconciles the far-flung family. As the prophetess explains, "sweet content" – on a gigantic scale – has arrived. Human agency contributes little to this resolution.

The recognition at the text's end, however, does not obviate the interpersonal horror of the preceding scene, in which three generations of men fight over Sephastia's body. In his attention to Sephastia's plight, Greene exceeds Sidney and Heliodorus: where they toy with various adulterous or extramarital affairs, Greene describes the son and father hacking each other with swords over the mother, with the grandfather's army waiting in the wings to crush the winner. As W. W. Barker notes, *Menaphon* takes the "familiar themes of familial and social love" and makes their reconciliation nearly impossible by confusing them in incest.[39] In a world this violent and threatening, conspiratorial "mendacity" seems as impotent as chivalric swords. Sephastia, in her pastoral disguise as Samela, can only resign herself to despair. She tells herself, "Unfortunate Samela, born to mishaps and forepointed to sinister fortunes, whose blooms were ripened by mischance and whose fruit is like to wither with despair" (165). This lament recalls the oracle, for which nothing less than the union of lion and lamb will suffice. The stakes in *Menaphon* – as in Greene's romances generally – are cosmic, not political or personal. Bad government is a problem, but political acumen never helps. Even the errant sea must be transfigured and "have neither ebb nor tide" for Arcadia to reach its

---

[39] "Rhetorical Romance," 84.

promised "happy time." Redemption in Greene's Arcadia is entirely supernatural, and the unlooked-for appearance of the prophetess gives proof to the proverb Greene later cites: "no heaven but Arcadia" (152).[40] The "heaven" that rescues Sephastia redeems both the Sphinxian riddle of human desire and the happy play of Roscius's comic pageantry.[41]

As in Sidney and Heliodorus, shipwreck underlines the intervention of unknowable powers into Greene's tale.[42] The arrival of Sephastia on Arcadian shores with her infant son Pleusidippus and her guardian Lamedon comes by the familiar wreck. This loss starts a slide into impotence that Greene's heroine never escapes. Like Heliodorus and Sidney, Greene begins from a minor character's point-of-view, that of the shepherd Menaphon, who spies Sephastia coming ashore and falls in love with her.[43] The shipwreck, which Sephastia thinks has killed Maximus (he washes up a bit farther down the shore, and disguises himself as a shepherd), appears with its Greek romance elements foregrounded: "Menaphon...casting his eye to the seaside, espied certain fragments of a broken ship floating upon the waves, and sundry persons driven up upon the shore with a calm, walking all wet and weary upon the sands. Wondering at this strange sight, he stood amazed" (101). The scene plays it both ways: Menaphon sees the "broken fragments" that testify to the violence of the storm, and also the "calm" that has allowed Sephastia and her companions to reach the shore. Menaphon sees nothing but wonder, and Greene's narrator pointedly notes that the three survivors are "preserved by some further forepointing fate" (101). This "fate," of course, is the plot of the book (*fabula*) as well as Providential destiny.

Menaphon's interpretation is so simplistic that Greene must remind the reader about "forepointing fate" himself. Sephastia's reaction, however, is more perceptive. In taking on a pastoral disguise, and later obtaining the help of the lovestruck Menaphon, she adopts Chariclea's indirect tactics. Unlike Sidney's

---

[40]   Lindheim takes Greene's demand for complete transformation to mean that he is an anti-romance writer, and she cites with approval C. S. Lewis's verdict that "There is a coldness, even a brutality, about Greene's mind, which unfits him for telling this sort of tale" (*English Literature in the Sixteenth-Century*, 423). This criticism ignores that Elizabethan readers, apparently, thought him perfectly fit for these sorts of tales, perhaps because of the call for metaphysical, rather than human, redemption. See "Lyly's Golden Legacy," 18, 20.

[41]   Kinney suggests that *Menaphon* purifies humanist rhetoric from baser commercial and frivolous elements: "humanist rhetoric is salvaged after being subjected to the terms of romance within the leisure of fiction" (*Humanist Poetics,* 183). I believe commercial elements never leave Greene's fiction.

[42]   Jordan suggests that the primary Greek romance influence on *Menaphon* is Longus's *Daphnis and Chloe,* translated into English by Angel Day in 1587. Scanlon counters that Sidney and Heliodorus are greater influences. See Jordan, *Robert Greene,* 39, and Scanlon, "Greene's Later Prose Romances," 11.

[43]   Despite the book's title, Menaphon remains a minor character, merely serving to solidify Greene's pastoral world. Sidney, by contrast, has no real shepherds in his Arcadia.

princesses, she has the benefit of good masculine advice, from her husband's uncle and co-survivor of the wreck, Lamedon. As Sephastia bewails her (supposedly) dead husband, Lamedon preaches the inconstancy of Fortune. He also suggests the nature of Fortune means her position will improve:

> Chance is like Janus, doubled-faced, as well full of smiles to comfort as of frowns to dismay; the ocean at his deepest ebb returns to full tide...so fareth it with Fortune who in her highest extremes is most unconstant; when the tempest of her wrath is most fearful, then look for a calm....Thus are the arrows of Fortune feathered with the plumes of the bird halcyon that changeth colors with the moon, which howsoever she shoots them pierce not so deep but they may be cured. (103-4)

As a primer in the correct attitude for a heroine of Greek romance, Lamedon's advice is straightforward: things will get better, preserve yourself, and wait. In espousing delaying tactics, he echoes a series of wise old men from Calasiris to Lyly's Eubulus, but Lamedon reprises this role without "showmanship." In Lamedon's explanation of shipwreck, the heroine's course of action is simple; all she has to do is to wait. (In Chariclea's words, "there bee some more hidden mysterie, which casteth into extreame perill, and when al hope is past, findeth a remedy" [216].) A simplified version of the Heliodoran model, this gloss on Fortune sets the stage for Sephastia's inactivity.

Part of Greene's alteration of Heliodoran romance is the attitude toward Chance that Lamedon's speech reveals. When Lamedon notes that Sephastia should not give up hope because "Chance is like Janus, double-faced," he celebrates the blind Chance that for Heliodorus is problematic. Greene's representations of Fate and Chance never abandons the point-of-view of the human actor caught up in confusing events. Unlike Calasiris or Pamela, Greene's characters speculate little on the divine order. Rather, they accept that divinity is just and also realize that from their point of view divine actions are indistinguishable from chance. The passivity of Greene's heroines is both an acquiescence to religious and social authority and part of Greene's sympathy with human weakness. Sephastia cannot differentiate between a shipwreck caused by chance and one caused by Providence or Tyche; she can only endure, and hope that by survival she will retrospectively demonstrate that the wreck was Providential. The turn from Sidney's active heroes to Greene's passive women entails a loss of agency, but a gain of sympathy with human powerlessness.

Sephastia never acts directly, but she is the oracle's "Arcadian wonder" who motivates the entire plot. Accepting Lamedon's advice, she settles in the countryside, saying, "I will imagine a small cottage to [be] a spacious palace, and think as great quiet in a russet coat as in royal habiliments" (105). The key term here is "imagine": Sephastia's pastoral retreat is an act of imagination. Greene's heroine is his ideal reader and in a real sense her solution is the "booke" celebrated in Greene's peritexts. (His ideal hero, who emerges later, is a fictionalized version of the author.) Sephastia steps into pastoral romance and waits for its plot to guide her home. Her focus at first is on her son, but when he (in another stock scene) is stolen by pirates (136-8), she continues in shepherd's weeds, turning down Menaphon's overtures and those of her husband Maximus, whom she does not recognize in his pastoral disguise. The patent absurdity that Sephastia should refuse her husband's (disguised) wooing in order to be faithful to her (missing) husband, like the later absurdity that three generations of men should fight over Sephastia without recognizing each other, underscores Greene's demotion of human agency. All action is errant, and passivity allows the story to unfold.

Like Greene's other heroines, Sephastia's virtue is constancy, not just to her missing husband but also to her son and even to her father Democles, who exiled her in the first place.[44] In denying Menaphon's suit, Sephastia uses Chariclean indirection. By extolling "equal fortunes" in love, Sephastia manipulates Menaphon, encouraging him not to pester her with proposals while securing his help to maintain her shepherdess's life. With sly indirection, she suggests that if Menaphon waits, she may favor him. Her speech, like Chariclea's or Zelmane's, is both literally true and utterly deceptive: "Give me leave then, Menaphon, first to sorrow for my fortunes, then to call to mind my husband's late funerals. Then, if the fates have assigned I shall fancy, I will account of thee before any shepherd in Arcadia" (116). She leaves herself two escapes, first by appealing to "the fates," whom she trusts will not assign her to Menaphon, and also by saying that she will prefer Menaphon to "any shepherd." Since she has just celebrated social equality as essential to any match, and since she is a princess, she knows that she will never "account of" any shepherd. Her deception plays on Menaphon's ignorance of her true identity and his hope that fate has reserved her for him.[45] It also manipulates the semi-elite position of Greene's intended readers, who enjoy seeing the shepherd's hopes dashed. The trick she plays on Menaphon is cruel, like the one Maria and Toby play on Malvolio in *Twelfth Night*. Cruelty is the price Greene pays for his attachment to social hierarchy, and his middlebrow audience seems to have loved it.[46] Her forced pastoral retreat makes deception her only weapon, and she uses it only to preserve herself for the tale's appointed ending.

The narrow horizons of solitude and disguise place greater constraints on Sephastia's agency than those of Chariclea or Sidney's princesses. Here *Menaphon's* middlebrow humility threatens to become self-abnegation. Greene also mutes his religious sub-text, so that the risks of Sephastia's despair are never

---

[44] Barbour argues that Greene's romances "preserve the order of...society" (*Deciphering Elizabethan Fiction*, 49). His further suggestion that Greene's writing creates a "narrative stability" (21, 43) supports my more claim of narrative coherence in Elizabethan fiction.

[45] Wolff notes Sephastia's "skill in dissimulation" and compares her to Chariclea in this regard (*Greek Romances in Elizabethan Prose Fiction*, 412, 424).

[46] The plot that married servant to master did not, however, have to wait until Richardson's *Pamela;* Thomas Deloney presented it in *Jack of Newbury* (1597-8).

emphasized.[47] As she bewails her desperate fortune, her passivity seems like surrender: "Dissembling heavens, where is your happiness? Unconstant times, what are your triumphs? Have you therefore hitherto fed me with honey that you might at last poison me with gall?" (141). At this point, she believes her story is the opposite of a romance. She despairs, and things only get worse. Pleusidippus returns, as does her father Democles, but each presses an incestuous suit. Greene's metaphor for their assault is the Medusa's paralyzing gaze: "Samela...stood amazed like Medusa's metamorphosis and blushing oft with intermingled sighs, began to think how injurious Fortune was to her, shown in such an incestuous father" (154-5). Forgetting Lamedon's advice, Sephastia has become convinced that fortune is "injurious," as her family comes to blows over her.

From Sephastia's perspective, she survives by refusing to break her personal vows. Imprisoned by Democles alongside Maximus, Sephastia does not reveal herself, which would expose Democles's lust as incest. Maximus, also, refuses to reveal his true identity. The impasse epitomizes the extreme passivity of Greene's characters. Sephastia's retreat from her public identity is Greene's version of Protestant internality; his characters name themselves only to themselves. Even threatened by death, his heroine will not expose herself: "Samela was so desirous to end her life with her friend that she would not reveal either unto Democles or Melicertus what she was, and Melicertus rather chose to die with his Samela than once to name himself Maximus" (172). The dilemma of Greene's plot can be solved only by supernatural intervention.

Notably, none of the principal characters makes a substantial speech after the prophetess appears. The family reconciles, Pleusidippus craves his father's pardon, and Democles seeks forgiveness from Maximus and Sephastia, which he obtains by naming their son his heir and making Lamedon a duke. The great reunion, however, calls up no celebratory rhetoric, not even a rehearsal of Lamedon's pieties about Fortune and Chance. The text retreats from social spectacle as if embarrassed, and closes instead with two country weddings, Menaphon's to his old love Pesana, and the shepherd Doron's to Carmela. The reunion of the end of romance has arrived, but Greene's focus on the unplotted marriages of the shepherds dims the political glow of the royal reunions.

Greene's apparent distaste for political rhetoric suggests that his investment in romance concludes before the dynastic marriage. This focus on the individual rather than the national matches Greene's social position as compared to Sidney's: Greene sought pleasure and profit, not political influence. It also reflects the social status of Greene's readers, whose marriages would not have been political events.[48]

---

[47] The threat of atheism, a potent subtext in Sidney, Lodge, and Nashe, never appears in Greene's fiction, although it does in his fictionalized autobiographies.

[48] Greene presents an alternative concluding movement in a poem inserted just before the final scene. This "sonnetto," the only one authored by Greene in his narrator-persona, has no connection to the plot, reconsiders erotic motivation:

The anti-epic project that Elizabethan writers found in Heliodorus, and that Sidney problematized by revising his *Arcadia*, finds here its clearest middlebrow expression.

---

> What thing is love? It is a power divine
> That reigns in us, or else a wreakful law
> That dooms our minds to beauty to incline;
> It is a star whose influence doth draw
>          Our hearts to love, dissembling of his might,
>          Till he be master of our hearts and sight. (170-1)

Like *Menaphon* itself, the poem explores love's influence rather than political realities. Sephastia's passivity seems tactically shrewd, given Love's capricious dominion. Her static nature, her refusal to talk to her husband, father, or son, makes her Greene's ideal heroine: she endures, preserves herself, and triumphs in the end. The sonetto suggests that love, and by extension all human desire, is untrustworthy and obscure: "It is a secret hidden and not known, / Which one may better feel than write upon" (171). For Greene, this "hidden" secret motivates his obsessive creation and re-creation of fictional avatars. His own love, however, is not for any one person but for the crowd itself, and the "secret" he pursues is the "love" of the market.

# Chapter 5

# The Homer of Women: Greene and the Novella

Tastes (i.e., manifested preferences) are the practical affirmation of an inevitable difference. It is no accident that, when they have to be justified, they are asserted purely negatively, by the refusal of other tastes.

Pierre Bourdieu, Distinction (56)

During the 1560s and 1570s, the most popular genre of Elizabethan fiction was the novella. Drawing on Italian writers from Boccaccio to Bandello, and their French translators and imitators from Belleforest to Margarite de Navarre, writers like William Painter, Jeffrey Fenton, George Pettie, and Barnebe Riche, produced dozens of book-length collections. The largest successes were Painter's 3-volume *Palace of Pleasure* (1566, 1567, and 1575), Pettie's *Petite Palace* (1576), and Fenton's *Certaine Tragicall Discourses* (1567). All three of these are in large part translations from Italian, French, or classical sources, but there was also a native vogue for this kind of fiction. The most well-known descendents of the Elizabethan novella are probably the fictions of Gascoigne and Lyly, but an influential example of the novella's authorial stance appears in Pettie's *Pettie Pallace*. For many reasons, not least of which being their shared motto, *Omne tulit punctum qui miscuit utile dulce*, Pettie makes an instructive comparison for Greene. Where Pettie remains fundamentally cynical, deploying his literary wares as part of a courtier's game, Greene's more brazen appeal to a middlebrow readership marks his novelle collections as Heliodoran narratives rather than products of academic humanism.[1]

The novella challenged humanist standards. Accounts of the genre emphasize both its roots in traditional medieval and post-classical narrative forms (joke tales, fabliaux, etc.) and also its radical nature. Tzvetan Todorov has suggested that the two basic storylines of *The Decameron* are "punishment avoided" and "conversion."[2] H. J. Neuschäfer has also suggested the novella combines compact

---

[1]   Salzman notes that Pettie's primary sources are Ovid, Livy, Tacitus, and Hyginus (14). Greene draws on these humanist authorities, but he shows greater interest in narrative variation.

[2]   For a narratological analysis of Boccaccio, see Tzvetan Todorov, *Grammaire du Décaméron*, (The Hague: Mouton, 1969).

linear plotting with dramatic reversals of traditional ethical norms.[3] The inverse relationship between narrative progression and moral context shadowed the novella's reception in Elizabethan England. Robin Kirkpatrick has emphasized the "ethical ambiguity" of the form, and numerous critics have commented on the anti-novella polemics of Ascham and others.[4] Even as writers like Fenton drew on the more heavily moralized French novelle, a hint of sophisticated depravity lurked in the genre.[5]

Part of the charge of Elizabethan novelle was their highly sexualized presentation. What Juliet Fleming has called the gendered ambivalence or "transvestism" of the "ladies' texts" emphasizes the deployment of gender as a rhetorical strategy which allows semi-elite male authors to divide their readers into two categories: the women to whom the texts are addressed, and the men who read them.[6] Fleming reads the "overt interpellation of a female audience" (160) as byproduct of the gender politics of the Elizabethan age; women readers so constructed get subsumed in a "deeply sarcastic...attack" on the Queen and her feminized court. Reading Riche as a writer of "protest," (166-7), however, Fleming overlooks the less aggressive implications of the two-headed volumes that addressed themselves sequentially to "Gentle Ladies" and "Gentlemen." The imaginatively bi-gendered audience that these works construct allowed Elizabethan writers to portray themselves as elite and popular at the same time. "Transvestism" seems a distinctly middlebrow strategy. The issue seems less masculine interpellation (though the power of author over reader is part of the fiction) than an elaborate rhetorical construction of diverse readers. Greene once again aims lower than his courtly rival. The split between Pettie and Greene thus recapitulates the distinction between elite separatism and middlebrow community. Pettie's cynicism about humanist ethics distinguishes him from Sidney, but neither plays to the semi-elite as broadly as Greene.

---

[3]   Quoted by Jauss, "Theory of Genres and Medieval Literature," *Toward an Aesthetic of Reception*, 92, 209n.

[4]   See Robin Kirkpatrick, *English and Italian Literature from Dante to Shakespeare: A Study of Source, Analogue, and Divergence*, (London: Longman, 1995) 225. See also Clubb, *Italian Drama in Shakespeare's Time*; Kinney, *Humanist Poetics*; and David Bevington, "Cultural Exchange: Gascoigne and Ariosto at Gray's Inn," *The Italian World of English Renaissance Drama: Cultural Exchange and Intertextuality*, Michele Marrapodi, ed., (Newark: University of Delaware Press, 1998).

[5]   Kirkpatrick emphasizes that French translators like Belleforest added "verbosity and didacticism" to their Italian sources, which English writers like Fenton kept (*English and Italian Literature from Dante to Shakespeare*, 228).

[6]   Fleming nicely captures the aggressiveness of the transvestite pose: "the enabling logic of the prodigal text itself... requires its female readers to attend to the story of their own rejection" ("The Ladies' Man and the Age of Elizabeth," *Sexuality and Gender in Early Modern Europe: Institutions, Texts, Images*, James Grantham Turner, ed., [Cambridge: Cambridge University Press, 1993] 161.)

The title of this chapter comes from Nashe's oblique attack on Greene in *The Anatomy of Absurditie* (1590). Nashe had made his print debut the previous year in his preface to *Menaphon*, but this professional debt did not deter his aggressive sniping. Nashe claims that Greene misuses humanist rhetoric to pander to women; after a diatribe against women from Antigone to Pasiphae, Nashe notes that "the *Homer* of Women has forestalled an obiection...[and claimed] that there be amongst them as amongst men, some good, some badde" (1:12). Nashe's description does not quite make Greene a proto-feminist, and in fact the portrait ends ambiguously: "some good, some badde." Greene's desire for a broad audience explains his desire to appeal to women readers. It is uncertain how many "women readers" there were in Elizabethan London, or how many women purchased books, but documents like Margaret Tyler's 1578 preface to *The First Part of the Mirrour of Princely deedes and Knighthood* suggests that there were some women who read fiction. Recent critics like Helen Hackett and Lori Newcomb observe that men, too, might be attracted to works advertised as "written for women."[7] Nashe's epithet, "Homer of women," links Greene to one audience out of several; Greene's prefaces suggest he sought many at once.

Pettie's authorial practice, by contrast, appeals to "Gentlewomen Readers" while surreptitiously creating a misogynistic bond with the male courtiers who were his true audience. Turning from his peritexts to his faux-classical tales reveals a shift from eroticized readers to bifurcated heroines who oscillate between marriage-centered chastity and a more destabilizing sexuality.[8] Pettie concludes each of his dozen tales with an explicit address to his women readers, and these addresses as often criticize the virtuous behavior of the tale's heroines as they reinforce it. Unlike the passive but deceptive heroines of Greene's faux-Heliodoran romances, Pettie's heroines are thoroughly ironized, in a tense dialogue with eroticized women readers who may choose not to follow their examples and the male readers who enjoy seeing female virtue under duress.

### Kissing the Reader: Pettie's Pleasures

> These be the inchantementes of *Circes*, brought out of *Italie*, to marre mens maners in England; much by example of ill life, but more by preceptes of fonde bookes, of late translated out of *Italian* into English, sold in euery shop in London, commended

---

[7]   Hackett observes, "The male reader may adopt a female persona in order to assess male writing apparently addressed to women, and to enjoy metaphoric access to women's bedchambers and other spaces of courtship" (*Women and Romance Fiction*, 12).

[8]   Jane Collins connects Pettie's heroines with Riche's and describes both as "represent[ing] a chaste female sexuality that supports marriage" ("Publishing Private Pleasures: The Gentlewoman Reader of Barnebe Riche and George Pettie," *Explorations in Renaissance Culture* 29 [2003]: 185). I argue that sexuality in these tales is more multifaceted.

by honest titles the soner to corrupt honest maners, dedicated ouer boldlie to
vertuous and honorable personages the easier to begile simple and innocent wittes.

Ascham, *The Scholemaster* (2)

The most dramatic case of Pettie breaking the frame of his fiction occurs in the
sixth story, "Ademetus and Alcest." After the pair has eloped and is about to be
secretly married, Pettie turns their illicit contact into an invitation to his female
readers: "But here [Ademetus] aptly ended his talke upon her mouth, and they
entred into such privy conference, their lips beeing joyned most closely together,
that I can not report the meaninge of it unto you, but if it please one of you to leane
hitherward a litle I will shew you the manner of it" (137). By this point (halfway
through the collection) the reader has become used to Pettie's intrusions into his
fiction, but this passage shocks and titilates male and female readers. Pettie
suggests that a lapse of his writerly powers – "I can not report the meaninge of it"
– must be supplemented by action: "I will shew you the manner of it." Whether we
believe Pettie to be showing off to a male audience, flirting with a female one, or
flattering a non-aristocratic female reader who would interpret the sexualized
Gentlewoman as a bad example, this passage emphasizes the sexual tension in the
reader-text relationship as Pettie constructs it.[9] His female readers, like Sidney's,
surround him, but he threatens to violate the courtly frame.

Moments in the *Pettite Pallace* when the author addresses the gentlewomen
readers are often opportunities to recast the tales' battles of the sexes. In the first
story, "Sinorix and Camma," the challenge to choose between male and female
characters is explicit:

> Therefore Gentlewomen I leave it to your judgements to give sentence, whether be more
> worthy reprehension, hee or she. He had the law of love of his side, shee had the lawe of
> men and of marriage on her part: love led him, which the goddes themselves cannot
> resist, chastitie guided her, which the goddes themselves have lost. (38-9)

The choice seems unfair: Camma does poison Sinorix, but only after he murdered
her husband. Posing this question facilitates a sly dig at the uselessness of chastity,
which even the gods lack. Pettie's attack on chastity is clearer in his version of the
Tereus and Progne story when he finally cannot decide "who more offended of the
husband or the wife" (55). That Tereus's rape precedes Progne's slaying of their
children seems not to matter, and Pettie interprets Ovid's tale as evidence that the
women are guilty: "as *Ovid* reporteth [they] were turned into birds, meaninge they
were not worthy humaine shape or the use of reason, which were sutch cruel
monsters altogether devoyd of ruth and reason" (55). Moments that in Greene
would produce sympathy with assailed chastity become in Pettie opportunities for

---

[9]    This last is Collins's reading: "Because the upper-class sexuality represented is illicit
and transgressive, the figure of the gentlewoman reader can offer readers of lower classes a
feeling of moral superiority" ("Publishing Private Pleasures," 189).

masculine barbs. While it is possible that some female readers might have enjoyed such counter-intuitive interpretations, it seems likely that Pettie is playing to his home audience of male courtiers.

The relationship between author and reader in the *Pettite Pallace* combines the kiss that Pettie solicits and the masculine chuckle that he hides. Given this juxtaposition, the tales' obsession with marriage seems a marked case of what Hutson has described as "the displacement of masculine agency from prowess to persuasion."[10] The tales assert that marriage is the most important moment in a man's life – "Of all the ordinary accidents incident to the lyfe of man, there is none of more moment to our prosperytie, or misery, than marriage" (210) – and all twelve center around erotic relationships. Marriage may be "a daungerous thinge" (257), but it is clearly the central thing. The tales bear out Hutson's claim that fictions of courtship emerge from the changing nature of masculinity in Elizabethan England, especially as "fictions of women" underlie masculine friendship. For Pettie the centrality of the heroine masks his portrait of a male career path, in which "the emergence of textual communication [becomes] the new medium in which manhood is to be tried."[11] Placing Pettie alongside Greene, however, suggests that this understanding of courtly misogyny was not the only position available in the 1580s and 1590s. Rather, within the rubric of fictions about marriage, the Heliodoran masterplot of deceptive constancy represents the plot not taken by Pettie.

Marriage shows two faces in Pettie's fiction. The first, which we might call the Greene/Heliodorus version, sees it as a gift from the gods which must be accepted and either endured or celebrated. The second, perhaps adapted from Boccaccio, sees marriage arising from individual choices that can be manipulated. Introducing the tale of Icilius and Virginia (in which Virginia's father slays her to preserve her virginity), Pettie's narrator muses, "I thinke love chiefly to bee grounded upon the similitude of manners shewed and signified by familiarity and abode together" (103). This pragmatic Boaccaccian outlook, which also appears when the narrator terms marriage a "trade of life" (66), asserts that marriage is secular, fungible, and subject to human manipulation. It contrasts sharply with the Greene-like assertion in the next tale that "Marriages are guided by destinie...I think they only bee not in our owne power or pleasure" (126). Pettie's narrator later cites the same metaphor from Ovid that Greene presumably has in mind when he calls love "a thing divine" in the sonnet at the end of *Menaphon*: "love is some heavenly influence and no earthly accident" (166). These contradictory positions produce an indeterminate figure; marriage seems both "trade" and miracle, the result of both destiny and "familiarity." The narrative flexibility thus preserved facilitates Pettie's ambiguous portraits of such women as Progne and Alexius: since love is divine, rapists like

---

[10]  Hutson, *The Usurer's Daughter*, 89.
[11]  Hutson, *The Usurer's Daughter*, 89.

Tereus cannot be completely blamed, but since it is also human, heroines should not resist seductive heroes.

In addition to marriage, chastity becomes for Pettie a social symbol ripe for debunking. Rather than attacking chastity directly, however, Pettie's text implies that its value is very limited. His first heroine, Camma, expresses skepticism about the social value of chastity when she debates committing adultery with Sinorix: "And what is that chastity which I seke so charily to keep, do not some men say that women alwaies live chastly inough, so that they live charily inough, that is so that they convay their matters so covertly that their dooinges bee not commonly knowne" (26). Camma will not reconcile herself to adultery, but the "some men" to whom she refers sound suspiciously like Pettie's gentlemen readers. Pettie's protestations that chastity is the highest virtue seem at odds with the advice he gives his readers at the end of "Scilla and Minos." First he advises them to accede to their fathers' wishes: "I am by this story chiefly to admonish you that you pull not of your fathers haire" (164). After elaborating this doctrinaire moral, however, the narrator continues, "But (Soveraigne) now your father is gone, I will give you more sound advice: I will admonishe you all not to pull of your owne haire, that is not to binde you selves to the froward fansi of your politique parents, but to make your choice in marriage to your own mindes" (164-5). Obedience, like chastity, becomes here (as in Boccaccio) a negotiable virtue rather than an absolute command.

Pettie's genuflections to his female readership seem an elaborate fictional performance, designed to be overheard by the male readers who are supposedly excluded. Thus when he appeals directly to his female readers – "Now I would heare your judgements..." (183) – he plays an intricate game: in appealing to female readers who may largely be constructs, he also appeals to male readers who enjoy the imaginative cross-dressing of the fictional frame. By constructing this two-leveled appeal, in which the overt approach to a named but imaginary female reader shadows a covert appeal to unnamed but implicitly male readers, Pettie carves out the elite, male, courtly readership that made this text popular in the 1570s and 1580s. In the last tale, "Alexius" (notably the only tale whose title does not refer to a woman as well as a man),[12] he writes an anti-prodigal narrative in which his scholar-hero takes his father's advice, marries well, and abandons his wife and child for solitary wandering. (The parallels with Greene's life must be coincidental; Pettie inverts the standard prodigal plot.) This story leads Pettie's narrator to apologize twice to his women readers: first for presenting Alexius's misogyny at such length (257), and second for praising women too excessively (268). The second apology comes with an attack on the reasoning behind the praise of women: "yet his general reasons are altogether sophisticall and full of fallacies,

---

[12]    The eleventh story, "Pigmalions friend, and his Image," comes very close to the all-male title of "Alexius," but of course Pigmalion's story ends in marriage.

set forth without any lively colour, only with fayning & painting" (268). The point seems to be that any praise of women includes both "fallacies" and "fayning."

Pettie plays his ending both ways, but unlike Greene's embrace of diverse reading practices Pettie's model mocks both male and female readers. The solitary Alexius, who "spent the remaindour of his life in pilgrimage & travel," is presented as a religious example – the reader is enjoined to "forsake wife and wealth, & take up the crosse of Christ and follow him as *Alexius* did" (270) – that Pettie's urbane courtiers seem very unlikely to follow. The Gentlewomen, likewise, are to conclude that they must not "repose any permanent plesure in practising with your husbands" and instead concentrate on "the true love which you ought to beare towards god" (271). Pettie's final joke, and the final words of his book, however, redirect this doctrinaire conclusion to an unexpected source of erotic pleasure. Pettie concludes, "I wil leave this text to maister parson, who while he is unmarried I warrant you will disswade you so earnestly from sutch idolatrous doting on your husbands…that you ought to have no respect of persons, but to love an other man or him self so well as your husbandes" (271). Virtue leads to adultery again, this time with clerical sanction and perhaps participation.[13] If the mood at the end of Heliodoran romance is amazement at the fortunate resolution, Pettie's text generates cynical amusement at a world whose characters are not any more moral than they should be.

## Escaping Italy: From Novelle to Romance in Gascoigne and Lyly

*Inglese Italianato é un diabolo incarnato.*

Ascham, *The Scholemaster* (2)

Pettie's style of novella gave to Heliodoran romance in the 1580s, and the progress of this shift reveals itself in the interaction between four popular fictions of the late 1570s, George Gascoigne's two versions of *The Adventures of Master F. J.* (1573 and 1575), and John Lyly's two volumes of *Euphues* (1578 and 1580). Writing in the wake of Painter, Fenton, and Pettie, both Gascoigne and Lyly began by modeling their fictions on the novella.[14] Revision for each entailed generic and

---

[13]  Pettie gestures toward the ending of *Lazarillo de Tormes* (1554), which ends with the picaro colluding in an affair between his wife and a clergyman. *Lazarillo* was translated by David Rowland in 1568-9. See Salzman, *English Prose Fiction*, 353.

[14]  On the novella's influence on Lyly, see John Dover Wilson, *John Lyly*, (New York: Haskell House, 1970), repr. of 1905 ed.; G.K. Hunter, *John Lyly: The Humanist as Courtier*, (London: Routledge and Kegan Paul, 1962); and Violet M. Jeffrey, *John Lyly and the Italian Renaissance*, (Paris: Champion, 1929). On Gascoigne, see Ronald Johnson, *George Gascoigne*, (Boston: Twayne, 1972); C.T. Prouty, *George Gascoigne: Elizabethan Courtier, Solider and Poet*, (New York: Columbia University Press, 1942); and Lynette McGrath,

cultural purification; dangerous Italian influences were purged, or at least concealed. The final text of the four, *Euphues and his England*, rejects the novella's labyrinth and helps establish the narrative conventions of Elizabethan romance. Taken together, these texts show that the mainstream genre of English prose fiction in the 1580s and 1590s – romance – arose to a significant extent as a reaction against the Italian features of the novelle. These four fictions portray, with explicit intertextual references that have gone unremarked, the shift away from the novella toward Elizabethan-Heliodoran romance.

Modern readers have often found an appealing sophistication and ironic detachment in the fictions of Gascoigne and Lyly. The complexity sixteenth-century readers would have termed Italianate, late twentieth-century criticism anachronistically called "modernist." James Joyce, in fact, became a touchstone in the 1970s for each author: Philmus titled his essay, "Gascoigne's Fable of the Artist as a Young Man," and Steinberg called Lyly's prose "the most peculiar style before *Finnegans Wake*."[15] Gascoigne's and Lyly's so-called "modernity," however, more precisely represents their struggles with the novella. Ambivalence toward this genre underpins their self-conscious uncertainty and skepticism.

Now that the passion for finding proto-modernism in Renaissance fiction has ebbed, it is possible to read the search for modernist analogues in Gascoigne's and Lyly's fictions as a sympathetic reaction to their strange, fractured nature. The cultural, stylistic and moral dislocations that twentieth-century critics deemed modern exhibit neither the alienation of high modernism nor the radical skepticism of postmodernity. Rather, they expose the generic aspect of what historicist readers have long seen in these fictions, the deliberate juxtaposition of Italian decadence and English moral frailty. English resistance to an Italian form underlies the dislocations legible to twentieth-century critics as modernist. Replacing the familiar stories of national or sectarian rivalry with a historically specific analysis of generic competition clarifies the place of these texts in early modern English fiction. By reframing the debate in terms of "Italy" rather than "modernity," and by looking at *Euphues and his England* as a turn toward romance rather than the modern novel, "Italy" and "the novella" represent a set of narrative and intellectual practices that early modern Englishmen found attractive but untrustworthy. Romance thrived as an antidote to this kind of Italy.[16]

---

"George Gascoigne's Moral Satire: The Didactic Use of Convention in *The Adventures Passed By Master F.J.*," *JEGP* 70 (1971): 432-50.

[15] Theodore L. Steinberg," The Anatomy of *Euphues*," *Studies in English Literature* 17 (1977): 27.

[16] I speculate that for Ascham, Italy had the same pernicious influence that conservative American thinkers attribute to Paris. On Renaissance humanist debates and the "theory wars," see Victoria Kahn, "Humanism and the Resistance to Theory," *Literary Theory/Renaissance Texts*, ed. Patricia Parker and David Quint, (Baltimore: Johns Hopkins University Press, 1986).

Lyly, writing five years after Gascoigne, took his predecessor as a counter-example. The three early texts – both versions of *F. J.* and the first Euphues volume – end with broken love affairs and disillusioned characters limping toward solitary deaths. In *Euphues and his England*, however, Lyly breaks this narrative dead end by updating a plot device he borrows from Gascoigne. Lyly's solution involves Mistress Frances, the English heroine who becomes Philautus's bride in the end. Lyly's Frances takes her name and character from Gascoigne's Frances, who crucially fails to attract F. J.'s love. (The intertextual relationship between these two characters has been noted recently, but its significance has gone unremarked.[17]) In the context of the struggle between fictional forms, the composite figure of Frances exemplifies Lyly's revisionary method and the genre of his final text.

The two characters named Frances are substantially the same: virtuous, constant, intelligent, and against all wisdom in love with the hero. Each author, however, treats her differently. In Gascoigne, Frances is the weak virtuous woman who cannot redirect F. J.'s lust away from the amorous Elinor. In Lyly, Frances becomes a shrewd practitioner of indirect persuasion who guides Philautus to a redemptive marriage. In narrative terms, the difference between the characters is simple: Lyly's Frances succeeds and Gascoigne's fails. The change of plot creates a change in genre; Frances draws Lyly's text out of the novella toward romance.

The two writers "escaped" Italianate fiction in opposite ways. Gascoigne's second version of *F. J.* washed his hands of his own tale, claiming that it is (and always was) not his invention but a translation "out of the Italian riding tales of Bartello."[18] (Bartello, whom I discuss below, is an invented character who did not appear in the 1573 edition.) The purported Italian author shifts responsibility away from Gascoigne; neither setting nor author is English any more. Absolved from blame for the ethical failings of his text, Gascoigne could revel in the racy tale while preserving English moral superiority.

*Euphues and his England*, by contrast, transforms Lyly's – and to some extent English fiction's – relationship with the novella. The rejection of the old genre is packaged as a geographic shift: the heroes leave the sin-city of Naples and go to London.[19] The English air mends the wanton courtiers' ways, so that the tale ends not with erotic betrayal but with marriage. The Italian courtier Philautus,

---

[17] Maslen, *Elizabethan Fictions*, 269, notes that Lyly borrows Frances from Gascoigne. Although Maslen considers Gascoigne's Francis at some length – he calls her "the champion of light and air" (146) and the sole Protestant" in a Catholic household (153) – he treats Lyly's Frances more briefly.

[18] Gascoigne, *The Adventures of Master F. J.*, *The Poesies*, John W. Cunliffe, ed. (New York: Greenwood Press, 1969). Further citations to the second version given in the text.

[19] He had promised his readers this move at the end of the first volume (*Euphues*, ed. Morris William Croll and Harry Clemans, [London: Routledge and Sons, 1916] 183). Further citations in the text.

Euphues's best friend, usurps the role of hero, and marries the English lady Frances. Euphues himself retreats to solitary meditation, as he returns to college in the first volume, but the Philautus-plot discovers a way out of the courtly impasse.[20] The solution Lyly proposes mirrors the shift in English fiction from novella to romance.

## *The Anatomy of Wit* (1578)

Lyly's *Anatomy of Wit* presents the novella as a genre that goes nowhere. Euphues, the Athenian whose post-university sojourn in Naples provides the core of the story, is the perfect student who learns nothing. He ignores the wise advise of Eubulus, whose name means "good counsel." [21] Eubulus mouths humanist moral precepts and recalls Roger Ascham, whose *Scholemaster* (1570) underlies much of Eubulus's speech.[22] Lyly took Euphues's name from Ascham, and Ascham in turn took it from Plato's *Republic*. For Ascham and Plato, *euphuia* is an admirable quality. An "Euphues," according to Ascham, is "he, that is apt by goodness of witte, and appliable by readiness of will, to learning."[23] Euphues typifies the ideal product of Elizabethan humanist education.[24] Lyly, a descendent of one of the founders of Tudor education, proceeds to show how morally impotent that education could be when its literary context is not an educational treatise but an erotic tale.

Euphues is Athenian, not English, but his position as a newly minted humanist with no clear place in life makes him an apt representative of Gascoigne and Lyly's generation.[25] When asked in Naples where he is from, Euphues mystifies the question: "What countryman am I not? If I be in Crete I can lie, if in Greece I can shift, if in Italy I can court it" (91).[26] Euphues's claim to be "citizen of the world" accents the cosmopolitanism of a generation brought up on international humanism. He imagines that his Athenian education has prepared him to enter a humanist world free of local barriers. His experience in Naples, however, reminds the reader that his ability to "court it" in Italy threatens the ethical basis of his education.

---

[20]   Euphues is now identified with Lyly (191), but his story no longer dominates the book.

[21]   See Kinney, *Humanist Poetics*, 162.

[22]   Kinney speculates that Eubulus represents William Lily (*Humanist Poetics*, 162).

[23]   See Ascham, *The Scholemaster*, 106.

[24]   On Lyly's use of the tropes of humanist education, see Richard A. McCabe, "Wit, Eloquence, and Wisdom in *Euphues: The Anatomy of Wit*," *Studies in Philology* 81 (1984), and Henderson, "Euphues and his Erasmus."

[25]   See Helgerson, *Elizabethan Prodigals*.

[26]   *Euphues: The Anatomy of Wit*, Salzman, ed., *An Anthology of Elizabethan Prose Fiction*, 91. Further citations given in the text. For the non-narrative sections of this book, I quote from Croll's edition.

Neither Euphues's apt intelligence nor his close friendship with Philautus stops him from using his wit to steal Lucilla, Philautus's fiancé. Lucilla betrays Philautus and Euphues in turn, and finally chooses Curio, "a gentleman of Naples of little wealth and less wit" (141). Lyly's plot (such as it is) reaches a narrative impasse after Lucilla's betrayal of Euphues short-circuits the erotic narrative. Melancholy Euphues flees Naples, and returns to school at Athens to fill the bulk of the text with letters and pedantic advice for Philautus, whom he has just betrayed. If these letters show, as the text claims, "what wit can and will do if it be well employed," (110), then the problem is that wit accomplishes very little.[27]

Many recent critics have seen *The Anatomy of Wit* as a critique, exposing the dangers of humanist rhetorical education.[28] Euphues does not use his wit properly, but the problem lies with wit itself, which is too plastic to be reliable. Some critics have accented the extent to which Lyly's critique is compatible with modernist or postmodernist attacks on Enlightenment rationality, but Lyly's criticism seems less broad: the problem with Euphues's wit is that it cannot shed the Italian coloring it acquires in Naples. Wit convinces Euphues to befriend Philautus on one page, and then betray him on the next. The elegant rhetorical style called "euphuism" loses its moral center in a decadent environment.

The environment that corrupts Euphues is Naples, but in generic terms, the problem is the novella. Readings that focus on Lyly's debunking of humanist rationality without considering his critique of the novella ignore the primacy of generic choice in the task of the Elizabethan writer. The tale's attacks on Italy shadow Lyly's attack on the novella, for which he as yet has not alternative. References to Italian decadence fill the text. Naples is "a place of more pleasure than profit, and yet of more profit than piety" (90). G. K. Hunter may be correct that Naples is an allegory of Elizabethan London.[29] But Naples is an Italianate London, quite different from the courteous city to which Euphues and Philautus travel in *Euphues and his England*. Even Euphues's repentance of his folly, after Lucilla abandons him for Curio, comes in geographic terms: "Ah, foolish Euphues, why didst thou leave Athens, the nurse of wisdom, to inhabit Naples, the nourisher of wantonness?" (145). Geography becomes shorthand for an cultural critique.

---

[27] Lyly is among the first English writers to oppose the word "wit" to wisdom. See Croll, int., 2n, and *OED* 7.

[28] Hunter sees *Anatomy* as displaying "the drying up of a tradition" (*Humanist as Courtier*, 35); Kinney as a "stalemate" between elegance and decadence ("Rhetoric and Fiction in Elizabethan England," *Renaissance* Eloquence, ed. James J. Murphy [Berkeley: University of California Press, 1983] 390); Steinberg as "an anti-courtesy book" ("Anatomy," 29); Stephanson emphasizes the irony, humor, and anti-humanism ("John Lyly's Prose Fiction: Irony, Humor, and Anti-Humanism," *English Literary Renaissance* 11 [1981] , and Gohlke reads anti-humanist sentiment in Lyly "a deep understanding...of one kind of human defense against [the] state of intense anxiety" caused by the "dominant reality of betrayal" ("Reading 'Euphues,'" *Criticism* 19 [1977]: 117).

[29] See *Humanist as Courtier*, 59.

Athens recalls Oxford as an idealized England, home of a serious, well-moralized humanism. Naples encompasses Italy and unidealized London, homes of sin and sophistication. Euphues's Athenian rhetoric, however, thrives even in the sinful city. The novella corrupts the classroom.

Euphuistic rhetoric, then, is a weapon that wounds its wielder when placed in the wrong context. The final image in *The Anatomy of Wit* is of the skilled rhetorician as self-contradictory recluse. Euphues flees to Athens to write polemics against Italy and Italian culture, but his style remains so obsessed with balance and shapeliness that he cannot conclude anything. His letter to "The Grave Matrons and Honest Maidens of Italy" (107-110) exposes his solipsistic logic. Not wanting to disparage all Italian women, even though he has seen few "grave matrons" or "honest maidens" in Naples, he writes four pages of balanced antitheses that add up to exactly nothing:

> I know that as there hath been an unchaste Helen...so there hath been also a chaste Penelope; as there hath been a prodigious Pasiphae, so there hath been a godly Theocrita... (108)

The list continues for four pages, but it does not teach anything, because every charm calls up its counter-charm.

The volume ends with Euphues and Philautus "ready to cross the seas for England" (183). The cultural symbolism of this geographic shift lays the ground for the successful plot resolution of the second volume. A crucial part of being English in the Elizabethan era seems to have consisted of thinking that England was morally superior (if perhaps rhetorically inferior) to Italy. Given this cultural divide, English writer-courtiers dramatized their ability to combine Italy's rhetorical prowess with an English notion of moral rectitude. The need to keep English society looking pure, in fact, had already been central in the scandal of Gascoigne's *Master F. J.*

## *The Adventures of Master F. J.* (1573 and 1575)

The first edition of *F. J.* has interested modern critics because of its complex narrative structure.[30] The split between the hero F. J., a rake and a poet, and the

---

[30] Much recent work centers on point of view (Leicester Bradner, "Point of View in George Gascoigne's Fiction," *Studies in Short Fiction* 3 (1965): 16-22), perspectivism (Paul Parrish, "The Multiple Perspectives of Gascoigne's 'The Adventures of Master F. J.,'" *Studies in Short Fiction* 10 [1973]: 75-84), the figure of the editor (Joseph Bloomfield, "Gascoigne's *Master F. J.* as Renaissance Proto-Novel: The Birth of the Judicious Editor as Narrator," *Essays in Literature* 19 [1992]: 163-72; Gregory Waters, "G.T .'s 'Worthless Enterprise': A Study of the Narrator of Gascoigne's 'The Adventures of Master F. J.,'" *Journal of Narrative Theory* 7 [1977]: 116-27), and the prehistory of the novel (Gordon Williams, "Gascoigne's *Master F. J.* and the Development of the Novel," *Trivium* 10

editor G. T., who narrates F. J.'s story, reflects the conflict between a courtier's practical humanism and a schoolteacher's moralistic vision.[31] G. T. espouses a cautious poetics and skeptical view of Italian culture, while F. J. steals his best lines from Ariosto and Petrarch. The summation that Kinney gives F. J.'s story, a "corruption of education by love," applies equally to this work and to Lyly's first *Euphues* volume.[32] F. J. and Euphues are both gifted, well-educated young men who cannot learn. The adulterous world of F. J.'s country estate is more erotic than Lyly's Naples,[33] but both heroes are equally foolish. Each knows his Petrarch, but neither can tell wit from wisdom.

In addition to F. J. and G. T., however, Gascoigne includes a reliable figure of virtue: Frances, whom F. J. ignores, and whom Lyly will borrow in his second volume. The etymology of "Frances," meaning "frank" or "honest," is ironic: Frances is as duplicitous and witty as her corrupt companions.[34] Her innovation combines Italian wit with English moral rectitude. This paradoxical union makes her the impotent moral heart of Gascoigne's text, and it is this ethical core that Lyly seizes in *Euphues and his England*. Frances makes distinctions where F. J. and Euphues cannot, and thus ties her courtly wit to a moral anchor. She steals F. J.'s sword the night he consummates his affair with Elinor, and the emasculating joke suggests she knows exactly what is going on. She has been to the same school as F. J. and Euphues, but the white light of sexual desire does not blind her.

Frances is a teacher, but not a pious bore like G. T. or Lyly's Eubulus. She tries to teach F. J. through fiction, by telling him a novella about an errant wife who redirects her love back to her husband after an adulterous affair. The moral fails to reach F. J., just as Eubulus's lecture fails for Euphues, but Frances's more dexterous tactics seem promising.[35] Frances's version of humanist education involves not pedantic lectures but entertaining stories and practical jokes. It

---

[1975]: 137-50 ; M. R. R. Philmus, "Gascoigne's Fable of the Artist as a Young Man," *JEGP* 73 [1974]: 13-31).

[31] On "old humanism" and courtiers, see Helgerson, *Elizabethan Prodigals*.

[32] See *Humanist Poetics*, 105. Henderson also links these works ("Euphues and His Erasmus," 144, 155).

[33] Jokes include F. J.'s curing of Elinor's mysterious nosebleed (13-14), remarks about the size of the secretary's "pen" (62), and elaborate discussions of the "naked sword" which F. J. takes with him for a midnight tryst with his lady.

[34] While Frances mediates between Italian decadence and English morality, the geographic pun – Frances meaning "France" – seems undeveloped. For a reading of Frances's "frank, open" nature as sexual availability, see Susan C Staub, "The Lady Frances Did Watch: Gascoigne's Voyeuristic Narrative," *Framing Elizabethan Fictions: Contemporary Approaches to Early Modern Narrative Prose,* Constance Relihan, ed., (Kent: Kent State University Press, 1996) 50.

[35] This novella, to which F. J. barely listens, suggests that not all Italianate fictions have dissolute morals.

promises a rapprochement between the court and academic humanism. Unfortunately, Frances's tactics do not work on F. J.

The "thriftless history" (80) of the first version of *Master F. J.* does not conclude so much as break off, the plot collapsing once F. J. learns that Elinor prefers her secretary's "pen" to his own. In the second version, Gascoigne notes that the first edition was "offensive for sundrie wanton speeches and lascivious phrases...the same hav[ing] been doubtfully construed and (therefore) scandalous" (3). The scandal apparently arose from its English setting; some readers claimed to recognize the principal characters.[36] In re-issuing the story, however, Gascoigne never addresses the scandal as such, nor does he force F. J. to see the error of his ways and ride off into the sunset with Frances. Rather, he simply Italianates the tale in context as well as content. He adds moralized fates for the protagonists: Frances the abandoned lover dies a consumptive death, and F. J. and Elinor lead dissolute and solitary lives. He also Italianizes his characters' names, so that F. J. becomes Ferdinando Jeronimi; Elinor, Leonora del Vasco; and Frances, Franceschina. He claims to have edited his text, and he uses a striking metaphor to describe the process: "my Poemes [are] gelded from all filthy phrases" (6). Gascoigne's presentation of himself as *poemata castrada* in the 1575 *Poesies* accents the helplessness of the literary courtier in Elizabethan England, and it has attracted attention from recent critics.[37] But while he omits the most offensive passages, including F. J.'s rape of Elinor, it is the same dissolute tale. The biggest revision cuts the editorial figure G. T., but in his place we have Gascoigne's new image of Italy: Bartello.

"Bartello" is a made-up name, perhaps chosen for its near-match with "Bandello." Gascoigne does not provide any information about this invented Italian source. The name alone created an Italian veneer that served to preclude any reflection on English aristocracy: F. J. is now an Italian courtier rather than an English one. It is hard to imagine that the Italian costume convinced anyone who was really scandalized by the earlier text; it was the same story, in mostly the same words. Bartello appears part of Gascoigne's elaborate dance around censorship, but the invented author looks suspiciously like a marketing gimmick, allowing the audience to revel in the Italianate tale without threatening English purity.[38] Gascoigne may not intend his audience to believe in Bartello.[39] The new internal

---

[36]   The initials probably added to the confusion, and may have been intended to do so.

[37]   See McCoy, "Poemata Castrada," and Wall, *Imprint of Gender*, 127-40.

[38]   On Gascoigne's attempts to clear his name in the 1575 *Poesies*, see Hughes, "Gascoigne's Poses," 5-6,. The attempt failed, and the *Poesies* was called in by the Stationers' Company in 1576. See McCoy, "Poemata Castrada," 22n.

[39]   In the poem, "The fruite of Fetters," which immediately precedes *F. J.* in the *Poesies*, Gascoigne describes his poetic alter-ego the Green Knight as "the knight on whom *Bartello* writes / All cladde in Greene, yet banisht from delights" (369). See Johnson, *George Gascoigne*, 15. Maslen concludes that Gascoigne does not intend careful readers to believe

author changes the text's narrative frame from pious humanism to Italianate "riding tales." Bartello defends Gascoigne by taking responsibility for the Italian tale upon himself. Once the tale has left the English countryside, it no longer matters that the hero and his lover are morally bankrupt. Fernando Jeronomi and Leonora now represent a foreign literary genre. Franceschina pays for the switch with her life, as the 1575 version consigns her to a consumptive death.

## *Euphues and His England* (1580)

When Lyly continues the story of Euphues, he reverses Gascoigne's geography and moves his heroes from Italy to England. Lyly's sequel rejects the didactic letters that conclude the *Anatomy of Wit* in favor of a new emphasis on plot.[40] The main story brings Philautus and Euphues to London, where Philautus finds his bride. The Italian courtier marries an English woman and sells his lands in Italy to settle in London. Euphues himself ends up in solitary retreat. The reader finds two endings: compromise and redemption for Philautus, constancy and sorrow for Euphues. The split parallels their relation to the new genre: Philautus accepts romance and is rewarded, while Euphues continues to suspect all forms of fiction and ends up alone. It is still Euphues's name in the title, but the plot shifts from his impasse to Philautus's success.

It seems odd that Philautus, the Italian courtier whose name means "self-love," should merit a virtuous English wife. It is equally strange that this volume, dedicated to the notoriously Italianate Earl of Oxford, should provide the redemptive plot that the openly humanist first volume abjured. Oxford's decadence has contributed to the split reception of *Euphues and his England*.[41] Skeptical proto-modernity, however, is notably absent in readings of this text. In contrast to the betrayals and counter-betrayals of Gascoigne's *F. J.* and *The Anatomy of Wit*,

---

in Bartello, and he emphasizes the "games with the question of authorship" (*Elizabethan Fictions*, 8n).

[40] The volume includes two inset tales: a prodigal-son story (205-25) and a tale of frustrated love (233-85). It thus remains a humanist compendium, as Henderson notes ("Euphues and his Erasmus," 150), but one interested in fictional as well as rhetorical variations.

[41] Many readers follow Albert Feuillerat who in 1910 condemned the sequel as a "moral regression" (83) linked to Oxford's circle (*John Lyly: Contribution à l'histoire de la Renaissance en Angleterre*, [Cambridge: Cambridge University Press, 1910]). See also Hunter, *The Humanist as Courtier*; Catherine Bates, "A Large Occasion of Discourse: John Lyly and the Art of Civil Conversation," *Review of English Studies* n. s. 42 (1991): 469-86; and Louise Schleiner, "Ladies and Gentlemen in Two Genres of Elizabethan Fiction," *Studies in English Literature* 29 (1989): 1-20. The alternative position treats the book as the redemptive half of the prodigal plot. Helgerson describes the "realism" of *England* as a step forward for Elizabethan fiction (*Elizabethan Prodigals*, 77), and Kinney accents the redemption of humanist rhetoric (*Humanist Poetics*, 178).

the plot becomes straightforward, almost too easy. Philautus re-makes himself by re-locating himself. Lyly's shift in genre gives narrative meaning to "England" and "Italy" as cultural symbols, and the novella's impasse becomes romance's triumph.

When Philautus arrives in London and falls in love with the unattainable Camilla, he knows his biggest problem is his nationality: "Thou art an Italian, Philautus, as much misliked for the vice of thy country as she [Camilla] marveled at for the virtue of hers [England]" (295). Philautus knows about Italianate Englishmen, and his task will be to invert the proverb and Anglicize his devilish Italian nature. He eventually succeeds by adopting a maneuver from romantic comedy – shifting one's passion from an unattainable love to an available one – but not before his Italian habits lead him astray. He twice attempts Italian love-trickery before he comes around to the English way. His first and most extreme tactic seeks out his countryman Psellus, an alchemist and sorcerer.[42]

The interview between Psellus and Philautus (323-37) occasions pages of elaborate euphuistic speech in a sequel that turns down the stylistic volume of its predecessor. Philautus explains his problem to Psellus by listing classical heroes laid low by love from Julius Caesar to Hercules. Even after he cites the three ways he knows to attract women – violence, great wealth, and sorcery – Psellus does not rise to the bait. In fact, Psellus's reply suggests that England has converted him: "Do you think, gentleman, that the mind being created of God can be ruled by man or that anyone can move the heart but He that made the heart?" (329). Since "moving the heart" is precisely the object of humanist persuasive rhetoric, Psellus's debunking makes explicit the critique of wit that *The Anatomy of Wit* discovered at great cost. Psellus trivializes euphuistic rhetoric, providing a mocking reprisal of Lyly's notorious "unnatural natural history": "If you take pepper, the seed of a nettle, and a pretty quantity of Pyretum, beaten or pounded together and put into wine of two years old, whensoever you drink to Camilla, if she love not you you lose your labour" (330). Euphuism is an old joke, no longer a persuasive strategy.[43]

Psellus's impotent magic metaphorically encompasses the self-defeating rhetoric of Lyly's first volume and Gascoigne's *F. J.* This magic is all that remains of the skepticism and uncertainty of the 1570s works; it is as close as this volume gets to *Finnegans Wake*. Psellus, however, rejects magic, noting that poisoning ladies for their love is not the fashion in England (336). He convinces Philautus to use only the English love-tactics of "faith, virtue, and constancy" (335). The Italian

---

[42] The name Psellus comes from a Greek verb meaning "to stammer," which accents his parody of Euphuistic rhetoric. Maslen draws attention (via C.S. Lewis) to Cornelius Agrippa's interest in a Greek mathematician named Psellus (*Elizabethan Fictions*, 275n). Maslen also convincingly pronounces Psellus Lyly's "self-parody" (276).

[43] This passage recalls Falstaff's parody of Euphues in *Henry IV, Part I*: "[F]or though the camomile, the more it is trodden on, the faster it grows, [yet] youth, the more it is wasted the sooner it wears..." (2.4.399ff).

convert Psellus here replaces the pious old humanist Eubulus, as well as the intrusive narrator G. T., as the older male advisor. The difference is that Philautus, finally, takes the hint.

Philautus's next trick, however, does not bring him all the way to English virtue. He eschews sorcerer's rhetoric for courtly intrigue, and adopts the tactics of F. J. by initiating a clandestine correspondence with his lady. He sends love letters to Camilla, concealing them in Italian fashion, first using a hollowed-out pomegranate (342), and then a volume of Petrarch (346). These courtly letters do not work, however, because Camilla loves a virtuous Englishman named Sirius.[44] At this point, Philautus does not know what to do. The move that will free him from Italy comes not from him, but from his English future wife, Frances.

Frances's presence makes solving the love problem simply a matter of shifting Philautus's love-object, but he does not initiate the shift himself. Rather, Frances takes the lead when she proposes a triangle as a metaphor for successful courtship: "There must in every triangle be three lines, the first beginneth, the second augmenteth, the third concludeth it a figure; so in love three virtues, affection which draweth the heart, secrecy which increaseth the hope, constancy which finisheth the work. Without any of these lines there can be no triangle, without any of these virtues no love" (401). Frances's tripartite love rehabilitates a crafty Italian virtue, secrecy, alongside the virtues of constancy and affection. While there is no sorcery at the English court, clandestine methods – even Philautus's pomegranate and volume of Petrarch – have their places.

Like Chariclea's, Frances's rhetoric is deceptive, perhaps more so than the stories of Gascoigne's Frances. Her metaphorical triangle mirrors Philautus's erotic triangle, in which he himself is the third point, connected to both Camilla and Frances. Frances's goal is to shift the triangle and become Philautus's sole mistress. Accomplishing this shift will re-make the triangle as a straight line, just as the public acknowledgment of love through marriage eliminates the need for secrecy and leaves the happy couple in a straight line of constancy and affection.[45] Frances's metaphor appears more subtle than anything Philautus, Euphues, or F. J. have tried so far. It is also the most successful rhetorical ploy in all four volumes. Persuaded by Frances, "Philautus...began to look askew on Camilla, driving out the remembrance of the old love with the recording of the new. Who now but his Violet, who but Mistress Frances?" (410). It takes a final nudge from Sirius to get Philautus to the altar, but Frances first catches him with her triangular gambit.

Switching from Camilla to Frances calls into question Philautus's constancy, presumably the most English of virtues. In fact, to the extent that Philautus turns to his most expedient suit, his love-making remains suspiciously corrupt. At this point he recalls F. J., who decides to woo Elinor instead of his Frances, "Because the one

---

[44] The pun in English ("serious") seems facile, but I do not think Lyly means to recall the dog star.

[45] Philautus's former love for Camilla must also remain secret after he switches to Frances.

is overcome with less difficulty than the other" (27). Yet the resolution of Philautus's story, his marriage and re-settling in London, suggests that Italian inconstancy gives way to English fidelity. As Euphues tells Philautus, "Touching thy proceedings in love, be constant to one and try but one; otherwise thou shalt bring thy credit into question, and thy love into derision. Wean thyself from Camilla, deal wisely with Frances" (413). This statement typifies Euphues's font-of-humanist-wisdom mode, but the irony that Philautus can be faithful to Frances only by being faithless to Camilla does not seem overwhelming. Euphues dismisses Philautus's Italianate love for Camilla as Lyly eschews the novella. The sense of loss that Philautus will not let himself feel for Camilla finds its echo in some readers' nostalgia for the harsher and more titillating world of *The Anatomy of Wit*. What emerges in *Euphues and his England* is a practical mean, equidistant from the extremes of cynical reliance on force, wealth, and sorcery, and also from foolish constancy in a fruitless passion. The foolishly constant figure is Euphues himself, whose piety leaves him exiled.[46] The main plot turns to Philautus's resettlement and its suggestion that the English court can cure residual Italian sin.[47]

Lyly's example would reverberate through the remaining decades of Elizabethan fiction. While *Euphues and his England* is not yet a full-blown Heliodoran romance like the *New Arcadia*, *Rosalynde*, or *Menaphon*, many of the plot conventions of the genre are present in embryo. The love triangle resolved by two marriages, the voyage by sea that stimulates radical change, the stubborn constancy of virtuous women who are rewarded in the end – these are the essential bones of Elizabethan prose romance, and they typify *Euphues and his England*'s departure from *The Anatomy of Wit* and *Master F. J.*

Lyly's text is only half a romance, as Euphues himself does not marry, but the new model is nearly in place. The widespread use of the name Euphues in the titles of later books represents publishers cashing in on Lyly's market success, but it also seems that writers understood that he was a valuable model.[48] Later Elizabethan writers would certainly have written romances without Lyly's example, but the model *Euphues and his England* provided for converting love into marriage was well-timed to shape the development of English prose fiction. The same year that

---

[46]   For a reading that values Euphues's "civil conversation" over Philautus's "bourgeois marriage," see Bates, "A Large Occasion of Discourse."

[47]   This plot needs constancy in its women, Frances and Camilla, to facilitate the happy ending. The sexual inequality which juxtaposes them against the inconstant men, however, seems more a convention of romance than a reprisal of the misogyny of the *Anatomy of Wit* or *Master F. J.*

[48]   For the use of the name "Euphues" in the titles of other books, see Hunter, *Humanist as Courtier*, 259. To take two examples, Lodge's *Rosalynd* (1590), subtitled *Euphues' Golden Legacie*, tells a story in which persuasive rhetoric brings about happiness, and Greene's *Menaphon* (1589), subtitled *Camilla's Alarum to Slumbering Euphues*, presents a world in which the virtuous heroine must endure suffering before being saved by Fate.

Greene's first romance was printed, Lyly demonstrated that the genre of romance could inoculate narrative fiction against the novella.

By transforming Philautus into an English courtier with newly-bought English lands Lyly pretends that escaping Italy also entails converting and purifying it. His Italian courtier resettles on English soil as Lyly rejects the novella for romance. The Italian courtier, stripped of his literary context, is no longer threatening. The struggle between the temptations of Italian fiction and the moral demands of English culture, between F. J.'s libidinous poetry and Euphues's moralistic piety, echoes through the two endings of *Euphues and his England*. The volume's resolution, however, suggests that some part of Italy is recoverable. Frances, the character Lyly salvaged from Gascoigne's narrative scrap-heap, combines Italianate education with English moral certainty to redeem the lusty and misguided Philautus. If weaned from sorcery, violence, and overwrought rhetoric, humanist culture and prose fiction could help courtiers seeking personal (and literary) fulfillment, at least if they seek it in Elizabethan London. Philautus's solution is a fantasy unavailable to real courtiers like Lyly and Gascoigne, but in literary terms his bi-national marriage would prove fruitful. In a sense, *Euphues and his England* paved the way for Greene's twelve-year experiment in romance, although Greene would negotiate his own solution to the lure of Italianate fiction.

## Novella against Epic: *Penelopes Web* (1587) and *Euphues his Censure* (1587)

> Poesie [is] an art not only of making, but also of imitation...Otherwise, how was it possible that *Homer*, being but a poore priuate man, and, as some same, in his later age blind, should so exactly set foorth and describe, as if he had bene a most excellent Cataine or Generall, the order and array of battels...the wrath of *Achilles*, the magnanimitie of *Agamamnon*, the prudence of *Menelaus*, the prowesse of *Hector*, the maiestie of king *Priamus*, the grauitie of *Nestor*, the pollicies and eloquence of *Vlysses*?
>
> George Puttenham, *The Arte of English Poesie*[49]

Greene experimented with novelle collections both early in his career (*Morando*, 1583) and late (*Opharion*, 1590), but his innovations differed from the cynicism of Pettie and Gascoigne and from Lyly's transformation. In fact, looking at Greene's novelle reveals that he never relinquished this form, but he transformed it to make it more Heliodoran. Unlike Lyly, Greene remade the novelle rather than escaping it. *Perimedes the Blacksmith* (1588) provides a catalog of Greene's formal strategies. The title page indicates that *Perimedes* contains multiple short tales organically connected: "Heerin are interlaced three merrie and necessarie discourses fit for our time: with certaine pleasant Histories and tragicall tales,

---

[49] *Elizabethan Critical Essays*, Smith, ed., 2:4.

which may breed delight to all, and offence to none" (7:3). The terms Greene uses for the stories – "discourses," "Histories," and "tales" – together with the varied descriptions he applies to these words – "merrie," "necessary," "fit for our time," "pleasant," and "tragicall" – indicate that this work will be a varied narrative feast. Greene as usual covers his marketing bases, with "tragicall" and "discourses" echoing Fenton's *Certaine Tragical Discourses* (1567) and "merrie...tales" recalling the perennially reprinted *Hundred Merrie Tales* (1525), but the term "interlaced" highlights his efforts to control his material. Narrative "interlace" is often associated with Ariosto and Tasso, but its elaborate cross-cutting between different narratives also has roots in medieval romance.[50] Interlace becomes for Greene another way to create the coherent plot that forms the core of his narrative product. The stories in *Perimedes* must be remade to make them coherent, since the first two are novelle drawn directly from *The Decameron* (2.6 and 5.2).[51]

The middlebrow ambition of Greene's novelle appears more clearly in two publications of 1587 which may have motivated the "Homer of women" accusation. Both *Penelopes Web* and *Euphues his Censure to Philautus* are novella-collections set within a Homeric frame. Like *Menaphon*'s promise of "a note beyond your reach," these books reveal Greene's ambition. He combines epic material and an Italian genre to carve out a market niche. Greene's relationship to humanist morality was not as cynical as Pettie's; his defenses of chastity, in particular, were more sincere. In formal terms, he attempted, through interlace and frame tales, to unify a collection of stories with more than a narrative voice. Greene's middlebrow readers here are imagined to combine the residually elite ( "Homer") with a self-consciously broad gender-based appeal ("of women").

The striking placement of Homeric material in these two tales recalls Heliodorus's use of the ghost of Odysseus in the *Aethiopian History*. In each case, these writers use Homer's cultural prestige to reformulate it: Heliodorus has Odysseus praise Chariclea to endorse his departures from Homeric epic, and Greene has Homeric characters espouse his a non-martial, indirect model of heroic agency. Greene's novelle collections thus have two generic objects in mind: they recast martial epic as an insufficient model, and they reimagine the novella as amenable to other kinds of social agency than the trickster's. The novella, like epic and romance, is a capacious form, and Greene demonstrated that it could be remade in the service of anti-epic classicism.

These two books emphasize the gendered divide in Greene's readership. In the Gentleman's letter prefaced to *Penelopes Web*, Greene explains the interest of male readers in the "womans prattle" of these collected tales by noting that "*Mars* will sometime be prying into *Venus* papers" (5:145). This gambit imagines two distinct readings practices – Mars prying, Venus reading – and also constructs a

---

[50]   On Renaissance interlace, see David Quint, *Cervantes's Novel of Modern Times: A New Reading of* Don Quijote, (Princeton: Princeton University Press, 2003) 3-7

[51]   See Wolff, *Greek Romances in Elizabethan Fiction*, 322, 345-6

mutually viable relationship between them. Men and women do not read together, but they read the same book. This assertion of commonality is the heart of Greene's fantasy about his readers; his long dalliance with the novella exploits the genre's popularity by recasting it. In focusing on reading as "prying," a description that makes it attractive and dangerous precisely because it is not authorized, Greene constructs a partly oppositional relationship to authorized texts like Homer and even Boccaccio.[52] Greene places a problematic genre in an authorized frame in order to steal the frisson of the one and the moral authority of the other for his own literary project. What emerges is a complex portrait of a readership that shares common cultural material and an authorial practice that manipulates how that material is consumed.

To the extent that the choice of genre signals participation in a formalized language, Greene shows himself in these books to be a master of generic positioning. He divides his epic frame into matching halves: *Penelopes Web* chooses the Ithaca-bound subplot of the *Odyssey*, the aspect of Homer's tale that most resembles romance, and *Euphues his Censure* explores an imagined truce that brings Achilles and Hector into a "philosophical combat" (6:149). The Ithacan volume, designed to appeal to ladies, invokes the shrewdness of Ulysses and chastity of Penelope to defend against the accusations of Ascham and other humanists. It seems likely, however, that Greene knew some readers sought *novelle* because Ascham condemned them. Greene's fantasy of literary community includes not just diverse readers but mutually exclusive ones: virtuous ladies who enjoy being praised, prurient gentlemen who laugh at this show of virtue, and even humanist critics who want to keep them separated.

The first multiplicity in *Penelopes Web* that invites readerly sharing is its three-headed front matter. Greene writes a dedication to two noble ladies (Margaret, Countess of Cumberland, and Anne, Countess of Warwick), follows that with a letter "to the Gentlemen Readers," and concludes with a third, significantly different, letter "To the Courteous and Courtly Ladies of England." The dedication to the Countesses refers to the book as "so precious a monument as the Web of Penelope, the only trophee of her chastitie" (5:141). This image of feminine virtue matches the virtuous lives of the Countesses, who exceed the "fiction" of the *Odyssey* with their own "vertuous resolutions" and "fame" (5:142).[53] Alongside this familiar praise, however, Greene distinguishes among his potential readers. He notes that Homer "penned his Odissea...because [Ulysses] was wise," but then

---

[52] Pettie's mockery of humanist pieties was not the only reading of Continental novelle. See Ullrich Langer, "The Renaissance Novella as Justice," *Renaissance Quarterly* 52 (1999): 311-41.

[53] On this dedication, see Georgiana Ziegler, "Penelope and the Politics of Woman's Place in the Renaissance," *Gloriana's Face: Women, Public and Private, in the English Renaissance*, S. P. Cerasano and Marion Wynne-Davies, eds., (New York and London: Harvester Wheatsheaf, 1992) 25-46.

states that he will write of Penelope "for that she was chast" (5:142). The contrast may be designed to flatter the Countesses, but it also suggests a distinction in different terms for male readers, who comfortably assume the superiority of wisdom to chastity. Greene here employs for the first time what will become a crucial term in *Penelopes Web*, "pollicie." The term describes the common humanist interpretation of Ulysses: "diuers [people] reading the Poets works did imitate his wisdome and spoke well of his pollicie" (5:142). Greene uses virtue of "pollicie" to define Penelope more than Ulysses; "pollicie" is the master-quality that links and regulates the feminine virtues of chastity, silence, and obedience. Greene preemptively attaches this virtue to Ulysses, gesturing toward humanist readings of Homer's hero by Elyot and Ascham. As the work continues, however, female policy takes center stage. Moreover, "pollicie," in addition to being shared by Odysseus and Penelope, is a hermeneutic virtue. Uncovered by "diuers" readings of Homer's poem, "pollicie" foregrounds the matching of fit audiences to well-constructed tales.

Balancing this appeal to women readers, *Euphues his Censure* is dedicated to a martial hero, Robert Earl of Essex, and it identifies itself as a warrior's text. These tales describes themselves as" the exquisite portraiture of a perfect martialist, consisting...in three principall points: wisedome to gouerne; fortitude to performe; liberalitie to incourage" (6:152). These male virtues mirror and trump the feminine trio of chastity, silence, obedience, but Greene's book draws not only from Homer but also from *Euphues*. Turning Lyly's Philautus – settled happily in England with Frances – into the "new chosen generall of certaine forces" (6:152) flatters underemployed courtiers whose hopes of military glory were seldom realized. The supposed martialism of *Euphues his Censure*, however, gets undercut by its appeal to humanist learning for its matter ("*philosophicall* combat") and its self-proclaimed textual models: "Tullies orator, Platoes comon wealth, and Beldesars courtier" (6:152). Greene's dedicatee is a soldier, but his imagined readers have different interests.

The Letter to the Gentlemen Readers in *Penelopes Web* transforms Greene's distinction between male wisdom and female chastity into a blatant appeal to male solidarity. "[T]he matter," Greene apologizes, "is womens prattle, about the untwisting of Penelopes Web" (5:145). But "womens prattle" has sex appeal for male readers: "But considering that...gentlemen [are] desirous to have the parlie of Ladies, I thought rather to write a lyne to much...then by leauing out one title, incurre your displeasures" (5:145). This claim for two distinct modes of reading stops short of Chartier's "sharing" because Greene postulates separate but unequal prefaces, segregated by gender. But part of the claim's charge surely lies in the unlikeliness that this segregation will be enforced: men reading this letter can imagine themselves "prying" into a private feminine discourse while also knowing that women have access to it and the letter addressed to them. The fiction of exclusivity, that Gentlemen should read one letter and Ladies another, flies in the face of likely reading practices. It seems possible that a male reader reading to "fair ladies" would omit the masculine preface, but anyone with access to the book itself would know that the two apparently incompatible prefaces share space. In *Euphues his Censure,* by contrast, there is only one letter following the dedication, titled "To the Reader," but begining with the word, "Gentlemen" (6:154). The point seems to be that gentlemen readers share a set of interests and ways of reading.

The final letter to the Ladies in *Penelopes Web* transforms "prattle" into virtue, thus continuing a split already noted on the title-page, which contrasts women's "vertues and graces" with their "Apparell, or Iewels." Greene apologizes for writing about women – "euery man hath his folly," (5:146) he says – and advances his fiction as a model of feminine perfection: "I reprehend not, as one thinking all generally to be vertuous, but perswade, as one wishing euery one should lyue well and dye better" (5:147). This persuasion converts chastity to wisdom via policy. His conclusion, "I wish you all such happie successe as you can desire and I can imagine" (5:147), places the author's imaginative powers at the ladies' service. These two collections are thus devoted to parsing of different, and differently feminized, heroic virtues. *Penelopes Web* focuses on the master-virtue of "pollicie," associated with Ulysses in numerous commentaries. *Euphues his Censure,* by contrast, explores the masculine virtues of wisdom, fortitude, and liberality in constructing the ideal soldier. To readers who associate the novella with licentiousness and corruption Greene offers Penelope as proof of the coexistence of "pollicie" and virtue. To those who see the exchanging of tales as a pale substitute to descriptions of combat, he suggests that even Hector and Achilles valued rhetorical warfare. Greene's idea of literary community – perhaps fantasy is more accurate – again includes diverse and mutually exclusive readers, including virtuous ladies, sophisticated gentlemen, and even humanist critics who want to keep these groups separated.

In *Penelopes Web*, the master-virtue of "pollicie" is attributed to Ulysses, but Greene re-applies it to Penelope early in the main text: her unweaving uses "pollicie to preuent that which the honest and honorable pretence of her chastite was not able to defend" (5:151). Here policy explicitly exceeds chastity; it is a strategic virtue that is more practical than traditional passivity. As an unweaver who wants to defer an unwelcome event, Penelope's situation parallels Greene's: he too wants to control how his symbolic material is consumed, and he too needs careful strategizing to avoid its getting out of his control. The three inset tales, told by Penelope to her maids and nurse over three nights, exemplify the virtues of obedience, chastity, and silence, but in each case, a heroine's "pollicie" transforms a virtue from a way to endure passively to a strategy for active triumph.

In the first tale, a virtuous queen must re-win her husband's affections after he strays into the arms of a courtesan. Barmenissa, the wife, accomplishes this counter-intuitively by encouraging the courtesan; after finding a damning letter to her husband the king, Barmenissa "thought not by reuenge to make requitall of such treacherie, but by a bountifull courtesie to shewe her enemies how little she esteemed of their practizes" (5:171). This passive style includes embracing her own exile from court, thus placing her in the wandering position common to romance heroines. One distinction between the heroine of romance and that of the novella is that when the novella-heroine returns to respectable society, there is often some ironic joke about her travels, such as the miraculously restored virginity of the Princess Alatiel (*Decameron* 2.7). Greene's heroine, however, seems clearly the romance version. She defends her exile as providing what she could never have at the court: "Content without plentie, Quiet without enuy, and Poverty without impatience" (5:186). Despite this embrace of liminality, Barmenissa does not relinquish her queenly status; when the king's lust cools he remembers her status as "the lawfull Queene of Egypt" (5:191). The "pollicie" that guides the exiled queen's career is a near-complete passivity, which the text terms "patient obedience" (5:192), but this passivity restores the kingdom. Greene's meta-generic point suggests that even in a novella, romance passivity remains potent.

Even when a heroine is more active, she seems less a trickster than a model of Chariclean active-passivity. The heroine of the second tale, Cratyna, must defend herself from the unwelcome attentions of her landlord. Like Barmenissa, she uses a delaying tactic, in this case the old expedient of disguise: "chaunging her apparell into the attyre of a man, and her head brauely shorne, she became a handsome stripling" (5:213). Cratnya's disguise makes her titular virtue, chastity, practical. Like Barmenissa's exile, Cratnya's removal of herself from her landlord's sight allows for the "remorse of conscience" (5:216) to operate in the male character. No further cleverness or manipulation is required of the heroine; she simply removes herself from sight and allows conscience to take its course. Disguise is a common tactic in drama and novelle, but in Greene's tale it becomes a form less of sly manipulation than passive acceptance.

The third sister, whose virtue is silence, provides the most stunning use of policy to make what might seem an impotent virtue powerful. In a scene with striking anticipation of the opening of *King Lear*, each of the wives of the King of Delphos's three sons must publicly speak about her own worth, with the kingdom going to the son with the wisest wife. The first two speeches are effusive, satiric reflections on self-interested courtly rhetoric. By contrast, the youngest sister's answer is "briefe and pithie. He that gaineth a Crowne getteth care: is it not follie then to hunt after losse?" (5:232). This backhanded answer and her refusal to elaborate – "whe[n] others talke, yet being a woman I can hold my peace" (5:232) – so impresses the King that the youngest son is made heir. The point is not simply that silence is an important component of female wisdom, but that the strategic refusal to speak is itself a cunning rhetorical ploy. The youngest daughter here seems closest to the manipulative heroine of the novella, although her anti-rhetoric matches even more closely with Chariclea's refusal to speak at the Aethiopian court. She remakes romance resignation as a tactic compatible with novelistic cunning.

These three examples of "pollicie" by Greene's heroines in *Penelopes Web* emphasize reversals: each heroine turns a feminine weakness into a practical strength. As a comment on Greene's authorial strategies, these versions of policy accent his attempts to regulate the consumption and interpretation of his material. Greene wants to frame the readings of his tales, so that gentlemen, scholars, courtiers, and noble ladies each have their own paths through his text. If it seems unlikely that his readership would have been as docile as he appears to have imagined, his success in print suggests that a readership that appreciated such tactics was emerging during the late Elizabethan period. The heterogeneous "sharing" that defines the popular consumption of literary texts was beginning to find authors who wrote explicitly for this diversity of reading.

The four tales told in *Euphues his Censure* treat a masculine trio of virtues, and the stories themselves are called "Tragedies," perhaps to increase their cultural heft. As allusions to Castiglione, Cicero, and Plato make clear, however, this volume addresses itself to the concerns of courtiers as much as warriors. The siege of Troy is suspended during the second year of war, and the tales are presented as a "Sophomachia" (6:156) featuring male and female aristocrats from both sides. The love of Achilles for Polyxena colors his presentation in terms that recall *Penelopes Web*: "*Achilles* who knewe as well how to tune the Lute with *Venus*, as to sound the Trumpet with *Mars*...subtelly singled him selfe with *Polixena*" (6:160). Even Achilles has entered the mixed-gendered world. The truce suspends martial epic and relocates its heroes in a courtly storytelling world, in which Achilles's lute sounds as loudly as his trumpet. Thus the male virtues presented by the storytellers (Hector on fortitude, Helenus on wisdom, Achilles on liberality) form an anti-epic whole: the perfect martialist is trained to be the ideal courtier. In fact, as will become clear, their exchange highlights the interpretation of tales as a key factor in male heroism.[54] Greene's hero is his ideal reader.

Before these figures offer their competing virtues, however, Ulysses opens the storytelling with a tragedy set in Ithaca that has a topical subtext. His tale of the adultery of Queen Maedina, who sails off with her lover Vortymus but is finally forgiven by her virtuous king, is a thinly-veiled allegory of the abduction of Helen. King Polumestor's offer to forgive his wife stakes out a reasonable compromise: "let mee say that loue as it is variable, so it is mighty inforcing his effect without deniall...so it hath tied mee perforce so partially to thinke of thy fault, as iniury offering no disparagement to affection I haue uppon they repentance resolued quite to fogiue & forget such folly" (6:193). The comment could be Menelaus forgiving Helen, as Ulysses's Trojan audience recognizes. The story is a warning to Troy not to persist in an ignoble cause: both Vortymus and Maedina die in exile. This message is not lost on Hector: "Although *Hector* perceiued that this Tragicall hystorie was induced in hope of a restitution of *Helena*, yet dissimuling the matter, hee onely gaue praise to *Ulisses* for his goode methode, yet superficially glauncing, hee said, that it ill fitted a subiect to be so treacherous" (6:199). Ulysses

---

[54] Hutson does not discuss Greene, but this work fits the thesis of *The Usurer's Daughter* closely.

offers a tale with an accessible meaning, but Hector chooses to dissemble. The other Trojan heroes also refuse the primary meaning: Troilus sees "the rubbing of this scarre" (6:199) as a provocation and evidence that Ulysses "had rather make a conquest of us with Philosophy, than the swoord" (6:199). To the extent that Troilus has correctly diagnosed Ulysses's story, he exposes not just his agenda but Greene's: to convert a story about swords into a tale of competing philosophies.

If Ulysses's tale seems an aggressive opening gambit, in which a story replaces the warfare that has been suspended, the next story told by Helenus about wisdom makes a suitable riposte. He describes a city willing to protect a stolen woman by all means possible: "But the Senators whose heads though not armed with helmets, yet stored with politicke foresight of their enemies caused the gates to be shut up, the Percullyzes to bee let downe, the walls to be countermured with rampiers of forces, and euery quarter of the city to bee gaurded with seuerall companies" (6:217-8). Rather than the moral resolution that Ulysses favors, in which the stolen woman returns to her husband, Helenus's tale accents the cost of attempting to recover her by force. When the bereft Rascianus takes the town and recovers his wife, she mixes poison with the victory wine: "after the pledge had passed, & *Cimbriana* saw hir purpose had taken effect; with a sterne countenance looking upon Rascianus, she told him that now shee had quitted hir cities spoyle with reueng, for know tyrant (quoth shee) that thou and all thy Lordes are impoysoned by the hands of women" (6:230). The story makes a thinly veiled threat and counter to Ulysses's tale, but perhaps more notably it posits Trojan women as a potential instrument of revenge. Greene's revised Trojan war mixes gender roles, and wisdom as Helenus describes it is not only a relatively feminized virtue, but a virtue that might enable a male hero to avoid being killed by (or over) women.

The final two storytellers, Hector and Achilles, turn their rhetoric back toward martial activity. Hector, extolling fortitude, tells the story of three brothers competing over their father's legacy, and the eldest son, the soldier triumphs over the politician and the philosopher. Coming home to find his two brothers' armies fighting over the kingdom, the soldier attacks "like a lyon massacring whom he met" (6:258) and slays each brother in turn. In its celebration of martial fortitude over political skill and philosophical depth Hector's tale comes close to being an outright threat. In fact, the Greeks respond to the story as if it were a threat: "*Hector* having ended his Tragedie. The Grecians noting in his countenance the very counterfayte of magnanimity, and in discoursing of valour, his very face presented a myrrour of fortitude, measuring his inward thoughts by his outward gestures, did both commend the Hystorie and alowe of censure: saying, that where courage manaceth reuenge with the Sworde, there it is folly to bring in wysedomes in his Purple Roabes" (6:259). Thus Hector's tale operates as a linguistic substitute for the martial activity that Greene's text excludes; it is, in Greene's language, a "counterfayte" and "myrrour" of the virtues needed on the battlefield. This tale is as close as these two volumes bring us to the battlefield itself.

The lovesick Achilles, in the final tale, shifts his internal audience. Discoursing on liberality, his tale emphasizes that soldiers will not fight for a leader who does not reward them; when the tight-fisted Athenian leader Clytomaches replaces the liberal Roxander, the army takes the city but grows dispirited when denied its reward: "the Souldiers thus couragiously hauing entred combat, and won the conquest as before time they had done, entring into euery house to feth out the spoile, generall proclamation was made that no man uppon paine of death should take one penny...which so amazed and discouraged the mercenary men, that with hartlesse groanes they went stragling to the tents" (6:275-6). The warning is directed to Agamemnon, not Troy. The return of the general Roxander and the killing of Clytomaches underscores Achilles's threat to the Greek hierarchy. This story highlights a storyteller's ability to shift his intended audience, and it also marks Greene's turn to a male courtly audience somewhat like Pettie's: the threat in Achilles's story is recognizable only to an audience familiar with Book 1 of the *Iliad* (which is to say, mostly male university-educated readers; Peele's *Tale of Troy* did not appear until 1589). The warrior-hero has become a master courtier, aiming veiled barbs at his own king.

Greene's volume ends with an attempt at interpretive unity by King Priam, who asserts that all these virtues are necessary for a soldier: "then of these premisses wee may conclude, that none can come to the perfection of a souldier, unlesse he be both wise, valiant, and liberall" (6:283). This easy moral, which Greene calls a "graue censure" (6:283), asserts that the disparate audiences of these tales – the beseiged Trojans warned by Ulysses, the overconfident Greeks threatened by Helenus, the argumentative armies challenge by Hector, and the Greek leadership destabilized by Achilles – can be unified. The model still seems to be many heads and wits being combined, though it is never clear exactly how Greene purports to bring these strands together. Greene continued to write novelle collections until 1590, and recognizable features of these tales also appear in the cony-catching pamphlets and *Greenes Groatsworth of Wit*. The internal tension between Greene's attempts to produce coherent books to represent a marketable persona, and the tendency of each story to become its own narrative world, was something with which he never ceased experimenting.

Chapter 6

# Fictions of Nostalgia: Lodge versus Greene

But beeing of simple nature, hee served but for a block to whet Robertoes whit on.

Robert Greene, *Groatsworth of Wit* (71)

Thomas Lodge began his career in fiction as a protégé of Robert Greene. Following *Pandosto* (1588) and *Menaphon* (1590), the two worked together on two romances published under Lodge's name, *Rosalynde* (1590) and *Euphues Shadow* (1592). Greene contributed a "To the Gentlemen Reader" epistle to each, and to *Rosalynde* he added a second epistle in the voice of Euphues. He may also have edited Lodge's prose.[1] They collaborated on a play, *A Looking-Glasse for London and England*, probably in 1586.[2] Their Arcadian romances *Menaphon* and *Rosalynde*, written one year apart and at the height of their profession alliance, represent the public high point of Elizabethan-Heliodoran prose romance.

Despite this close collaboration, their relationship deteriorated in the early 1590s. The seeds of their split were literary and philosophical; Lodge, like Sidney, remained tied to medieval and chivalric narrative forms. Even early works like *Forbonious and Prisceria*, Lodge's first fiction, and *Rosalynde*, the romance that Greene may have substantially re-written, bear traces of Lodge's later repudiation of his mentor. The distinction is both formal (Lodge prefers medieval settings and sources) and religious (his narratives turn on Catholic penance rather than Protestant repentance). Lodge's interest in human depravity and penance contrast with Greene's rhetorical play and last-minute performative repentances. After 1590 the split became obvious: each wrote fictions of prodigality, but Lodge portrays lengthy acts of penance, rejecting Greene's model. *Robin the Devil* (1591), was a veiled attack on Greene himself, and *A Margarite of America* (1596) rejects Elizabethan-Heliodoran prose romance for a tragic reinterpretation of Iberian chivalry.

---

[1]  Donald Beecher, sees Greene's authorial hand in the similes, sub-title, front matter, and concluding paragraph. See Beecher, ed., *Rosalind: Euphues' Golden Legacy Found After His Death in His Cell at Silexedra (1590)*, (Ottawa: Dovehouse Editions, 1997) 65, 71, 231n.

[2]  See Testumaro Hayashi, ed., *A Looking Glasse for London and England*, (Metuchen: Scarecrow Press, 1970) 13.

Lodge's life was as dominated by romance *topoi* as Greene's. He was the eldest son of Sir Thomas Lodge, a leader of the Grocer's Guild and Lord Mayor of London.[3] Rejecting his family's preference for a legal career, Lodge turned to the book market to see if he, like Greene, could live by his pen. Despite his family's wealth and prosperity, he lived among poor publishers and writers, apparently lodging with John Busby for a period of time.[4] Whatever money he had, he spent; perhaps £1,000 between 1579-83, when £40 was a comfortable year's wage. His struggles with his family were protracted and well-known; parallels between his life and the plight of the outcast brother in *Rosalynde* (and *As You Like It*) have been made since his lifetime.[5]  Since Lodge's religious model required public penance, he could not simply repent his sins on his deathbed. Instead, Lodge's penance was conversion to Catholicism and temporary exile from his native land. He became a Catholic around 1600, went to France, and earned a Medical degree at Avignon. He lived on the continent for a decade before returning to England in 1611, inheriting his family's depleted estate from his younger brother, and finally dying in 1625, impoverished and intestate.[6]

As this biography shows, Lodge was a Prodigal Son par excellence. When he took up this theme in fiction, he remade it to reject Greene's Protestant model. For Lodge, as Helgerson notes, Greene's internal and/or rhetorical repentances seemed too easy. Lodge's fiction describes lengthy conversions that go beyond repentance to significant penitent action. They tell the story of the efficacy of human works, rejecting Calvinist self-examination for Catholic penance.[7] Helgerson observes, "Chivalric romance and Catholicism are to Lodge as Greek romance and Calvinism were to Greene."[8] The debate between these two men centers on conversion: what it is, how it can be described, and what its consequences are.

## Lodge's Heliodorus: *Forbonius and Prisceria*

In his earliest fiction, *The Delectable Historie of Forbonius and Prisceria*, published as the second part of *An Alarum for Usurers* (1584), Lodge had not yet

---

[3]   See Charles J. Sisson, "Thomas Lodge and his Family," *Thomas Lodge and Other Elizabethans*, (Cambridge: Harvard University Press, 1933) 17.
[4]   See N. Burton Paradise, *Thomas Lodge: The History of an Elizabethan*, (New Haven: Yale University Press, 1931) 38n; Wesley D. Rae, *Thomas Lodge*, (Boston: Twayne Publishers, 1967); Elaine Cuvelier, *Thomas Lodge: Témoin de son temps (c. 1558-1625)*, (Paris: Didier Érudition, 1984); and Beecher's Appendix to *Rosalind*, 253-44.
[5]   See Sisson, "Thomas Lodge," 102-3.
[6]   See Sisson, "Thomas Lodge," *passim*.
[7]   On Catholicism and Lodge's authorial persona, see R. W. Maslen, "Lodge's *Glaucus and Silla* and the Conditions of Catholic Authorship in Elizabethan England," *EnterText* 3 (2003): 59-100.
[8]   *Elizabethan Prodigals*, 121.

split with Greene's Heliodoran model. In fact, like Greene, Lodge mentions Theagenes and Chariclea by name in his first work.[9] Lodge's debt to Heliodorus is even more explicit than Greene's. His heroine Prisceria is Chariclea's grand-daughter, and her advisor, Appollonius the Gymnosophist, mirrors Calasiris. Lodge's references to Heliodorus, however, seem confused. Jumbling his source's Egyptian and Aethiopian settings, Lodge sets his romance "In Memphis (the chiefest citie of Aegypt)...at such time as Sisimithres was head Priest of the same, & Hidaspes gouernour of the Prouince."[10] Beyond misreading Chariclea's homeland as Egypt, Lodge jumbles his chronology. Hydaspes is Chariclea's father, but Lodge carelessly allows his rule to continue into the life of his own heroine, the daughter of "Valduuia, daughter and heire of Theagines of Greece, the copartner of sorrow with Caricleala [sic], the straunge borne childe of the Aegyptian King" (1:54). The life-span is impossible unless Hydaspes is another Methuselah. Lodge remembers that Chariclea is "straunge borne," but misspelling her name is just one of a series of errors.[11]

These errors lend credence to Wolff's contention that Lodge's allusions prove nothing other than the popularity of the *Aethiopian History* in the 1580s. Wolff notes, "Lodge would have no motive for professing to continue a story that was not widely and favorably known." Wolff's further comment, however, that "Lodge's own story...shows no other trace of Heliodorus," ignores the cultural meanings of Heliodoran fiction.[12] Heliodorus's non-martial, deceptive version of heroism situates Lodge generically and philosophically. Given that the *Alarum against Usurers* was an exposé of London life intended to defend Lodge against rumors of ill-living, the romance interlude seems out of place. The story is not distinctive; it follows the two lovers as they maneuver past Prisceria's father to marriage. The Heliodoran frame gives stock material intellectual and social provenance, as well as guiding it to a potential market niche.

The cultural milieu at which Lodge aimed appears in his dedicatee, Philip Sidney. While its uncertain whether Lodge would have read, or heard rumors of, Sidney's *Arcadia* by 1584, the dedication places the text in the Sidney circle, Protestant, literary, and chivalric.[13] Lodge asks Sidney for future help as well as

---

[9]   See Wolff, *Greek Romances in Elizabethan Prose Fiction*, 381. Lodge makes only one subsequent reference to Theagenes and Chariclea, in *Robin the Devil*, which I discuss below.

[10]  Thomas Lodge, *An Alarum against Usurers*, *The Complete Works of Thomas Lodge*, Edmund Gosse, ed., (Glasgow: The Hunterian Club, 1883) 1:53. Further citations given in the text.

[11]  Calasiris is the *Aethiopian History*'s central Egyptian character, and perhaps Lodge's attraction to this priest-figure shapes his erroneous citations.

[12]  *Greek Romances in Elizabethan Prose Fiction*, 459.

[13]  Salzman notes that Beaty fails to show that *Forbonius and Prisceria* imitates Sidney. If, however, Lodge had not read the *Arcadia* but merely heard that Sidney wrote a Heliodoran romance, that might help explain his gestures toward this model. See Frederick L. Beaty,

protection from malicious rumors (1:3). Although nothing came of this appeal for patronage (Sidney would be dead in two years), it places Lodge's Heliodoran superstructure in Elizabethan context. By the time of Lodge's central years as a romance writer (the early 1590s), Sidney's and Heliodorus's names were intertwined. By citing both writers in his first romance, Lodge appears to have made this connection in 1584.

There is little action in *Forbonius and Prisceria*; like the early Greene, Lodge follows the Euphuistic formula, and his characters debate nothing so much as Fortune. Where Fortune in Heliodorus or Sidney is a mysterious dispensation that motivates intense debate, in Lodge it is comparatively simple: falling in love is following Fortune. Forbonius, who, in another slight misreading of Heliodorus, is a non-shipwrecked mariner, falls in love with Prisceria because of Fortune. Like Greene's Mamillia, he discovers that the proper reaction is passivity: "at last finding out his mistres aloted him by fate, [he] yeelded willinglye unto importunitie of the Destinies" (1:54). By accepting divine power, Forbonius needs neither repentance nor Chariclean indirection. He must only "yeeld" to Fortune. When Prisceria's father hides her in the country, Forbonius dresses as a shepherd to woo her. Much more simply than in the *Old Arcadia*, his swain's disguise and pastoral eclogues win her heart.

Forbonius's guide is the priest-magician Appollonius, who reveals divine law in no uncertain terms: "If all things be ordered by the higher powers, it is vayne you must conclude to infringe what is concluded on, if the destenies have appoynted" (1:60). Lacking "showmanship," Appollonius provides straightforward philosophical help. He isolates constancy, the virtue of Greene's Mamillia, as Forbonius's ethical key. "[B]y onely continent forbearaunce," Appollonius advises the hero, "thou shalt be disburdened of many misfortunes" (1:60). While Lodge, unlike Greene, does not privilege his heroine over his hero, he does value constancy above all.

Prisceria, convincing her father not to kill Forbonius, defends their love as a gift from Fortune. There is nothing indirect or dissembling about her rhetoric: "Who seeketh O father, to preuent the destinies, laboreth in vaine, and who indeauoureth to alter nature, as he striueth against the streame, so much he perish in his own ouerweening: the Gods have concluded our loue, and will you being a creature seeke to infringe it?" (1:81). In the pseudo-theological language of Greek romance, Prisceria imagines love and Fortune as synonyms. Lodge's concern to preserve human agency would lead him to break with Greene's and Sidney's semi-Calvinist models, but in this early work he allots all agency to Fortune. Between the naive romance of *Forbonius and Prisceria* and the Catholicism he would arrive at in 1596, lie Lodge's Arcadian romances of the late 1580s. In these texts,

---

"Lodge's *Forbonius and Prisceria* and Sidney's *Arcadia*," *English Studies* 49 (1968): 38-45, and Salzman, *English Prose Fiction*, 71-2.

especially *Rosalynde*, Lodge struggled with the Heliodoran model, attempting to turn it toward his particular obsessions.

## Lodge for Sale: *Rosalynde*

Living and writing in Greene's shadow, Lodge's sole commercial triumph was *Rosalynde* (1590).[14] That this text has remained popular into the twentieth century owes much to Shakespeare's *As You Like It*, but *Rosalynde* was a media event in its own right, going through nine editions between 1590 and 1634. The four most prominent members of the Ling-Busby consortium – Nicholas Ling, John Busby, Thomas Gubbins, and John Smethwicke – published all nine editions.[15] For a time, the text dominated Elizabethan fiction. Even as Ponsonby's editions of the *Arcadia* continued to sell in their more expensive format, *Rosalynde* enabled Ling and his allies to make their publishers' marks symbols for middlebrow prose romance.

*Rosalynde*, as its subtitle shows, is a hybrid text. The full title, *Rosalynde: Euphues' Golden Legacy Found After His Death in His Cell at* Silexedra, invokes both *Euphues* and *Menaphon*. Borrowing from Lyly and Greene, *Rosalynde* marks the high point of the Greene-Lodge collaboration. (That *Rosalynde*'s success might sell more copies of *Menaphon* cannot have been far from Greene's mind.) The prefatory epistle, perhaps written by Greene in the voice of Euphues, accents the collaboration: "Thou hast sons by Camilla, as I hear, who being young in years have green thoughts...I have bequeathed them a golden legacy because I greatly love thee" (96).[16] Lodge's primary source is an anonymous fourteenth-century Middle-English verse romance, *The Tale of Gamelyn*, but with Greene's revisions *Rosalynde* became an ideal fiction, with touches of Lyly, Greene, and Sidney.

Greene's editing and influence, however, cannot overshadow Lodge's departure from his and Sidney's examples. *Rosalynde* problematizes the passivity of Heliodoran romance. "Patience" is an ideal, but the key motif for Lodge's fiction, and the key to his departure from Greene, is penance. In Lodge's Arden, a jailhouse conversion eclipses the pastoral frolics of the other characters. Saladyne, the hero's brother, makes an abortive turn from villainy to penitent labor that prefigures Lodge's later revisions of Elizabethan prose romance.

The dual nature of *Rosalynde* – at once the most popular text of Ling's consortium, and also the start of Lodge's emancipation from Greene – appears in its three-headed front matter. The first letter, by Lodge himself, dedicates the text

---

[14] Helgerson accents the failure of Lodge's other publications (*Elizabethan Prodigals*, 122).

[15] The first edition (1590) was published by Gubbins and Busby, and then Gubbins and Busby again in 1592, Ling and Busby in 1596, Ling and Gubbins in 1598, Ling alone in 1604, and the last four editions (1609, 1612, 1623, and 1634) by Smethwicke.

[16] Beecher identifies Greene as the author of this passage.

to Henry Carey, Lord of Hundson. The second addresses "The Gentlemen Readers" in Greene's style, and was likely written by Greene. The third letter, the dying words of Euphues, written by Greene for the 1592 edition, places the tale in a fictional frame.[17] The tension between Lodge's social deference and Greene's marketing savvy describes *Rosalynde*'s entrance into St. Paul's. What Lodge's dedication describes as a decorous chivalric totem becomes a market property. Lodge's moral ambition and Greene's obsession with the consumer duel in the peritexts.

Lodge's plea for patronage includes a biographical note that makes more pointed his departure from Greek romance. Lodge describes himself as a sailor experienced in storms: "Having with Captain Clarke made a voyage to the islands of Terceras and the Canaries, to beguile the time with labor I writ this book, rough – as hatched in the storms of the ocean – and feathered in the surges of many perilous seas" (93).[18] A sea-traveler like Chariclea and Sephastia, Lodge connects his prose to the "storms" and "surges" of his Atlantic voyage. Like *A Margarite of America* (1596), which Lodge would claim was a translation of a manuscript he discovered in South America,[19] *Rosalynde* appears to have been born at sea. Lodge describes himself in a romance-scene, thus prefiguring the union of author and hero that occupied Greene in the early 1590s.

Lodge's description of the writing process, however, does not fit Greene's model. A romance should be written "to beguile the time," but adding, "labor," breaks the mold. Greene was famous for writing quickly and carelessly, and Lodge's admission of labor may have made him wince.[20] Thematically, Lodge's emphasis on "labor" reveals a departure from Greene: both describe the recovery of prodigals, but Lodge's heroes "labor" for their reformation, while Greene's simply repent and are transformed.

Recasting the submissive tone of Lodge's letter, which was apparently written two to three years before publication, the second letter "To the Gentlemen Readers" takes Greene's direct approach.[21] Always careful to lower the bar for his

---

[17] This letter misreads *Euphues and his England*, addressing Philautus's "sons by Camilla," not remembering that Philautus married Frances, not Camilla. See Bates, "A Large Occasion of Civil Discourse."

[18] Citations are from Beecher's edition and cited in the text. See Sisson, "Thomas Lodge," 106-7, on Lodge's sea voyages.

[19] The Spanish or Portuguese source has never been found and is presumably part of the fiction. See Donald Beecher, "The Fiction of Symbolic Forms: Mythological Drifting in Lodge's *A Margarite of America*," *Critical Approaches to English Prose Fiction*, Donald Beecher, ed., (Ottawa: Dovehouse Editions, 1998) 219.

[20] In the epistle to *Menaphon*, Nashe praises Greene's "extemporal vein" (82) and in *Strange Newes* he notes that, "In a night & a day would he haue yarkt up a pamphlet as well as in seauen yeare" (1:287).

[21] Beecher observes that Lodge omitted the titles Carey obtained in August 1589 (*Rosalind*, 229n).

audience, Greene cautions the reader not to look for "any springs of Pallas' bay tree, nor ... the humor of any amorous laureate, nor the pleasing vein of any eloquent orator" (95). By pointedly refusing Lodge the very terms of praise (eloquence and humor) that Nashe gave *Menaphon*, Greene defends his own dominant position while praising Lodge's sea-borne style: "To be brief, Gentlemen, room for a soldier and a sailor that gives you the fruits of his labors that he wrought in the ocean, when every line was wet with a surge and every humorous passion counterchecked with a storm. If you like it, so; and yet I will be yours in duty, if you be mine in favor" (95). Recalling Lodge's assertion that the book was borne at sea, Greene makes the location part of the sales pitch. Born in a romance setting, the story must appeal to readers of Heliodorus, Sidney, and Greene himself. In Greene's epistle, the word "labors" does not evoke sustained effort, but rather the "fruits" of the powerful storm, which "wet" every line and "counterchecked" every passion. As Greene imagines it, the sea collaborates with the author, and the text is produced with minimal human labor. Greene makes Lodge into a romancer like himself and imagines *Rosalynde* continuing the project of *Forbonius and Prisceria*.

The third letter attached to *Rosalynde*, also written by Greene, claims to be the final words of Euphues: "The Schedule Annexed to Euphues' Testament, the Tenor of his Legacy, the Token of his Love" (97). Greene applies his usual Horatian criteria to the text, saying that Euphues sends the tale to Philautus's sons so that they may "profit by it" (97). Profit (in both moral and financial senses) motivates and rewards the writing process, and becomes a synonym for writing itself. The appeal to Philautus's sons, "who being young in years have green thoughts," makes a further pun on "Greene's" influence. The letter shapes *Rosalynde* to appeal to those who have "green/Greene" thoughts and tastes.

*Rosalynde*, however, suspects Greene's prodigality. Greene's Euphues explains the narrative as the product of repentance: "I feel death that summoneth me to my grave, and my soul desirous of his God. Farewell, Philautus, and let the tenor of my counsel be applied to thy children's comfort" (96). In 1590, Greene had just begun turning from *Menaphon*'s celebration of passive virtue to his first literary repentance in *Greenes Mourning Garment* and *Greenes Never Too Late* (both 1590). *Rosalynde* anticipates Greene's career path by combining a conversion narrative with a Greek-romance storyline.

The central plot of *Rosalynde*, however, does not really lend itself to the prodigality-repentance mode that both Lodge and Greene would use later.[22] The reunion of the estranged brothers Rosader and Saladyne, and their marriages to the court ladies Rosalind and Alinda, is a straightforward pastoral tale that Lodge treats leisurely, with Euphuistic speeches and pastoral lyrics. The play between Euphuism and the easy solutions of romance has led Lindheim to see *Rosalynde* as

---

[22]  Repentance figures more directly in *A Looking Glasse for London and England*, which rewrites Jonah's warning to Nineveh a cautionary tale for Elizabethan London.

a rejection of Lyly's more skeptical fiction: "Inherent in the very fabric of the romance world, therefore, are suppositions about reality and perfection which force that author to modify and soften the kind of antithesis and paradox at the heart of *Euphues.*"[23] Lyly's skepticism, according to Lindheim, does not mesh with the idealism of romance. Romance, however, is more complex than she allows. The Heliodoran tradition, in particular, places "antithesis and paradox" at the heart of its ethical vision. Lodge downplays this tension, but this shift indicates his departure from, not slavish imitation of, mainstream Elizabethan-Heliodoran romance. Lodge short-circuits romance, and in doing so modifies its ideals. As Walter Davis has noted, Arden is a simplified Arcadia, where Nature's bounty replaces Fortune's mystery as the guiding force.[24] Once in Arden, the central characters have little trouble, either erotic or political. Rosader and Saladyne find Rosalind and Alinda, and even exiled King Gerismond has only to wait for the Twelve Peers of France to help him re-conquer his kingdom in the final pages.

Lodge's term for human virtue in Arden is "patience." Contrasting with the active conspiracy of Heliodorus, Greene, and Sidney, Lodge's characters submit completely; even Sephastia's deception of Menaphon is beyond them. Rosader, exiled by Saladyne, "brooked all the injuries of fortune with patience" (140). The departure from the Heliodoran model is subtle, for Chariclea also brooks injuries with patience, but Rosader never actively deceives. Even Rosalind retreats to patient passivity once she arrives in the forest. Alinda maintains that "the sweetest salve for misery was patience" and therefore advises her to "be patient, Rosalind" (121-2). In their patient, passive states, Rosalind and Alinda adapt disguises that do not strain their own courtly identities. As Charles Larson suggests, the tale "discourage[s] role playing" in favor of a "new and clearer definition of the self."[25] Unlike Shakespeare's Rosalind, Lodge's heroine does not critique gender conventions but accepts wooing-play as part of her pastoral interlude.[26]

Following *Menaphon* in refusing to distinguish chance from Providence, Lodge accents coincidence in his plot. In Arden chance is always Providential. When Rosader and Adam are starving, Rosader happens upon Gerismond's camp "by chance fortune" (144). The meeting between Rosader, Rosalind, and Alinda also comes about "by good fortune" (149). There is no distinction between "chance" and "good" fortune. Even the lovers' names announce their compatibility; *Ros*ader

---

[23] "Lyly's Golden Legacy," 11.

[24] See "Masking in Arden: The Histrionics of Lodge's *Rosalynde*," *Studies in English Literature* 5 (1965): 151-63.

[25] "Lodge's *Rosalind*: Decorum in Arden," *Studies in Short Fiction* 14 (1977): 126, 118. Larson emphasizes the text's "essential conservatism" (118).

[26] The differences between *Rosalynde* and *As You Like It* cannot be stressed enough. Lodge's romance lacks the skeptical playfulness Jacques and Touchstone bring to the play, and his Rosalind is much less of an actor. Charles Whitworth, Jr., reveals how the "white light" of Shakespeare has lead scholars to misread Lodge ("*Rosalynde:* As You Like It and as Lodge Wrote It," *English Studies* 58 [1977]: 114-17).

marries *Ros*alind. Lodge simply identifies chance with Providence; his tale contains no evil coincidences. Even Rosader's discovery of Saladyne, still a villain at this point, comes about by fortune's "smile" (171), when Saladyne is beset by a lion and no threat. Fortune wears the happiest face possible; the stormy sea appears only in the prefatory letters.

Lodge's tale accents the distinction between two romance spaces, the wood and the sea. In Greene and Sidney, the sea threatens on a cosmic scale, while the wood is a place of human treachery. Lodge, following the notion that dry land is safe, emphasizes the idyllic pastoral wood to the exclusion of the violent sea.[27] In the forest of Arden, storms are passing problems, and supernatural forces never threaten. The problems that exist are domestic, matching wooer to beloved, rather than the cosmic crises of Greene and Heliodorus.

In addition to its pastoral plot, however, *Rosalynde* gestures toward more serious concerns. The heart of *Rosalynde*, and the change it marks from the *New Arcadia* and *Menaphon*, occurs in the minor characters Adam Spencer and Saladyne, not the romance principals. The tale's critique of fortune comes from Adam, the loyal servant who nearly starves in the forest. Adam employs the language of Greek romance by comparing his world to the sea: "Oh, how the life of man may be well compared to the state of the ocean seas, that for every calm hath a thousand storms, resembling the rose tree that for a few fair flowers hath a multitude of sharp prickles" (141). Adam turns his metaphor from the unknowable sea to a domestic English flower, the rose. By displacing this lament from master to servant, Lodge implies that Rosader does not need the advice such a monologue produces, since his Fortune must be good.

Adam does not discover any way to mediate Fortune's storm. Instead, he resolves to "thwart [Fortune] with brooking all mishaps with patience. For there is no greater check to the pride of fortune than with a resolute courage to pass over her crosses without care" (142). Relying on patience, Adam maintains a steadfast passivity, refusing worry or "care." The reference to Fortune's "crosses" highlights the religious subtext that Lodge would sound later in his career. More than any other character, Adam demonstrates that replacing the stormy sea with happy Arden is an arbitrary generic decision, not a reward for human virtue. His lament casts a shadow Rosalind and Rosader's adventures in the forest.

Adam's monologue reverses itself at its end. By this time, the speech has moved from an initial lament against fortune, to a celebration of patience, to, finally, near despair.[28] Seeing Rosader starving, Adams turns his assault from

---

[27] A counter-tradition does exist. The threatening forest of Virgil's Nisus and Euryalus (*Aeneid* 9) and of Dante's *Inferno* (1) typify the haunted romance-wood. Spenser's *Faerie Queene* explores this wood more, perhaps because it follows the tradition of verse romance from Virgil and Dante to Ariosto and Tasso.

[28] Lindheim suggests that Lodge's romance never contains a Lylian "major-alternative soliloquy" (in which real alternatives are debated) ("Lyly's Golden Legacy," 12-13).

Bordeaux's Fortune to Arden's Nature: "Nature hath prodigally enriched [Rosader] with her favors...and now, through the decree of the unjust stars, to have all these good parts nipped in the blade and blemished by the inconstancy of fortune" (142-3). This lament leads Adam to offer his body as food, in a dark parody of Christian communion and   a jarring insertion of cannibalism within pastoral romance.[29] Adam wrestles with loss like no other character in *Rosalynde*; he describes what the forest would be without the "chance fortune" that brings Rosader to Gerismond. In a dark wood, Adam struggles with loss of hope, at last concluding, "Ah, despair is a merciless sin" (143). "Despair," a spiritual sin that Rosalind and Rosader never discover, hovers on the edge of Lodge's romance, providing a foretaste of the less hopeful fictions of the later 1590s.

Even more than Adam's monologue, *Rosalynde*'s departure from romance pieties lies with Saladyne. A villain who tries to kill his brother and drives him to Arden when that fails, Saladyne is imprisoned and exiled by the usurper Torismond. In prison, Saladyne begins the journey from prodigality to penance that typifies Lodge's later fiction and his own life. Saladyne's prison monologue sounds an explicitly religious theme: "There is no sting [like] to the worm of conscience, no hell to a mind touched with guilt....Be penitent and assign thyself some penance to discover thy sorrow and pacify [Rosader's] wrath" (147).[30] Saladyne's reformation and marriage to Alinda sew up the comic ending of the tale, but his turn from evil comes by way of "penitence" rather than "patience." [31] In this near-pun, Lodge devises a new version of romance, which centers on sinful humanity's purging itself of sin.

Compared with Saladyne, Rosader and Rosalind seem lightweights, frolicking in the forest when they should be examining "the worm of conscience." Arriving in Arden to be saved from a lion by Rosader, Saladyne dedicates his life to penance, telling his unrecognized brother: "Passionate thus with many griefs, in penance of my former follies, I go thus pilgrim-like to seek out my brother, that I may reconcile myself to him in all submission and afterward wend to the Holy Land to end my years in as many virtues as I have spent my youth in wicked vanities" (176). The true hero of the text, as these sentences make clear, is Saladyne, not Rosader or Rosalind. His resolve does not affect the pastoral plot so much as provide an alternative to it. Saladyne and Adam suggest that Lodge was not

---

Adam's monologue, however, fits her model much better than the speeches of Alinda, Rosader, and Rosalynde that she considers.

[29] Lodge became fascinated with cruelty in the 1590s, especially in *Robin the Devil* (1591), *A Margarite of America* (1596), and *The Wounds of Civil War* (1594). Elaine Cuvelier comments on his "Senecan horror" in "Horror and Cruelty in the Works of Three Elizabethan Novelists," *Cahiers Elisabethains* 19 (1981): 40.

[30] Although the words "penitent" and "penance" carry Catholic subtexts, Lodge's theology remains broad enough her to avoid upsetting Protestant authorities. Later his Catholicism became more pointed.

[31] Shakespeare, interestingly, omits the repentance episodes I discuss.

content with pastoral. Having stripped romance down to the bare essentials of "patience" and "good Fortune," Lodge found that this core did create narrative tension.

The pastoral superstructure of *Rosalynde* finally smothers its serious characters. Adam fades into the background as soon as he is fed and finally disappears as "captain of the king's guard" (227). Saladyne becomes a lover after meeting Alinda. His love-discourse, however, when compared to Rosader's, highlights Saladyne's moral seriousness. He likens constancy in love to "heavens eternal course" and tells his story of becoming a loving "forester" as a version of a prodigal's repentance (197-9). More than any other character, Saladyne recognizes that the magic of Arden is moral clarity, not rhetorical play. What he finds in the forest is truth, first about his own betrayal of Rosader, and then about his feelings for Alinda. He woos as bluntly as he can, saying, "seeing in many words lies mistrust and that truth is ever naked, let this suffice for a country wooing: Saladyne loves Aliena and none but Aliena" (199).[32] While not quite the final word on courtship, Saladyne's anti-rhetoric suggests Lodge's distrust of romance models. The future of his fiction lies with the despairing self-examination of Adam and Saladyne, not the manipulations of Rosalind or the heroics of Rosader.

After *Rosalynde*, Lodge's output increased. He published nine volumes between 1591-6, of which four were fiction, each departing from the Greene-Sidney-Heliodorus model.[33] Lodge's career became schizophrenic in the turbulent mid-1590s; he followed *Rosalynde* by attempting to make himself Greene's heir, but he was increasingly skeptical of Greene. For Lodge, the problem with prodigal romances was that they celebrated irreligion. Religion, which for Lodge always meant the Catholicism he encountered as a student at Oxford,[34] dominated Lodge's post-*Rosalynde* output. Lodge's religious turn produced quite different results from Greene's.

---

[32] That Saladyne makes this avowal to the false name Aliena, is one of Lodge's rhetorical tricks. Unlike Shakespeare's play, however, Lodge emphasizes the truth in bluntness, not that which emerges only through disguise.

[33] The nine volumes are *Catharos: Diogines in his singularitie* (1591), *Robin the Devil* (1591), *Euphues' Shadow* (1592), *William Long beard* (1593), *Phillis: honoured with pastoral sonnets* (1593), *Wounds of Civil War*, (1594), *A Fig for Momus* (1595), *A Margarite of America* (1596), *Prosopopeia* (1596), and *Wits Miserie* (1596). *A Looking Glasse for London and England* was also published in 1594. John Busby published three of the four fictional works.

[34] See Paradise, *Thomas Lodge*, 17-8. Cuvelier's biography also considers religion in detail, and Kinney, notes Catholic elements in his fiction (*Humanist Poetics*, 374, 405, 411).

## Rejecting Greene: *Robin the Devil*

The play that Lodge wrote with Greene, *A Looking Glasse for London and England*, prefigures their split. A dramatic account of the Old Testament prophet Jonah, the play has as its refrain, "Repent, or else thy judgment is at hand."[35] This sentence seems to have meant different things to the two authors. Whereas for Greene repentance is a sudden internal clarity, Lodge's model is more laborious. Lodge's Catholic emphasis on penance, public devotional practices, and the authority of Rome, contrasts sharply with Greene's internalized Protestantism. Lodge's break with Greene appears most strikingly in a historical romance of 1591, *The famous, true and historicall life of Robert second duke of Normandy.* This work's alternate title, *Robin the Devil*, captures Lodge's new opinion of Greene.

In place of Greene's reliance on Heliodorus, Lodge's fiction includes a serious penitential phase and transformation from sinner to saint. As in *Rosalynde*, Lodge takes a medieval source, in this case a French chronicle history "drawne out of the old and ancient antiquaries" (2:4) and published in English by Wynken de Worde in the early sixteenth century.[36] This source underlines Lodge's medievalism, as opposed to Greene's classicism. The horror of Robin's early crimes leads Beecher to conclude that the text is "a parody of a saint's life."[37] The disparity between the devilish and saintly halves of Robin's career appears designed to appeal, as Beecher suggests, to a sensationalist reader.[38] Stories of repentant saints often work in exactly this way, with early wickedness emphasizing God's grace in redeeming sinners. (The tradition owes much to Greek romance, as medieval scholars note.)[39] As Lodge puts it in the text's closing phrases, "[Robin] became of an irreligious

---

[35] Some variation of this phrase, addressed to Niniuie or London, appears nine times. See Hayashi, ed., *A Looking Glasse*, 101, 116, 127, 136, 143, 153-4, 158, 167, 175.

[36] Busby's edition of *Robin the Devil* was modeled on de Worde's 1510 edition, according to the *STC*. Claudette Pollack suggests that Lodge's use of de Worde and French versions of Robert's history make this text the first "historical romance" in English literature. See "Romance and Realism in Lodge's *Robin the Devil*," *Studies in Short Fiction* 13 (1976): 491-97.

[37] Appendix to *Rosalind*, 260.

[38] John Selzer emphasizes that the disparity between the aims and techniques of Lodge's fiction has led to confusion: "Too often the fiction betrays either an indecision about aim or, when its purpose is consistent, an inconsistency in the means chosen to accomplish that aim. In other words, there is an imprecision in either the tenor or the vehicle." I suggest that this "imprecision" is exactly what romance enables: a way of thinking about hard questions in the assurance that the genre will prevent tragic conclusions. See "The Achievement of Lodge's *Robin the Devil*," *Texas Studies in Language and Literature* 26 (1984): 19.

[39] Greek romance prototypes are particularly influence the stories of nautical saints like St. Mary Magdalene and St. Martha. See Thomas J. Heffernan, *Sacred Biography: Saints and Their Biographers in the Middle Ages*, (Oxford: Oxford University Press, 1988).

person, the onley royall paragon of the world" (2:89). What John L. Selzer calls the "devotional purpose" of the text works because of, not despite, Robin's early wickedness.[40] The romance *topoi*, including a supernatural hermit, a Spenserian *bois du temptacion*,[41] a journey to a holy city, and Robin's final triumph over the Sultan of Babylon, shift from the vaguely Protestant world of Elizabethan-Heliodoran romance to the Catholicism of saints' lives.

The text's front matter, written entirely by Lodge,[42] dedicates the volume to Thomas Smith, the "true Moecenas of learning" (2:3). The emphasis on learning and self-improvement signals a change from the happy paradise of Arden: "Seeing in these our days, men rather seek the increase of transitorie wealth, than the knowledge of deuine wisedome, preferring stuffed baggs, before studious bookes" (2:3). The jab aims at market-oriented writers like Greene and also at publishers like Busby who demand "transitorie wealth" from an author's pen. Greene, who proudly declared himself *Utriusque Academiae in Artibus magister* on his title pages, was vain about his learning, and Lodge's appeal to moral rather than financial acumen highlights his attempt to separate himself from part of Greene. He remained loyal to the Master of Arts, but rejected the marketplace hack.

In his second prefatory epistle, "To the curteous Reader whatsoeuer," Lodge notes that he publishes the medieval French legend "uppon the earnest request of some my good friends" (2:4). While he presumably includes Greene among this number, he goes on to note that he publishes "as much as I haue read, and not so much as they haue written"(2:4). Lodge wants to reign in the narrative impulse, "to applie all things that tend to good, to their end, which is vertue, and esteeme them" (2:4). Despite the dullness such an introduction promises, *Robin the Devil* is a wide-ranging fiction, taking up the dangers and temptations of vice only to redeem the devil by means of a seven-year vow of silence and a pilgrimage to Rome.[43]

Robin's birth occasions a significant addition to the supernatural infrastructure of Elizabethan romance. To the Chance-Providence dialectic, Lodge adds a third term: the Devil. Frustrated by her inability to conceive, Robin's mother calls on the Devil, and in doing so changes the moral world of Lodge's fiction. "Well you

---

[40]     "The Achievement of Lodge's *Robin the Devil*," 21-2. Kinney suggests *Robin the Devil* is Lodge's "first fiction with a decided Catholic orientation" (*Humanist Poetics*, 405).

[41]     Pollack, "Romance and Realism," 492, accents Lodge's use of Spenser's 1590 *Faerie Queene*.

[42]     Lodge's next fiction, *Euphues Shadow*, contains front matter by Greene, perhaps because the commercial failure of *Robin the Devil* sent Lodge scurrying back to his friend's embrace. Even Greene's name, however, could not save *Euphues' Shadow* from the ignominy that all Lodge's later texts shared; none were reprinted in his lifetime.

[43]     While some recent critics share my positive evaluation of *Robin the Devil*, earlier judgments were dismissive. J. Payne Collier called it the "dryest and dullest of Lodge's productions" which "bears strong evidence of poverty of pocket, which occasioned poverty of the imagination" (cited by Pollack, "Romance and Realism," 491). Salzman calls it a "mishmash of legend, romance, novella, and allegory" (*English Prose Fiction*, 76-7).

heauens," she cries, "since you neglect me, I respect you not, if God vouchsafe me no sonne, the Deuill send me one" (2:9). In the Providential monotheist universe of romance from Heliodorus to Greene, the intrusion of evil supernatural power marks a metaphysical crisis.[44] Unlike Rosalind and Rosader, or Forbonius and Prisceria, Robin emerges under the sign of Evil. The task of redeeming him becomes less the recovery of a prodigal from error than a true expiation of original sin. Unlike Saladyne, Robin will have to complete his atonement, because there is real evil to be defeated.[45]

Robin's early career is brutal, as one would expect from the Devil's influence. Close examination of Robin's habits, however, reveals a second model for his behavior: Robert Greene. When he is not biting the nipples off his wet-nurse (2:11) or raping nuns (2:17-19), Robin misapplies the teachings of the "man of good life and great learning" (2:12) his mother finds to teach him. Robin becomes a demon-student, perverting instruction to his own ends:

> Robert by nature inclined to vice, coulde in no wise be induced by aduice; hee was in wit pregnant, but applied the same to looseness, reioycing as much at diuelishnes as others in their doctrine; in reading the Poets he despised the precepts of worth, and delighted in poems of wantounes; hee was eloquent, but in impietie; diligent, but in mischiefe, hauing nothing in more estimate than murther, flying nothing more earnestly than modestie... (2:12)

The terms Lodge uses are those with which Greene describes himself in his repentance pamphlets: "in wit pregnant," "looseness," "wantounes." Like Greene, Robin is a talented student who misuses his gifts. His "pregnant" wit recalls his mother's Devil-inspired conception, but Greene's wit is also pregnant. Robin's "eloquent...impietie" recalls Greene's "no less wittie than pleasant" style.

Lodge's dedication to the "Moecenas of learning" takes on new resonance when placed beside this lament of misused education. Even though Robin's crimes are sexual and violent, the text emphasizes his fluency in rhetoric.[46] Having poisoned his tutor's child, he defends himself by claiming to have learned the art of poison from his teacher: "Master...I haue but put into practise that which you have taught me in precept" (2:13). Humanist education has become a course in poisoning. Greene's influence on Lodge is noted by critics, but the emphasis on

---

[44]  This supernatural birth recalls Chariclea's. On *Robin the Devil* and unnatural childbirth, see Brenda Cantar, "Monstrous Conception and Lodge's *Robin the Devil*," *Studies in English Literature* 37 (1997): 42-3.

[45]  Selzer notes similarities between Robin and Saladyne, and suggests that "Lodge this time refuses to subordinate repentance to any other thematic purpose" ("Achievement," 22-3). Selzer's misreading of Lodge's religion as Protestant, however, leads him to misidentify Robin's pilgrimage.

[46]  Helgerson suggests that Robin and *A Margarite of America*'s Arsadachus exemplify the "anti-type of the poet" (*Elizabethan Prodigals,* 117).

Robin's rhetorical training adds a new twist to this subtext.[47] Robin the demon-student echoes Greene the Master of Arts who eschews sobriety for pleasure. Lodge's portrait of the prodigal student as devil may have been intended to point Greene back toward moral fictions.[48]

Robin's repentance begins in a forest where, wounded in the thigh, he hears the voice of conscience. The wood reprises Arden, but the scene recalls Saladyne's solitary recollection of sins rather than a pastoral frolic. Lodge has recreated Arden as *selva oscura*. Hearing voices in his ears that say, "the reward of sinne is death," Robert makes full confession: "Lord it is iustice," he says, "I merite condemnation, I deserue affliction and no fauour, damnation & no preseruation, commination from thee, not combination with thee" (2:30-1). Self-castigation modulates into absolution, as a holy Hermit finds Robin "ouercome with dispayre" (2:32), heals his wound, and provides him with spiritual guidance. Under the Hermit's teaching, Robin agrees "for pennance to goe barefoote to Rome on Pilgrimage" (2:34). Unlike Greene's prodigals, whose repentance either transforms their lives in an instant or comes just too late to do so, for Robin repentance is the first step on an arduous journey. The form of *Robin the Devil* is a diptych, as critics have noted,[49] and the parallel between Robin's fall and his rise allows Lodge to devote considerable narrative space to the slow process of penance.

The key character in the redemptive half of *Robin the Devil* is the Sultan of Babylon, Robin's rival for the hand of Princess Emine. Robin's vow of silence cedes the rhetorical field to the Sultan tale. As a lover and courtier, the Sultan recalls Greene's Maximus or Lodge's Rosader: he writes sonnets to his beloved and builds a temple to her and Cupid (2:49-55). His speech of love explicitly invokes Theagines and Chariclea: "Princes wonder not," the Sultan says to the Roman court, "Theagines a Greeke, loued Cariclia a Moore, & your Souldan a Mohometist, his Emine a Christian" (2:52). The reference to Heliodorus, the final one in Lodge's corpus, underlines how far Lodge has come from his early imitation of Heliodoran romance. Theagenes and Chariclea are now rhetorical tools for a faithless Sultan. In contrast to the Sultan's honey-tongued oratory, his Altar, and his sonnets, Robin loves Emine mutely, feeds with the Emperor's dogs, and lives in "a cabbin under the staiers of the Emperours pallace, where for seauen yeres space he cotinually slept with ye hound, refusing all other content or

---

[47] Pollack suggests that "Robert seems...close to the repentant rogue of Greene's pamphlets" (Pollack, "Romance and Realism," 497); Selzer sees Greene as a larger influence than Spenser or Lodge's French source ("Achievement," 22); and Kinney sees *Robin the Devil* as a revision of fiction itself: "By explicitly linking his history of Robert with the prodigal son stories of Lyly and Greene, [Lodge] has returned them to the religious context from which they have been disjoined" (*Humanist Poetics*, 409).

[48] It may even have succeeded, although Greene's final repentances were not as sincere or straightforward as Lodge's.

[49] Cantar, "Lodge's *Robin the Devil*," 40.

delectation" (2:48). This juxtaposition rejects courtly and rhetorical prowess as "Mahometism."

By the time the Sultan and Robin come into direct conflict, the Sultan has taken over the role of demon-rhetorician. The resemblance between them reveals that in fighting the Sultan, Robin fights his former self. Since Robin, I have argued, represents Greene, the conflict allows Lodge to defeat his former mentor. Selzer's thorough summary of the parallels between Robin and the Sultan thus elicits a subtext that Selzer does not emphasize. Robin in the second half of the story exemplifies the direction Lodge wants his fiction to go, and the Sultan represents the old Greene:

> Robin and the Sultan foil each other in many ways. Both are great princes, strong and valiant warriors, who carry the fate of their nations on their shoulders. Both travel to Rome to attain their heart's desires – the sultan, to obtain Emine; Robin, to attain forgiveness. Both are sonneteers: the sultan addresses his to Emine; Robin, to God. Both incur thigh wounds in the final episode, the sultan dishonorably, Robin honorably. Both claim the title of White Knight: the sultan illegitimately, through "negromancy"; Robin legitimately, through providence. The sultan feigns conversion to Christianity to win Emine; Robin repents to win heaven. The sultan trusts fortune; Robin trusts providence. It is as if the sultan become a kind of infernal substitute for Robin after his repentance, a kind of satanic embodiment of Robin's early values. By allowing Robin to battle the sultan, his shadow, Lodge gives his hero the opportunity to win out completely and dramatically over his old self.[50]

At every point in Selzer's summary, the sultan's errors – obsession with human desire, erotic excess, mistrusting providence, and a false conversion – duplicate the errors of Greene's fiction as Lodge now perceives them. Even the Sultan's "Mahometism" may point to Protestantism as errant theology. Not only does Robin's victory represent a triumph over his former self; it also shows Lodge's defeat and escape from his own professional idol, Robin Greene.

### Farewell to Fiction: *A Margarite of America*

Lodge's assault on Greene is at once too aggressive and too veiled to have been acknowledged publicly. In fact, 1592 would see Greene again acting as Lodge's proto-publisher, writing epistles for *Euphues Shadow*. Greene wrote the front matter because Lodge was again at sea, and this journey, plus Greene's death, prevented the two from meeting again. Lodge continued to write fiction until 1596, before turning exclusively to history, satire, and Catholic devotional literature. *A Margarite of America*, Lodge's last fiction, extends another attack on Greene, the

---

[50]   Selzer, "Achievement," 30.

untrustworthy master of rhetoric.[51] Fiction for Lodge always involves Greene's legacy. Cantar links Lodge's "violent repression of the 'otherness' of the imagination"[52] to anti-maternal images in his fiction, but it might more directly be an attempt to repress Greene, his tutor and demon Other, whose dedication to market values and rhetorical "looseness" made romance such a troubling genre for Lodge. Lodge's rejection of Green foreshadows his rejection of fiction itself.

Often cited as one of the first works of English literature at least partially written in the New World (when Lodge visited South America with Cavendish), *A Margarite of America* unravels the idealism of *Rosalynde* by discounting the possibility of conversion and the agency of virtue. Kinney suggests that among Elizabethan fiction only Nashe's works and William Warner's *Pan his Syrinx* are comparably bleak[53] What has largely gone overlooked, however, is the cultural meaning of the putatively chivalric nature of the work. Especially since no single source exists for the tale, Lodge's claim to be working from a Spanish manuscript he discovered "in the librarie of the Iesuits in *Sanctum*" has special import. The purported Spanish author may have been a screen behind which Lodge could hide his responsibility for such a dark tale (like Gascoigne's Bartello), but by linking *Margarite* to the language of Amadis and his descendents, Lodge turns in his last fiction to a tragic revision of chivalry.[54]

The Spanish qualities of the story begin with its purported origins, but do not end there. In fact, the mixing of generic signals implies that Lodge intends *Margarite* as a summatory comment on the types of fiction then prevalent in England. He opens, like Sidney's *Arcadia* or Greene's *Menaphon*, with a description of pastoral perfection:

> The blushing morning gan no sooer appeare from the desired bed of her old paramour, & remembring hir of hir *Cephalus*, watered the bosom of sweete floures with the christal of hir teares... (3:5)

This opening recalls the Sanazzaran pastoral tradition behind Sidney and Greene. As the sentence continues it abandons pastoral for a military setting:

> ...but both the armies (awaked by the harmonie of the birds, that recorded their melody in euery bush, began to arme them in their tents, & speedily visit their trenches... (3:5)

---

[51] On *Margarite* as an anti-romance, see Josephine A. Roberts, "Lodge's *Margarite of America*: A Distopian Vision of the New World," *Studies in Short Fiction* 17 (1980): 407-14.

[52] "Lodge's *Robin the Devil*," 51.

[53] *Humanist Poetics*, 403-4.

[54] Ann Falke suggests that the last book of Malory's *Le Morte d'Arthur* may have been a structural model. See "The 'Marguerite' and the 'Margarita' in Thomas Lodge's *A Margarite of America*," *Neophilologus* 79 (1986): 142-52.

The shift from pastoral to war that takes three books in the *New Arcadia* appears in a single sentence. The harmonious pastoral serves as a cue for the war plot, as soldiers happily waking to birdsong think not of lovers, flocks, or poetic contests, but arms and trenches. Pastoral is not the opposite of war, but its trusty servant, ensuring the battle will begin on time. With this sentence Lodge signals that the happy fictions of the 1580s are gone.

This amalgamation of pastoral and martial elements does not lead to catastrophe in the opening of *Margarite*, because Lodge's opposed emperors, of Moscow and Cusco have learned policy. Their teacher is an "old man, whose sober lookes betokeneth his seuere thoughts, whose morneful garments, shadowed, his melancholie minde" (3:5); this wise figure recalls the hermit of *Robin the Devil* and Calasiris. Citing Plutarch, Plato, and Aristotle, he convinces the emperors to patch up their differences with an arranged marriage, linking the two kingdoms through Margarite of Moscow's engagement to Arsadachus of Cusco. Margarite's marriage and sojourn in Cusco explains the "America" of the book's title, and again the Spanish nature of the South American setting seems important. The old-world heroine's voyage to a Spanish colony defines the cultural task of this text; the tragic failure of the marriage reveals not just Arsadachus's villainy, but also the moral failure of the Spanish imperial project.

In the post-Armada 1590s, English anti-Catholicism was largely focused on Spain. Lodge's public conversion to Catholicism was several years away when he wrote *Margarite*, but his growing discontent shows in his continued assault on the Protestant models of Greene and Sidney. By typing Catholic vice as a feature of New World Spanish society, Lodge distinguish the Spanish empire from the France to which he would emigrate in 1600. Arsadachus is in many ways a typical Machiavel – his ally "had Machiavles Prince in his bosome" (3:20) – but by labeling him Spanish Lodge implies that some Catholic cultures might be more virtuous than others. He had already attacked Spain in a prefatory poem to Greene's *The Spanish Masquerado* (Thomas Cadman, 1589), in a poem significantly written in French. Lodge in this poem aligns himself with Greene's anti-Catholic attack on "gens seditieux" (treasonous men), but by choice of language he signals his cultural affinities.[55] Lodge's presence in Greene's book may have been intended for public consumption, but it demonstrates a clearly demarked contrast between France and Spain.

Margarite, while Russian rather than French, bears traces of the old Catholicism that Lodge linked to French culture. On her wedding day, Margarite appears as a medieval heroine, but her Machiavellian husband misreads her allegorical costume. She is a picture of virtue: "on that day hir apparel was so admirable, hir carriage & behavior so execelent, that had the wisest *Cato* beheld her, he would haue in some parte dismissed his stoical seueritie" (3:26). Her challenge to Stoic asceticism defines Margarite as a heroine not subject to

---

Thomas Lodge, prefatory sonnet to Greene, *The Spanish Masquerado*, 5:240.

skepticism about human virtue, either in its classical form or its early modern (Machiavellian or humanist) versions. As the description becomes more elaborate, however, the reader finds that some suspicion may be warranted:

> hir golden haires curled in rich knotes, and enterlaced with rich bands of diamonds and rubies, seemed to staine *Appolos* golden bush; enuironed with hir wreath of christoles, her eies like pure carbuncles, seemed to smile on the roses of her cheekes, which consorted with the beautie of the lillie, made her beutie more excelent, her eies, briars like the net of *Vulcan*, polished out of refined threeds of fine ebonie, her alabaster neck was encompassed with a coller of orient pearle, which seemed to smile on her teeth when she opened her mouth, claiming of them some consaguinitie; her bodie was apparrelled in a faire loose garment of greene damaske, cut upon cloth of tissue, and in euerie cut, was inchafed a most curious Iewelll, wherein all the escapes of *Iupiter*, the wanton delights of *Venus*, and the amorous deceits of *Cupid* were cunningly wrought. (3:26)

The slow movement from perfect virtue to "amorous deceits" describes Margarite's fall into history; she begins in the realm of Cato and slowly becomes an early modern woman subject to the skeptical gaze of her husband (and the reader).

Arsadachus, who arrives dressed "in red coth of golde, betokening reuenge" (3:26), reads her frailty, not her virtue. The marriage of medieval virtue and early modern vice is not, however, simply a matter of Arsadachus assailing his bride, though the tale does descend into a level of bloodshed seldom matched in Elizabethan fiction. Rather, Arsadachus seduces Margarite through the early modern science of shows. Like Robert Greene or Robin the Devil, he creates a beguiling exterior to entrap his audience. In fact, when he arrives at a tournament in Mosco before bringing Margarite back to Cusco, his exaggerated version of the chivalric ensemble recalls the chivalric combats of the *New Arcadia* and Nashe's parody of them in *The Unfortunate Traveler*. Arsadachus portrays himself as faithful to Margarite, but also as all-powerful:

> Arsadachus in his triumphant chariot drawn by foure white unicornes entred the tilt-yard, under his seate the image of fortune, which he seemed to spurne, with this posie, *Quid haec?*, on his right hand enuy, whom he frowned on by hir this posie, *Nec haec*; on his left hand the portraiture of *Cupid*, by whome was written this posie, *Si hic*; ouer his head the picture of *Margarita* with this mot, *Sola haec*. (3:46)

His devotion to Margarite is a sham – Lodge's narrator has already revealed that his lovemaking was "nothing but falsehood" (3:20) – but she "was not alittle tickled with delight to behold the excellencie of his triumph" (3:46). The Renaissance villain hoodwinks the medieval heroine.

Arsadachus finds a better match in his lover Diana, who leads him to destroy the kingdom and kill most of the principal characters. Brought to Arsadachus by her ambitious father, Diana is the artful mistress of calculated display that Margarite is not. She wears the mask of the goddess who is her namesake, but her attire is not designed to preserve chastity: "her haire scattered about her shoulder, compassed with a siluer crownet, her neck decked with carkanets of pearle, her daintie body was couered with a vaile of white net-worke wrought with wiers of siluer, and set with pearle, where through the milke white beauties of the sweete Saint gaue so heavenly a reflexion, that it was sufficient to make *Saturne* merry and mad with loue, to fixe his eie on them" (3:64). The contrast with Margarite seems clear: what was static and virtuous becomes unstable and untrustworthy. Even Margarite's signature pearls contribute to a game of partial visibility, showing through Diana's "vaile of white net-worke" to incite Arsadachus's lust.

Diana, even more than Arsadachus, drives the tale's apocalyptic conclusion. Her father uses her beauty to advance himself at court, but he soon dies, and Diana's ambitions are more grandiose. After encouraging Arsadachus to murder the emperor (who advised his son to return to Margarite), Diana becomes a goddess in show as well as name: Arsadachus "honoured her as a godesse, causing his subiects to erect a shrine, and to sacrifice unto her; and such was his superstitious and besotted blindness, that he thought it the only paradise of the world to be in her presence" (3:74). A series of plot twists follow, including a magic box that drives Arsadachus to kill Diana and their son, but the failures of Diana and Arsadachus seem complete. In worshipping Diana as a false goddess, Arsadachus represents himself as a chivalric knight, worshipping a lady other than his wife. This Iberian custom, Lodge suggests, is fundamentally corrupt.

In some versions of this plot, we might expect Margarite to redeem her errant husband, or at least the kingdoms, as Samela redeems her family in *Menaphon*. *Margarite*'s world is much less friendly. A reference to the lion in *Rosalynde* makes this point explicit. In Lodge's Greene-modeled fiction, Saladyne's being beset by a lion provides an opportunity for his brother to rescue him.[56] That lion is docile both by nature ("for that lions hate to prey on dead carcasses") and because of fortune's will ("fortune, that was so careful over her champion, began to smile" [171]). The lion that surprises Margarite and her friend Fawnia on their long journey from Mosco to Cusco, however, is deadly. Fawnia – her name comes from the daughter in *Pandosto* – gets killed by the lion because, despite being "a faithfull follower" of Margarite, she "had tasted too much of fleshly loue" (3:80-1). The stain of sexual license here spreads to Margarite's companions, and she expects to die at the claws of the beast as well.

While Fawnia has been corrupted by sexual adventurism, Margarite's encounter with the lion emphasizes that she hails from a different generic world. She is a medieval virgin (despite her marriage), and her virtue converts the violent lion of *Margarite* to the tame one of *Rosalynde*: "but see the generositie and vertue of the beast insteede of renting her limmes he sented her garments, in the place of

---

[56]  Lodge, *Rosalynde,* 171.

tearing her peecemeale, hee laied his head gentlie in hir lap, licking her milkewhite hand, and shewing al signes of humilitie, in steede of inhumanitie" (3:81). As the only conversion in this text, this moment has special significance, although Margarite is only saved temporarily. (Arsadachus kills her in the end.) In a world that has become violent and destructive, Margarite's virtue calms the savage beast, only for a moment. The failure of this static virtue within *Margarite* spells out Lodge's growing conviction that he could not tell the story he wanted. After the happy conversion of Saladyne and the unlikely one of Robin the Devil, *Margarite* presents only this mini-conversion of a blood-stained lion. Lodge's ability to replace Greene's last-minute repentances with the Catholic trope of penitent conversion seems to have worn thin.

# Chapter 7

# Dishonest Romance: Greene and Nashe

> Many are honest because they know not how to be dishonest.
>
> *The Unfortunate Traveler* (306)

The last of Greene's life, 1592, was his high-water mark in terms of the number of titles published. Despite dying on September 3rd, he published more than ten books this year, including several cony-catching pamphlets (at least four, possibly all six), the satire *A Quip for an Upstart Courtier* (entered 21 July), the romance *Philomela* (ent. 1 July), and the three repentance tracts, *Greenes Vision* (not entered), *The Repentance of Robert Greene* (ent. 6 Oct), and *Greenes Groatsworth of Wit* (ent. 20 Sept).[1] This massive surge in publications, some of which saw print after Greene's death, represents the clearing out of his papers as well as a series of attempts (some contradictory) to codify his literary reputation. These books largely lack the high-minded ambition of *Menaphon* or the critical attitude toward classical epic of *Penelopes Web* and *Euphues his Censure*. Instead they demonstrate that Greene and his posthumous publishers settled on one final narrative trope to cement his career: repentance.

The published repentances of Robert Greene took place twice in the early 1590s. They began with a series of books published in 1590 in which Greene eschewed the romance fictions that had made him "a second Ouid" (9:121) and turned to prodigal-son tales. This movement may have been initiated by *Greenes Farewell to Folly* (ent. 1587; pub. 1591). Whatever the reason for the delay between entry to publication, Greene is clearly aware when he penned the letter "To the Gentlemen Students" that literary repentances were becoming au courant: "Gentlemen and Studentes (my olde friendes and companions) I presented you alate with my Mourning garment...but the Printer hath past them all out of his shop, and the Pedlar founde them too deare for his packe, that he was faine to bargain for the life of Tom-liuclin to wrappe up his sweete powders in those unsauorie papers" (9:230). The reference to another early repentance pamphlet, *Greenes Mourning Garment* (1590) is chronologically confusing – the *Farewell* was entered earlier and published later, and the letter seems to have been written afterwards – but in any case these books, along with the two parts of *Greenes*

---

[1]   See Allison, *Bibliographical Catalogue*, 10-11. The *Notable Discovery* and *The Second Part of Cony-catching* are dated 1591 in their first editions, but that refers to old-style dating, in which the new year begins on March 25.

*Never Too Late* (1590), make up Greene's initial literary repentance.[2] By suggesting that the *Farewell to Folly* will displace *Tom a Lincoln* (assuming that is what "Tom-aliuclin" means), Greene shows himself to be aware of the competitive nature of Elizabethan fiction: he targets a native chivalric romance.[3] Following a six-volume diversion into London's cony-catching underworld – itself sold as a social repentance – Greene would repent in print again, posthumously, in *Greenes Vision* (1592),[4] *The Repentance of Robert Greene, M.A.* (1592), and *Greenes Groatsworth of Wit* (1592). That Greene's repentance should be repeated twice in three years weakens the case for autobiographical sincerity; instead this pattern reveals that Elizabethan-Heliodoran romance, as Greene transformed it, became less about the constancy of a virtuous woman (a plot he downplayed after *Menaphon*) and more about the repentance of a wanton hero (the semi-autobiographical storyline that dominates his last three writing years).[5] Greene claimed that his repentance emerged from contrition and self-examination, but it also followed a market turn toward repentance in the early 1590s.

It explains little to read these final pamphlets as concessions to, or even manipulators of, popular taste. Greene's love-affair with the book market reached its apex in these years when he fictionalized his own mortality. He re-wrote his life story to steal (and sell) Death's sting. Greene's solution to waywardness was repentance: not an Augustinian volte-face, but repeated attempts to re-make and re-create himself, to shape his career into a tale that followed recognizable generic rules. Greene's repentances define themselves not through Protestant prayer or Catholic penance, but through renewed appeals to his readers. By recreating Heliodoran romance as a story about a repentant hero, Greene derived "profit" (in the financial and Horatian senses) from his assumed contrition.

Repentance, as Greene knew well from the Calvinist sermons he heard in Norwich as a boy, develops in Christian doctrine from the Old Testament's call to "circumcise the heart" (Deut. 30.6; Jer. 4.4) to Gospel admonitions to repent before entering the Kingdom of God (Mark 1.14; Matt. 3.2; Luke 5.32).[6] The doctrine of

---

[2]   Carmine di Biase, following Helgerson, notes that "Repentances had become something of a fashion by 1590," ("The Decline of Euphuism: Robert Greene's Struggle Against Popular Taste," *Critical Approaches to English Prose Fiction*, 90.)

[3]   On *Tom a Lincolne* as "essentially a moral work" and thus a response to humanist criticism of chivalric romances, see Richard S. M. Hirsh's edition, *The Most Pleasant History of Tom a Lincolne*, (Columbia: University of South Carolina Press, 1978) xii.

[4]   This text was composed in 1590, as numerous critics have proved from internal evidence. See Nicholas D. Ranson, "The Date of Greene's 'Vision' Revisited," *Notes and Queries* n. s. 22 (1975): 534-5. It is unclear why it was not published in 1590, but Newman brought it out in 1592 to ride the wave of posthumous repentance tracts.

[5]   Alwes has recently advanced the most extreme reading, that all three repentance tracts are insincere or forgeries (*Sons and Authors in Elizabethan England*, 144-6).

[6]   See Paula Fredricksen, "Repentance," *The Oxford Companion to the Bible*, Bruce M. Metzger and Michael D. Coogan, eds., (New York: Oxford University Press, 1993) 646-7.

repentance was crucial to the Protestant departure from Catholic orthodoxy. Luther emphasized repentance in the first of his Ninety-Five Theses: "When our Lord and Master, Jesus Christ, says 'Repent', he means that all the life of the faithful man should be repentance."[7] At issue textually is the Greek word *metanoeite*, which the Vulgate had rendered in Latin as "poenitentiam agite" ("do penance"). Protestants like Luther, and translators like Tyndale, believed that the Greek word meant "repent inwardly," and that faith in penitential works was based on errant translation of Scripture.[8]

Sermons of repentance sounded out from pulpits across Tudor England.[9] The theme was a favorite, often preached before the crown. In the early sixteenth century, John Fisher of Rochester emphasized the omnipresence of sin and the need for repentance.[10] During Elizabeth's reign, when the presses of St. Paul's produced more volumes of theology than any other genre of fiction or non-fiction, repentance sermons were gobbled up by a nation hungry for salvation. Perhaps the most popular of these tracts, judging by number of editions, was Arthur Dent's *Sermon of Repentance*, preached before Elizabeth in 1582. At least thirty-eight separate editions of Dent's sermon appeared between 1582 and 1638.[11]

Dent's sermon, like Greene's fiction, was published to maximize its appeal. The book advertised its popularity in its title, which reads in part, "published at the request of sundry godly and well disposed persons."[12] The front matter includes, among other things, a celebratory Latin poem by G. Pewdaeus, followed by an English translation, in case prospective readers lacked Latin. The poem lauds the persuasive power of Dent's words: "Some that haue heard this read of late, / lamenting much their sinne: / Haue changde their former manners, / and a new life now begin" (A2r). Dent's "To the Reader" epistle follows, and in the familiar modesty *topos* it expresses his regret that he should stoop to print publication. Like

---

Fredricksen notes that Augustine deemed despair the one unforgivable sin because it precludes repentance (647).

[7] See Richard Marius, *Martin Luther: The Christian Between God and Death*, (Cambridge: Belknap Press, 1999) 140. The translation is Marius's.

[8] See Carter Lindberg, *The European Reformations*, (Oxford: Blackwell, 1996) 314. The Greek word, μετα–νοεω, is translated in Liddel and Scott's *Greek-English Lexicon*, (Oxford: Oxford University Press, 1980) as "to change one's mind or purpose" (Plato, Xenophon) or "repent" (Thucydides).

[9] See Ashley Null's unpublished dissertation, "The Rise of Repentance: Towards a Recovery of Anglican Identity," Yale Divinity School, 1989.

[10] See Christopher Haigh, *English Reformations: Religion, Politics, and Society under the Tudors*, (Oxford: Clarendon Press, 1993) 10-11.

[11] For a survey of other sermons, see Millar McClure, *Register of Sermons Preached at Paul's Cross, 1534-1642*, Jackson Campbell Boswell and Peter Pauls, eds., (Ottawa: Dovehouse Editions, 1989).

[12] Arthur Dent, *A Sermon of Repentance...*, (London: [J]ohn Harison, 1598), sig. A1r. Further citations given in the text by signature.

so many Elizabethan writers, Dent claims that his private readers gave him no choice: "I did at the last yeeld to their request, and so this untimely fruit is come abroad, to bee solde in open marketes" (A3r-v). The reference to "open markets" seems strange for a godly sermon. Records show, however, that the book market was eager for texts that were – or pretended to be – "godly."[13] These "markets" were the common ground of Dent's sermon and the romances of Greene, Lodge, and Nashe.

Dent provides a definition of repentance which seems quite compatible with Greene's final books: "Repenta[n]ce is an inward sorrowing, and continuall mourning of the hearte and conscience for sinne, ioyned with faith, and both inward and outward amendment" (A6r). Notably repentance requires little overt action. Dent's definition supports understandings of English Protestantism that rely on "inwardness" as a defining characteristic, and it opens the door for fictions like Greene's based on internal submission.[14] In these terms, it is almost impossible to distinguish true from false repentance as the eternally re-repenting Greene demonstrates. Dent's desire to pass judgment is balked by his certainty that only God knows what is true in the soul. The dilemma leads to tautology. Dent writes, "For where Repentance is, there bee the qualities of Repentance, and where the qualities bee absent, there is no true repentance" (B5r). The qualities of true repentance – indignation, fear, desire, zeal, and desire for revenge, all psychological states – are signs of the undetectable truth of the repentant heart.

Dent accepts "outwarde amendment" as a sign of repentance, but he attributes this change to divine intervention, not human will. "[T]he conuersion of a sinner is a worke supernaturall" (B3v), he writes. Repentance imposes divine order on human passivity. Like romance characters, Dent's believers are victims whose challenge is to wait for divine rescue. When Dent lists the nine things that can move people to repentance, they include five examples of God's power (his "bountinesse," his "iudgementes," his "word," the "day of iudgement," and "helles torments") and four of human impotence (the "infinite number of [our] sinnes," the "shortnesse of our life," the "small number of those who shalbe saved," and "death.")[15] The division is absolute: total strength and agency is God's, and total weakness man's.[16] Like romance heroes adrift in stormy seas, Dent's readers must submit to unseen powers. Not my way but Thine: this motto applies to Protestants

---

[13] See Blayney, "Publication of Playbooks."

[14] See, for example, Stephen Greenblatt's reading of Wyatt, "Power, Sexuality, and Inwardness in Wyatt's Poetry," *Renaissance Self-Fashioning: From More to Shakespeare*, (Chicago: University of Chicago Press, 1989) 115-56.

[15] See Dent, "A Sermon," C5v-D1r.

[16] The seven "special lets, and hindrances unto repentance" with which Dent concludes his sermon, by contrast, all describe man's grasping at potency or knowledge that he cannot have. They are, "unbeelfe," "presumption of Gods mercy," "the example of the multitude," "long custome of sinne," "long escaping of punishment," "beholding of other mens ends," and "hope of long life." See *A Sermon*, D3r-D7r.

from Luther to Sidney and romance characters from Chariclea to Sephastia. Even such unlikely heroes as Nashe's Jack Wilton, as we shall see, follow this dictum.

Greene, like Sidney, used romance to soften the hard truths of Calvinism. Greene's model abjures outward heroism, and instead promotes internality – constancy for his heroines, and repentance for his heroes. Helgerson emphasizes that Greene's repentances are entirely internal, but need not be sincere. Neither Greene's repentant heroes and nor his chaste heroines conquer enemies themselves, but rather the over-magic of Fortune (or the plot) does so for them. Helgerson concludes, "Virtue remains as passive and powerless in victory as in defeat," and he convincingly argues that the ultimate source of order is the author's belief in predestination and divine control.[17] Greene's repentance tracts relate human experience to predestination. Helgerson suggests that for Greene's characters, "Repentance is the acceptance of inevitability in one's own life."[18] Repentance thus becomes the axis around which Greene's Providential plot rotates, the crucial expression of an inscrutable, faux-Calvinist Providence.

The two phases of Greene's repentance chose different literary material. The early texts rework standard prodigal plots. In 1590, fresh from the successes of *Menaphon* and *Tullies Love*, Greene signaled a change with a new title page motto: *Sero sed serio*.[19] The newly moral author, "late but in earnest," offers more than the old romancer, because he has found a moral center in "unfeined repentance" (9:120). These prodigal narratives gave Greene another opportunity to rehearse old plots, thus pleasing his former audience as well as expanding to a morally conservative readership. Having divided his readership into three parts – the wanton, the grave, and the wise – Greene devised a two-part narrative to appeal to all three. [20] The wanton enjoy the prodigal's initial excess; the grave cherish the justice of his fall; and the wise follow the moral logic of the tale's turn around repentance. Greene still follows his old maxim, "So many heads, so many wittes": the later fictions no less than the earlier aspire to be all things to all readers. His prodigal heroes are not as constant as his heroines, but their redemptions are miracles, rather than their own achievements.

In 1592, with illness making future pamphlets a poor bet, the weight of penitent transformation came to bear on Greene himself. Facing the end of his life, he produced fictional autobiographies invoking a double audience, God and the market. As he notes in his letter "To all the wanton youths of England" in *The*

---

[17] See *Elizabethan Prodigals*, 81, 79-104.
[18] *Elizabethan Prodigals*, 104.
[19] Jordan divides Greene's career into three phases, each indicated by a new Latin tag: romances in the *Omne tulit punctum* phase, moral fictions in the *Sero sed serio* phase, and London exposés in the *Nascimur pro patria* phase. While later critics, notably Pruvost, have added detail, Jordan's model has the advantage of using Greene's terms to indicate his intentions, even if Greene did not use these terms in precisely the order Jordan suggests. See Jordan, *Robert Greene, passim*.
[20] See Di Biase, "Decline of Euphuism," 93, 96.

*Repentance of Robert Greene*, he narrates his plea for "Gods grace" in order to expose his edifying deathbed to his readers: "Accept it in good part, and if it may profit anie I haue my desire" (12:160). Death gave a new earnestness to Greene's prose in 1592, and well-founded suspicion about Greene's sincerity and the texts' authenticity should not blind us to the pathos of these final texts, even if this pathos was calculated.[21] Greene reacted to mortality with desperate rhetorical tricks, conjuring market success out of his shroud. As Barker has observed, the "unseriousness" of Greene's death is "devastating"; he turned mortality itself into "a last-ditch effort to provide a remarkable entertainment."[22] Even in these tales, Greene provided coherent plots of passive resistance and internal repentance staving off disaster. His masterplot now redeemed him, as it had his chaste heroines. Greene's final texts personalize the masterplot of romance.

*Greenes Vision*, written around 1590 but published in 1592, explicitly explores the future of Greene's fiction. It also demonstrates structural similarities between the 1590 prodigal tales and the 1592 fictionalized autobiographies. It narrates a dream in which Chaucer, Gower, and Solomon appear as possible models. Greene rejects Chaucer's "Amorous workes" as "nothing but smoke" (12:273) and chooses "Father Gower." This choice has lead to controversy among modern critics. Kinney and Miller argue that Greene's new moralism is heartfelt, while Helgerson and di Biase see an ironic defense of Greene's Chaucerian fiction.[23] Attempts to fix Greene in one position or the other – either genuinely anti-Chaucer or subversively ironic – ignore Greene's most consistent trait, his attempt to be all things to all people. Di Biase, for example, sees Greene as a writer who "began to search for a more honest approach to his art, ...[feeling] shackled by the demands of th[e] reader, whose affected taste he had actually help to form."[24] Greene's professional and psychological investment in marketability, I argue, was much greater than any desire to create "honest" art.

The two medieval poets narrate competing stories of wives accused by jealous husbands. Chaucer's wife tricks her husband by having an affair with a scholar, and Gower's wife remains constant through her trials. In neither case, notably, does repentance reform the errant husband. Each tale is simple and old-fashioned: Chaucer imitates Italian novelle, and Gower writes a saint's life. Chaucer's attack

---

[21] Nineteenth- and early twentieth-century criticism saw these pamphlets as emotionally powerful; J. J. Jusserand, for instance, believed Greene was "repentant and sorrow-stricken" and wrote "with the utmost sincerity" (*The English Novel in the Time of Shakespeare*, Elizabeth Lee, trans., [London: Fisher Unwin, 1899] 151). Contemporary critics are skeptical about Greene's tendency to exaggerate and fictionalize, but Greene's Elizabethan readers, in all likelihood, were not. See also di Biase, "Decline of Euphuism," 90n.

[22] Barker, "Rhetorical Romance," 97.

[23] See Kinney, *Humanist Poetics*, 227-9; Miller, *The Professional Writer in Elizabethan England*, 86-7; Helgerson, *Elizabethan Prodigals*, 100; Di Biase, "Decline of Euphuism," 91, 101.

[24] Di Biase, "Decline of Euphuism," 105.

on Gower notably centers on the tale's market failures, not its morals: "these are not pleasant [tales], they breed not delight, youth wil not like of such a long circumstance" (12:270). Implicitly placed against Chaucer's novella and Gower's saint's life is *Greenes Vision* itself, the story of a wanton author-hero whose tale moves from a novella to a saintly end. The point of *Greenes Vision* is not to choose one narrative over the other, but to construct a composite genre that draws on both models.

*Greenes Vision* does not end with the choice of Gower. Instead, a third model appears in Solomon, who advises Greene to reject secular morality for religion: "be a Deuine my Sonne" (12:279). Solomon is not the "final authority," marking Greene's reconciliation with "Christian humanism,"[25] since his advice is absurdly impractical. Both Chaucer and Gower suggest focusing on types of fiction that Greene has already written, but Solomon's injunction would have Greene leave fiction entirely for the "mother of all knowledge...Theologie" (12:279). There was little chance of that, although Greene may have recalled Sidney's translations of Mornay and wanted to advertise similar impulses. Greene, however, grappled with theology only in the loose and forgiving format of romance. When confronted with opposing demands, he re-contextualized them so that they were compatible. The prodigal tales he published in 1590, which he advertises in the *Vision*,[26] combine the delight of Chaucer (in the prodigal author's London life), the morality of Gower (in the punishments visited on him), and the religion of Solomon (in the focus on repentance as the only escape from sin).

Solomon's teachings have pride of place in closing the volume, and linking theology to the "end" of the story re-affirms the near-congruence of theological ends and romance narratives. Solomon advises Greene to "enter into the consideration, what the end of all is" (12:278). Greene imitates this "end" in the last-minute conversions of his final tales. Greene's repentance tracts parallel Sidney's *New Arcadia* not only because they are incomplete, but because their incompleteness highlights the importance of closure in the Aristotelian-Heliodoran paradigm. The reformed wanton's story ends at the instant of his (supposed) reformation, with religion's triumph forever deferred. The instant of reformation is as far as Greene takes his hero, both because repentance never completes itself in his career (witness his multiple shifts of genre), and because a truly religious "end" would eliminate fiction altogether.

*The Repentance of Robert Greene* puts into practice the techniques of *Greenes Vision*. Perhaps the last complete work from Greene's pen,[27] the *Repentance* tells

---

[25] See Kinney, *Humanist Poetics*, 227-28.

[26] He notes, "looke as speedily as the presse wil serue for my mourning garment" (12:274), an ironic advertisement since *Greenes Vision* was not published until two years after *Greenes Mourning Garment*.

[27] Its entry in the Stationers' Register is October 6th, and *Greenes Groatsworth of Wit*'s is September 20th. It remains unclear which of the texts has true priority. *Groatsworth* has

the story of his life, dressed up with a list of maxims, a deathbed melodrama, a letter to his estranged wife,[28] and a final prayer. Decorating his deathbed with the accouterments of romance, Greene makes himself a male counterpart for Mamillia and Sephastia. His self-portrait never equals the high moral standard of his heroines, but he describes himself in terms he has previously reserved for them. Returning to the simile Mamillia used to describe her love for Pharicles (2: 64), Greene describes his youth as susceptible to evil influence: "[L]ike as waxe is ready to receiue euerie new fourme, that is stamped into it, so is youth apt to admit of euery vice that is obiected unto it, and in young yeares wanton desires is cheefely predominate" (12:158). Like a romance heroine falling in love, Greene is "stamped" with the wanton desires that precipitate his loose London years. He has no will to choose either sin or virtue for himself.

Unlike Mamillia, however, Greene changes. His turn to vice makes his final repentance seem inevitable; since vice was imprinted on him, not chosen by him, his reformation is just returning to what he would have been had his "waxe" been properly "stamped." Thus the too-easy quality of Greene's repentances (both his own, and those of his fictional criminals)[29] are explicable because they return to a previous virtue. Greene's wax-impression model of human character occludes the role of choice in moral decisions. Characters are given desires so strong they eliminate free will, and the tactical challenge, for prodigal heroes or chaste heroines, is to endure these desires.

The wanton life Greene describes seems both a more or less factual account of his youth (as far as we can tell) and also a tale framed to appeal to English readers in 1592. He relates that he picked up sinful ways in Cambridge "amongst wags as lewd as my selfe," and then hardened into sin in Italy and Spain (12:172). Returning to London, he became a hard-drinking, gambling writer who devised a new morality based on financial gain:

> I became an Author of Playes, and a penner of Loue Pamphlets, so that I soone grew famous in that qualitie, that who for that trade growne so ordinary about London as Robin Greene. Yong yet in years, though olde in wickedness, *I began to resolue that there was nothing bad that was profitable.* (12:173; italics added)

The book market now represents the errancy-phase of his own romance, and St. Paul's is the site of youthful error. Written by a dying man, however, this final

---

been under an authorship cloud since its first publication, with Henry Chettle being suspected of writing the text as well as editing it. Computerized authorship studies favor Chettle, although mixed authorship seems likely. See Mentz, "Forming Greene."

[28] The letter is dated September 2, 1592 (12:185-6), and Greene probably died on September 3rd.

[29] For a skeptical reading of Greene's repentant English courtesan, see Virginia Macdonald, "Robert Greene's Courtesan: a Renaissance Perception of a Medieval Tale," *Zeitschrift für Anglistik und Amerikanistik* 32 (1984): 217.

rejection of his "trade" has no teeth; despite its message, this book was designed to sell. This passage contributed to the notoriety of "Robin Greene" in a way that made his publishers happy. The prodigal author was inextricably linked to the penitent moralizer, and both are, he takes pains to emphasize always "profitable."

Greene's description of his life, however, is much more than a simple recounting of financial successes. The marketplace romance that supported his early fictions now leads to atheism. The most scandalous of Elizabethan social crimes, atheism logically follows from Greene's spendthrift life: "From whordome I grew to drunkennes, from drunkennes to swearing and blaspheming the name of God" (12:174). This accusation ups the stakes, and Greene carefully foregrounds it, calling himself "a mere Atheist" (12:162) on the first page of the main text. As Sidney's Cecropia makes clear, the sin of atheism denies the existence of Providence, but for a romance writer to deny Providence is to deny plot itself.[30] As nominal atheist, Greene rejects the miraculous plot-turns of his pastoral romances and also the repentances of his final texts. From this far point of nihilism, repentance rescues Greene, returning Providence to the center of his world.

Greene creates some suspense in this predetermined narrative. Like Lodge in *Robin the Devil*, he introduces "Sathan" (12:88) to disrupt Fortune. A sermon in Norwich converts him, although he later backslides (12:175-6).[31] He uses Biblical language when he refers to his "heart hardened with Pharao" (12:174),[32] but then turns to the tactics of Sephastia when he becomes "most patient and penitent" (12:184). Faced with inevitable closure of death, Greene found a way for even that interruption to have narrative allure. The unfinished feeling of his repentance tracts, the implied wish that Greene be given just one more try, resonates with the unfinished romances of Sidney and Spenser. Ending is the moment of generic crisis for Elizabethan romance, when the broad parallels between the narrative paradigm and the religious masterplot break down. Greene's deathbed conversions are perhaps the most inventive solution to this technical problem that Elizabethan fiction produced.

The most famous of the deathbed pamphlets is *Greenes Groatsworth of Wit*, which contains the first mention in print of the emerging dramatist William Shakespeare.[33] The *Groatsworth* retreads familiar ground, providing slightly divergent versions of his the *Repentance* and the prodigal romances of 1590. The main narrative, in which Roberto, his brother Luciano, and the courtesan Lamia

---

[30] Greene is presumably thinking of Marlowe's supposed atheism, to which he refers in *Groatsworth*.

[31] Manley suggests that prodigal son tales were meant to displace sermons: "the prodigal's perspective is offered as an implicitly critical alternative or supplement to the ineffectual guidance of the clergy" (*Literature and Culture*, 316).

[32] This episode from Exodus (9:12) played a major role in debate about the nature of free will and divine grace. See *Luther and Erasmus: Free Will and Salvation*, E. Gordon Rupp and Philip S. Watson, eds., (Philadelphia: Westminster Press, 1969) 64-66, 219.

[33] See *Groatsworth*, 83-5, and Carroll's extensive notes.

double-cross each other over the rich estate of Gorinus, parallels the two parts of *Greenes Never Too Late*. Even the two beast fables, one from Aesop and the other perhaps a revision of Spenser's *Mother Hubbards Tale*, do not depart far from his previous work.[34] There is little original or unique about *Groatsworth* – even the accusation that Greene and his dramatic friends practiced atheism also appears in *Repentance*.[35]

Henry Chettle (the chief candidate for alternative author) admitted to having scrounged these pages from Greene's disorganized papers.[36] What he found (or invented) is a mélange of Greene themes, yoked together by the repentance plot that occupied his last years. The very success of *Groatsworth* testifies to the presence of Greene as a quasi-literary character in 1592; he was so well-known that any traces of him, spurious or not, were snatched up by publishers.[37] *Groatsworth* appears a composite text, not just because it may have been written by Chettle, but because it recapitulates the literary career of Robert Greene. My proposed solution to the authorship problem is simple: I believe that the narrator as we have him, the "Greene" whose Groatsworth of Wit is the text, is a fictional character created by at least two authors: Chettle and Greene himself.[38] This "Greene" is partly produced by his own literary history, partly shaped by Chettle, and partly molded by common knowledge of Greene's life. (To use Wayne Booth's term, the "implied author" of *Groatsworth* is a literary and historical amalgam of Greene.) The book is an unwieldy mixture, and one of its primary accomplishments seems to be retracing Greene's career. Published posthumously, *Groatsworth* makes an odd *summa*: it is both the culmination of Greene's previous publications and their recapitulation.

What is most striking about the text, and what makes it a fitting end to Greene's career, is the author's overt identification with his fictional persona. This identification has been building since Greene began writing about a writer-hero in *Tullies Love*, but it reaches a new level when Greene, or Greene/Chettle, abandons fictional pretense:

---

[34]   See *Groatsworth*, 107-14, on the political implications of Lamia's tale.

[35]   *Groatsworth*, 80-1.

[36]   Commenting on how he assembled *Groatsworth*, Chettle writes that he "stroke out what then, in conscience I thought, he in some displeasure writ: or had it beene true, yet to publish it was intollerable." See *Kind-Hearts Dreame*, G.B. Harrison, ed., (London: Bodley Head, 1923) 6.

[37]   Of the three 1592 repentance pamphlets, only *Groatsworth* saw subsequent editions, published by Richard Olive in 1596, and Henry Bell in 1617, 1621, 1629, and 1638.

[38]   See *Groatsworth of Wit*, 13-14. Carroll's suggestion that this pamphlet may have been modeled on published accounts of Richard Tarlton's death underlines the notion that *Groatsworth* owes more to professional judgments of fictional value than to factual accuracy.

> Here (Gentlemen) breake I off *Robertoes* speech; whose life in most parts agreeing with mine, found one self punishment as I have doone. Heereafter suppose me the said *Roberto*, and I will goe on with that hee promised: *Greene* will send you now his groats-worth of wit, that never shewed a mites-worth in his life: and though no man now bee by to doo me good: yet ere I die I will by my repentaunce indevour to doo all men good. (75)

The long-awaited shift is complete: Greene the writer has merged with Roberto the fictional character. The work of his repentance is internal – "no man now bee by" – but Greene seeks an outward result, the "good" his book will do its readers. Unlike the "inward amendment" of Dent's sermon, this repentance is measured by its impact on readers. By the alchemy of fiction, Greene makes his "groats-worth of wit" worth whatever the market will bear.

Having lived for the market, Greene died for it. After his death, Elizabethan prose romance changed. The fictions of the later 1590s betray the malaise of these years of uncertain succession. Lodge, Nashe, and later Dekker broke away from Arcadian pastoral and the self-as-market fantasy that Greene embodied. Greene's embrace of the "many heads" of the buying public allowed him to re-create himself with each new literary fad, but this capacity for renewal foreclosed any lasting personal stance of his own.

## Dishonest Romance in *The Unfortunate Traveler*

> Gentle readers (look you be gentle now, since I have called you so), as freely as my knavery was my own, it shall be yours to use in the way of honesty.
>
> *The Unfortunate Traveler* (262)

Unlike *Menaphon* or the *Arcadia,* Nashe's *The Unfortunate Traveler* (1594) is not usually classified as a romance. Nashe skeptically modifies the genre he inherits from Greene and Sidney.[39] Emphasizing the artificiality of Elizabethan prose romance, he plays a deeply ironic game with its conventions. Perhaps because of its atypical nature, *The Unfortunate Traveler* has come to typify the dislocation and alienation central to revisionist readings of the 1590s. Critics have called Nashe a proto-postmodernist and suggested that his text marks the turn from romance to the complex fictions that culminate in the "modern novel." For these critics, the Nashe problem distinguishes his work from the overly conventional narratives of his peers.[40] The split in reading Nashe's fiction, which I outline below, defines the

---

[39] On Nashe, skepticism, and romance, see Mentz, "The Heroine as Courtesan," 339-47. Part of this article in reproduced below.

[40] On the "Nashe problem," see Crewe, *Unredeemed Rhetoric*, 1. Crewe begins with C. S. Lewis's famous pronouncement that "In a certain sense of the word 'say,' if asked what

changing reputation of *The Unfortunate Traveler*. The text appropriates not only the disparate romance modes of Greene, Sidney, and Lodge, but also every other type of fiction available: the *novelle* of Bandello, jest books, chronicle history, humanist debate, and Spanish picaresque, among others.

*The Unfortunate Traveler* is a self-conscious *summa* of Elizabethan prose fiction, an attempt to distill and critique it at the same time. Efforts to wring coherence from this unwieldy text have long recognized Nashe's debts to his predecessors, especially Sidney, but have not considered how thoroughly Nashe interrogates the fiction of his day. *The Unfortunate Traveler* is a dishonest romance: both dishonest in itself, and the cause that we can recognize the dishonesty of other fictions. Nashe, more explicitly than any other Elizabethan writer, exposes the connection between dishonesty and the conventions of Heliodoran romance. His fiction places strategic dishonesty at its conceptual center. When Jack first meets his future wife, Diamante, he observes, "Many are honest because they know not how to be dishonest" (306). This distinction between savvy dishonesty and naive honesty defines Nashe's sense of his genre.[41] Nashe fills his generic vessel with surprises: a rogue hero, a courtesan heroine, a virtuous matron raped and mocked. The greatest surprise of all, however, is that these unorthodox elements do not preclude Jack and Diamante's marriage, the final plot-twist that brings the text in line with the major narrative tropes of Elizabethan prose romance.[42]

Honesty, as William Empson has pointed out, is a fraught term in Elizabethan literature.[43] In *The Unfortunate Traveler*, this term appears as central and problematic as it is in *Othello*.[44] Honesty denotes chastity on one level, but in Nashe's text, as in Heliodoran romances, "honest" rhetoric is less practical than strategic half-truths and manipulations. Diamante is literally "dishonest" in the sense of unchaste, and she is rhetorically dishonest and scheming. She is also Nashe's explicit link to Heliodorus; her names comes from an unchaste Greek

---

Nashe 'says,' we should have to reply, 'Nothing'" (*English Literature in the Sixteenth Century*, 416).

[41] Jack makes this statement when he seduces Diamante in a Venetian prison; I discuss its context below.

[42] Attempts to read Nashe as a post-modernist *avant la lettre* tend to ignore the marriage. See Crewe, *Unredeemed Rhetoric*; Ann Rosalind Jones, "Inside the Outsider: Nashe's *Unfortunate Traveler* and Bahktin's Polyphonic Novel," *English Literary History* 50 (1983): 61-81; Michael Keefer, "Violence and Extremity: Nashe's *Unfortunate Traveler* as an Anatomy of Abjection," *Critical Approaches*, 183-218; and Kiernan Ryan, "The Extemporal Vein: Thomas Nashe and the Invention of Modern Narrative," *Narrative: from Malory to Motion Pictures*, Jeremey Hawthorn, ed., (London: Edward Arnold, 1995), 41-54.

[43] See *The Structure of Complex Words*, (New York: New Directions: 1951) 185-249.

[44] See Empson, *Structure of Complex Words*, 228-9, 235. Empson's argument that *Othello* produces a linguistic "test" (229) for the link between honesty and honor makes a suggestive parallel to *The Unfortunate Traveler*.

woman in the *Aethiopian History*, spelled "Demeneta" by Underdowne. She and Jack fail the test of honesty in social terms. As Empson emphasizes, "honest" derives from the Latin *honestus*, meaning honor, both social and personal, and neither Nashe's hero (a page) nor heroine (a courtesan) measure up. As the narrative unfolds, however, their dishonest qualities do not hinder them from receiving the prototypical romance ending. Jack and Diamante become hero and heroine despite refusing to toe the generic line.

Modern critical solutions to the Nashe problem fall roughly into four camps. Before 1970 critics emphasized Nashe's inconsistencies in theme, character, and authorial attitude, and deemed the work an artistic failure.[45] During the 35 years this reading has been challenged in three distinct ways. Some see Nashe as a proto-postmodernist who anticipates thinkers like Bahktin or Kristeva.[46] A second group sees him as a precursor of modern journalists or travel writers.[47] A third group, to which I am most sympathetic, rejects high theory and anachronism. Keeping Nashe firmly in sixteenth-century context, it argues that he knowingly dissents from the humanist norms of his age.[48] As anti-humanist, Nashe exposes skepticism and nihilism that render the familiar portrait of Elizabeth's "golden age" untenable.

---

[45] See Alexander Leggat, "Artistic Coherence in *The Unfortunate Traveler*," *Studies in English Literature* 14 (1974): 31-46; Richard Lanham, "Tom Nashe and Jack Wilton: Personality as Structure in *The Unfortunate Traveler*," *Studies in Short Fiction* 3 (1967): 201-16; G. R. Hibbard, *Thomas Nashe: A Critical Introduction* (Cambridge: Harvard University Press, 1962); and David Kaula, "The Low Style in Nashe's *The Unfortunate Traveler*," *Studies in English Literature* 6 (1966): 43-57.

[46] For Bahktinian readings, see Hutson, *Thomas Nashe in Context*; and Ann Rosalind Jones, "Inside the Outsider." On Kristeva's notion of "abjection," see Keefer, "Violence and Extremity." For a Derridean reading, see Crewe, *Unredeemed Rhetoric*. For a post-structural Marxist reading, see Ryan, "The Extemporal Vein."

[47] On Nashe as a journalist, see Donald J. McGinn, *Thomas Nashe* (Boston: Twayne, 1981); Charles Nicholl, *A Cup of News: The Life of Thomas Nashe* (London: Routledge & Kegan Paul, 1984); and G. R. Hibbard, *Thomas Nashe*. On travel writing, see Philip Edwards, "Unfortunate Travelers: Fiction and Reality," *Huntington Library Quarterly* 50 (1987): 295-307; and Jennifer Turner, "Jack Wilton and the Art of Travel," *Critical Approaches*, 123-56.

[48] See Barbour, *Deciphering Elizabethan Fiction*; Stephen Hilliard, *The Singularity of Thomas Nashe* (Lincoln: University of Nebraska Press, 1986); Kinney, *Humanist Poetics*; Ferguson, "Newes of the Maker,"; Madelon S. Gohlke, "Wits Wantoness: *The Unfortunate Traveler* as Picaresque," *Studies in Philology* 73 (1976): 397-413; Neil Rhodes, "Nashe, Rhetoric, and Satire," *Jacobean Poetry and Prose: Rhetoric, Representation, and the Popular Imagination*, Clive Bloom, ed. (London: Macmillan, 1988) 25-43; Louise Simons, "Rerouting *The Unfortunate Traveler*: Strategies for Coherence and Direction," *Studies in English Literature* 28 (1988): 18-38; Susan Harrington and Michael Bond, "'Good Sir, Be Ruld by Me': Patterns of Domination and Manipulation in Thomas Nashe's *The Unfortunate Traveler*," *Studies in Short Fiction* 24 (1987): 243-50; and Mihoko Suzuki, "'Signiorie ouer the Pages': The Crisis of Authority in Nashe's *The Unfortunate Traveler*,"

Even this third mode usually reads Nashe's fiction as distinct from his literary peers. Nashe questioned the generic assumptions of popular romance along with the truisms of humanist practice. He parodies the conventions of romance as his own plot moves from trickster episodes to a pseudo-romance on Italian soil. The final gestures of the plot – Jack's marriage and return to his liege-lord – define the tale retro-actively as a romance. *The Unfortunate Traveler* is be best read, I believe, not as a polyphonic protonovel nor a work of journalism *avant la lettre*, but as critical presence in the literary world of his day. He arrived in London in 1588 to make a name and place for himself in the literary scene, and that literary scene is what, *pace* Lewis, his fiction appears fundamentally about.

Like Greene and Lodge, Nashe lived inside the bustling world of St. Paul's in its Elizabethan boom, and like Lodge's his most productive years coincide with the *fin de siècle* malaise of the 1590s.[49] Entering the fiction market two years after the death of Greene, Nashe signaled his mixed feelings with *The Unfortunate Traveler*'s double-talking front matter.[50] Greene's market success led him to mock pleas for patronage, but Nashe's marginal position – one success in ten books – made him more desperate.[51] Nashe never attracted reliable patronage, and one of his early patrons, Bishop Whitgift, signed the 1599 order banning his books. In 1594, *The Unfortunate Traveler* exposed Nashe's dissatisfaction with patronage. The text is dedicated to the Earl of Southampton, but Nashe's attitude toward the dedicating act is ambivalent at best. "Ingenuous honourable lord," he writes, "I know not what blind custom methodical antiquity hath thrust upon us, to dedicate such books as we publish to one great man or other" (251). He appears barely able to stomach his own "blind" appeal. This sentence captures Nashe's dishonest

---

*Studies in Philology* 81 (1984): 348-71. A related school emphasizes parody. See Anges Latham, "Satire on Literary Themes and Modes in Nashe's *Unfortunate Traveler*," *English Studies* 1 (1948): 85-100; Katherine Duncan-Jones, "Nashe and Sidney: The Tournament in *The Unfortunate Traveler*," *Modern Language Review* 63 (1968): 3-7; Werner von Koppenfels, "Two Notes on *Imprese* in Elizabethan Literature: Daniel's Additions to *The Worthy Tract of Paulus Iovius*; Sidney's *Arcadia* and the Tournament Scene in *The Unfortunate Traveler*," *Renaissance Quarterly* 24 (1971): 13-25; and Raymond Stephanson, "The Epistemological Challenge of Nashe's *The Unfortunate Traveler*," *Studies in English Literature* 23 (1983): 21-36.

[49] Nashe lived and worked for the printer John Danter from 1593-5, during which time he most likely wrote *The Unfortunate Traveler*. See Hibbard, *Thomas Nashe*, 233; and Nicholl, *Cup of News*, 24-31.

[50] See Edwin Haviland Miller, "The Relationship of Robert Greene and Thomas Nashe (1588-1592)," *Philological Quarterly* 33 (1954): 353-67.

[51] The one success was *Pierce Penniless* (1592), which was reprinted four times: three by Busby (1592, 1592, and 1593), and one by Ling (1595). Of Nashe's other works, only *Christes Teares ouer Ierusalem* (1593) and *Strange Newes* (1592) were printed more than once in the Elizabethan era. On the commercial failure of *The Unfortunate Traveler*, see Stephanson, "Epistemological," 36.

method; he contaminates his own dedication with an ironic twist. Punishing itself for following convention, *The Unfortunate Traveler*'s dedication appeals to and insults Southampton at the same time.[52]

Rejecting patronage, Nashe clutched the book market, Greene's escape route. Nashe's obsession with the market underlies his metaphors. He calls his book "goods uncustomed" and asks Southampton to "set any price on them" (251). He suggests that he has been driven to write by "divers of my good friends" (251); this phrase, perhaps lifted from *Robin the Devil* (2:4), places him among commercial writers. While asking for Southampton's approval, Nashe applies to the market for alternate succor.

Beyond its veiled aggression toward patronage, Nashe's dedication reveals *The Unfortunate Traveler*'s hybrid nature. Nashe gives the text a mixed generic heritage from the start, calling it a "fantastical treatise," which conveys both "history, and a variety of mirth" (251). Farther down the page he suggests that without Southampton's approval the text will be "shipwrecked" and become "waste paper" (251-2).[53] (The reference to shipwreck, a narrative convention Nashe does not use, recalls how much Nashe knowingly rejects in the popular romances of his day.) Later he puns on the "handful of leaves" he offers the Earl (252). The extended organic imagery ("with [Southampton's] juice and sap they [will] be evermore recreated and nourished," [252]) marks a striking contrast to the "goods" and "price" with which he opens the dedication. Nashe cannot decide what he wants his text to be: leaves or pages, a "fantastical" or historical treatise, "mirth" or seriousness, aristocratic fiction (like Sidney's) or fodder for the urban market (like Greene's). Critics, too, cannot decide if the text is parody or celebration, experiment or pastiche.

The ambivalent peritexts veil the controlling logic behind Nashe's career. If his principle was "innovation" and he never wrote a text without entering new generic terrain, as Philip Schwyzer claims, then *The Unfortunate Traveler*'s variation on romance marks simply another way-stage on his stylistic journey.[54] But by turning to prose romance, the mode of Greene and Sidney, Nashe interrogates his two most prominent peers. While romance in the Heliodoran mode relies on Fortune or Providence, Nashe makes this passive stance look like bad faith. Resigning agency

---

[52] On Nashe's mockery of patronage, see Ferguson, "Newes of the Maker," 167; Gohlke, "Wits Wantoness," 398-9; Relihan, "Rhetoric, Gender," 142; Suzuki, "Signiorie," 350-1; and Crewe, *Unredeemed Rhetoric*, 76.

[53] The image of a book becoming waste paper is one of Nashe's favorites, and he uses it again in his introductory epistle (253). It emphasizes the physicality of Nashe's conception of the book trade: he is less interested in ideas than in things, which can become either "profit" or waste. Julian Yates's reading of *The Unfortunate Traveler* in terms of the physicality of print unfortunately came to my attention too late to influence my argument. See *Error, Misuse, Failure: Object Lessons from the English Renaissance*, (Minneapolis: University of Minnesota Press, 2003) 101-42.

[54] Schwyzer, "Summer Fruit," 585.

to Providence allows the malicious tricks of an anti-hero like Jack, as well as the brutality of villains like Cutwolfe, Juliana, and Esdras, to become inconsequential, since the genre seizes agency in the end. Nashe critiques predestination in its hard Calvinist core, and dispenses with even the active-passive agency to which Sidney's heroes and heroines cling.[55]

Faced with this bleak restriction of human agency, *The Unfortunate Traveler* recreates the compensatory fiction of Heliodoran romance. Ironizing the passivity-reward model, Nashe explores a series of compensatory mechanisms: jest book tricks underlie Jack's adventures in and around Henry VIII's camp in France; Senecan tragedy and Bandellan novelle color his travels across Europe; and romance conventions retrospectively organize his Italian adventures. Nashe participates in the each literary mode, but always dishonestly: as he plays at wit, revenge, and Italianized romance, he cannot resist pointing out how absurd these games are. Jack's sudden marriage and last-minute reformation solidify romance as the master-genre, but many readers distrust Jack's conversion. Nashe hides Jack's character under the cloak of marriage on the final page, but neither the character nor the text seems finally transparent.

The first section of *The Unfortunate Traveler* follows Jack's adventures in the camp of Henry VIII, demonstrating how "a certain kind of appendix or page" (254) can create, by wit and ruthlessness, an alternative power-center in Henry's army. Jack's wit revises romance's anti-epic heroism. Having set the scene by describing Henry VIII as the "terror of the world" who rules through "full-sailed fortune" (254), Jack usurps Henry's power and terrorizes in his own right. A warlike King like Henry would make an ideal epic hero, but Nashe replaces him hero with a witty rogue who subverts power rather than wielding it.

The heart of Jack's "wit" is verbal play. What Margaret Ferguson calls the "'Newes of the Maker' game" entails manufacturing of titles for Jack out of pure stylistic invention. Thus the introduction of Henry VIII gives rise to corresponding mock-honorifics for the page-hero: "sole King of Cans and Black-jacks, Prince of the Pigmies, County Palatine of Clean Straw and Provant, and...Lord High Regent of Rashers of the Coals and Red-herring Cobs" (254). These titles set up Jack as an alternative locus of power, a "keisar" whose subjects owe him "liquid allegiance" (255).[56] Jack's disruptive wit orchestrates a variety of episodes: he tricks a "Lord of misrule" (255) into giving away his cider, sends a rival dice-player to the French camp as an incompetent spy (262-9), and seduces a "Switzer captain" by dressing

---

[55] On Nashe's anti-Puritanism, presumed to have begun in Cambridge, see Nicholl, *Cup of News*, 25; Hilliard, *Singularity*, 27-8, 29-30; Kinney, *Humanist Poetics*, 315-18. On the Munster massacre as a satire of English Puritanism, see Hutson, *Thomas Nashe*, 231.

[56] Jack makes this competition explicit: "The Prince could but command men spend their blood in his service; I could make them spend all the money they had for my pleasure" (255).

as a "half-crown wench" (270). Jack impersonates entrepreneur, spymaster, and camp follower with equal ease.

Like Chariclea's Jack's master-art is the "art of dissembling" (265), but unlike Chariclea Jack deceives in order to attack. The qualities Jack seeks in a spy parody the virtues of romance heroes or courtesy manuals like Castiglione's. Jack asks the spy-Captain to imitate a wolf, a hare, and an eagle, and tells him "how he must be familiar with all and trust none; drink, carouse and lecher with him out of whom he hopes to wring any matter, [and] swear and forswear rather than be suspected" (264-5). These techniques, reminiscent of the Italianate vices Ascham decries in *The Scholemaster*, describe Jack more than the hapless Captain. They parody the discrete mendacity of romance heroines. Jack will become passive once he arrives in Italy, but earlier he is too active to fit the Heliodoran mold.[57]

The episode in which Jack' most clearly engages the Heliodoran tradition is his cross-dressing seduction of the Switzer Captain. A burlesque of Zelmane's seduction of Basilius, this scene mocks romance sentiments: Jack covets the Switzer's purse, not his heart.[58] The feminine disguise is purely practical: "I came disguised unto him in the form of a half-crown wench, my gown and attire according to the custom then in request" (270). The sharpest joke of the passage comes at its close: Jack, having received six crowns from the lusty Switzer, feigns "an impregnable excuse to be gone" (270). The pun on "impregnable" – Jack, not really a woman, is literally impregnable – mocks not just the Switzer, but also Jack's delusions of power. Jack receives no insight into human weakness through his female garb. He wins six crowns, but these matter little as the stakes of his journey rise.

Unlike Chariclea's mendacity, Jack's wit lacks staying power. Jack tricks the Cider-Lord, the Captain, and the Switzer, but each triumph gets reversed. He is "pitifully whipped" (261) for cheating the Cider-Lord; the Captain returns to the English camp and Jack, presumably, is punished for his deceit;[59] and six crowns are not much of a triumph for a "keisar." After he leaves the army camp, Jack criss-crosses Europe from England to France to the Low Countries to Germany to Italy, giving geographic expression to his boundless wit.[60] Unlike the castaways of

---

[57] See Ferguson, "Newes," 178; and Gohlke, "Wits Wantoness," 407.

[58] Nashe enjoyed parodying of famous romances; in *Lenten Stuffe* (1599) he burlesques Marlowe's *Hero and Leander*.

[59] Jack notes that the Captain "was turned on the toe" (269) for his treachery, but since he had exposed Jack to the French court, it seems likely that he exposed him to King Henry. The Latin tag that ends this episode, *Plura dolor prohibit* ("Grief prevents more"), suggests that Jack grieves for his own punishment as well as his victim's.

[60] Jack's mirror image is Cutwolfe, whose pursuit of his former partner Esdras across Europe is a dark parody of travel as education: "Twenty months together I pursued him, from Rome to Naples, from Naples to Caiete, passing over the river, from Caiete to Sienna, from Sienna to Florence, from Florence to Parma, from Parma to Pavia, from Pavia to Sion,

Greek romance, Jack travels by land only. This switch implicitly rejects romance's shipwreck motif. Drawing on controversies over the Elizabethan grand tour and on the careers of individual travelers, the wandering phase of Jack's story lacks Heliodoran-Aristotelean coherence.[61]

As Jack travels across Europe, his adventures switch from witty tricks to scenes of punishment, often divinely sanctioned. Jack jokes that he is "God's scourge" (271) because his tricks punish the proud and foolish. Leaving Henry's camp for Europe, however, Jack discovers scourges that exceed him in destructive power. These events reorient the tale to emphasize Jack's weakness. Plagues mutilate human bodies; Anabaptists sacrifice themselves; Surrey defeats Italian knights for Geraldine; and Cutwolfe imagines that revenge will bring him to heaven: "of hell I do esteem better than heaven, if it afford me revenge. There is no heaven but revenge" (367). Alongside these rivals, Jack's passivity allows Nashe to extend romance's rearticulation of heroic power.

Nashe's key trope for impersonal divine power – forces which are typically benevolent in Heliodoran fiction – is disease. Jack encounters two separate diseases: the sweating sickness in England (274-6) and plague in Rome (330-1). The sweating sickness exemplifies the function of disease in Nashe's text. Jack has been reveling in London ("how oft I was crowned King of the Drunkards with a court cup" [273]) when the sweating sickness ends his festivity. The epidemic displays Nashe's rhetoric at its most perverse: fat sweaty men coming near the King are guilty of "high treason"; cooks dissolve into sweat when basting their meats; tailors cut the "slightest and thinnest" garments to clothe a wasting populace (273-4). The most famous passage describing the death of an old woman has become a signature example of Nashe's style:

> I have seen an old woman at that season, having three chins, wipe them all away one after another, as they melted into water, and left herself nothing of a mouth but an upper chap. (274)

This passage isolates Nashe's most perplexing stylistic traits: comedy mixed with horror, a brutal pun ("melting") operating as both metaphor and literal description, and a grotesque image of bodily dismemberment. Most disturbing is the light touch, the spirit of verbal play and exuberance.[62] The irony perpetuates the wide discrepancy in critical interpretations of Nashe; Hibbard suggests it is "obviously

---

from Sion to Geneva, from Geneva back again towards Rome, where in the way it was my chance to meet him in the nick here in Bologna" (364).

[61] For the controversy over travel, see Turner, "Jack Wilton," 123-5. For the historical figure of Antony Knivet as a model, see Edwards, "Unfortunate Travelers," 296.

[62] Nashe may be influenced by Sidney's famously light-hearted description of slaying rebellious peasants (*New Arcadia*, 378-87). See Stephen Greenblatt, "Murdering Peasants: Status, Genre, and the Representation of Rebellion," *Representations* 1 (1983): 1-29.

meant to amuse," while Stephanson reads it as displaying an "epistemological crisis."[63] Nashe plays for laughs as he plays on the reader's heartstrings.

The sweating sickness emphasizes rhetorical instability and also produces one of many crises for humanist learning. Early modern medicine fails against this plague: "Galen might go shoe the gander for any good he could do....Hippocrates might well help almanack-makers....Paracelsus...could not so much as say 'God amend him' to the matter" (275). The failure of these talismanic names underlines the crisis of humanism in Nashe's text. The old humanist models can do nothing; there can be no "profit" in the humanist sense.[64] Nashe invokes the great names of humanism and dismisses them. Erasmus, More, Luther, Carolostadius, Cornelius Agrippa, Surrey: each trots across Nashe's page and fails to live up to the legend of his name. The great hope of Nashe's teachers at Cambridge becomes a target for belittling satire. As Jack has scourged the soldiers of Henry's camp, Nashe scourges the heroes of humanism.

At first glance Nashe's undermining his own fiction looks like a rarefied form of satire, as Latham suggested some time ago.[65] Satire, however, even of an all-inclusive kind, presupposes a target, and a separation between the satirist and that target. Nashe's ever-broadening attacks and his identification with his targets suggest that his project is more complex and ambivalent than satire. He might be considered to write pastiche in the contemporary (Jamesonian) sense, but to the extent that such a model removes Nashe from his sixteenth-century context it obscures more than it reveals.[66] Looking at the earl of Surrey, one of Jack's major rivals and companions, suggests that any simple reading – in which Surrey is either an idealized version of Sidney or a parody of the chivalric ideal – cannot adequately explain the text.

Surrey's status as poet, knight, lover, and chivalric quester reveals Nashe's engagement Sidney. Duncan-Jones concedes that Nashe parodies Sidney, but argues that it is "parody of the best sort," more admiring than critical.[67] The crucial question of tone remains vexed: the references seem clear, but their oscillation

---

[63] See Hibbard, *Thomas Nashe*, 152; Stephanson, "Epistemological," *passim*.

[64] The anti-humanist satire continues in Wittenberg with Vanderhulke's mock-Cicerionian oration (292-4) and a brief appearance by the ghost of Tully himself, conjured up by Cornelius Aggrippa (296-8). Tully's declamation of his notorious defense of a murderer, *pro Roscio Amerino*, accent the amoral power of rhetoric. This Tully recalls no one so much as Greene, chronicler of *Tully's Love*: "in entered Tully, ascended his pleading-place, and declaimed verbatim the forenamed oration, but with such astonishing amazement, with such fervent exaltation of spirit, with such soul-stirring gestures, that all his auditors were ready to install his guilty client for a god" (297-8).

[65] See "Satire," *passim*.

[66] On pastiche, see Frederic Jameson, *Postmodernism, or The Cultural Logic of Late Capitalism*, (Durham: Duke University Press, 1991) 16-19.

[67] "Nashe and Sidney," 5.

between admiration and critique is hard to assimilate.[68] In addition to Sidney the Elizabethan celebrity, however, Nashe explores the literary legacy Sir Philip bequeathed to England. Surrey resembles both the Petrarchan sonneteer Nashe admires (and attacks) in his preface to *Astrophil and Stella* and also, especially in the tournament scene, a romance hero from the *Arcadia* itself.

When Jack first meets Surrey, the Earl is "liberality itself" (287). Jack having just described himself as a "knight-arrant infant" (286), Surrey becomes an instant father-figure, the first authority that Jack has not instinctively attacked.[69] Echoing Sidney's *Defence*, Jack links Surrey's poetic power to divinity: "None come so near to God in wit, none more contemn the world....[his] thoughts are exalted above the world of ignorance and all earthly conceits" (287). Reworking Jack's strength, Surrey exalts "wit" from mere trickery to divine creation. He unifies divinity and poetry, making them into "this supernatural kind of wit" (287). Answering Jack's dilemma at Munster, Surrey suggests that divinity and poetry can be combined, and their combination produces a new generic model, the erotic quest.

Praising Surrey activates Jack's competitive instincts. Unwilling to criticize his "heroical master" (287), Jack breaks off his encomium: "Let me not speak any more of his accomplishments for fear I spend all my spirits in praising him, and leave myself no vigour of wit or effects of a soul to go forward with my history" (287). Surrey's "supernatural wit" saps Jack's "vigour of wit." Rivalry subtends their relationship, surfacing when Jack woos Diamante in prison and when they switch identities. Jack follows Surrey to Italy, but his service is ambivalent. He chooses Surrey's company only after hearing of the "unexpected love story" (290) between him and Geraldine. The Earl's rejection of the "nice terms of chastity and constancy" (290) inspires Jack's loyalty. Keeping these two characters together allows Nashe to juxtapose Surrey's chivalry with Jack's cynicism.

Jack and Surrey switch places by agreement the first time, in order to allow the Earl "to take more liberty of behaviour" (298) in Vienna. From this point, Jack considers Surrey both mark and rival. Surrey, however, is not a foolish Cider-Lord or Switzer captain; he is an educated courtier who "could counterfeit most daintly"

---

[68]   Critics who believe Surrey is a hero emphasize the quality of his sonnets, which were reprinted in *England's Parnassus* (1600) under Nashe's name. These critics also emphasize Sidney's parodies of chivalric virtue. See Duncan-Jones, "Nashe and Sidney"; Jones, "Inside the Outsider," 75; von Koppenfels, "Two Notes," 23; Crewe, *Unredeemed*, 82; Hilliard, *Singularity*, 127-30, and Kinney, *Humanist*, 311. The alternative view emphasizes Surrey's foppishness, the exaggerated tournament, and Nashe's rivalry with Sidney. See Lanham, "Tom Nashe," 213; Rhodes, "Rhetoric and Satire," 28-9; Schwyzer, "Summer Fruit," 585; Suzuki, "Signiorie," 365-6; Turner, "Jack Wilton," 146n, 148; Barbour, *Deciphering Elizabethan Fiction*, 72; and Hibbard, *Thomas Nashe*, 251.

[69]   Jack's attitude toward Surrey contrasts with his rivalry with Henry VIII, the various officers in the English camp, the humanists at Wittenberg, and the Italian noblemen. Surrey is the only character (except possibly Diamante) whom Jack admires.

(302). Imprisoned by a Venetian ruse, the two leave Surrey's chivalry for Jack's underworld. Their escape comes from Jack, not Surrey. Pietro Aretino frees them, occasioning a digression in praise of the writer, one of Nashe's models.[70] Jack wins their freedom, Diamante's love, and (with more help from Aretino) her fortune, while Surrey can only make impotent verses.

With Diamante's riches, Jack now has the trapping of a "keisar." His triumph, however, does not come as Jack Wilton; rather, he dresses as "another Earl of Surrey" (312). Instead of praising himself, he praises his disguise: "my pomp, apparel, train, and expense were nothing inferior to [Surrey's], my looks were as lofty, my words as magnifical" (312). On one level this disguise is sincere praise: with Diamante's money and his wit Jack could be anything, and he chooses to be Surrey. Nashe elevates Surrey to supreme object of desire and devalues nobility by suggesting that it consists entirely of pomp, apparel, trains, and expenses.

By the time Surrey catches them, Jack and Diamante appear as the prototypical decadent nobles, Antony and Cleopatra: "Overtake me at Florence [Surrey] did, where, sitting in my pontificalibus with my courtesan at supper, like Antony and Cleopatra when they quaffed standing bowls of wine spiced with pearl together" (312). What began as a parody of Surrey's opulence ends by making Jack look like a nouveau riche who cannot spend tastefully. Rather than recognize the rivalry in Jack's appropriation of his name, Surrey greets the tableau with laughter, and he accepts Jack's praise at face value. Surrey welcomes Jack's adoration – "as what nobleman hath not his ape and his fool?" (314) – but advises him to dispense with Diamante. A second rivalry is set up, between Surrey and Diamante, and for a moment Jack chooses Surrey over his courtesan.

The tournament that follows has long been considered a mock-reprise of the tournaments of the *New Arcadia*. The arms and armor of the knights are ridiculous, and their tilting awkward and unskilled.[71] Only Surrey, who easily wins, "observed the true measures of honour" (323). By this time, however, he has ceased to be a model for Jack: as a jouster he has left Jack's milieu. Called back to England by his King, Surrey abandons Jack to Italy, where he is paired not with an English knight but an Italian courtesan.

After Surrey leaves the scene, Jack discovers a second male rival, Cutwolfe, who typifies Jack's desire for outlaw power as Surrey typifies his literary and artistic ambitions. Cutwolfe is the mirror opposite of Surrey. A cobbler instead of a knight, intent on murder not chivalric combat, Cutwolfe culminates Jack's career as "God's scourge." Like Jack, who claims to be a "keisar," Cutwolfe believes he

---

[70] On the influence of Aretino, see Rhodes, *Elizabethan Grotesque*, 26-36; Hutson, *Thomas Nashe*, 238; Turner, "Jack Wilton," 150-4; and Nicholl, *Cup of News*, 4.

[71] The mock-imprese include "*Victrix fortunae sapientia*" (321). Properly translated as "Wisdom, conqueror of fortune," this motto recalls the advice of Lyly's Eubulus or Greene's Lamedon. Interestingly, Nashe mistranslates it as "Providence prevents misfortune" (321), suggesting that all human agency must be resigned to "Providence."

is a god among men. "The soul which is in me," he says, "is the very soul of Julius Caesar by reversion" (363). Cutwolfe's triumph, his revenge on Esdras, is brutal: he makes the thief foreswear God's mercy, then shoots him in the throat to preclude any later words of repentance. This execution forestalls the repentance that dominated Greene's fiction in the early 1590s.

Cutwolfe's revenge is the final event in the text except Jack's marriage. Neither Providence nor repentance can assimilate his violence. By shooting away Esdras's ability to repent, Nashe signals his rejection of the easy repentance of Greene and the more involved penance of Lodge. Before dying, however, Esdras notes that Cutwolfe acts out Providence's revenge for his rape of Heraclide. "In revenge of [Heraclide]," Esdras notes, "God hardens this man's heart against me" (365-6). This cruel execution, and Cutwolfe's later mutilation by the executioner in Bologna, mark the end-point of Jack's revenge fantasies. Cutwolfe claims revenge is the highest expression of God's will, but his death leaves the reader desiring another face for Providence. Heraclide has been revenged, but poetic justice appears worth very little.

Jack's arrival in Italy and his voyage to Rome force his travels into a retrospective quest-shape.[72] *The Unfortunate Traveler* assumes new structure in its final section, turning from picaresque episodes to what sixteenth-century writers called a "continuate history." Three episodes reveal what Nashe makes of the conventions of romance in Italy: a pair of semi-allegorized houses define "dishonest" artistry, the rape and suicide of Heraclide demonstrate the perils of too-rigid chastity, and Diamante's rescue of Jack shows the courtesan's versatility as romance heroine. The tale concludes with Diamante, and by romance's "end-determined" logic she assumes final control. Italian sophisticate, deceitful wife, courtesan, and romance heroine, Diamante illuminates Nashe's complex understanding of his genre.

Part of the challenge of Nashe's ending is its incongruity. Jack has alternated between punishing fools and being punished himself (i.e., between being the scourge of satire and the rogue of picaresque), and it is disconcerting to imagine him as the happy bridegroom of romance. Diamante, also, seems the wrong bride for a supposedly reformed English hero: an Italian who betrayed her first husband, she has been jailed, raped, and enslaved over the course of the story.[73] With this pair as hero and heroine, the reader can never be certain how to understand the conclusion. In conventional narrative terms, however, the events are

---

[72] Cervantes's more directly Heliodoran *Persiles y Sigusmunda* involves a pilgrimage to Rome without Nashe's satire of that destination.

[73] The misogynistic fantasies implicit in this narrative seem clear. Attacks on women appear often in Nashe's work, and he often associates women with traditional (i.e., honest) romance narratives. Relihan notes that, because of its apparent misogyny, *The Unfortunate Traveler* "has not been a focus for feminist scholarship" ("Rhetoric," 141), unlike other Elizabethan fictions.

straightforward. Jack's marriage to Diamante matches Nashe's to his genre; each union is ambivalent, unexpected, and, apparently, conclusive.

A new understanding of plot marks the final section of *The Unfortunate Traveler* as Nashe's tribute to Heliodoran romance. Romance in this context means not just a loss-wandering-recovery plot, but also adhering to the Aristotelian/Heliodoran law of narrative coherence. Things that happen to Jack matter, because the Italian world he has entered is a literary one, in which apparent accidents are ways for the author to reveal things his characters cannot know. In the traditions of Elizabethan and Greek romance, the generic imperatives of the plot declare themselves as the laws of Fate, immutable and all-powerful. Signifiers from previous romances rush into Nashe's text, each one is slightly off-kilter. Jack's lover is a "courtesan." Rome is an unholy city. The defeat of the arch-villain Cutwolfe involves Jack not at all. Providence, as usual, triumphs in the final movements, but her development is unusually obscure.[74]

Most Elizabethan prose romances present their readers with a Providential plot and highly virtuous characters, with the heroines embodying chastity. Nashe disjoins these two aspects of the genre. Jack and Diamante's actions have no impact on their final reward. They need not be "honest" because their actions do not cause their reward; their marriage is generically predetermined. Characters propose, but Providence – and romance – disposes. Diamante's marriage shocks readers who imagine that a heroine must be chaste to triumph, but it also teaches them that they have been deluding themselves, because last-minute reprieves are generic imperatives, not rewards for good behavior. Nashe makes his story's marriage problematic not because he rejects the structuring principles of romance, but because he understands them. Like Shakespeare, who makes the "not naturally honest" thief Autolycus contribute to the reunion of the kingdoms in *The Winter's Tale*, Nashe places dishonest characters at the heart of his redemptive plot.[75]

Diamante's dishonesty typifies the tactics of the romance writer: he, too, is both courtesan (selling his texts to the highest bidder) and potential bride (hoping for a reliable patron-husband). Diamante's marriage and *The Unfortunate Traveler*'s genre embody Nashe's career fantasies. He would re-imagine commercial writing as prostitution in *Have With You To Saffron-Walden* (1596), in a passage with striking reference to Diamante's story:

As newfangled and idle, and prostituting my pen like a Curtizan...well it may and it may not bee so, for neither will I deny it nor will I grant it; onely thus farre Ile go with you,

---

[74] Schwyzer notes how the distance of Nashe's God from the text creates artistic space: "Striking as it is, the absence of an interpretable God from Wilton's world is not the 'point' of *The Unfortunate Traveler*. It is simply the prerequisite for Nashe's experiment with openness and closure, leveling the field for play" ("Summer Fruit," 603).

[75] On Autolycus and romance, see Steve Mentz "Wearing Greene: Autolycus, Robert Greene, and the Structure of Romance in *The Winter's Tale*," *Renaissance Drama* 30 (1999-2001): 73-92.

that twise or thrise in a month, when...the bottome of my purse is turned downward, & my conduit of incke will no longer flowe for want of reparations, I am faine to...follow some of these new-fangled *Galiardos* and *Senior Fantasticos*, to whose amorous *Villanellas* and *Quipassas* I prostitute my pen in hope of gaine. (3:30-1)

Nashe refuses to "deny" or "grant" the charge he finally embraces. He claims to write in popular forms like romance only for money. Later in *Have With You*, he denies the charge of imitating Greene, but the denial focuses on Greene's cony-catching pamphlets and his prose style, not on his primary genre, prose romance. The phrase "prostituting my pen like a Curtizan" points to Diamante and her Greene-like tale of repentant rogues.[76] Nashe describes Jack and Diamante's tale as his previous attempt to redeem a dishonest profession.

In the last third of *The Unfortunate Traveler*, Nashe eschews stitched-together episodes for a coherent narrative form. Jack's arrival in Rome gives the story the retrospective shape of a quest. Rome was the second holy city in Christendom after Jerusalem, but Tudor anti-Papist culture transformed it into a demonic city.[77] The Roman episodes, in which Heraclide and Diamante are raped, Zadoch and Cutwolfe tortured, and Jack threatened by lustful Italians and bloodthirsty Jews, give the text new narrative coherence. Jack is under siege, and when he is rescued from these perils by his future wife, the narrative re-organizes itself retrospectively as the story of their courtship.[78]

In generic terms, Nashe's ending is conclusive, but its tone remains opaque. Jack receives romance's reward, marrying Diamante and returning to his liege lord, but he has not followed the ethical code that usually accompanies this ending. Entering Italy with nothing, Jack leaves with a wife and supposedly reformed morals. The text finally questions whether Diamante's behavior casts a shadow over the hero's (and text's) reformation. Diamante brings skepticism and erotic license to the surface of Elizabethan romance. Her "dishonesty" redefines and revitalizes the genre.

The earliest sign that Italy, Diamante's homeland, intensifies Nashe's investment in generic convention is the change in scenery. Jack's rambles have taken him across Europe, but except for a few battlefields and a cider-house, the places are undescribed. Even the lecture hall at Rotterdam where Jack meets Erasmus and More and the university hall in which Cornelius Agrippa raises Tully's ghost are featureless. Nashe caricatures people but leaves the space around them blank. In Italy, however, the physical world becomes three-dimensional and

---

[76] The reference to "*Senior Galiardo*" recalls Spanish picaresque. On the same page of *Have With You*, also, Nashe calls his antagonist Gabriel Harvey "My Doctour *Vanderhulk*" (3:31), a name that Nashe coined in *The Unfortunate Traveler*.

[77] See Antony Munday, *The English Romayne Life*, Philip J. Ayres, ed., (Oxford: Clarendon, 1980).

[78] Ferguson notably posits Dante's *Commedia* as an inverted model giving structure to this section of Nashe's text ("News of the Maker," 178).

ornate. Two buildings present a self-conscious elaboration of Nashe's dishonesty: Tabitha the Temptress's house in Venice (300-1) and the summer banqueting house in Rome (327-30). The latter, especially, has been a crux for critical readings of *The Unfortunate Traveler*. The two houses urbanize a common *topos* of Elizabethan romance, the ideal country estate.

Tabitha's house establishes the contradiction between outside and inside that typifies Italian artifice. Surrey has previously said that he values Italy as much for its art as for Geraldine: "The fame of Italy and an especial affection I had unto poetry, my second mistress...had wholly ravished me unto it" (289). The art Jack finds in Italy, however, is not just Petrarchan sonnets or even Surrey's tournament. Rather, he finds a thoroughgoing architecture of misdirection:

> The place...was a pernicious courtesan's house named Tabitha the Temptress's, a wench that could set as civil a face on it as chastity's first martyr, Lucretia. What will you conceit to be in any saint's house that was there to seek? Books, pictures, beads, crucifixes, why, there was a haberdasher's shop of them in every chamber. I warrant you should not see one set of her neckercher perverted or turned awry, not a piece of a hair displaced. On her beds there was not a wrinkle of any wallowing to be found; her pillows bare out as smooth as a groaning wife's belly, and yet she was a Turk and an infidel, and had more doings that all her neighbors besides. (300)

The contrast between a pleasing outside and perverse inside seems straightforward enough. Unlike Spenser's House of Pride, however, there seems no way to recognize the evil. (The reader is not even given a chance to try, as Nashe reveals Tabitha's evil immediately.) Tabitha looks exactly like the goodness she mimics. Nashe's text breaks the link between human virtue and Providential favor, so that sinners and saints appear interchangeable. The comparison to Lucretia foreshadows the upcoming appearance of Heraclide, and it also emphasizes how hard it is to find Tabitha out. Nashe's rhetoric warns the reader to trust nothing Italian and to assume the worst, and Tabitha's house reinforces this cultural prejudice. In this description, Nashe toys with the radical skepticism he will later nuance. If all Italian houses resembled Tabitha's, Jack and the reader would be unable to trust anything, and Nashe's romance would be unfathomable.

Tabitha's house makes an essential counterpoint for the most celebrated building in *The Unfortunate Traveler*, the summer banqueting house in Rome. Criticism remains divided about whether this house is Nashe's ideal or his version of the Bower of Bliss.[79] The description alludes specifically to Kalander's house, one of the most important houses in Elizabethan romance and the first building

---

[79] Critics who attack the house as an example of "bad art" or a "counterfeit Eden in Rome" (Simons, 31) include Crewe, *Unredeemed Rhetoric*, 85-6; Hilliard, *Singularity*, 125-6; and Leggat, "Artistic Coherence," 32-3. Alternative suggestions of a true, if complex, idealization include Hibbard, *Thomas Nashe*, 166; Barbour, *Deciphering Elizabethan Fiction*, 87; and Koppenfels, "Two Notes," 24-5.

described in the *New Arcadia* (73-5). Nashe both pays tribute to and revises Sidney:

> I saw a summer banqueting house belonging to a merchant, that was the marvel of the world, and could not be matched except God should make another paradise. It was built round of green marble like a theatre without; within there was a heaven and earth comprehended both under one roof. The heaven was a clear overhanging vault of crystal, wherein the sun and moon and each visible star had his true similitude, shine, situation, and motion, and, by what enwrapped art I cannot conceive, these spheres in their proper orbs observed their circular wheelings and turnings....For the earth, it was counterfeited in that likeness that Adam lorded over it before his fall. A wide, spacious room it was, such as we would conceit Prince Arthur's hall to be, where he feasted all his Knights of the Round Table together every Pentecost. (327)

The description continues for three pages and is by far the longest descriptive passage in the text. That the house belongs to a "merchant" places it in the world of new money and mercantile ideas, the buying and selling world in which Nashe struggled to advance his literary career. The anonymous "merchant" never appears, and he represents the ideal patron Nashe never found: rich, tasteful, and absent. To secure such patronage would be Nashe's equivalent of Diamante's marriage, washing clean the stigma of literary prostitution. The merchant's wealth produces a perfect literary object, an ideal "theatre" of "heaven and earth." Up until now, "art" has been a species of "wit," useful for tricking army captains or English earls. In the banqueting house, representation ascends to loftier subjects. Everything inside is doubled: the house is "another" Paradise; it pairs heaven and earth; and it brings Adam and Arthur together. Recalling the "artificial heau'n" with which Nashe described *Astrophel and Stella*, the house sets a new standard for artistic representation.[80]

The key terms in the description are "enwrapped art" and "counterfeited." These words foreground the architect's dishonesty and simultaneously limit it. Ambiguity clung to the word "art" (like the word "wit") in early modern period. In Nashe's description, however, the duplicity and artificiality of "art" are presuppositions, not fatal flaws. The house's art is "enwrapped" from the start, rather than falling from a pure state. The building mirrors Nashe's dishonest romance, since its very artifice – its manipulation of its own form – enables something created (a "similitude") to become "true." The apparently harsher term, "counterfeited," carried in the sixteenth-century the dual meaning that "art" maintains in contemporary usage: to "counterfeit" could mean to imitate with intent to deceive (*OED* 1-4) or without that intent (*OED* 7-9).[81] Counterfeit – a word Nashe may have drawn from Greene's prefatory epistles – complements

---

[80] Nashe, "Somewhat to read for them *that list*," 3:329. On this preface, see Mentz, "Selling Sidney," 163-69.

[81] The *OED* cites Chaucer and Milton each using the word in both senses.

dishonesty as terms of art for Nashe's romance. The banquet house counterfeits one of the standard *topoi* of Elizabethan romance. Jack counterfeits romance roles from Surrey to Mark Antony to Diamante's husband. The banqueting house, like Nashe's text, is a skeptical revision that expands and enriches a generic ideal. The house's bivalent artifice replaces the inside-outside dichotomy of Tabitha's house. The two houses clarify Nashe's effort to distinguish artistic dishonesty – the balance and nuance of the banqueting house – from the nihilistic uncertainty of Tabitha's house.[82]

The literary figures this description invokes, Adam and Arthur, appear before their celebrated falls. Part of the appeal of the banqueting house is its prelapsarian quality, which seems out of place in a Rome that contains "Pontius Pilate's house" (325), a lecherous Pope, and his cruel mistress. The ideal the house presents is religious; even Arthur, a national and secular hero, appears at a Pentecostal feast. The description climaxes with explicit reference to religious controversy: "Oh Rome, if thou hast in thee such soul-exalting objects, what a thing is heaven in comparison of thee....Yet this I must say to the shame of us Protestants: if good works merit heaven, they do them, we talk of them" (330). The question of good works meriting heaven invokes one of the central conflicts of the Reformation, but the appeal to Protestant shame and Catholic benevolence gestures toward a broad understanding of Christian community. A committed anti-Puritan, Nashe does not embrace Catholicism, but he evinces nostalgia for a unified Church. The Rome Jack sees is a divided place, in which the banqueting house abuts Pontius Pilate's and "richly furnished" (330) hospitals rub shoulders with the Pope's mistress's palace. It is not simply contemporary evil versus ancient glory, nor religious hypocrisy versus noble generosity. The Pope, Juliana, Zachary, and Zadoch embody Italianate corruption, and the banqueting house, Heraclide, and the banished English earl appeal to a unified moral code. Caught in the middle, Jack finds a third way, of sophisticated and knowing dishonesty.

In Rome, Jack and Diamante play out stock episodes from Elizabethan romance. First, they witness the brutal rape of Heraclide during a plague, Diamante is captured, and Jack arrested for the crime. Next, Jack escapes from prison, falls into the captivity of Zachary and Juliana, and finally escapes with Diamante's help. These two episodes might be termed the Rape of the Virtuous Woman and the Escape from Captivity.[83] They continue Nashe's increasingly overt turn back to Elizabethan prose romance.

Heraclide's rape defines the consequences of Nashe's version of romance for the only character in *The Unfortunate Traveler* who might be at home in Sidney's

---

[82] I depart from several recent critics who link Nashe with nihilism: see Suzuki, "Signiorie Ouer the Pages," 359-63; Ferguson, "Newes of the Maker," 174; and Gohlke, "Wits Wantoness," 403.

[83] Jack's fear that Zachary and Juliana will consume his body, Zachary in medical experiments and Juliana to sate her lust, evoke the romance motif of cannibalism.

*Arcadia.* She is a perfectly "honest" woman, the chaste heroine Diamante conspicuously fails to be, and her suicide closes the door on ethical rectitude. Her rape strains Jack's descriptive powers, no mean feat given his eager descriptions of the massacred Anabaptists and the sweating sickness. The violent clichés of tragic melodrama mute his tongue, marking his progressive conversion from a rogue to a romance-hero. The rape of Heraclide, like Cutwolfe's execution and the massacre of the Anabaptists, forces Jack to realize that there are things about which he does not want to talk: "Conjecture the rest, my words stick fast in the mire and are clean tired; would I had never undertook this tragic tale" (336). Jack's generic signals have changed; his tale is now "tragic" where it had been a "fantastical treatise" (251) or a "holiday lie" (261). Newly sensitive to emotional drama, Jack now calls his story an "elegiacal history" (336), a particularly potent phrase if "history" implies a generic connection to romance, as it does in the *Aethiopian History*.

Diamante is also raped during the attack on Heraclide's house, but unlike Heraclide's her rape goes undescribed and largely unremarked. Jack reacts to it with confusion and dismay, but no purple prose. The courtesan survives on her own terms, flaunting the convention that the story's heroine cannot suffer rape.[84] Even Jack's frantic plea, "Save her, kill me! And I'll ransom her with a thousand ducats" (332), focuses not on her but on his conflicted position between self-sacrificing romance hero and mercenary rogue.[85] Jack's position, moreover, is ridiculous because it is Diamante's money he offers the rapist, extracted from the estate of her dead husband.

Heraclide's debate on suicide, on the other hand, recapitulates classical and romance precedents from Lucretia to Book 4 of the *Old Arcadia*. In explaining her decision to kill herself, she considers predestination from a human perspective: "The serpent in Paradise is damned sempiternally: why should not I hold myself damned (if predestination's opinions hold) that am predestinate to this horrible abuse?" (337). By holding predestination – i.e., Providence – responsible for the crime against her, she exposes the consequences of Nashe's romance for everyone except the hero and heroine. Her reading of predestination reinforces the misogynist canard that makes a woman culpable for her own rape, and Nashe's strange classical parallels – Cephalus after killing his wife, Oedipus after killing his father (337) – highlight her guilt.

Her choice of suicide, Lucretia's solution to the same problem, had been debunked by no less an authority than St. Augustine.[86] Humanist thinkers like Juan

---

[84] Diamante's reticence on this matter may be her version of the modesty of the romance heroine, but it emphasizes her departure from Heraclide's norm.

[85] The monetary reference recalls the mercantile world of *Lazarillo de Tormes*, a constant *bete noir* of Nashe's text. Jack, unlike Lazarillo, has money to offer, but money does not play a role in the solution he finds.

[86] See *City of God*, 1:24, Marcus Dods, trans., (New York: Modern Library, 1950) 29-30. Schwyzer concludes that Nashe gives more weight to Augustine's theological example than the numerous Lucrecia-figures of early modern literary culture. See "Summer Fruit," 601n.

Luis Vives in his *Instruction of a Christian Woman* (1529), however, argued in support of Lucretia's suicide.[87] Nashe's anti-humanist critique underlines Heraclide's fallacious reasoning; she makes the (rational) mistake of judging predestination on the basis of local human experience. Ironically, Esdras makes the same error in assuming that his run of luck has given him "a charter above scripture" (333). These characters believe they can extrapolate the shape of Fate from what has happened to them recently. Jack's sympathy, and the reader's, is overwhelmingly drawn to Heraclide, but her understanding of Providence is no clearer than Esdras's.

Romance-plots punish characters who prejudge the Providential plan, and here *The Unfortunate Traveler* pushes the convention to its extreme. Cutwolfe's killing of Esdras comes as belated revenge for his rape of Heraclide. Heraclide's punishment, however, comes much sooner, by way of one of Nashe's macabre jokes. Her melodramatic suicide – "Point, pierce, edge, enwiden, I patiently afford thee a sheath" (339) – becomes comic when her falling body awakens her seeming-dead-but-only-sleeping husband. Nashe marks this anticlimax by returning to a mocking style: "So, thoroughly stabbed, fell she down and knocked her head against her husband's body, wherewith he, not having been aired his full four-and-twenty hours, start[s] as out of a dream" (339). The dead man's revival, another *topos* from romance, comes too late, transforming tragedy into farce. The joke might return the text to its trickster mode, but this abrupt turn – from death to life, from tragedy to comedy – is the essence of Nashean romance. Nashe's version of the genre encompasses Heraclide's tragedy and the comic farce of her husband's revival. Jack recognizes the strangeness of this moment and says, "Here beginneth my purgatory" (339). Invoking both more torment and the beginning of a reformed self, Jack eases the text toward a redemptive ending.

Heraclide's rhetorical lead-up to suicide combines theological error with a misreading of the genre of her fictional universe. Her dilemma, however, is the basic one in Nashe's fiction, as in all romance: how to endure the world's inconstancy. Unlike Jack's witty aggression and revenge-fantasies, Heraclide's solution is self-mortification: "The only repeal we have from God's undefinite chastisement is to chastise ourselves in this world" (339).[88] Heraclide represents a passive extreme, in which repentance becomes suicide: "nought but death be my penance" (339). When Jack nearly stops his narrative after her death, Nashe flirts with a literary analogue to suicide. Jack's turn back to Diamante mediates between

---

Gohlke praises Heraclide's "faith in eventual retribution" (Gohlke, "Wits Wantoness," 404), but Ferguson rebuts this position sharply ("Newes of the Maker," 179n).

[87] Relihan cites Vives in support of Lucretia's (and, she extrapolates, Heraclide's) suicide. See "Rhetoric," 148, 238n. Relihan's focus on early modern misogyny, however, leads her to exaggerate the anti-woman sentiment of many popular writers, including Robert Greene. I discuss Relihan's perceptive reading of Diamante below.

[88] Suicide often tempts romance heroines, but, like rape, it is typically a threat, not reality.

Esdras's refusal to repent and Heraclide's maximal penance for no sin of her own.

As Constance Relihan has observed, Diamante is the only female character in the text who does not threaten Jack, and who instead offers him help in need.[89] Relihan also notes that Diamante's first appearance in the text, during Jack's imprisonment in Venice, marks a crucial shift in tone, as the trickster tale becomes a romance.[90] Called a "courtesan" even though she gives Jack money, Diamante carves out a space for erotic self-interest in the role of romance heroine.[91] She is, as Relihan observes, "a source of consolation and safety" for Nashe's threatened hero, but she is only an "unlooked-for source" if the reader assumes that Nashe's fiction is absolutely different from Sidney's or Greene's.[92] For Nashe's transfiguration of Elizabethan-Heliodoran romance, Diamante's prominence makes perfect sense. Romances need heroines. Diamante exposes things her exemplars hide, but she affects the plot exactly as a heroine should.

Nashe introduces her through detailed allusion to his most-admired English author, Chaucer. The "English Homer" gives Nashe a widely admired precursor who is also unconventional in his female protagonists.[93] Describing Diamante for the first time, Nashe produces a series of allusions to two of Chaucer's unruly women, the Wife of Bath and Alison of "The Miller's Tale":

> As glad were we almost as if they had given us liberty, that fortune lent us such a sweet pew-fellow. A pretty round-faced wench was it, with black eyebrows, a high forehead, a little mouth, and a sharp nose; as fat and plum, every part of her, as a plover, a skin as sleek and soft as the back of a swan; it doth me good when I remember her. Like a bird she tripped it on the ground, and bare out her belly as majestical as an estrich. With a lickerous rolling eye fixed piercing in the earth, and sometimes scornfully darted on the t'one side, she figured forth a high discontented disdain; much like a prince puffing and storming at the treason of some mighty subject fled lately out of his power. Her very countenance repiningly wrathful, and yet clear and unwrinkled, would have confirmed the clearness of her conscience to the austerest judge in the world (306).

Chaucer permeates this passage. The central phrase, "it doth me good when I remember her," echoes the Wife of Bath's ecstatic recollection of her sexual past: "But – Lord Crist! – whan that it remembreth me / Upon my yowthe, and on my

---

[89]   Relihan notes that Heraclide, despite her virtue, threatens Jack "because he is charged with the crime and sentenced to be hanged" ("Rhetoric," 147).

[90]   The distinction she makes between the two halves of the text involves a change in narrative voice and the positing of a solitary reader ("Rhetoric," 146).

[91]   Jack repeatedly calls Diamante a "courtesan," but she does not appear to ply the trade. She is a "courtesan" in the same sense that Nashe is "dishonest": they reshape conventions and open themselves up to criticism, but finally return to convention in the end.

[92]   "Rhetoric," 151.

[93]   Nashe calls Chaucer the "English Homer" in *Strange Newes* (1:299) and praises him often. See 1:258, 316-7; 3:123, 176, 322.

jolitee, / It tikleth me aboute my herte roote" (D.469-71).[94] Nashe's word "lickerous" is also Chaucerian, appearing twice in the Wife's Prologue (D.167, 611) and once in the description of Alison (A.3244). Like Alison, Diamante has black brows (A.3245-6) and a roving eye (A.3244). Diamante imports Chaucer's view of female sexuality into Nashe's romance. She also embodies Nashe's double-talk: prince-like but in prison, "lickerous" but "scornful," "wrathful" but "clear" of conscience. Even her eyes are both "fixed" and "rolling." When Jack replaces her lost "subject," he switches his own status from would-be dominator to faithful ally, and from predatory trickster to potential husband and hero.

Diamante adds the sexual assertiveness of the Wife of Bath to the romance heroine. Instead of an orphaned princess, she is a magnifico's wife, jailed on false suspicion of adultery by a jealous husband. Jack diagnoses her fealty to her husband as lack of experience and observes, "Many are honest because they know not how to be dishonest" (306). This sentence, which I invoked earlier as Nashe's comment on his literary method, converts Diamante from mistreated wife to heroine. Her erotic appetite is weak at first; Jack remarks, "she thought there was no pleasure in stolen bread because there was no pleasure in an old man's bed" (306).[95] Jack, however, introduces her to "stolen bread," and if her virtue had been due to ignorance, adultery transforms her into a witty deceiver worthy of Jack Wilton.[96]

Diamante remains mysterious to the reader. Parts of her story, in particular her recovery from rape, remain untold. In crucial moments, however, she frees Jack from persecution and poverty. After her husband dies, she obtains his property, her own freedom, and "invested [Jack] in the state of a monarch" (312).[97] Later, Diamante betrays her mistress Juliana, frees Jack, and they "courageously rob her and run away" (361). Her betrayal of Zadoch also occasions his execution. Their voyage up the Tiber takes Jack and Diamante to Bologna for Cutwolfe's execution, and eventually out of Italy. By this time Diamante has become, as Jack says, "my redeemer" (358): she advances the Providential plot that enables him to marry and escape.

---

[94] Geoffrey Chaucer, *The Riverside Chaucer*, 3rd Edition, Larry Benson and F. N. Robinson, eds., (Boston: Houghton Mifflin, Co., 1987). Citations to Chaucer given in the text by group letter and line number.

[95] These lines again recall the Wife of Bath, who also abandons an older husband: "For wynnyng wolde I al his lust endure, / And make me a feyned appetit; / And yet in bacon [i.e. old meat] hadde I nevere delit" (D.416-8).

[96] Jack describes Diamante as a courtesan for practical reasons: "It is almost impossible that any woman should be excellently witty and not make the utmost penny of her beauty" (306). Here Nashe anticipates his description of writing as prostitution in *Have With You*.

[97] At this point she "proved to be with child," but this child never returns to the scene. There is no hint at the tale's conclusion that Jack must marry her to give legitimacy to his child, although that appears a possibility, unless Nashe simply forgot that Diamante was pregnant.

Diamante is a thoroughly unconventional heroine, deceiving nearly everyone in the text. She is raped by Bartol and seen by Jack "kissing very lovingly with a prentice" (347) in Zadoch's house. (The identity of this prentice is never explained, nor is Diamante's presence in Zadoch's house.) More sexually durable and less chaste than her predecessors, Diamante is the heroine as courtesan, playing out the possibilities Chariclea flirted with in deceptive rhetoric. Not bound by conventional moral codes, Diamante maneuvers through the urban squalor of Italy to wealth, marriage, and a rogue who may be her match. Her pursuit of pleasure along with security revitalizes the happy marriages with which romances are required to end.[98]

Several critics suggest that the ending may not be straightforward. They insist that true reform cannot be as easy as saying, with Jack, "that ere I went out of Bologna I married my courtesan, performed many alms-deeds, and hasted...out of the Sodom of Italy" (370).[99] If endings recapitulate the essence of a plot, as Kermode suggests, this final turn reveals the controlling force of the Diamante subplot.[100] Nashe calls attention to the unsatisfactory nature of his ending on the last page, writing, "All the conclusive epilogue I will make is this: that if herein I have pleased any, it shall animate me to more pains of this kind" (370). Faced with what looks like the promise of a sequel, critics point to the commercial failure of *The Unfortunate Traveler*, and argue that a happier bottom line would have seen Jack ditch Diamante and take to the highways again. The reference to Jack dimly remembering Diamante is also hard to explain.[101] Hibbard attributes it to Nashe's carelessness and his incomplete sense of Diamante when he first describes her, and Relihan argues that it "subtly unravels the text's conclusion" by destabilizing the marriage.[102] Assuming it is not Nashe's carelessness, this phrase may cast doubt on Jack's marital happiness, but it also reminds the reader that time has not stopped after the final page. In a last dig at the faux-theological structure of romance, which wraps everything up on the last page, Nashe adds a pair of hints about his

---

[98] Relihan describes the marriage as revealing a "dirty little secret – that marriage not only provides a satisfying, comforting means of fulfilling masculine desire but that it also presents one of the few strategies by which the male can insulate himself from a hostile world" ("Rhetoric," 144).

[99] Critics who doubt about Jack's conversion include Crewe, *Unredeemed*, 87; Hilliard, *Singularity*, 148; Hutson, *Thomas Nashe*, 243; Leggat, "Artistic," 40; and Turner, "Jack Wilton," 150. Ambivalent views appear in McGinn, who argues that Nashe is not really an anti-romancer (*Thomas Nashe*, 98) and Schwyzer, who suggests that Nashe "submits to convention" in his ending ("Summer Fruit," 606). Only Relihan argues for a cautiously optimistic view.

[100] See *The Sense of an Ending*, 53.

[101] When introducing Diamante, Jack remarks, "it doth me good when I remember her" (306). As noted above, this phrase echoes Chaucer, and its awkwardness might be due to a half-remembered quotation.

[102] See Hibbard, *Thomas Nashe*, 161, and Relihan, "Rhetoric," 238n.

hero's afterlife. He does not close with his own death, like Greene, nor abandon his tale before closure, like Sidney, but he makes his ending problematic.

The problem with full-throated generic identification is not that romance elements are not present, but that they assume their places only in retrospect. Nashe practices genre designation by back-formation, and his widely ranging tones make this method feel unstable. His rebellious acquiescence reveals a passive-aggressive relationship toward his precursors in the book market and Elizabethan prose romance in general. Desperate to produce another marketable commodity five years after *Pierce Penniless*, Nashe seized on romance as a viable mode, but he could not resist sending up its follies while borrowing its formal structure. Torn between his satiric instincts and his social conservatism, between his need for market success and his competitive nature, Nashe devised dishonesty as a way to write a romance that critiques romance, a boisterous tale with nihilistic coloring, and a tribute to Greene and Sidney riddled with barely concealed hostility.

Nashe's divided image of romance would find distinguished parallels in the following century. A split in his fictional structure divides his female characters into Heraclide and Diamante, his symbolic settings in the banqueting house and Tabitha's house, and his hero's rivals into Surrey and Cutwolfe. The division exposes a fundamental tension between the ideals of romance (Heraclide, the banqueting house, Surrey) and their anti-romance reflections (Diamante, Tabitha's house, Cutwolfe). The paradox of the abrupt ending, in which the anti-romance characters conform to romance conventions, emphasizes the interdependence between idealism and realism that would flower in early seventeenth-century masterpieces like *Don Quixote* and *The Tempest*. Paired characters like Quixote and Sancho and Prospero and Caliban extend Nashe's fascination with mismatched absolutes and unlikely couplings. Nashe's achievement, however, remains Jack and Diamante, who become a mobile middle term that expands romance to include its skeptical undercurrents. Jack and Diamante, like Nashe himself, cash in on romance's promise when it is offered, but, again like their creator, they make sure to get their satiric knocks in first. They expose the naiveté of all previous heroes and heroines of romance. Their dishonest triumph opens the door for the increasing self-consciousness of romance and its interaction with more heterogeneous kinds of prose fiction.

# Conclusion

# Greene's Ghosts and the Middlebrow Author

[W]hat Cesars might, or Catoes integrity, or what Saints deuotion can stop such mouths?

Gabriel Harvey[1]

Robert Greene's death had more than just symbolic importance for narrative fiction in early modern England. The dead writer had a lively literary afterlife. Greene's demise generated his own posthumous works and a series of responses by Harvey, Nashe, Dekker, Chettle, Barnebe Riche, John Dickenson, Samuel Rowlands, and others.[2] The reactions to Greene's passing reveal an ongoing debate over what it meant to be an author of printed fiction in late Elizabethan London. These responses comprise a communal and competitive attempt to theorize the place of narrative fiction in early modern English culture. They describe a genre that recognizes its potential to disrupt existing cultural rules, celebrates its own staying power, and acknowledges that its "author" was new to English literature. Greene's afterlife provides evidence that his peers thought his career both distinctive and lasting. Works like Harvey's salacious account of Greene's "fatall banquet," the cony-catching sequels of Dickenson and Rowlands, and Dekker's, Riche's, and Middleton's descriptions of Greene's and Nashe's ghosts in Hell reveal how early modern English authors imagined his legacy. The combined portrait is more cultural fantasy than reliable history, but read as a meta-literary commentary it articulates a provisional definition of the early modern prose fiction Author. Greene became many things to his heirs in popular prose: an immoral influence, a cash cow, fertile soil for later writers, and a symbol of ceaseless mischief and disorder. At the risk of anachronism, I suggest that the reactions to Greene's death produced a proleptic announcement of the central position printed fiction would assume in English literary culture.

---

[1]    Harvey, *Foure Letters*, 17. Further citations in the text.
[2]    On texts that discuss or allude to Greene's death, see Manley, *Literature and Culture in Early Modern London*, 320-40

Chettle struck early in the battle for Greene's legacy, registering the *Groatsworth* just weeks after Greene's death. Nashe and Harvey, too, were off the mark quickly. Harvey's *Foure Letters*, with its detailed account of Greene's death, appeared in late September 1592, and Nashe's reply, *Strange Newes, or the Foure Letters Confuted*, saw print in early 1593. The multivolume Nashe-Harvey controversy which followed soon left Greene behind, but elegiac works like R. B.'s (Richard Barnfield's?) *Greenes Funerals* (1594) and Barnebe Riche's *Greenes News Both from Heaven and Hell* (1593) used the dead author's name to make bids for market share. Other writers kept his name on readers' lips into the next decade, with titles like Dickenson's *Greene in Conceipt, Newly Raised from the Grave* (1598) and Rowlands's *Greenes Ghost Haunting Cony-Catchers* (1602). The trend continued in the early seventeenth century, with Nashe's ghost joining Greene's in Dekker's *A Knight's Conjuring* (1606), Middleton's *Black Book* (1604), and the anonymous *Tom Nash his Ghost* (1642). These texts reveal a self-consciousness group of writers with close experience of the early phases of English narrative culture's accommodation with the marketplace of print using Greene's model to define their own cultural status. Read as proto-critical summa they outline five qualities that define the author of middlebrow Elizabethan prose fiction: 1) Greene is the prototypical author, 2) the author destabilizes existing cultural structures, 3) the author's moral example is problematic, 4) the author lives and dies in poverty, and 5) the author's readers control his meaning. Together these five qualities portray a new figure, the Author in Print, who would cast a long shadow on English literary culture.

## Greene "the Author"

The most aggressive and counterproductive attempt to bury (not praise) Greene was Harvey's *Foure Letters*. Harvey's attack notably concurs with much other evidence regarding Greene's position as "the" popular author in 1592. It is Harvey, not one of Greene's defenders, who terms him, along with the balladeer Elderton, "the very ringleaders of the riming, and scribbling crew" (15). As the epigram to this chapter attests, Harvey pays tribute to Greene's cultural power by suggesting that neither Caesar, nor Cato, nor any Saint can "stop" his dead mouth. Beginning a series of fantastic coinages that Nashe would turn against him, Harvey calls Greene the "Scrivener of Crosbiters [and] ... the Patriarch of Shifters" (33). He further suggests that these titles are not his invention but part of the groundswell that wants to remake Greene: "How shal cosenage do for a new Register: or Phantasticalitye for a new Autor. They wronge him much with their Epitaphes, and other solemn deuises, that entitle him not at the least, The second Toy of London; the Stale of Poules, the Ape of Euphues, the Vice of the Stage, the mocker of the simple world: the flowter of his friendes, the Foe of himselfe: and so foorth" (39-40). Harvey surely intends his audience to contrast Greene with Spenser, called "the new poete" in the *Shepheardes Calendar* (1579),[3] but he perhaps inadvertently emphasizes Greene's popularity. Later Harvey terms Greene one of our "new-new writers, the Loadstones of the Press" (82), "your Onely Pregnant Autor" (86), and "your greenest Flower" (88). He pointedly contrasts him with his own ideal poets: "the Countesse of Pembrookes Arcadia is not greene inough for queasie stomackes, but they must haue *Greenes* Arcadia: and I beleeue most eagerlie longed for *Greenes* Faerie Queene" (41). Harvey's invective condemns Greene, but it also establishes him as the most popular print author of his era. Despite Harvey's intentions, it fixes Greene's ringleader status.

Nashe entered the fray to defend his dead friend from Harvey's slander. Nashe may have felt obliged to defend himself as well, since Harvey had placed him at the banquet with Greene, or to defend the ringing endorsement he had given *Menaphon* in 1589. In any case, he seems more determined to situate Tom Nashe as heir to Greene's literary prowess than to defend Robin Greene's morals. He describes Greene as a man who "inherited more vertues than vices" (1:287) but he accents Greene the writer not Greene the man: "In a night & a day would he haue yarkt up a Pamphlet as well as in seauen yeare, and glad was that Printer that might bee so blest as to pay him deare for the very dregs of his wit" (1:287). For Nashe, as for Chettle, Greene's success was above all financial; he is paid "deare" by the happy printer-publisher for the "dregs" of his wit – and *Groatsworth*, as Chettle had all but admitted, was the very dregs indeed.

The Harvey-Nashe controversy obscures the extent to which Greene's larger-than-life stature had becdame accepted at the end of the sixteenth century. Chettle's claim in *Kind-Hearts Dream* (1592) that Greene was "the only Comedian of a vulgar writer" further accents his primacy, although this may be a defense of Chettle's interest in *Groatsworth*.[4] Later in this text, Chettle describes Greene's ghost appearing to Pierce Pennilesse (i.e., Nashe) and responding to attackers like Harvey by suggesting that his literary output be judged rather than his personal conduct: "For my Bookes, of what kind souer, I refer their commendation or dispraise to those that haue read them" (35). Chettle's defense of Greene's literary productions parallels Francis Meres's description of Greene in *Palladis Tamia* (1598) as one of "the best for Comedy amongst us."[5] The shadow into which the rise of Shakespeare would cast Greene had not yet appeared in the late 1590s.

Samuel Rowlands's *Greenes Ghost haunting cony catchers* (1602) demonstrates that the marketability of Greene's name continued into the following century. A decade after Greene's death, his authorial persona was still hot property. Imitating and competing with Greene's own authorial voice, Rowlands's title-page claims that his own book is "Ten times more pleasant than any thing yet published

---

[3]  See *The Yale Edition of the Shorter Poems of Edmund Spenser,* William A. Oram, et al., (New Haven: Yale University Press, 1989) 13.

[4]  *Kind Heartes Dream,* 13.

[5]  Francis Meres, *Palladis Tamia, Elizabethan Critical Essays,* 2:319-20.

of this matter."[6] Rowlands's letter to his readers apes Greene's habit of appealing to a broad swath of readers, addressing "All Gentlemen Merchants, Apprentices, Farmers, and plaine countreymen" (3). Also, like the master thief in Greene's *Second Part of Cony Catching* (10:114), Rowlands's criminals "proceed Doctor" (4) in their arts. Greene appears in Rowlands's book as "the Author" (7): the man who established the form in which Rowlands writes. Rowlands suggests a few additions to spruce up Greene's franchise (including exposés of false pride and "the abuse committed by such as sell bottle ale" [9]) and adds some new technical terms ("batfowling" for "conycatching," etc.) but he imagines that Greene has defined the basic authorial function: "But my meaning in this is, but to chase the game which others haue rowsed; and execute them outright which Conicatching only hath branded" (25). The Author has begun the task, and Rowlands will complete it. Rowlands's celebration may be tactical, designed to latch onto Greene's marketplace success, but this practical purpose underscores the extent to which the fiction market was typed "Greene" in 1602.

Even more hagiographically, the author "R. B." (probably Richard Barnfield) published in 1594 a set of sonnets entitled *Greenes Funerals*. As expressions of grief the poems were two years late, but as attempts to fix Greene's theoretical meaning and pursue his readership they reveal the continued obsession with the dead man and his works. R. B.'s ninth sonnet describes Greene in evocative terms: "Greene, gave the ground, to all that wrote upon him."[7] This metaphor literalizes Greene's name, so that he becomes the fertile soil for succeeding generations. Like Shakespeare's sonnets, R. B.'s describe artistic immortality: "For though his Art be dead, yet shall it euer abide" (80). In conventional language R. B. rejects Harvey's attack on Greene. A further sonnet makes explicit what Greene's art was by cataloging "certain of his Bookes" (but none of his plays). The list is incomplete, and it wrongly calls *Mamillia* "Camilla," but it attests to Greene's prolific career by listing 16 titles, from the earliest to the latest.[8] R. B.'s portrait makes Greene the font and origin of printed popular fiction. Greene is the ground, and new writers are ready to spring up everywhere.

---

[6]    Samuel Rowlands, *Greenes Ghost haunting cony-catchers*, *The Complete Works of Samuel Rowlands*, 3 volumes, (Glasgow: Hunterian Club, 1880) 1:1. Titles in the volume paginated separately. Further citations in the text.

[7]    R. B., *Greenes Funerals*, R. B. McKerrow, ed., (London: Sidgwick & Jackson, 1911) 81.

[8]    Harrison suggests that the reference to "the Death of him," the last title listed, refers to *A Maidens Dreame*, published on the death of Christopher Hatton in 1591, but it seems as likely to refer to *The Repentance of Robert Greene* or *Groatsworth*, both of which refer to Greene's death. See *Greenes Funerals*, 92.

## The Author's Power

When these references established Greene as "the Author" of Elizabethan fiction, he became a danger for other ambitious writers. Nashe recognized that his own reputation was at risk if he seemed too indebted to his friend, and his response to Harvey is aggressive: "Wherein haue I borrowed from *Greene* or *Tarlton, that I should thanke them for all I haue*? Is my stile like *Greenes*, or my ieasts like *Tarltons*? Do I talke of any counterfeit birds, or hearbs, or stones, or rake up an newfound poetry from under the wals of Troy?" (1:318-19). The attack seems directed against lingering euphuism in Greene's style rather than Nashe's more palpable debt to Greene's anti-Harvey satire (*A Quip for an Upstart Courtier*, 1592) or the cony-catching or repentance pamphlets. Nashe does not quite refuse all literary influence, but he is determined to emphasize his singularity. He admits that he read *Euphues*, "when I was a little ape at Cambridge, and then I thought it was *Ipse ille*: it may be excellent good still, for ought I know, for I lookt not on it this ten yeare" (1:319). He does not really deny that his own style and burgeoning celebrity build on the examples Greene and Tarlton (more than Lyly); instead he suggests that he is more current than Greene, and owes less to passé fads like euphuism.[9] It is Greene's metamorphic example, in which euphuism gives way to pastoral, cony-catching, satire, and repentance, that guides Nashe's career as print author.

Barnebe Riche, like Greene a prolific fiction writer, produced the most substantial and suggestive portrait of Greene the author in *Greenes News both from Heauen and Hell*. This narrative follows Greene's ghost through the afterlife from the gates of Heaven to the fires of Hell to his final place as a "restless sprite."[10] For Riche, like Harvey, Greene's legacy seems morally and socially problematic, although Riche sympathizes with the wandering Greene rather than the authorities who reject him. First St. Peter and later Lucifer expel him from their respective final resting places. Riche's Greene embodies the uncomfortable position of early modern prose fiction, which can rest in neither a humanist's heaven nor an outlaw's hell.

Greene's notoriety precedes him in the afterlife, so that St. Peter condemns him for the dishonesty of his literary trade: "I must tell you," he says, "heaven is no habitation for any man that can looke with one eye and wincke with the other, for there must none rest there that dooth use to haulte, but such as be plaine and true dealing people" (18). St. Peter's critique suggests that all literary narrative – or at least all fiction that follows Greene's example – is culturally untrustworthy; this

---

[9]   The identity of the poetry "from under the wals of Troy" remains uncertain: McKerrow doubts that it is Peele's *Tale of Troy* (1589) and suggests instead a lost work of Tarlton's (3:189, 460). Greene's *Euphues his Censure* seems possible, though it is not in verse.

[10]   Barnebe Riche, *Greenes News both from Heauen and Hell*, R. B. McKerrow, ed., (London: Sidgwick & Jackson, 1911) 60. Further citations in the text.

kind of writing always looks with one eye and winks with the other. This heavenly critique follows one strain of criticism of narrative fiction, that which descends from Harvey and other university moralists, in which a low style and an author's lowlife habits mandate moral condemnation of these works.

Lucifer's subsequent reading of Greene, however, does not really oppose St. Peter's. Hell's readers casts Greene out as well. This time Greene is castigated because of the moral veneer of his tales. Greene's project of exposing criminals and protecting honest citizens finds no sympathy in infernal regions. Hell, according to Riche, teems with criminals whose methods and secrets have been exposed by Greene's works. These angry thieves and coseners want to torture Greene's ghost by cutting out his tongue or his eyes – so that he either cannot see their crimes, or at least cannot talk about them. (The irony, of course, is that it has been Greene's pen that has done the damage.) Only Lucifer's sentence of exile spares Greene their cruel intentions. Caught between the heavenly moral reader, sitting in Harvey's place, and the hellish multitude, who like Nashe do not want their tricks exposed, Greene's shade has no place to go. He ends up a "walking spyrite, restlesse and remedilesse to wander through the world" (60-1). The author of prose fiction has no place in the old cultural order.

In his liminal state of eternal motion, Greene's ghost becomes responsible for a wide variety of tricks and mischief. He frightens young women by posing as Robin Goodfellow, and in other guises he infects men with Avarice and women with Lust, as well as preying on lawyers, the court, and the clergy. (These three social categories may be singled out by Riche because they are all highly literate, and thus at risk for being corrupted by popular print.) It is not just that Greene embodies misrule, a spirit of chaos that disrupts urban life. He further embodies the particular kinds of misrule associated with popular print: he seduces innocent women readers with erotic tales, and distracts male readers away from their proper duties into licentiousness and greed. Greene's ghost becomes a metaphor for the social impact of prose fiction and popular print in general. Like Greene's spirit, popular prose fiction was beginning at the end of sixteenth-century England to destabilize a literary culture long been dominated by patronage and court circles. Greene's marketplace of print established an alternative space for the professional writer who sold his name on the printed page, directly to his readers. The man Harvey called a "ringleader" of popular print became for Riche an eternally marginal and disruptive spirit.

This image of Greene as restless and disorderly was extended in the first decade of the seventeenth century. Dekker, in a "To the Reader" epistle in *The Wonderful Yeare* (1603) that mocks Greene's peritextual letters, describes popular print authors without naming Greene explicitly: "But those Goblins whom I now am coniuring up, haue bladder-cheekes puft out like a *Swizzers* breeches (yet being prickt, there come out nothing but wind) thin headed fellowes that liue upon the scraps of inuention, and trauell with such vagrant soules, and so like Ghosts in white sheetes of paper, that the Statute of Rogues may worthily be sued upon them

because their wits haue no abiding place, and yet wander without a passe-port."[11]
That these wandering ghosts include Greene (and, after his death, Nashe) seems
clear from the oft-quoted scene in *A Knight's Conjuring* (1606) in which the
recently deceased Nashe joines "Marlow, Greene, and Peele" in Hell to rail against
the failure of patrons to support them (quoted in Nashe, 5: 152).[12] A poem prefaced
to the anonymous *Tom Nashe his Ghost* (1642) also links print authorship and
cultural instability: the poem begins, "I am a Ghost, and Ghosts doe feare no
Lawes" and contains an description of the ghost's powers that echoes Riche and
Dekker's portraits of Greene: "For (being now invisible, a Spirit) / I cut through th'
Ayre, and in the Earth can ferrit, / And in an Augure hole my selfe can hide, / And
heare their knaveries and spie unspide."[13] The image of prose authors as ghosts and
goblins emphasizes their hidden cultural force and its destabilizing impact on older
traditions of patronage and courtly writing.

## The Author's Morality

Alongside this consensus about the cultural force of Greene the author came
persistent anxiety about the moral rectitude of his life and works. While his most
famous motto, *Omne tulit punctum*, is impeccably Horatian, Greene's blurring of
the line between "profit" and "pleasure" corrupted this doctrinaire sentiment.
Harvey, especially, declared Greene morally corrupt and a symbol of all that was
dissolute about London's literary culture. In a lengthy summary of the rumors
concerning Greene's life, Harvey carefully links the failings of the writer to the
sins of the man:

> I was altogether unacquainted with the man, & neuer once saluted him by name: but
> who in London hath not heard of his dissolute, and licentious liuing: his fonde
> disguisinge of a Master of Arte with ruffianly haire, unseemely apparell, and more
> unseemelye Company: his vaineglorious and Thrasonicall brauinge: his piperly
> Extemporizing, and Tarletonizing: his apish counterfeiting of euery ridiculous, and
> absurd toy: his fine coosening of Iuglers, and finer iugling with cooseners: hys

---

[11] Thomas Dekker, *The Wonderful Year. 1603, The Non-Dramatic Works of Thomas
Dekker*, Alexander Grosart, ed., 4 volumes, (London: Huth Library, 1884) 1:79-80.

[12] Dekker's diatribe against failed patronage suggests how writing for print has become
frustrating: "Nay (sayes he) into so lowe a miserie (if not contempt,) is the sacred Arte of
Poesie falne, that tho a wryter (who is worthy to set at the table of the Sunne,) wast his
braines, to earne applause from the more worthie Spirits, yet when he has done his best, hee
workes but like Ocnus, that makes ropes in hell; for as hee twists, an Asse stands by and
bites them in sunder, and that Asse is no other than the Audience with hard hands" (quoted
in Nashe, 5:152). Dekker's Nashe does not share Greene's happy fantasy about his
relationship with his audience.

[13] *Tom Nashe his Ghost*, quoted in Nashe, 5:46.

villainous cogging, and foisting; his monstrous swearinge, and horrible forswearing; his
impious profaning of sacred Textes: his other scandalous, and blasphemous rauinge; his
riotous and outrageous surfeitinge; his continuall shifting of lodginges: his plausible
musteringe, and banquetinge of roysterly acquaintaunce at his first comminge; his
beggarly departing in euery hostisses debt; his infamous resorting to the Banckeside,
Shorditch, Southwarke, and other filthy hauntes: his obscure lurkinge in basest corners:
his pawning of his sword, cloak, and what not, when money came short; his impudent
pamphletting, phantasticall interluding, and desperate libelling, when other coosening
shiftes failed: his implyinge of Ball (surnamed, cuttinge Ball) till he was intercepted at
Tiborne, to leauy a crew of his trustiest companions, to gaurde him in daunger of
Arrestes: his keeping of the foresaid Balls sister, a sorry ragged queane, of whome hee
had his base sonne, *Infortunatus Greene*: his forsaking of his owne wife, too honest for
such a husband: particulars are infinite: his contemning of Superiours, deriding of other,
and defying of all good order? (19-20)

This passage shifts registers several times, attacking Greene's disorderly hair, his
clothes, his sexual practices, his unseemly company, wide-ranging literary style,
and illegitimate child. Harvey shows his hand, however, when after noting that
"particulars are infinite," he concludes the passage by figuring Greene as a
corruptor of the social order, "contemning of Superiours ... and defying of all good
order." For Harvey, Greene's personal and literary disorder threatens the social
order; like Ulysses in *Troilus and Cressida*, he insists that any crack in the social
façade will lead to disintegration.[14] Thus failings that might seem purely personal
or professional (Greene's hair, or his aping of Lyly and Tarlton) are fundamentally
moral for Harvey: the disorder this author represents threatens the social order
itself.

   Against Harvey's assault Greene's defenders offered several different replies.
Nashe defended Greene's financial status but disassociated himself with his work,
calling *Groatsworth* a "scald, trivial, lying pamphlet" (*Pierce Pennilesse*, 50).
Writers like Dickenson, who relied on Greene's name to authorize their works,
defended him in the terms he had made familiar in his own prefaces.[15] In what
Dickenson calls "An aduertisement to the Reader," he writes that Greene appeared
to him in a dream and defended himself against Harvey: "I am hee, whose pen was
first emploied in the aduancement of vanitie, and afterward in the discouering of
villianie. Ioyne the two, and they will serue thee for the *Periphrasis* of my name.
In the former of which, I confesse I haue offended, yet who knoweth not, that

---

[14]   For comparable reasons, presumably, Harvey notes his approval of Augustus's decision
to exile Ovid (42).
[15]   Dickenson's previous fiction, *Arisbas: Euphues amidst his slumbers* (1594), also
borrowed the names of other writers: he alludes to Lyly in his subtitle, dedicates the volume
to Edward Dyer, and mentions Sidney in his "To the Gentlemen-Readers" epistle (31).
Salzman claims that his real model is Lodge's *Rosalynde* (*English Prose Fiction*, 81-2).

Fiction the godmother of Poesie makes her the shadow of Philosophie."[16] The two-part defense of Greene's vain-then-virtuous career is familiar; Dickenson may have adapted it from *Greenes Vision, Greenes Never Too Late*, or several other volumes of late Greene. In these terms, Harvey's reading of Greene's work is not exactly false – Greene and Dickenson concur that the early works are "emploied in the advancement of vanitie" – but Greene transformed himself and shored up the social order after 1590.

A more daring and less explicit defense of Greene's career suggests that broad popularity was his defining feature, and his appeal to heterogeneous readers helped create a new kind of literary celebrity. The concluding anecdote of Samuel Rowlands's *Greenes Ghost haunting cony catchers* (1602) focuses on the career of Doctour Pinchbacke, a cony catcher who becomes a symbol for a new kind of popular author and thus another commentary on Greene. In order to establish his authority, Pinchbacke first has his servant steal a "gilt goblet," then after a great show of magic-making that recalls Calasiris's "showmanship" – "Two hours hee stayed alone by himselfe tosting him by a good fire till he sweat againe, than painting his face with a deadish colour, which hee caried alwaies about him for such a purpose" (47) – he locates the goblet, after which he becomes an honored guest and much sought-after advisor for the neighborhood. The gambit of committing a crime in order to solve it parallels Greene's two-part career strategy: first he seduces his readers with love-pamphlets, then he corrects them with tales of repentance. The creation of Pinchebacke as minor celebrity turns him into a symbol of Greene's newfound authorial power: "the people diuersely talked of the Doctors skill and cunning, and that he could do anie thing, or tell anie thing that was done in anie place" (49). The language recalls the wandering placenessness of Greene's ghost, and it makes that wandering a source of public power, rather than disgrace. While Pinchebacke is eventually executed for a murder he may not have committed (51-2), Rowlands's tale emphasizes his ability to authorize himself, to become a figure of authority among common people. Rowlands judges this career with the familiar metaphor from the preface to *Mamillia*: "And in a word, so manie men, so manie mindes, but the greater part of the countrey admired his deepe knowledge, and published his excellent learninge, so that he became famous amongst the people" (50). "Published" here means "made widely known" and need not refer to print, but surely Rowlands is thinking about Greene's (and his own) print circulation.

---

[16]   John Dickenson, *Greene in Conceipt, Occasional Issues of Unique or Very Rare Books*, Alexander Grosart, ed., 16 volumes, (London: Private Subscription, 1878) 5:97.

### The Author's Poverty

Even for Harvey, Greene's name signifies market value, but it is crucial to Harvey's attack that Greene died poor. Harvey's *Foure Letters* are worth reading, according to their own sub-title, because they are "especially touching Robert Greene, and other parties by him abused." Harvey's personal invective attempts to establish boundaries between the Cambridge Don and the London writer, but the conversation, as Nashe would demonstrate, drags Harvey into his opponents' mud. Harvey wanted Greene's readers to buy his book – hence he names Greene on his title-page – but by entering into the dialogue on Greene's death, he mixed with a rougher level of company than he was able to manage. Harvey, the Cambridge Don, was angry with Greene for precisely the reason that his career is so important to scholars of English narrative: over his twelve-year career, Greene became a public symbol of narrative fiction, and the new medium of print spread his personal fable throughout the city. "Euery priuate excesse is dangerous," Harvey writes, "but such publike enormities [are] incredibly pernitious, and insupportable" (16). The "enormities" Harvey describes embody the errors humanists like Harvey associated with popular print culture and by extension with narrative fiction itself.

A key part of Harvey's attack on Greene consists in emphasizing his deathbed poverty. Despite being a calling-card for printed fiction, Greene died in debt (if we can trust Harvey), and this financial crisis loomed large in Harvey's attack on him. His assault on Greene's character thus dissects his clothes: "he was faine poore soule, to borrow [mistress Ball's] shirte, whiles his owne was a washing: and how his dublet and hose, and sword were sold for three shillinges: and beside the charges of his windinge sheete, which was foure shillinges: and the charges of hys buriall yesterday in the New-churchyard neere Bedlam, which was six shillinges, and foure pence; how deeply hee was indebted to her poore husbande" (22). The charge of indebtedness, and obligation to his mistress's husband, leads Harvey to quote (his version of) Greene's abject final letter to his wife, asking her to settle his debts.[17] Making the widely-read author destitute allows Harvey to insist that Greene's version of authorship can never become respectable.

Nashe, while careful to distinguish himself from Greene, insists on contradicting this point. He reminds his readers that Greene's literary proclivity created financial success, and asserts that the doublet Greene wore to the fatal banquet alone would fetch 30 shillings from a cloth broker (1:288). He also memorably asserts to Harvey that "in one yeare [Greene] pist as much against the walls, as thou and thy two brothers spent in three" (1:287). Nashe does not deny Greene's profligacy – presumably undeniable in 1590s London – but he claims that drink and an unthrifty life are necessary for the poet: "that Poet or nouice, be hee what he will, ought to suspect his wit, and remaine halfe in a doubt that it is not authenticall, till it hath beene seene and allowd in unthrifts consistory," and "I

---

[17]    Alternate versions of this letter exist in both *Groatsworth* and *Repentance*.

protest I should neuer haue writ passion well, or beene a peece of a Poet, if I had not arriu'd in those quarters" (1:310). The point is familiar from Rabelais and Nashe's preface to *Menaphon* – "no man can write with conceit except he take counsel of the cup" (91) – and Nashe uses it here to respond to Harvey's snobbery.

Nashe's defense of proto-Bohemianism resonates oddly with his own description of Greene's prosperity. Faced with this choice, most of Greene's defenders opted to paint him as much less destitute than did Harvey, or indeed Greene's own deathbed tracts. Chettle describes Greene's ghost as a thoroughly reputable scholar with unruly hair: "a man of indifferent yeares, of face amible, of body well proportioned, his attire after the havite of a schollerlike Gentleman, onely his haire was somewhat long" (*Kind-Hartes Dreame*, 13). Dickenson is presumably copying Chettle when he describes Greene as "well proportioned" (97). This prosperous figure seems very unlike both Harvey's wastrel and Nashe's satiric roisterer: for these authors, each of whom hitched his literary career to Greene's reputation, the dead man was a perfectly respectable figure in changing literary culture.[18]

## The Author's Readers

Greene's most distinctive contributions to the profession of print author were his numerous attempts to ingratiate himself with his imaginary readers; from *Mamillia* until after his death, Greene stood for a way of making printed fiction available and attractive to heterogeneous middlebrow readers and reading practices. Looking at the fate of the reader after the death of this author demonstrates that Greene's techniques for assimilating his readership – techniques that, I have argued, he adapted from Heliodorus among other places – became widely distributed among his self-nominated heirs in popular fiction. I have discussed above how Nashe's *Unfortunate Traveler* and Lodge's *Robin the Devil* and *Margarite of America* rely on and transform Greene's legacy, and how in each case they enact distinctly Greenian strategies in their peritexts. Turning to Chettle, R. B., and Rowlands reveals that these writers, too, recognized that Greene had something particular to offer in terms of reimagining the relationship between author, book, and readers.

---

[18] The figure of the impoverished dying writer has considerable iconic value, and Middleton's depiction of Nashe's deathbed in *The Black Book* (1604) extends portraits of the dying Greene: "In this unfortunate tiring-house lay poor Pierce upon a pillow stuffed with horse-meat; the sheets smudged so dirtily, as if they had been stolen by night out of Saint Pulcher's churchyard when the sexton had left a grave open, and so laid the dead bodies wool-ward: the coverlet was made of pieces a' black cloth clapt together, such as was snatched off the rails in King's-street at the queen's funeral..." *The Works of Thomas Middleton*, A. H. Bullen, ed., 8 volumes, (Boston: Houghton Mifflin, 1886) 8:25.

Chettle's *Kind-Hartes Dreame* seems in many ways a score-settling text, particularly if we accept that there is an apology to Shakespeare in its prefatory letter.[19] Whatever Chettle's role in the *Groatsworth*, Greene clearly is Chettle's model for how an author should approach his readers. The letter Chettle pens from Greene's ghost to Nashe contains a typical bit of doublespeak in which the author, having given, takes away: "All this had I intended to write, but now I wil not giue way to wrath, but returne it unto the earth from whence I tooke it" (37). The two-part maneuver is familiar to readers of Greene: he offers the alluring but troubling matter (love stories, or, in this case, incitements for Nashe to attack Harvey in print), then hides it under the cover of moral restraint, but of course the cat has left the bag. Chettle, an astute reader of Greene, plays to both sides, and appeals to both readers who desire and those who deplore the flyting match that would follow between Harvey and Nashe.

In *Greenes Funerals*, the writer's consciousness of his readers appears by way of Greene's familiar metaphor of heads and wits. In the second sonnet in the collection, R. B.'s concluding couplet embraces multiple heads explicitly: "No Booke pleases all that come: / None so bad but pleases some" (72). In the context of a poem about fortune –" Greene loude *Fortune* foolish Man" (72) – this couplet suggests that the power of reader over author is analogous to the power of Fortune in a Greene romance: it is mysterious, uncontrollable, and, after many hardships, finally beneficent.

The most sophisticated exploration of what Greene's example suggests for the relationship between reader and author appears in Rowlands's *Greenes Ghost haunting cony-catchers*. Concerned about the social impact of writing yet another cony-catching pamphlet, Rowlands writes, "I would bee loth by this my publisht Discouerie to corrupt the simple, or teach them knauerie by my book, that els would haue beene honest, if they had neuer seene them" (25).[20] The problem Rowlands identifies centers on the consumption of his narrative: if readers want to use the information for anti-social ends they would be able to. His solution invokes the wise and discreet reader. Rowlands seems to have learned from Greene that authors rely on readers to complete their work: "But imagine the Reader to be of this wisdome and discretion, that hearing some laid open, he can discerne it to be sinne, and can so detest it, tough he be not cloid with a common place of exhortation. And sooth to say, I thinke euery man to bee of my minde" (25). Here, more explicitly than in Nashe's or Lodge's competitive fictions, is Greene's fantasy laid bare: the ideal Reader is wise, discrete, and of the same mind as his

---

[19]  For the countersuggestion that Peele, not Shakespeare, receives the apology, see Lukas Erne, "Biography and Mythography: Rereading Chettle's Alleged Apology to Shakespeare," *English Studies* 79 (1998): 430-40.
[20]  On cony-catching pamphlets as an urban conduct books, see Craig Dionne, "Fashioning Outlaws: The Early Modern Rogue and Urban Culture," *Rogues and Early Modern English Culture*, 33-61.

author.[21] Rowlands finishes what the prefatory letters to *Mamillia* began: a long-wandering romance between Author and Reader.

I close by reflecting on the value for scholars of early modern English narrative culture of treating Greene as "the Author" of Elizabethan prose fiction. The obsessive struggle in the 1590s to give meaning to Greene's name and legacy helps define changes in the cultural status of middlebrow prose fiction during the English Renaissance. Prose fiction has long been the ignored little sibling of drama and verse in Renaissance studies, and although emerging interest in the history of the book and print culture is inspiring a return to fiction, this return will be incomplete without considering these texts not simply as attractive back alleys of Elizabethan literary culture but as major developments in the history of English narrative. The texts that rescue Greene from his deathbed and transform him into a wandering spirit of prose fiction reveal a powerful cultural fantasy about the newfound energy and destabilizing social consequences of inexpensive printed fiction. The place of this narrative form in the history of English fiction should not remain marginal much longer.

---

[21] Greene was not the only early modern author who fantasized about his readers. On Ben Jonson's construction of an ideal audience, see Stanley Fish, "Author-Readers: Ben Jonson's Community of the Same," *Representations* 7 (1984): 26-58.

# Bibliography

Adams, Robert P. "Bold Bawdry and Open Manslaughter: The English New Humanist Attack on Medieval Romance." *Huntington Library Quarterly* 23 (1959-60): 33-48.

Agnew, Jean-Christophe. *Worlds Apart: The Market and Theater in Anglo-American Thought*. Cambridge: Cambridge University Press, 1986.

Allison, A. F. *Robert Greene, 1559-1592: A Bibliographical Catalogue of the Early Editions in English (to 1640)*. Old Woking: Pall Mall Bibliographies, 1975.

Althusser, Louis. *Reading Capital*. Brewster, Ben, trans. London: Verso, 1979.

Alwes, Derek B. "Robert Greene's Dueling Dedications." *English Literary Renaissance* 30 (2000): 373-97.

_____. "'To Serve Your Prince by…an Honest Dissimulation': The *New Arcadia* as a Defense of Poetry." *Explorations in Renaissance Culture* 29:2 (Winter 2003): 147-69.

_____. *Sons and Authors in Elizabethan England*. Newark: University of Delaware Press, 2004.

Anderson, Michael J. "The ΣΟΦΡΟΣΥΝΗ of Persinna and the Romantic Strategy of Heliodorus' *Aethiopica*." *Classical Philology* 92 (1997): 303-22.

Arber, Edward, ed. *Transcript of the Register of the Stationers' Company*. Five volumes. London: Private Printing, 1875.

Ariosto, Ludovico. *Orlando Furioso*. Reynolds, Barbara, trans. Two volumes. New York: Penguin, 1973.

Aristotle. *Poetics*. Ingram Bywater, trans. New York: Modern Library, 1954.

Augustine, Saint. *City of God*. Dods, Marcus, trans. New York: Modern Library, 1950.

Bahktin, Mikhail. *The Dialogic Imagination: Four Essays*. Holquist, Michael, ed. Emerson, Caryl, and Holquist, Michael, trans. Austin: University of Texas Press, 1981.

Bal, Mieke. *Narratology: Introduction to the Theory of Narrative*. 2nd ed. Toronto: University of Toronto Press, 1997.

Ballaster, Ros. *Seductive Forms: Women's Amatory Fiction from 1684 to 1740*. Oxford: Clarendon Press, 1992.

Barbour, Reid. *Deciphering Elizabethan Fiction*. Newark: University of Delaware Press, 1993.

Barker, W. W. "Rhetorical Romance: The 'Frivolous Toyes' of Robert Greene." *Unfolded Tales: Essays on Renaissance Romance*. Logan, George M., and Gordon Tesky, eds. Ithaca: Cornell University Press, 1989: 74-97.

Barthes, Roland. *S/Z: An Essay*. Miller, Richard, trans. New York: Hill and Wang, 1974.

Bartsch, Shadi. *Decoding the Ancient Novel*. Princeton: Princeton University Press, 1989.

Bates, Catherine. "'A Large Occasion of Civil Discourse': John Lyly and the Art of Civil Conversation." *Review of English Studies* n. s. 42 (1991): 469-86.

Beaty, Frederick L. "Lodge's *Forbonius and Prisceria* and Sidney's *Arcadia*." *English Studies* 49 (1968): 38-45.

Beecher, Donald. "The Fiction of Symbolic Forms: Mythological Drifting in Lodge's *A Margarite of America*." *Critical Approaches to English Prose Fiction*. Beecher, Donald, ed. Ottawa: Dovehouse Editions, 1998: 219-39.

Beer, Gillian. *The Romance*. London: Methuen, 1970.

Beier, A.L. "New Historicism, Historical Context, and the Literature of Roguery: The Case of Thomas Harman Re-opened." *Rogues and Early Modern English Culture*. Dionne, Craig and Steve Mentz, eds. Ann Arbor: University of Michigan Press, 2004: 98-119.

Bergbush, Martin. "Rebellion in the *New Arcadia.*" *Philological Quarterly* 53 (1974): 29-41.

Bergvall, Åke. "The 'Enabling of Judgement': An Old Reading of the *New Arcadia.*" *Studies in Philology* 85:4 (Fall 1988).

_____. "Reason in Luther, Calvin, and Sidney." *Sixteenth-Century Journal* 23 (Winter 1992): 115-27.

Bérubé, Michael. "There is Nothing Inside the Text, or, Why No One's Heard of Wolfgang Iser," *Postmodern Sophistry: Stanley Fish and the Critical Enterprise.* Olsen, Gary A. and Lynn Worsham, eds. Albany: State University of New York Press, 2004: 11-26.

Bevington, David. "Cultural Exchange: Gascoigne and Ariosto at Gray's Inn." *The Italian World of English Renaissance Drama: Cultural Exchange and Intertextuality.* Marrapodi, Michele ed. Newark: University of Delaware Press, 1998.

*Bibla Sacra: Iuxta Vulgatam Versionem.* 2nd Edition. Stüttgart: Württembergische Bibelanstalt, 1975.

Blagden, Cyprian. *The Stationers' Company: A History 1403-1959.* Cambridge, MA: Harvard University Press, 1960.

Blayney, Peter. *The Texts of "King Lear" and Their Origins.* Volume 1. Cambridge: Cambridge University Press, 1979.

_____. *Nicholas Oakes and the First Quarto.* Cambridge: Cambridge University Press, 1982.

_____. *The Bookshops in Paul's Cross Churchyard.* London: Bibliographical Society, 1990.

_____. "The Publication of Playbooks." *A New History of Early English Drama.* Cox, J. C., and Kastan, David S. eds. New York: Columbia University Press, 1997: 383-422.

Bourdieu, Pierre, *Distinction: A Social Critique of the Judgement of Taste.* Nice, Richard, trans. Cambridge: Harvard University Press, 1984.

_____. *Practical Reason: On the Theory of Action.* Shapiro, Gisele, trans. Stanford: Stanford University Press, 1988.

Bowie, Ewen. "The Readership of Greek Novels in the Ancient World." *The Search for the Ancient Novel*. Tatum, James, ed. Baltimore: Johns Hopkins University Press, 1994: 435-59.

Bloomfield, Morton W. *Essays and Explorations: Studies in Ideas, Language, and Literature*. Cambridge, MA: Harvard University Press, 1970.

Briggs, William Dinsmore. "Political Ideas in Sidney's *Arcadia*." *Studies in Philology* 28 (1931): 137-61.

Brink, Jean. "Materialist History of the Publication of Spenser's *Faerie Queene*," *Review of English Studies* 54: 213 (Feb 2003): 1-26.

Brooks, Douglas A. *From Playhouse to Printing House: Drama and Authorship in Early Modern England*. Cambridge: Cambridge University Press, 2000.

Brooks, Peter. *Reading for the Plot: Design and Intention in Narrative*. Cambridge, MA: Harvard University Press, 1984.

Brown, Cedric C., and Arthur F. Marotti, eds. *Texts and Cultural Change in Early Modern England*. New York: St. Martin's Press, 1997.

Bruster, Douglas. *Shakespeare and the Question of Culture: Early Modern Literature and the Cultural Turn*. New York: Palgrave, 2003.

Burke, Séan. *The Death and Return of the Author: Criticism and Subjectivity in Barthes, Foucault, and Derrida*. 2nd ed. Edinburgh: Edinburgh University Press, 1998. First ed. 1992.

Burton, Robert. *The Anatomy of Melancholy*. Holbrook Jackson, ed. London: J.M. Dent & Sons, 1932.

Cantar, Brenda. "Monstrous Conception and Lodge's *Robin the Devil*." *Studies in English Literature* 37 (1997): 39-53.

Cave, Terence. *Recognitions: A Study in Poetics*. Oxford: Clarendon Press, 1988.

_____. 'Suspendere animos': Pour une histoire de la notion de suspens," *Les commentaires et la naissance de la critique littéraire, France/Italie (XIVe-XVIe siècles)*. Mathieu-Castellani, Gisèle, and Michel Plaisance, eds. Paris: Amateurs de Livres, 1990.

Cervantes, Miguel de. *Don Quixote*. Shelton, Thomas, trans. New York: P. F. Collier & Son, 1937. Translation originally published 1612.

_____. *The Trials of Persiles and Sigusmunda*. Waller, Celia Richmond, and Clark A. Colahan, trans. Berkeley: University of California press, 1989.

_____. *Novelas Ejemplares I*. Sieber, Harry, ed. Madrid: Editiones Cátedra, S.A., 1995.

_____. *Don Quixote*. Starkie, Walter, trans. New York: Signet, 1964, 2001.

Charles, Casey. "Heroes as Lovers: Erotic Attraction between Men in Sidney's *New Arcadia*." *Criticism* 34 (1992).

Chartier, Roger. *The Cultural Uses of Print in Early Modern France*. Cochrane, L. G., trans. Princeton: Princeton University Press, 1987.

_____. *The Order of Books: Readers, Authors, and Libraries in Europe between the Fourteenth and Eighteenth Centuries*. Cochrane, L. G., trans. Cambridge: Polity Press, 1994.

_____ and Guglielmo Cavallo, eds. *A History of Reading in the West*. Amherst: University of Massachusetts Press, 1999.

Chaucer, Geoffrey. *The Riverside Chaucer*. Benson, Larry, and F. N Robinson, eds. Boston: Houghton Mifflin Co., 1987.

Cheney, Patrick. *Sepnser's Famous Flight: The Renaissance Idea of a Literary Career*. Toronto: University of Toronto Press, 1993.

_____. *Marlowe's Counterfeit Profession: Ovid, Spenser, Counter-Nationhood*. Toronto: University of Toronto Press, 1997.

Chettle, Henry. *Kind-Hearts Dreame (1592)*. Harrison, G. B., ed. London: Bodley Head, 1923.

Clements, Robert J. and Joseph Gibaldi. *Anatomy of the Novella: The European Tale Collection from Boccaccio and Chaucer to Cervantes*. New York: New York University Press, 1977.

Clubb, Louise George. *Italian Drama in Shakespeare's Time*. New Haven: Yale University Press, 1989.

Colie, Rosalie. *The Resources of Kind: Genre-Theory in the Renaissance.* Lewalski, Barbara K., ed. Berkeley: University of California Press, 1973.

Collins, Jane. "Publishing Private Pleasures: The Gentlewoman Reader of Barnebe Riche and George Pettie." *Explorations in Renaissance Culture* 29:2 (Winter 2003): 185-210.

Craig, D. H. "A Hybrid Growth: Sidney's Theory of Poetry in *An Apology for Poetry.*" *Sidney in Retrospect: Selections from* English Literary Renaissance. Kinney, Arthur F., ed. Amherst: University of Massachusetts Press, 1988: 62-80.

Cressy, David. *Literacy and the Social Order.* Cambridge: Cambridge University Press, 1980.

_____. "Gender Trouble and Cross-Dressing in Early Modern England." *Journal of British Studies* 35 (1996).

Crewe, Jonathan. *Unredeemed Rhetoric: Thomas Nashe and the Scandal of Authorship.* Baltimore: Johns Hopkins University Press, 1982.

Croxall, Samuel. *A Select Collection of Novels and Histories.* London: John Watts, 1720.

Crupi, Charles W. *Robert Greene.* Boston: Twayne Publications, 1986.

Cuvelier, Elaine. "Horror and Cruelty in the Works of Three Elizabethan Novelists." *Cahiers Elisabethains* 19 (1981): 39-51.

_____. *Thomas Lodge: Témoin de son temps (c. 1558-1625).* Paris: Didier Érudition, 1984.

Danby, John F. *Poets on Fortune's Hill: Studies in Sidney, Shakespeare, Beaumont and Fletcher.* London: Faber & Faber, 1952.

Danson, Lawrence. *Shakespeare's Dramatic Genres.* Oxford: Oxford University Press, 2000.

Darnton, Robert. *The Great Cat Massacre and Other Episodes in French Cultural History.* New York: Basic Books, 1984.

_____. *The Kiss of Lamourette: Reflections on Cultural History.* New York: Norton, 1990.

Davis, Walter. *A Map of Arcadia: Sidney's Romance in its Tradition*. New Haven: Yale University Press, 1965.

_____. "Masking in Arden: The Histrionics of Lodge's *Rosalynde*." *Studies in English Literature* 5 (1965): 151-63.

_____. *Idea and Act in Elizabethan Fiction*. Princeton: Princeton University Press, 1969.

De Certeau, Michel. *The Practice of Everyday Life*. Rendall, Steven, trans. Berkeley: University of California Press, 1984.

DeJean, Joan E. *Tender Geographies: Women and the Origins of the Novel in France*. New York: Columbia University Press, 1991.

Dekker, Thomas. *The Wonderful Year. 1603. The Non-Dramatic Works of Thomas Dekker*. Alexander Grosart, ed. Four volumes. London: Huth Library, 1884.

Dent, Arthur. *A Sermon of Repentance...* London: [J]ohn Harison, 1598.

Di Biase, Carmine. "The Decline of Euphuism: Robert Greene's Struggle with Popular Taste." *Critical Approaches to English Prose Fiction 1520-1640*. Beecher, Donald, ed. Ottawa: Dovehouse Editions, 1998: 85-108.

Dickenson, John. *Greene in Conceipt. Occasional Issues of Unique or Very Rare Books*. Grosart, Alexander, ed., 16 volumes. London: Private Subscription, 1878.

Dipple, Elizabeth. "'Unjust Justice' in the *Old Arcadia*." *Studies in English Literature* 10 (1970): 83-101.

Doody, Margaret. "Heliodorus Rewritten: Samuel Richardson's *Clarissa* and Frances Burney's *Wanderer*." *The Search for the Ancient Novel*. Tatum, James, ed. Baltimore: Johns Hopkins University Press, 1994: 117-31.

_____. *The True Story of the Novel*. New Brunswick: Rutgers University Press, 1996.

Dowden, Edward. *Shakspere*. London: Macmillan, 1877.

Dubrow, Heather. *Genre*. London: Methuen, 1982.

Dudley, Edward. *The Endless Text:* Don Quixote *and the Hermeneutics of Romance*. Binghampton: State University of New York Press, 1997.

Duncan-Jones, Katherine. "Nashe and Sidney: The Tournament Scene in *The Unfortunate Traveler*." *Modern Language Review* 63 (1968): 3-7.

_____. *Sir Philip Sidney: Courtier Poet*. New Haven: Yale University Press, 1991.

Dunn, Kevin. *Pretexts of Authority: The Rhetoric of Authorship in the Renaissance Preface*. Stanford: Stanford University Press, 1994.

Duplessis, Robert S. *Transitions to Capitalism in Early Modern Europe*. Cambridge: Cambridge University Press, 1997.

Eco, Umberto, "The Myth of Superman." *The Role of the Reader: Explorations in the Semiotics of Texts*. Bloomington: Indiana University Press, 1979.

Eden, Kathy. *Hermeneutics and the Rhetorical Tradition: Chapters in the Ancient Legacy and its Humanist Reception*. New Haven: Yale University Press, 1997.

Edwards, Philip. "Unfortunate Travelers: Fiction and Reality." *Huntington Library Quarterly* 50 (1987): 295-307.

Eichner, Hans, ed. *'Romantic' and Its Cognates: The European History of a Word*. Toronto: University of Toronto Press, 1972.

Eisenstein, Elizabeth. *The Printing Press as an Agent of Change: Communications and Cultural Transformations in Early-Modern Europe*. Two volumes. Cambridge: Cambridge University Press, 1979.

Ellrich, Robert J. "Prologomenon: or, Preliminary Musings to make the gentle reader think, or fume, or snort. In which we modestly propose to deal with the origin, history, and meaning of Romance." *Para-doxa* 3 (1997): 239-85.

Elton, William. King Lear *and the Gods*. San Marino: Huntington Library Press, 1968.

Empson, William. *The Structure of Complex Words*. New York: New Directions 1951.

Erasmus, Desiderius. *The Adages of Erasmus: A Study with Translations*. Phillips, Margaret Mann, ed. Cambridge: Cambridge University Press, 1964.

Erne, Lukas. "Biography and Mythography: Rereading Chettle's Alleged Apology to Shakespeare." *English Studies* 79 (1998): 430-40.

_____. *Shakespeare as Literary Dramatist.* Cambridge: Cambridge University Press, 2003.

Farrell, Joseph. "Classical Genre in Theory and Practice." *New Literary History* 34:3 (Summer 2003): 383-408.

Febvre, Lucien, and Henri-Jean Martin. *The Coming of the Book: The Impact of Printing 1450-1800.* Gerard, David, trans. Geoffrey Nowell-Smitth, and David Wooton, eds. London: NLB, 1976.

Felperin, Howard. "Romance and Romanticism: Some Reflections on *The Tempest* and *Heart of Darkness,* Or When is Romance No Longer Romance?" *Shakespeare's Romances Reconsidered.* Hay, Carol McGinis, and Henry Jacobs, eds. Lincoln: University of Nebraska Press, 1979.

Ferguson, Margaret. "Nashe's *Unfortunate Traveler*: The 'Newes of the Maker' Game." *English Literary History* 11 (1981): 165-82.

Field, B.S., Jr. "Sidney's Influence: The Evidence of the Publication History of the History of Argalus and Parthenia." *English Language Notes* 17 (1979): 98-102.

Fielding Henry. *The History of Tom Jones, a Foundling.* Baker, Sheridan, ed. 2nd ed. New York: Norton, 1995.

Fish, Stanley. "Author-Readers: Ben Jonson's Community of the Same." *Representations* 7 (Summer 1984): 26-58.

Fishelov, David. *Metaphors of Genre: The Role of Analogies in Genre Theory.* State College: Penn State University Press, 1993.

Fleming, Juliet. "The Ladies' Man and the Age of Elizabeth." *Sexuality and Gender in Early Modern Europe: Institutions, Texts, Images.* Turner, James Grantham, ed. Cambridge: Cambridge University Press, 1993: 158-181.

Forcione, Alban. *Cervantes, Aristotle, and the 'Persiles.'* Princeton: Princeton University Press, 1970.

Fowler, Alastair. *Kinds of Literature: An Introduction to the Theory of Genres and Modes.* Cambridge, MA: Harvard University Press, 1982.

_____. *Renaissance Realism: Narrative Images in Literature and Art*. Oxford: Oxford University Press, 2003.

_____. "The Formation of Genres in the Renaissance and After." *New Literary History* 34:2 (Spring 2003): 185-200.

Frederickson, Paula. "Repentance." *The Oxford Companion to the Bible*. Metzger, Bruce M., and Michael D. Coogan, eds. New York: Oxford University Press, 1993.

Fry, Paul. *A Defense of Poetry: Reflections on the Occasion of Writing*. Stanford: Stanford University Press, 1995.

Frye, Northrop. *Anatomy of Criticism: Four Essays*. Princeton: Princeton University Press, 1957.

_____. *The Secular Scripture: A Study of the Structure of Romance*. Cambridge, MA: Harvard University Press, 1976.

Genette, Gerard. *Paratexts: Thresholds of Interpretation*. Lewin, Jane E., trans. Cambridge: Cambridge University Press, 1997.

Girard, René. *Deceit, Desire, and the Novel: Self and Other in Literary Structure*. Freccero, Yvonne, trans. Baltimore: Johns Hopkins University Press, 1965.

Godshalk, William Leigh. "Sidney's Revision of the *Arcadia*, Books III-V." *Philological Quarterly* 43 (1964): 171-84.

Goldhill, Simon. *Foucault's Virginity: Ancient Erotic Fiction and the History of Sexuality*. Cambridge: Cambridge University Press, 1995.

Golkhe, Madelon S. "Wits Wantoness: *The Unfortunate Traveler* as Picaresque." *Studies in Philology* 73 (1976): 397-413.

Gracia, Jorge. *A Theory of Textuality: The Logic and Epistemology*. Albany: State University of New York Press, 1995.

_____. *Texts: Ontological Status, Identity, Author, Audience*. Albany: State University of New York Press, 1996.

Grafton, Anthony. *Commerce with the Classics: Ancient Books & Renaissance Readers*. Ann Arbor: Michigan University Press, 1997.

Grafton, Anthony, and Lisa Jardine. "'Studied for Action': How Gabriel Harvey Read His Livy." *Past and Present* 129 (1990): 30-78.

Greenblatt, Stephen. "Sidney's *Arcadia* and the Mixed Mode." *Studies in Philology* 70 (1973): 269-78.

_____. *Renaissance Self-Fashioning: From More to Shakespeare.* Chicago: University of Chicago Press, 1980.

_____. "Murdering Peasants: Status, Genre, and the Representation of Rebellion." *Representations* 1 (1983): 1-29.

_____. *Shakespearean Negotiations: The Circulation of Social Energy in Renaissance England.* Berkeley: University of California Press, 1988.

Greene, Robert. *The Complete Works in Prose and Verse of Robert Greene, M.A.* Grosart, Alexander B., ed. Fourteen volumes. London: Huth Library, 1881-86.

_____, and Thomas Lodge. *A Looking Glasse for London and England.* Hayashi, Testumaro, ed. Metuchen: Scarecrow Press, 1970.

_____. *Greenes Groatsworth of Wit, Bought with a Million of Repentance.* Carroll, D. Allen, ed. Binghamton: Medieval and Renaissance Texts and Studies, 1994.

_____. *Menaphon: Camilla's Alarm to slumbering Euphues in his melancholy cell at Silexedra.* Cantar, Brenda, ed. Ottawa: Dovehouse Editions, 1996.

_____. *Gwyndonius, or The Card of Fancy.* Di Biase, Carmine, ed. Ottawa: Dovehouse Editions, 2001.

Greenhalagh, Darlene G. "Love, Chastity, and Women's Erotic Power: Greek Romance in Elizabethan and Jacobean Contexts." *Prose Fiction and Early Modern Sexualities in England, 1570-1640.* Relihan, Constance C., and Goran Stanivukovic, eds. New York: Palgrave Macmillan, 2003: 15-42.

Greville, Sir Fulke. *The Prose Works of Fulke Greville Lord Brooke.* Gouws, John, ed. Oxford: Clarendon Press, 1986.

Guillén, Claudio. *Literature as System: Essays toward the Theory of Literary History.* Princeton: Princeton University Press, 1971.

Hackett, Helen. *Women and Romance Fiction in the English Renaissance.* Cambridge: Cambridge University Press, 2000.

Hägg, Tomas. *The Novel in Antiquity.* Berkeley: University of California Press,1983.

Haigh, Christopher. *English Reformations: Religion, Politics, and Society under the Tudors.* Oxford: Clarendon Press, 1993.

Halasz, Alexandra. *The Marketplace of Print: Pamphlets and the Public Sphere in Early Modern England.* Cambridge: Cambridge University Press, 1997.

Halpern, Richard. *The Poetics of Primitive Accumulation: English Renaissance Culture and the Genealogy of Capitalism.* Ithaca: Cornell University Press,.

Hamilton, A. C. "Sidney's *Arcadia* as Prose Fiction: Its Relation to Its Sources." *English Literary Renaissance* 2 (1972): 29-60.

_____. "Elizabethan Romance: The Example of Prose Fiction." *English Literary History* 49 (1982): 287-99.

_____. "Elizabethan Prose Fiction and Some Trends in Recent Criticism." *Renaissance Quarterly* 37 (1984): 21-33.

Hardison, O. B., Jr. "The Two Voices of Sidney's *Apology for Poetry.*" *English Literary Renaissance* 2 (1972): 83-99.

Harrington, Susan M., and Bond, Michael N. "'Good Sir, Be Ruld by Me': Patterns of Domination and Manipulation in Thomas Nashe's *The Unfortunate Traveler.*" *Studies in Short Fiction* 24 (1987): 243-50.

Harvey, Gabriel. *Foure Letters and certaine Sonnets.* Hardison, G. B., ed. London: Bodley Head, 1922.

Hayes, Gerald R. "Anthony Munday's Romances of Chivalry." *The Library.* 4th ser. 6 (1925-6): 57-81.

Heffernan, Thomas J. *Sacred Biography: Saints and Their Biographers in the Middle Ages.* Oxford: Oxford University Press, 1988.

Heisermann, Arthur. *The Novel Before the Novel.* Chicago: University of Chicago Press, 1977.

Helgerson, Richard. *The Elizabethan Prodigals*. Berkeley: University of California Press, 1976.

_____. *Self-Crowned Laureates: Spenser, Jonson, Milton, and the Literary System*. Berkeley: University of California Press, 1983.

_____. *Forms of Nationhood: The Elizabethan Writing of England*. Chicago: University of Chicago Press, 1992.

Heliodorus. *L'Histoire Aethiopique de Heliodorus*. Amyot, Jacques trans. Paris: Estienne Groulleau, 1547.

_____. *Aethiopicae Historiae*. Warschewiczki, Stanislaus, trans. Basel: Johannes Oporinus, 1552.

_____. *An Aethiopian Historie*. Underdowne, Thomas, trans. London: Francis Coldocke, 1569.

_____. *An Aethiopian Historie*. L'Isle, William, trans. London, 1638.

_____. *An Aethiopian Historie of Heliodorus*. Underdowne, Thomas, trans. George Saintsbury, ed. London: Simpkin, Marshall, Hamilton, Kent, and Co., 1925.

_____. *Le Ethiopiche di Eliodoro*. Colonna, Aristide, ed. Torino: Unione Tipografico-Editrice Torinese, 1987.

_____. *An Ethiopian Story*. Morgan, J. R., trans. *Collected Ancient Greek Novels*. B. P. Reardon, ed. Berkeley: University of California Press, 1989: 349-588.

Hernadi, Paul. *Beyond Genre: New Directions in Literary Classification*. Ithaca: Cornell University Press, 1972.

Hibbard, G. R. *Thomas Nashe: A Critical Introduction*. Cambridge, MA: Harvard University Press, 1962.

Hilliard, Stephen. *The Singularity of Thomas Nashe*. Lincoln: University of Nebraska Press, 1986.

Hirsh, E. D. *Validity in Interpretation*. New Haven: Yale University Press, 1967.

Hornat, Jaroslav. "*Mamillia*: Robert Greene's Controversy with *Euphues*." *Philologica Pragensia 5* (1963): 210-18.

Huet, Pierre-Daniel. "The History of Romances." *Select Collection of Novels and Romances*. London: John Watts, 1720.

Hughes, Felicity. "Gascoigne's Poses." *Studies in English Literature* 37 (1997): 1-19.

Hutson, Lorna. *Thomas Nashe in Context*. Oxford: Clarendon Press, 1989.

_____. "Fortunate Travelers: Reading for the Plot in Elizabethan England." *Representations* 41 (1993): 83-103.

_____. *The Usurer's Daughter: Male Friendship and Fictions of Women in Sixteenth-Century England*. London: Routledge, 1994.

Iser, Wolfgang. *The Implied Reader: Patterns of Communication in Prose Fiction from Bunyan to Beckett*. Baltimore: Johns Hopkins University Press, 1974.

_____. *The Act of Reading: A Theory of Aesthetic Response*. Baltimore: Johns Hopkins University Press, 1978.

Jameson, Frederic. *The Political Unconscious: Narrative as a Socially Symbolic Act*. Ithaca: Cornell University Press, 1981.

_____. *Postmodernism, or the Cultural Logic of Late Capitalism*. Durham: Duke University Press, 1991.

Jauss, Hans Robert. *Toward an Aesthetic of Reception*. Bahti, Timothy, trans. Paul de Man, intro. Minneapolis: University of Minnesota Press, 1982.

Javitch, Daniel. "Italian Epic Theory." *The Cambridge Companion to Literary Criticism, Volume 3: The Renaissance*. Norton, Glyn P., ed. Cambridge: Cambridge University Press, 1989.

Jayne, Edward. *Negative Poetics*. Iowa City: University of Iowa Press, 1992.

Jeffrey, Violet. *John Lyly and the Italian Renaissance*. Paris: Champion, 1929.

Johns, Adrian. *The Nature of the Book: Print and Knowledge in the Making*. Chicago: University of Chicago Press, 1998.

Johnson, Gerald D. "John Busby and the Stationers' Trade, 1590-1612." *Library* 6th series 7 (1985): 1-15.

Johnson, Richard. *The Most Pleasant History of Tom a Lincolne.* Hirsh, Richard S. M., ed. Columbia: University of South Carolina Press, 1978.

Jones, Ann Rosalind. "Inside the Outsider: Nashe's *Unfortunate Traveler* and Bahktin's Polyphonic Novel." *English Literary History* 50 (1983): 61-81.

Jonson, Ben. *The Complete Poems of Ben Jonson.* Parfitt, George, ed., Harmondsworth: Penguin, 1975.

Jordan, John Clark. *Robert Greene.* New York: Oxford University Press, 1915.

Jusserand, J. J. *The English Novel in the Time of Shakespeare.* Lee, Elizabeth, trans. London: Fisher Unwin, 1899.

Kahn, Victoria. "Humanism and the Resistance to Theory." *Literary Theory/Renaissance Texts.* Parker, Patricia, and David Quint, eds. Baltimore: Johns Hopkins University Press, 1986.

_____. "Margaret Cavendish and the Romance of Contract." *Renaissance Quarterly* 50: 2 (1997): 526-66.

Kastan, David Scott. *Shakespeare and the Book.* Cambridge: Cambridge University Press, 2001.

Kaufmann, Linda S. *Discourses of Desire: Gender, Genre, and Epistolary Fictions.* Ithaca: Cornell University Press, 1986.

Kaula, David. "The Low Style in Nashe's *The Unfortunate Traveler.*" *Studies in English Literature* 6 (1966): 43-57.

Keefer, Michael. "Violence and Extremity: Nashe's *Unfortunate Traveler* as an Anatomy of Abjection." *Critical Approaches to English Prose Fiction.* Beecher, Donald, ed. Ottawa: Dovehouse Editions, 1998: 183-218.

Kenyon, Frederick G. *Books and Readers in Ancient Greece and Rome.* Oxford: Oxford University Press, 1951.

Ker, W. P. *Epic and Romance: Essays on Medieval Literature.* New York: Dover Publications, 1957. Repr. of 1905 ed.

Kermode, Frank. *The Sense of an Ending: Studies in the Theory of Fiction*. Oxford: Oxford University Press, 1966.

Kiefer, Frederick. "Fortune and Providence in the *Mirror for Magistrates*." *Studies in Philology* 74 (1977): 146-64.

Kinney, Arthur F. *Humanist Poetics: Thought, Rhetoric, and Fiction in Sixteenth-Century England*. Amherst: University of Massachusetts Press, 1986.

_____. "Intimations of Mortality: Sidney's Journey from Flushing to Zutphen." *Sir Philip Sidney: 1586 and the Creation of a Legend*. Dorston, Jan van, Baker-Smith, Dominic, and Arthur Kinney, eds. Amherst: University of Massachusetts Press, 1986: 125-48.

_____. "Marketing Fiction." *Critical Approaches to English Prose Fiction 1520-1640*. Beecher, Donald, ed. Ottawa: Dovehouse Editions, 1998: 45-61.

Kinney, Claire. "Chivalry Unmasked: Courtly Spectacle and the Abuses of Romance in Sidney's *New Arcadia*." *Studies in English Literature* 35 (1995): 35-52.

Kirkpatrick, Jean. *English and Italian Literature from Dante to Shakespeare: A Study of Source, Analogue, and Divergence*. London: Longman, 1995.

Konstan, David. *Sexual Symmetry: Love in the Ancient Novel and Related Genres*. Princeton: Princeton University Press, 1994.

Koppenfels, Werner von. "Two Notes on *Imprese*: Daniels' Additions to *The Worthy Tract of Paulus Iovius*; Sidney's *Arcadia* and The Tournament Scene of the Unfortunate Traveler." *Renaissance Quarterly* 24 (1971): 13-25.

Kusakawa, Sachiko. *The Transformation of Natural Philosophy: The Case of Philip Melanchthon*. Cambridge: Cambridge University Press, 1995.

Lamb, Mary Ellen. "Exhibiting Class and Displaying the Body in Sidney's *Countess of Pembroke's Arcadia*." *Studies in English Literature* 37 (1997): 55-72.

Lamberton, Robert. *Homer the Theologian: Neoplatonist Allegorical Reading and the Growth of the Epic Tradition*. Berkeley: University of California Press, 1989.

Langer, Ullrich. "The Renaissance Novella as Justice." *Renaissance Quarterly* 52:2 (Summer 1999): 311-41.

Languet, Hubert, and Sidney, Sir Philip. *The Correspondence of Sir Philip Sidney and Hubert Languet*. Pears, Seuart A., ed. London: William Pickering, 1845.

Lanham, Richard. "Personality as Structure in *The Unfortunate Traveler*." *Studies in Short Fiction* 3 (1967): 201-16.

Larson, Charles. "Lodge's *Rosalind*: Decorum in Arden." *Studies in Short Fiction* 14 (1977): 117-27.

Laslett, Peter. *The World We Have Lost: England Before the Industrial Age*. 2nd ed. New York: Charles Scribner's Sons, 1971.

Latham, Agnes. "Satire on Literary Themes and Modes in Nashe's *Unfortunate Traveler*." *English Studies* 1 (1948): 85-100.

Lawry, Jon S. *Sidney's Two Arcadias: Pattern and Proceeding*. Ithaca: Cornell University Press, 1972.

Leggat, Alexander. "Artistic Coherence in *The Unfortunate Traveler*." *Studies in English Literature* 14 1974): 31-46.

Levi-Strauss, Claude. "How Myths Die." *Structural Anthropology*, Volume 2. Layten, Monique, trans. New York: Basic Books, 1963.

_____. *The Savage Mind*. Chicago: University of Chicago Press, 1966.

Lewis, C. S. *English Literature in the Sixteenth Century, Excluding Drama*. Oxford: Clarendon, 1954.

Lindberg, Carter. *The European Reformations*. Oxford: Blackwell, 1996.

Lindenbaum, Peter. "Sidney's *Arcadia* as Cultural Monument and Proto-Novel." *Texts and Cultural Change in Early Modern England*. Brown, Cedric C., and Arthur F. Marotti, eds. New York: St. Martin's Press, 1997: 80-94.

Lindheim, Nancy. "Vision, Revision, and the 1593 Text of Sidney's *Arcadia*." *English Literary Renaissance* 2 (1972): 136-47.

_____. "Lyly's Golden Legacy: *Rosalynde* and *Pandosto*." *Studies in English Literature* 15 (1973): 3-20.

—————. *The Structures of Sidney's* Arcadia. Toronto: University of Toronto Press, 1982.

Lodge, Thomas. *The Complete Works of Thomas Lodge.* Gosse, Edmund, ed. Five volumes. Glasgow: The Hunterian Club, 1883.

—————. *Rosalind: Euphues' Golden Legacy Found After His Death in His Cell at Silexedra (1590).* Beecher, Donald, ed. Ottawa: Dovehouse Editions, 1997.

Loewenstein, Joseph. "The Script in the Marketplace." *Representations* 12 (Fall 1985): 101-14.

—————. *Ben Jonson and Possessive Authorship.* Cambridge: Cambridge University Press, 2002.

—————. *The Author's Due: Printing and the Prehistory of Copyright.* Chicago: University of Chicago Press, 2002.

Lowe, N. J. *The Classical Plot and the Invention of Western Narrative.* Cambridge: Cambridge University Press, 2000.

Lucas, Caroline. *Writing for Women: The Example of Woman as Reader in Elizabethan Romance.* Philadelphia: Open University Press, 1989.

Lucian. *A True Story.* B.P. Reardon, trans. *Collected Ancient Greek Novels.* B. P. Reardon, ed. Berkeley: University of California Press, 1989: 619-649.

Lukács, Georg. *The Theory of the Novel: A Historico-Philosophical Essay on the Forms of Great Epic Literature.* Bostock, Ann, trans. Cambridge, MA: MIT Press, 1994.

Luther, Martin, and Erasmus, Desiderius. *Luther and Erasmus: Free Will and Salvation.* Rupp, E. Gordon, and Philip S Watson, eds. Philadelphia: Westminster Press, 1969.

Lyly, John. *Euphues.* Croll, Morris William, and Harry Clemons, eds. New York: E. P. Dutton & Co., 1916.

—————. *Euphues: The Anatomy of Wit. An Anthology of Elizabethan Prose Fiction.* Salzman, Paul, ed. Oxford: Oxford University Press, 1987.

MacAlister, Suzanne. *Dreams and Suicides: The Greek Novel from Antiquity to the Byzantine Empire.* London: Routledge, 1996.

MacDonald, Virginia. "Robert Greene's Courtesan: A Renaissance Perception of a Medieval Tale." *Zeitschrift für Anglistik und Amerikanistik* 32 (1984): 210-19.

Machiavelli, Niccoló. *The Prince.* Ricci, Luigi, and E. P. R. Vincent, trans. Gauss, Christian, intro. New York: Times Mirror, 1952.

Manguel, Alberto. *A History of Reading.* New York: Viking, 1996.

Manley, Lawrence. *Literature and Culture in Early Modern London.* Cambridge: Cambridge University Press, 1995.

Margolies, David. *Novel and Society in Elizabethan England.* London: Croom Helm, 1985.

Marius, Richard. *Martin Luther: The Christian Between God and Death.* Cambridge, MA: Belknap Press, 1999.

Marrotti, Arthur F. *Manuscript, Print, and the English Renaissance Lyric.* Ithaca: Cornell University Press, 1995.

Maslen, Robert W. *Elizabethan Fictions: Espionage, Counter-Espionage, and the Duplicity of Fiction in Early Elizabethan Prose Narrative.* Oxford: Clarendon Press, 1997.

_____. "Lodge's *Glaucus and Silla* and the Conditions of Catholic Authorship in Elizabethan England." *EnterText* 3.1 (Spring 2003): 59-100.

Masten, Jeffrey. *Textual Intercourse: Collaboration, Authorship, and Sexualities in Renaissance Drama.* Cambridge: Cambridge University Press, 1997.

May, Stephen W. "Tudor Aristocrats and the Mythical 'Stigma of Print.'" *Renaissance Papers* 10 (1980): 11-18.

McCanles, Michael. "Oracular Prediction and the Fore-conceit of Sidney's *Arcadia.*" *English Literary History* 50 (1983): 233-44.

_____. *The Texts of Sidney's Arcadian World.* Durham: Duke University Press, 1989.

McClure, Millar. *Register of Sermons Preached at Paul's Cross, 1534-1642.* Boswell, Jackson Campbell, and Peter Pauls, ed. and augmented. Ottawa: Dovehouse Editions, 1989.

McCoy, Richard. *Sir Philip Sidney: Rebellion in Arcadia.* New Brunswick: Rutgers University Press, 1979.

_____. "Gascoigne's 'Poemata castrada': The Wages of Courtly Success." *Criticism* 27 (1985): 29-55.

_____. *The Rites of Knighthood: The Literature and Politics of Elizabethan Chivalry.* Berkeley: University of California Press, 1989.

McDermott, Hubert. *Novel and Romance: The* Odyssey *to* Tom Jones. London: Macmillan, 1989.

McGinn, Donald J. *Thomas Nashe.* Boston: Twayne Publications, 1981.

McKeon, Michael. *The Origins of the English Novel 1600-1740.* Baltimore: Johns Hopkins University Press, 1987.

McPherson, C. B. *The Political Theory of Possessive Individualism.* Oxford: Oxford University Press, 1962.

Melanchthon, Philip. *Commentarii ad Epistolam Pauli ad Romanos. Melanchtons Werke.* Gütersloh: Gütersloher Verlagshaus Gerd Mohn, 1965.

Mentz, Steve. "Selling Sidney: William Ponsonby, Thomas Nashe, and the Boundaries of Elizabethan Print and Manuscript Cultures." *TEXT* 13 (2000): 124-47.

_____. "Wearing Greene: Robert Greene, Autolycus, and the Structure of Romance in *The Winter's Tale.*" *Renaissance Drama* 30 (1999-2001): 73-92.

_____. "The Heroine as Courtesan: Dishonesty, Romance, and the Sense of an Ending in *The Unfortunate Traveler.*" *Studies in Philology* 98 (2001): 339-58.

_____. "The Thigh and the Sword: Gender, Genre, and Sexy Dressing in Sidney's *New Arcadia.*" *Prose Fiction and Early Modern Sexualities.* Relihan, Constance and Goran Stanivukovic, eds. (New York: Palgrave, 2003) 77-91.

_____. "Reason, Faith, and Shipwreck in Sidney's *New Arcadia.*" *Studies in English Literature* 44:1 (Winter 2004): 1-18.

_____. "Escaping Italy: From Novella to Romance in Gascoigne and Lyly." *Studies in Philology*, 101:2 (Spring 2004) 253-71.

_____. "Magic Books: Cony-Catching and the Romance of Early Modern London." *Rogues and Early Modern English Culture*. Dionne, Craig, and Steve Mentz, eds. Ann Arbor: University of Michigan Press, 2004: 240-58.

_____. "Forming Greene: Theorizing the Early Modern Author in the *Groatsworth of Wit*." *Robert Greene: Page and Stage*. Gieskes, Edward, and Kirk Melinkoff, eds. Aldershot: Ashgate Publishing, forthcoming.

Mentz, Steve and Craig Dionne, eds. *Rogues and Early Modern English Culture*. Ann Arbor: University of Michigan Press, 2004.

Meres, Frances. *Palladis Tamia. Elizabethan Critical Essays*. Smith, G. Gregory, ed., Two volumes. Oxford: Oxford University Press, 1904.

Merkelbach, Reinhold. *Roman und Mysterium in der Antike*. Munich: Bech, 1962.

Middleton, Thomas. *The Black Book. The Works of Thomas Middleton*. Bullen, A. H., ed. 8 volumes. Boston: Houghton Mifflin, 1886.

Miller, Edwin Haviland. "The Relationship of Robert Greene and Thomas Nashe (1588-1592)." *Philological Quarterly* 33 (1954): 353-67.

_____. *The Professional Writer in Elizabethan England*. Cambridge, MA: Harvard University Press, 1959.

Montalvo, Garci Rodrígez de. *Amadis of Gaul*. 2nd ed. Place, Edwin B., and Herbert C. Behm, trans. Lexington: University Press of Kentucky, 2003.

Montaigne, Michel de. *The Complete Essays of Montaigne*. Frame, Donald M., trans. Stanford: Stanford University Press, 1958.

Morgan, John R. "A Sense of the Ending: The Conclusion of Heliodoros' *Aethiopika*." *Transactions of the American Philological Association* 99 (1989): 299-320.

_____. "The Story of Knemon in Heliodoros' *Aethiopika*." *Journal of Hellenic Studies* 109 (1989): 99-113.

_____. "Reader and Audience in the *Aithiopika* of Heliodoros." *Groningen Colloquia on the Novel* IV (1991): 85-102.

Mornay, Philip du Plessis. *A Woorke Concerning the Trewnesse of the Christian Religion*. Delmar, NY: Scholars's Facsimiles and Reprints, 1976.

Mowat, Barbara. "Rogues, Shepherds, and the Counterfeit Distressed: Texts and Infracontexts of *The Winter's Tale* 4.3." *Shakespeare Studies* 22 (1994): 58-76.

_____. "The Theater and Literary Culture." *A New History of Early English Drama*. Cox, J. C., and David S. Kastan, eds. New York: Columbia University Press, 1997: 213-30.

_____. "'What's in a Name?': Tragicomedy, Romance, or Late Comedy." *A Companion to Shakespeare's Works, Volume 4: The Poems, Problem Comedies, Late Plays*. Dutton, Richard, and Jean E. Howard, eds. Oxford: Blackwell, 2003.

Munday, Anthony. *Zelauto: The Fountaine of Fame (1580)*. Jack Stillinger, ed. Carbondale: Southern Illinois University Press, 1963.

Nashe, Thomas. *The Works of Thomas Nashe*. McKerrow, R. B., ed. F. P. Wilson, rev. Oxford: Oxford University Press, 1966.

_____. *The Unfortunate Traveler and Other Works*. Steane, J. B., ed. New York: Penguin, 1985.

_____. "To the Gentlemen Students of Both Universities." *Menaphon*. Cantar, Brenda, ed. Ottawa: Dovehouse Editions, 1996: 81-94.

Newcomb, Lori Humphrey. *Reading Popular Romance in Early Modern England*. New York: Columbia University Press, 2002.

_____. "Gendering Prose Romance in Renaissance England." *The Blackwell Companion to Romance*. Saunders, Corinne, ed. (London: Blackwell, 2004).

Nicholl, Charles. *A Cup of News: The Life of Thomas Nashe*. London: Routledge and Keegan Paul, 1984.

Null, Ashley. "The Rise of Repentance: Towards a Recovery of Anglican Identity." Unpublished Dissertation. New Haven: Yale Divinity School, 1989.

O'Connor, John Joseph. *'Amadis de Gaulle' and Its Influence on Elizabethan Literature*. New Brunswick: Rutgers University Press, 1970.

Orgel, Stephen. "Shakespeare and the Kinds of Drama." *Critical Inquiry* 6 (1979): 107-23.

*Oxford Classical Dictionary*. Hammond, N. G. L., and H. H. Scullar, eds. 2nd edition. Oxford: Clarendon Press, 1970.

*Oxford Companion to the Bible*. Metzger, Bruce M., and Michael D. Coogan, eds. Oxford: Oxford University Press, 1993.

*Oxford English Dictionary*. 2nd Edition. Oxford: Clarendon Press, 1989.

Paradise, N. Burton. *Thomas Lodge: The History of an Elizabethan*. New Haven: Yale University Press, 1931.

Parker, Patricia. *Inescapable Romance: Studies in the Poetics of a Mode*. Princeton: Princeton University Press, 1979.

Patchell, Mary. *The* Palmerin *Romances in Elizabethan England*. New York: Columbia University Press, 1937.

Patterson, Annabel. *Censorship and Interpretation: The Conditions of Reading and Writing in Early Modern England*. Madison: University of Wisconsin Press, 1984.

_____. *Reading Holished's Chronicles*. Chicago: University of Chicago Press, 1994.

Pavel, Thomas. "Literary Genres as Norms and Good Habits." *New Literary History* 34: 2 (Spring 2003): 201-210.

Pearson, Nicholas Holmes. "Literary Forms and Types; or, A Defence of Polonius." *English Institute Annual 1940*. New York: AMS Press, 1965.

Perry, B. E. *The Ancient Romances: A Literary-Historical Account of Their Origins*. Berkeley: University of California Press, 1967.

Pettie, George. *A Petite Pallace of Pettie His Pleasure*. Hartman, Herbert, ed. New York: Barnes and Noble, 1970. Repr. of Oxford University Press, 1938.

"Philip the Philosopher." "An Interpretation of the Modest Chariclea from the Lips of Philip the Philosopher." Lamberton, Robert, trans. *Homer the Theologian: Neoplatonist Allegorical Reading and the Growth of the Epic Tradition*. Berkeley: University of California Press, 1989: 306-11.

Pierce, Frank. *Amadis de Gaula.* Boston: Twayne, 1976.

Pinhiero, Marilla Futre. "Calasiris' Story and its Narrative Significance in Heliodorus' *Aethiopica.*" *Groningen Colloquia on the Novel* IV (1991): 69-83.

Pollack, Claudette. "Romance and Realism in Lodge's *Robin the Devil.*" *Studies in Short Fiction* 13 (1976): 491-97.

Polyani, Karl. *The Great Transformation.* New York: Rinehart and Company, 1944.

Propp, V. *Morphology of the Folktale.* Scott, Laurence, trans. Louis A Wagner, ed. Svatava Pirkova-Jacobson, and Alan Dundes, intro. Austin: University of Texas Press, 1968.

Pruvost, René. *Robert Greene et ses romans: Contributions à l'histoire de la Renaissance en Angleterre.* Paris: Société d'Editions 'Les Belles Lettres,' 1938.

Quint, David. *Epic and Empire: Politics and Generic Form from Virgil to Milton.* Princeton: Princeton University Press, 1993.

_____. *Cervantes's Novel of Modern Times: A New Reading of* Don Quijote. Princeton: Princeton University Press, 2003.

"R. B." *Greenes Funerals.* Harrison, G. B. ed. London: Sidgwick & Jackson, 1911.

Radway, Janice. *Reading the Romance: Women, Patriarchy, and Popular Literature.* Chapel Hill: North Carolina University Press, 1984, 1991.

_____. *A Feeling for Books: The Book-of-the-Month Club, Literary Taste, and Middle-Class Desire.* Chapel Hill: University of North Carolina Press, 1997.

Rae, Wesley D. *Thomas Lodge.* Boston: Twayne Publishers, 1967.

Ranson, Nicholas D. "The Date of Greene's 'Vision' Revisited." *Notes & Queries* n. s. 22 (1975): 534-5.

Raymond, Joad. *Pamphlets and Pamphleteering in Early Modern Britain.* Cambridge: Cambridge University Press, 2003.

Reardon, B. P, ed. *Collected Ancient Greek Novels.* Berkeley: University of California Press, 1989.

_____. *The Form of Greek Romance*. Princeton: Princeton University Press, 1991.

Reed, Walter L. *An Exemplary History of the Novel: The Quixotic versus the Picaresque*. Chicago: University of Chicago Press, 1981.

Rees, Joan. *Sir Philip Sidney and Arcadia*. Cranbury, NJ: Associated University Presses, 1991.

Relihan, Constance. *Fashioning Authority: The Development of Elizabethan Novelistic Discourse*. Kent: Kent State University Press, 1994.

_____. "Rhetoric, Gender, and Audience Construction in Thomas Nashe's *The Unfortunate Traveler*." *Framing Elizabethan Fictions: Contemporary Approaches to Early Modern Narrative Prose*. Relihan, Constance, ed. Kent: Kent State University Press, 1996: 141-52.

_____. "Humanist Learning, Eloquent Women, and the Use of Latin in Robert Greene's *Ciceronis Amor/Tullie's Love*," *Explorations in Renaissance Culture* 27:1 (Summer 2001): 1-19.

Rhodes, Neil. "Nashe, Rhetoric, and Satire." *Jacobean Poetry and Prose: Rhetoric, Representation, and the Popular Imagination*. Bloom, Clive, ed. London; Macmillan, 1988: 25-43.

Rhu, Lawrence F. *The Genesis of Tasso's Narrative Theory: English Translations of the Early Poetics and a Comparative Study of Their Significance*. Detroit: Wayne State University Press, 1993.

Ribner, Irving. "Machiavelli and Sidney: The *Arcadia* of 1590." *Studies in Philology* 47 (1950): 152-72.

Richardson, Brenda. "Robert Greene's Yorkshire Connections: A New Hypothesis." *Yearbook of English Studies* 10 (1980): 160-80.

Richardson, Samuel. *Clarissa, or The History of a Young Lady*. Ross, Angus, ed. New York: Penguin, 1985.

Riche, Barnebe. *Greenes News both from Heaven and Hell*. McKerrow, R. B., ed. London: Sidgwick & Jackson, 1911.

_____. *His Farewell to Military Profession*. Beecher, Donald, ed. Ottawa: Dovehouse Editions, 1992.

Richetti, John J. *Popular Fiction Before Richardson: Narrative Patterns, 1700-1739*. Oxford: Clarendon Press, 1969.

_____ and Paula R. Backscheider, eds. *Popular Fiction by Women 1660-1730: An Anthology*. Oxford: Clarendon Press, 1996.

Riffaterre, Michael. *Fictional Truth*. Baltimore: Johns Hopkins University Press, 1990.

Roberts, Josephine. "Lodge's *Margarite of America:* A Distopian Vision of the New World." *Studies in Short Fiction* 17 (1980): 407-14.

Roberts, Sasha. *Reading Shakespeare's Poems in Early Modern England*. New York: Palgrave, 2003.

Rose, Mary Beth. *Gender and Heroism in Early Modern England*. Chicago: University of Chicago Press, 2002.

Rose, Mark. "Sidney's Womanish Man." *Review of English Studies* n. s. 15 (1964): 353-63.

Rowlands, Samuel. *The Complete Works of Samuel Rowlands*. Three volumes. Glasgow: Hunterian Club, 1880.

Ryan, Kiernan. "The Extemporal Vein: Thomas Nashe and the Invention of Modern Narrative." *Narrative: from Malory to Motion Pictures*. Hawthorn, Jeremey, ed. London: Edward Arnold, 1995: 40-54.

Salzman, Paul. *English Prose Fiction, 1558-1700: A Critical History*. Oxford: Clarendon, 1985.

_____. "Theories of Prose Fiction in England: 1558-1700." *The Cambridge History of Literary Criticism*, Volume 3. Norton, Glyn P., ed. Cambridge: Cambridge University Press, 1999.

Sandy, Gerald N. "Characterization and Philosophical Décor in the *Aethiopica*." *Transactions of the American Philological Association* 112 (1982): 141-67.

_____. *Heliodorus*. Boston: Twayne Publishers, 1982.

Saunders, J. W. "The Stigma of Print: A Note on the Social Bases of Tudor Poetry." *Essays in Criticism* 1 1951): 139-59.

Saupe, Karen. "Trial, Error, and Revision in Sidney's *Arcadia*s." *Sidney Newsletter and Journal* 12.2 (1993): 22-29.

Scaliger, Julius Caesar. *Poetices libri septum.* Stuttgardt: fromman-holzbog, 1987.

Scanlon, Paul. "A Checklist of Prose Romances in English, 1474-1603." *The Library* n. s. 33 (1978): 143-52.

_____. "Greene's Later Prose Romances." *Cahiers Elisabethains* 24 (1983): 3-15.

Schleiner, Winfried. "Differences in Theme and Structure of the Erona Episode in the *Old* and *New Arcadia*." *Studies in Philology* 70 (1970): 377-91.

_____. "Male Cross-Dressing and Transvestitism in Renaissance Romance." *Sixteenth-Century Journal* 19 (1988): 605-19.

Scholes, Robert, and Robert Kellogg, *The Nature of Narrative.* New York: Oxford University Press, 1966.

Schwyzer, Philip. "Summer Fruit and Autumn Leaves: Thomas Nashe in 1593." *English Literary Renaissance* 24 (1994): 583-619.

Scudéry, Mlle de. *Artamène ou Le Grand Cyrus.* Ten Volumes. Paris, 1649-53.

Selzer, John L. "The Achievement of Lodge's *Robin the Devil*." *Texas Studies in Language and Literature* 26 (1984): 18-33.

Shakespeare, William. *The Riverside Shakespeare.* Evans, G. Blakemore, and J. J. M. Tobin, eds. 2nd Edition. Boston: Houghton Mifflin, 1996.

Shapiro, Susan O. "Herodotus and Solon." *Classical Antiquity* 15 (1996): 348-64.

Sheavyn, Phoebe. *The Literary Profession in the Elizabethan Age.* New York: Haskell House, 1964. First edition 1909.

Sherman, William. *John Dee: The Politics of Reading and Writing in the English Renaissance.* Amherst: University of Massachusetts Press, 1995.

*A Short-Title Catalogue of Books Printed in England, Scotland, & Ireland, and of Books Printed Abroad 1475-1640.* Pollard, A. W., and G. R Redgrave, eds. 2nd Edition. W. A. Jackson, F. S. Ferguson, and Katherine F Pantzer, rev. Three volumes. London: Bibliographical Society, 1986.

Sidney, Sir Philip. *The Countess of Pembroke's Arcadia (The Old Arcadia)*. Robertson, Jean, ed. Oxford: Oxford University Press, 1973.

_____. *The Countess of Pembroke's Arcadia*. Evans, Maurice, ed. New York: Penguin, 1977.

_____. *The Old Arcadia*. Duncan-Jones, Katherine, ed. Oxford: Oxford University Press, 1985.

_____. *The Countess of Pembroke's Arcadia (The New Arcadia)*. Skretkowicz, Victor, Jr., ed. Oxford: Oxford University Press, 1987.

_____. *Sir Philip Sidney: A Critical Edition of the Major Works*. Duncan-Jones, Katherine, ed. Oxford: Oxford University Press, 1989.

Simons, Louise. "Rerouting *The Unfortunate Traveler*: Strategies for Coherence and Direction." *Studies in English Literature* 28 (1988): 18-38.

Sinfield, Alan. *Literature in Protestant England, 1560-1660*. London: Croom Helm, 1983.

Sisson, Charles J. *Thomas Lodge and Other Elizabethans*. Cambridge, MA: Harvard University Press, 1933.

Skretkowicz, Victor, Jr. "Sidney and Amyot: Heliodorus in the Structure and Ethos of the *New Arcadia*." *Review of English Studies* n. s. 27 (1976): 171-4.

Spenser, Edmund. *The Faerie Queene*. Hamilton, A. C., ed. London: Longman, 1977.

_____. *The Yale Edition of the Shorter Poems of Edmund Spenser*. William A. Oram et al., eds. New Haven: Yale University Press, 1989.

Spufford, Margaret. *Small Books and Pleasant Histories: Popular Fiction and its Readership in Seventeenth-Century England*. Athens: University of Georgia Press, 1982.

Stanford, W. B. *The Ulysses Theme*. 2nd ed. Ann Arbor: University of Michigan Press, 1968.

Stechow, Wolfgang. "Heliodorus' *Aethiopica* in Art." *Journal of the Warburg and Courtauld Institutes* 16 (1953): 144-52.

Steinman, Martin. *Johannes Oporinus: Ein Basler Buchdrucker um die Mitte des 16. Jahrhunderts.* Basel, 1967.

Stephanson, Raymound. "The Epistemological Challenge of Nashe's *The Unfortunate Traveler.*" *Studies in English Literature* 23 (1983): 21-36.

Stern, Tiffany. "'A small-beer health to his second day': Playwrights, Prologues, and First Performances in the Early Modern Theater." *Studies in Philology* 101:2 (Spring 2004): 172-99.

Stephens, Susan A. "Who Read Ancient Novels?" *The Search for the Ancient Novel.* James Tatum, ed. Baltimore: Johns Hopkins University Press, 1994: 405-18.

Stone, Lawrence. *The Crisis of the Aristocracy, 1558-1641.* Oxford: Clarendon, 1965.

Suzuki, Mihoko. "'Signiorie Ouer the Pages': The Crisis of Authority in Nashe's *Unfortunate Traveler.*" *Studies in Philology* 81 (1984): 348-71.

Tatum, James, ed. *The Search for the Ancient Novel.* Baltimore: The Johns Hopkins University Press, 1994.

Thomas, Keith. *Religion and the Decline of Magic.* New York: Charles Scribner's Sons, 1971.

Tilley, Morris Palmer. *A Dictionary of the Proverbs in English in the Sixteenth and Seventeenth Centuries.* Ann Arbor: University of Michigan Press, 1950.

Todorov, Tzvetan. *Grammaire du Décaméron.* The Hague: Mouton, 1969.

_____. *The Fantastic: A Structural Approach to a Literary Genre.* Richard Howard, trans. Ithaca: Cornell University Press, 1975.

Traister, Daniel. "Reluctant Virgins: The Stigma of Print Revisited." *Colby Quarterly* 26 (1980): 75-86.

Tribe, Keith. *Genealogies of Capitalism.* London: Macmillan, 1981.

Trimpi, Wesley. "Sir Philip Sidney's *An Apology for Poetry.*" *The Cambridge History of Literary Criticism. Volume 3: The Renaissance.* Norton, Glyn P., ed. Cambridge: Cambridge University Press, 1999: 187-98.

Turner, Jennifer. "Jack Wilton and the Art of Travel." *Critical Approaches to English Prose Fiction.* Beecher, Donald, ed. Ottawa: Dovehouse Editions, 1998: 123-56.

Turner, Henry. "Plotting Early Modernity." *The Culture of Capital: Property, Cities, and Knowledge in Early Modern England.* Turner, Henry S., ed. London: Routledge, 2002: 85-127.

Turner, Myron. "The Heroic Ideal in Sidney's Revised *Arcadia.*" *Studies in English Literature* 10 (1970): 63-82.

_____. "The Disfigured Face of Nature: Image and Metaphor in the Revised *Arcadia.*" *English Literary Renaissance* 2 (1972): 116-35.

Vinaver, Eugéne. *The Rise of Romance.* Oxford: Clarendon Press, 1971.

Virgil. *The Aeneid.* Fitzgerald, Robert, trans. New York: Vintage, 1980.

Visser, N. W. "The Generic Identity of the Novel." *Novel* 11 (1978): 101-14.

Walker, D. P. *The Ancient Theology: Studies in Christian Platonism from the Fifteenth to the Eighteenth Century.* London: Duckworth, 1972.

Wall, Wendy. *The Imprint of Gender: Authorship and Publication in the English Renaissance.* Ithaca: Cornell University Press, 1993.

Warkentin, Germaine. "Patrons and Profiteers: Thomas Newman and the 'Violent Enlargement' of *Astrophil and Stella.*" *Book Collector* 34 (1985): 461-87.

Warner, William B. *Licensing Entertainment: The Elevation of Novel-Reading in Britain, 1684-1750.* Berkeley: University of California Press, 1988.

Watt, Ian. *The Rise of the Novel: Studies in Defoe, Richardson, and Fielding.* Harmondsworth: Penguin, 1963.

Watt, Tessa. *Cheap Print and Popular Piety, 1550-1640.* Cambridge: Cambridge University Press, 1992.

Weimann, Robert. *Author's Pen and Actor's Voice: Playing and Writing in Shakespeare's Theater.* Cambridge: Cambridge University Press, 2000.

Weinberg, Bernard. *A History of Literary Criticism in the Italian Renaissance.* Chicago: University of Chicago Press, 1960.

Weiner, Andrew. *Sir Philip Sidney and the Poetics of Protestantism*. Minneapolis: University of Minnesota Press, 1978.

Wellek, René, and Austin Warren. *Theory of Literature*. New York: Harcourt Brace, 1949.

Wells, Stanley. "Shakespeare and Romance." *Later Shakespeare*. Brown, John Russell, and Bernard Harris, eds. London: Edward Arnold, 1966: 49-80.

Weston, Jessie. *From Ritual to Romance*. Cambridge: Cambridge University Press, 1920.

Whitmarsh, Tim. "Heliodoros and the Genealogy of Hellenism." *Studies in Heliodorus*. Hunter, Richard, ed. *Cambridge Philological Society Supplementary Volume* 21 (1998): 93-124.

_____. "Reading for Pleasure: Narrative, Irony, and Eroticism in Achilles Tatius." *The Ancient Novel and Beyond*. Panayotakis, Stelios, Maaike Zimmerman, and Wytse Keulen, eds. Leiden: Konninklijke Brill, 2003: 191-205.

Whitworth, Charles Jr. "*Rosalynde*: As You Like It and As Lodge Wrote It." *English Studies* 58 (1977): 114-17.

Wiles, A. G. D. "Sir Philip Sidney: The English Huguenot." *Transactions of the Huguenot Society of South Carolina* 45 (1940): 24-37.

Wiles, David. *Shakespeare's Clown: Actor and Text in the Elizabethan Playhouse*. Cambridge: Cambridge University Press, 1987.

Williams, Joan. *Novel and Romance 1700-1800: A Documentary Record*. London: Routledge and Kegan Paul, 1970.

_____. *The Idea of the Novel in Europe, 1600-1800*. New York: Macmillan Press, 1979.

Wilson, Adrian. "Foucault on the 'Question of the Author.'" *Modern Language Review* 99: 2 (April 2004): 339-63.

Winkler, John J. "The Mendacity of Kalasiris and the Narrative Strategy of Heliodoros' *Aithiopika*." *Yale Classical Studies* 27 (1982): 93-158.

_____. *The Constraints of Desire: The Anthropology of Sex and Gender in Ancient Greece*. London: Routledge, 1990.

_____. "The Invention of Romance." *The Search for the Ancient Novel*. Tatum, James, ed. Baltimore: Johns Hopkins University Press, 1994: 23-28.

Wofford, Susanne. *The Choice of Achilles: The Ideology of Figure in the Epic*. Stanford: Stanford University Press, 1992.

Woodhuyson, H. R. *Sir Philip Sidney and the Circulation of Manuscripts, 1558-1640*. Oxford: Clarendon Press, 1996.

Wolff, Samuel L. *The Greek Romances in Elizabethan Prose Fiction*. New York: Columbia University Press, 1902.

Worden, Blair. *The Sound of Virtue: Philip Sidney's* Arcadia *and Elizabethan Politics*. New Haven: Yale University Press, 1996.

Wright, Louis B. *Middle-Class Culture in Elizabethan England*. Ithaca: Cornell University Press, 1948. Repr. of 1935 ed.

Wyatt, Sir Thomas. *The Complete Poems*. Rebholz, R. A., ed. New York: Penguin, 1978.

Ziegler, Georgiana. "Penelope and the Politics of Woman's Place in the Renaissance." *Gloriana's Face: Women, Public and Private, in the English Renaissance*. Cerasano, S. P. and Marion Wynne-Davies, eds. New York and London: Harvester Wheatsheaf, 1992: 25-46.

Zwicker, Steven N. "The Reader Revealed." *The Reader Revealed*. Baron, Sabrina A., ed. Washington: Folger Library Press, 2002: 11-17.

# Index